Public Policy and Politics

Series Editors: Colin Fudge and Robin Hambleton

Public policy-making in Western democracies is confronted by new pressures. Central values relating to the role of the state, the role of markets and the role of citizenship are now all contested and the consensus built up around the Keynesian welfare state is under challenge. New social movements are entering the political arena: electronic technologies are transforming the nature of employment; changes in demographic structure are creating heightened demands for public services; unforeseen social and health problems are emerging; and, most disturbing, social and economic inequalities are increasing in many countries.

How governments – at international, national and local levels – respond to this developing agenda is the central focus of the Public Policy and Politics series. Aimed at a student, professional, practitioner and academic readership, it aims to provide up-to-date, comprehensive and authoritative analyses of public policy-making in practice.

The series is international and interdisciplinary in scope, and bridges theory and practice by relating the substance of policy to the politics of the policy-making process.

Public Policy and Politics

Series Editors: Colin Fudge and Robin Hambleton

PUBLISHED

Danny Burns, Robin Hambleton and Paul Hoggett, *The Politics of Decentralisation: Revitalising Local Democracy*

Stephen Glaister, June Burnham, Handley Stevens and Tony Travers, *Transport Policy in Britain* (second edition)

Christopher Ham, *Health Policy in Britain: The Politics and Organisation of the National Health Service* (sixth edition)

Ian Henry, *The Politics of Leisure Policy* (second edition)

Christopher C. Hood and Helen Z. Margetts, *The Tools of Government in the Digital Age*

Peter Malpass and Alan Murie, *Housing Policy and Practice* (fifth edition)

Robin Means, Sally Richards and Randall Smith, *Community Care: Policy and Practice* (fourth edition)

David Mullins and Alan Murie, *Housing Policy in the UK*

Gerry Stoker, *The Politics of Local Government* (second edition)

Marilyn Taylor, *Public Policy in the Community* (second edition)

Keiron Walsh, *Public Services and Market Mechanisms: Competition, Contracting and the New Public Managment*

Public Policy and Politics
Series Standing Order

ISBN 0–333–71705–8 hardcover
ISBN 0–333–69349–3 paperback
(outside North America only)

You can receive future titles in this series as they are published by placing a standing order. Please contact your bookseller or, in case of difficulty, write to us at the address below with your name and address, the title of the series and the ISBN quoted above.

Customer Services Department, Macmillan Distribution Ltd
Houndmills, Basingstoke, Hampshire RG21 6XS, England

Public Policy in the Community

2nd edition

Marilyn Taylor

palgrave
macmillan

First edition 2003
Second edition 2011

Published by
PALGRAVE MACMILLAN

Palgrave Macmillan in the UK is an imprint of Macmillan Publishers Limited, registered in England, company number 785998, of Houndmills, Basingstoke, Hampshire RG21 6XS.

Palgrave Macmillan in the US is a division of St Martin's Press LLC, 175 Fifth Avenue, New York, NY 10010.

Palgrave Macmillan is the global academic imprint of the above companies and has companies and representatives throughout the world.

Palgrave® and Macmillan® are registered trademarks in the United States, the United Kingdom, Europe and other countries.

ISBN-13: 978–0–230–24264–7   hardback
ISBN-10: 0–230–24264–2   hardback
ISBN-13: 978–0–230–24265–4   paperback
ISBN-10: 0–230–24265–0   paperback

This book is printed on paper suitable for recycling and made from fully managed and sustained forest sources. Logging, pulping and manufacturing processes are expected to conform to the environmental regulations of the country of origin.

A catalogue record for this book is available from the British Library.

A catalog record for this book is available from the Library of Congress.

10   9   8   7   6   5   4   3   2   1
20 19 18 17 16 15 14 13 12 11

Printed in China

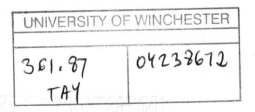

Contents

List of Figures, Tables and Boxes

Figures

Tables

Boxes

Preface to the Second Edition

When I wrote the first edition of *Public Policy in the Community*, ideas of 'community' had moved to the centre of the political agenda in many parts of the world, along with 'social capital', 'civil society', 'participation' and 'empowerment'. I warned then that those of us who welcomed this new direction in policy at national and international level might want to wait before rolling out the welcome mat. We had, after all, been here before. My own interest in community began in the early 1970s, when there was also considerable interest in ideas of community and participation in the public policy field. At that time, however, the interest proved to be short-lived. Community programmes introduced with a flourish in the 1960s were buried in the 1970s with little trace. The market revolution that followed was to prove a much more hardy creature and to bring with it a more individual and consumerist approach.

Perhaps I was unduly pessimistic. Since that first edition was published, 'community' has maintained its high profile in policy across the globe and been sustained across ideological divides. Other ideas in the community portfolio I discussed at that time – civil society, social capital, networks, empowerment and participation – are also still very much part of the policy discourse. Since 2002, however, when I finished writing the book, the context for community policy and practice has changed significantly. Then, we were in a long period of economic growth; as I write now, we are coming out of a major recession with continued uncertainty about our economic future. Then, September 11 had only just happened; since then, the 'war on terror' has led to widespread concerns about civil liberties, community cohesion and religious discrimination. In 2002, the election of Barack Obama as US president with his mixed-race heritage and history of community organising was almost unthinkable; now the UK government is proposing to train 5000 community organisers. Then, the immense potential of Web 2.0 had yet to be discovered – mobile phone technology was a long way from where it is now. And although environmental concerns were gaining in importance in 2002, climate change was still a specialist concern.

Then, in my country the headlines were dominated by race riots in the North of England and I based my conclusions around recent demonstrations against paedophiles. These particular events now belong more comfortably in historical references – although the issues raised still remain highly relevant and large-scale public expenditure cuts may trigger further unrest. Here, too, policies that were still relative shiny and new in 2002 (the National Strategy for Neighbourhood Renewal, for example) are now in their terminal stages. The language continues to change and evolve – 'community resilience' and 'localism' are currently in vogue and, in England, the new coalition government is pinning its hopes on the 'Big Society'. On the world stage, since 2002, advocates of community policies in the global North have discovered that there is a great deal to learn from the South. Participatory budgeting – a model developed initially in Brazil – has been rolled out not only in the UK but also in several European countries. However, global economic crisis has again changed the context in which concepts of community are applied, with public investment in community programmes and services to disadvantaged communities particularly at risk.

In the preface to the first edition, I described the book as an odyssey – a journey through experience, discussion and reading to explore the complexities of community and power over 40 years. As I said there, I came to this journey from a number of different directions. I grew up in a New Town in the UK, a manufactured 'community' that demonstrated just how difficult community is to build. In the 1970s and 1980s, I worked in the community development field as a researcher and policy analyst. But I also had 'hands-on' experience as a tenant on a public housing estate in London. Here, I was heavily involved in community activity as well as participating in a partnership between the local authority and local community organisations that in some ways was ahead of its time. Since 1990, I have been an academic, but one of a growing number who are trying to build bridges between the world of ideas and the world of practice in the community empowerment field.

The first edition built on all that I had learnt from experience and practice over those years. But since 2002, I have read more widely and a lot more has been written about the concepts I explored then. There is more theoretical work to draw on and there is more evidence on the achievements and challenges of community policies and practice as well as partnership working. I have further developed my own ideas and research – particularly in relation to power – and I also have new empirical data, from the UK and beyond. I am also aware of the need to engage more deeply with a number of the challenges highlighted in the first edition – particularly that of diversity.

In writing the second edition, I have tried as far as possible to maintain the structure of the first but to develop the arguments as necessary. It was particularly difficult, however, to know how much to update without writing a completely new book. The pace of change is such that language that was highly topical in 2002 is now somewhat passé, while new policies have replaced those that were topical then. But community approaches to social exclusion are still going to be needed. A friend told me recently that her young colleagues never read anything that is more than three years old. Well, as a US philosopher, George Santayana, put it: 'Those who do not remember the past are condemned to repeat it.' So, while I have included many new references, I have kept faith with the many older studies and references that have inspired me over the years.

Finally, there are more people to add to the Acknowledgements below, including the several colleagues I have worked with on research projects since 2002. In this respect, I would like to single out in particular Jo Howard, Derrick Purdue and Mandy Wilson, who have been colleagues in many of the studies referenced here. I would also like to acknowledge the support of John Low at the Joseph Rowntree Foundation, Ben Cairns and the staff of the Institute for Voluntary Action Research, with whom I have found a new second home, Carl Milofsky, who is always willing to answer queries and put me in touch with relevant work, Chris Miller and colleagues on the editorial board of the *Community Development Journal* and John Lever to whom I owe in particular an introduction to the work of Nick Crossley and several helpful texts on Foucault and Bourdieu. Thanks are also due to the staff at Palgrave Macmillan for their support in bringing this second edition into being.

Marilyn Taylor
Bristol, UK
February 2011

Acknowledgements*

Since this book describes a personal journey, it owes a great deal to the many people I have worked with over the years and reflects many conversations with them. I would particularly like to acknowledge my debt to Al Kestenbaum and Brian Symons, who started me off on this journey, to colleagues in the Community Development Foundation and the National Council for Voluntary Organisations (NCVO) with whom I worked over the 1970s and 1980s, to fellow community activists in Kings Cross and to the many people in communities who have participated in research I have done over the years and shared their learning and ideas with me. The Joseph Rowntree Foundation has supported a great deal of the work I have drawn on here and I owe it a great deal. I would also like to acknowledge my debt to Murray Stewart, Lucy Gaster, Paul Hoggett, Robin Hambleton and Julian Le Grand, with whom I worked at the School for Advanced Urban Studies at Bristol, to Perri 6 who persuaded me that I had something to say, and to my colleagues on the Board of the *Community Development Journal*, in particular Gary Craig and Marj Mayo, who provided valuable comments on the final text. I have drawn on research carried out with other colleagues in the body of the book, and along with those already mentioned, would like to acknowledge the contribution of Danny Burns, Surya Monro, Linda Seymour, Diane Warburton and Mick Wilkinson to the work reported here. More recent acknowledgements for the second edition are given in the Preface to this edition.

This book has drawn on material that I have published elsewhere over the years, particularly on work published by the Policy Press, the Joseph Rowntree Foundation, the Community Development Foundation and SQW. I have also drawn on articles I wrote for *Urban Studies* (2007) and the *Journal of Civil Society*

---

* This Acknowledgements relates mainly to the first edition, although the permissions to publish have been updated. Further acknowledgements to colleagues are given in the Preface to the Second Edition.

(2010) as well as chapters contributed to two edited collections: *Urban Governance, Institutional Capacity and Social Milieux* (Cars et al., 2002) published by Ashgate and the *Handbook of Community Movements and Local Organisations* (Cnaan and Milofsky 2007) published by Springer. The author and publishers would also like to thank the following for permission to reproduce copyright material. The Policy Press for permission to reproduce Table 7.2 on p. 124, Figure 7.1 on p. 127 and the material on Box 10.2 on p. 194; the Joseph Rowntree Foundation for permission to reproduce Figure 6.1 on p. 90; Taylor & Francis (http://www.informaworld.com) for permission to reproduce Figure 6.2 on p. 95; the Community Development Foundation for permission to reproduce the material in Box 6.2; Earthscan Publications for permission to publish Figure 8.1 on p. 144; Taylor & Francis for permission to reproduce Figure 8.3 on p. 153; John Gaventa for permission to reproduce Figure 8.4 on p. 156 the King's Fund for permission to reproduce Figure 13.1 on p. 279; and Local Governance Innovation and Development Ltd for permission to reproduce Figure 13.2 on p. 284. I would also like to acknowledge the following for permission to draw on their experience for boxed case studies: East Brighton New Deal for Communities for Boxes 10.6 and 11.4; Capital Action also for Box 10.6; Coin Street Community Builders for material in Box 11.1; Novas Scarman for Box 11.3; John Gaventa for Box 11.5; Yorkshire and Humber Empowerment Partnership for Boxes 12.2 and 12.4; Nick Acheson and Carl Milofsky for Box 12.3 and Carl Milofsky for Box 12.6. Every effort has been made to contact all the copyright holders, but if any have been inadvertently omitted the publishers will be pleased to make the necessary arrangement at the earliest opportunity.

There are, of course, many others to thank, not least my colleagues over the years in the field of third-sector research and current colleagues in Brighton and Hove. Peter Ambrose has been a recent source of inspiration, keeping my attention firmly fixed on the values that community participation should promote. I am also indebted to Mary Jacob and Tessa Parkes – whose postgraduate research kept me in touch with recent developments in the empowerment literature – and to Liz Cunningham who has been assiduous in keeping me up to date with the international literature and developments in the field of participatory research. An eleventh-hour conversation with John Gaventa and

Juliet Merrifield was particularly helpful in giving me a sense of the international relevance of the issues covered here. On the international front, I also owe a debt to Ralph Kramer, Carl Milofsky and Les Salamon, who over the years have provided a wider perspective, given me confidence in my ability to make a significant contribution and provided invaluable practical advice on how to realise a project that turned out to be much more ambitious than I originally anticipated. Finally, I would like to thank my publisher, Steven Kennedy, for his support and patience while I learnt to juggle different demands on my time.

MARILYN TAYLOR

Chapter 1

Introduction

We can learn a great deal about a society from the words that crop up again and again in government policy documents, that are *de rigueur* in the top circles and that mark the insiders from the outsiders. In the 1980s, that language was the language of the market and those who wanted to get on in any sphere of public life went to business school to learn it. Every organisation got its 'mission statement'; people who used to suffer poor quality public services suddenly became 'customers' – even those on welfare benefits, who were hardly in a position to exercise much choice. Public sector services were 'outsourced', bureaucracies were 'downsized', departments became 'cost centres'. The development of a new approach to public management placed 'performance' and 'efficiency' at the top of the agenda.

During the 1990s, however, a new vocabulary began to emerge – of community, civil society, participation and empowerment – along with a set of ideas that also included 'communitarianism', 'social capital', 'networks', the 'social economy', 'mutuality', 'partnership' and 'civic engagement'. First, Etzioni's communitarian manifesto seized the attention of leading politicians and institutions. Shortly afterwards, Robert Putnam popularised the idea of 'social capital', capturing the attention of the World Bank among many others. By the end of the decade, a UN document commented:

> It is difficult to think of an academic notion that has entered the common vocabulary of social discourse more quickly than the idea of social capital. Not only do academic journals devote special issues to discuss the concept, journalists make frequent references to it, and politicians pay homage to it. (Dasgupta and Serageldin 1999)

At the same time, following the fall of the Berlin Wall, the concept of 'civil society' was rediscovered. Initially it was promoted

1

as an alternative to the state but then, as the 1990s progressed, commentators also saw it as an alternative to the market. Similarly, the World Bank and International Monetary Fund began to require community participation as a condition of debt relief, stressing the 'need to engage the energies and enthusiasm of those at the grass-roots as a key to market success' (Salamon 1995, p. 257). This led to a range of flagship initiatives to foster social capital, self-help and community participation (see, for example, Box 1.1). As Cornwall and Coelho argued in their 2003 book on participation (2003, p. 4), 'The last decade has been one in which the voices of the public and especially the 'poor' have been increasingly sought'.

BOX 1.1   Community Driven Development

Community Driven Development (CDD) is an approach to development that supports participatory decision-making, local capacity building, and community control of resources. The five key pillars of this approach are:

- Community empowerment
- Local government empowerment
- Realigning the center
- Accountability and transparency
- Learning by doing.

With these pillars in place, CDD approaches can create sustainable and wide-ranging impacts by mobilising communities, and giving them the tools to become agents of their own development.

Support to CDD usually includes:

- Building capacity of community groups
- Promoting an enabling environment through policy and institutional reform (decentralisation, sector policies, etc.)
- Strengthening local governance relationships, including forging linkages between community based organisations and local governments.

Source: World Bank 2010a.

It is not that the language of the market has disappeared – far from it. But the rediscovery of 'community' over recent years has been heartening to many who despaired of the individualism and competitiveness fostered by the market, the dominance of structural adjustment policies and the priority given to economic over social agendas. After years of market supremacy, it has been encouraging to see policymakers and academics across the world pay attention to the need to invest in 'social capital' as well as the individual skills and financial resources that are needed to combat social, economic and political exclusion. It has also been encouraging to see worldwide recognition of the territory between the state and market, which tended to be lost in many of the ideological battles between right and left in the twentieth century. Increasing attention to social alongside market enterprise offers the potential to bridge the chasm between market definitions of value and the values of those concerned with social justice. Indeed, the award of the 2009 Nobel Memorial Prize in Economic Sciences to Elinor Ostrom, famous for her work on 'the commons', reinforces the sense that the hegemony of the neo-liberal economics of the 1980s has at least been tempered. We have a President in the White House in the US with a history of community organising and in the UK a right-of-centre coalition government committed to the Big Society – a commitment that invokes community, devolution of powers and mutualism (See Box 1.2). The emphasis on community empowerment and participation from the World Bank down to local governments in many parts of the globe has the potential to offer a voice to those who have been most marginalised and silenced by the supremacy of the market or indeed by authoritarian states.

This widespread adoption of the language of 'community' holds much promise. But its very popularity – and its adoption across significant ideological divides – also urges caution. The frequent and interchangeable use of the different terms in the community portfolio as a 'spray-on' solution to cover the fault lines of economic decline and social fragmentation has attracted considerable criticism, and threatens to devalue a set of ideas that could offer a great deal in addressing the complexities of the global society in which we live. It fails to acknowledge the considerable complexities and contradictions within this set of ideas. The language of community empowerment, too, often fails to grapple with the realities of power. Is there not something

---

BOX 1.2   Building the Big Society

The Big Society was a central theme in the election manifesto of
the Conservative party in 2010 and has taken centre stage in the
opening months of the coalition government that came to power
after that election. While the language has changed from that of
the previous New Labour administration, many of the Big Society's features are familiar and demonstrate the cross-party appeal
of the 'community' portfolio. It makes a commitment to:

1. Give communities more powers
*   In the planning system
*   To save local facilities and services and to take over state-run
    services
*   Through training 'a new generation' of community organis-
    ers to support the creation of neighbourhood groups, espe-
    cially in deprived areas.

2. Encourage people to take an active role in their communities
*   Encourage volunteering and involvement in social action
*   Encourage charitable giving and philanthropy
*   Introduce a National Citizen Service aimed at 16-year olds

$\longrightarrow$

---

paradoxical in the idea that one set of people can empower others? In the context of savage public expenditure cuts in many
countries, many also fear that, as used in policy, 'community' is
a codeword for the continued assault on the state as the guaran-
tor of social justice and the welfare of its citizens.

As someone with nearly 40 years of experience in this field,
I am still convinced of the potential of these ideas to create
real and lasting change in tackling the marginalisation of many
people across the globe. However, I also believe that the language of 'community' and the ideas associated with it will only
deliver on its promise and the expectations that surround it if
its use is based on a robust understanding of these ideas and the
contradictions and paradoxes within them. This understanding
needs to be informed by communities themselves, by experience
in both the global North and the global South, by theories of
community and power and by a continuing dialogue between the

3. Transfer power from central to local government
- Devolve power and introduce greater financial autonomy
- Introduce a general power of competence (which UK local government does not have)
- Return regional powers in housing and planning to local authorities

4. Support local co-operatives, mutuals, charities and social enterprises
- Encourage much greater involvement in the running of public services
- Support public sector workers in creating their own employee-owned co-operatives
- Use dormant bank accounts to establish a Big Society Bank to invest in neighbourhood groups, charities, social enterprises, etc.

5. Publish government data
- Create a new 'right' to government-held datasets
- Publish local crime data statistics

Source: Adapted from Cabinet Office 2010.

experience of the past and the aspirations, energies and hopes of the present.

In the mid 1990s, Murray Stewart and I reviewed the experience of community empowerment in the UK and beyond for the Joseph Rowntree Foundation (Stewart and Taylor 1995). At that time, we commented on the failure of government and others to learn from the past and the tendency to 'reinvent the wheel'. With the renewed interest in community and participation across the globe since that time, there may be a real opportunity to build on this past experience and move forward. This book is therefore an odyssey. In part, it revisits and reassesses the experience and debates of the past 40 years or so to see what they have to offer in the new political environment; in part, it explores current debates and their potential to 'make a difference' this time. It asks whether the prominence of these ideas in current policy and debate will have more than symbolic value and whether 'community' policies and practice have the potential to achieve what states and markets alone have failed to do: to change the balance of power in society; to reduce exclusion and polarisation; and to deliver sustainable improvements in the quality of life of the world's poorest citizens. In doing so, it draws on work that I and colleagues have published over the years; but also on the much larger body of theory and experience that I have found useful in trying to understand better how these ideas can be made to work.

My search for understanding began in the UK, but while there are obvious differences between countries and communities, due to different political structures and traditions as well as different economic profiles, the common themes that resonate across countries and the potential of learning across these different traditions are striking. My journey has been informed by the themes and concerns voiced in international debates, by more informal conversations with academics and practitioners from other countries, and by literature from across the globe. And while this book is aimed principally at readers from what is variously called the global North, the developed world, OECD or advanced capitalist countries, it has also been guided by the growing recognition in the North of the need to learn from the rest of the world. As such, while recognising the different contexts in which much of this learning has taken place, it draws from time to time on some of the best-known examples of effective community policy and practice in the South.

I begin, in Chapter 2, by tracking the fortunes of 'community' over recent years and asking why it has seized the attention of policymakers across the globe. I set out three scenarios for the future: optimistic, pessimistic and pragmatic. I move on, in Chapter 3, to explore the way that 'community' has been applied in policy over the past four decades and the different assumptions that lie behind community policies, exploring the rationales for different forms of community intervention and the different roles that communities are expected to play. Chapters 4 and 5 then take a step back in order to unpack in more detail the set of ideas that have clustered around community, social capital, civil society and related concepts: their ambiguities, the potential they offer, the pitfalls to be avoided and the challenges they pose. Chapter 6 explores more closely the relevance of these ideas for tackling poverty and social exclusion.

Chapters 7, 8 and 9 take a similar look at concepts of power, participation and empowerment. Chapter 7 examines different ways of understanding power and empowerment, while Chapter 8 looks in more detail at the policy process, the new political opportunities that have opened up over recent years and some frameworks for assessing levels of empowerment within them. Chapter 9 then explores the challenges that community empowerment policies and initiatives have faced over the past four decades and the tensions they have had to resolve.

Chapters 10 and 11 take up the challenges posed in the previous six chapters. They set out the elements of a strategy to tackle exclusion and to make participation and empowerment policies work. Chapters 12 and 13 then discuss in more detail the contradictions and tensions inherent in community work and partnership and how these can be addressed.

The final chapter considers the prospects for community empowerment and participation and the extent to which policies that seek to promote these aims offer genuine and sustainable opportunities for change. It reviews the optimistic, pessimistic and pragmatic scenarios set out in Chapter 2 in the light of the evidence presented in the body of the book. It ends by assessing the challenges that still need to be addressed if the resources of communities which have been marginalised and excluded by economic change are to make a full contribution to the search for sustainable solutions to the problems of the twenty-first century.

Many terms have been used to describe community interventions, often meaning different things in different countries or policy fields. This poses significant dilemmas in relation to the terminology this book will use. I have decided to use the terms community policy and community practice to cover external policies and interventions in the community and, where appropriate, action taken from within. I have focused mainly, too, on policies that seek to support those in disadvantaged and socially excluded communities to achieve social justice and a better quality of life. I have also referred throughout to 'communities' as either agents or objects of policies. I acknowledge that in doing so, I am falling prey to the criticisms I will make of others in using 'community' as a blanket term. But in the absence of suitable alternatives I use it in a purely descriptive sense to mean communities of place, identity or interest who take collective action or who are the targets – or potential beneficiaries – of policy.

One other set of terms I probably need to justify is the use of 'global North and global South' to describe what used to be called the developed and developing (or even 'third') world. I recognise that richer and poorer countries are not conveniently grouped to the North and South of the Equator respectively – Australia and New Zealand are, for example, very much part of what used to be called the developed world. I also recognise that the issues affecting community politics and policy *within* North and South are very different. But the terms global North and South are familiar in the development studies literature on which I have drawn and seem to have the fewest normative implications attached to them.

Chapter 2

The Changing Fortunes of 'Community'

In the heady days of the 1960s, it was possible to be optimistic about the prospects for 'community' and 'empowerment'. These were the years when the civil rights, peace and feminist movements in the North were challenging the post-war consensus, while, behind the Iron Curtain, the Prague Spring of 1968 briefly defied Soviet totalitarianism. Northern governments were introducing programmes – such as the War on Poverty in the USA and the National Community Development Project in the UK – that worked with communities to tackle the problems of poverty and alienation that persisted despite the growth of the welfare state and the economy. Change was in the air.

Community lost

The new dawn was to be short-lived, however. The oil crisis of the mid-1970s triggered recession, which brought with it rising unemployment and public expenditure cuts. In the Soviet bloc, the Prague Spring had been ruthlessly suppressed. Outside the communist world, increasing dissatisfaction with state welfare in many countries provided fertile ground for the rapid advance of a neoliberal ideology of welfare, based on the market. Government sponsors of community development programmes had their fingers burnt as they discovered that community responses were more radical than they had bargained for (Marris and Rein 1967; Moynihan 1969; Loney 1983; Lawrence 2007) so they looked elsewhere for solutions. In the global South, structural adjustment policies subordinated state welfare to economic growth, reproducing on a global scale the increasing polarisation, disenfranchisement and social division that the market was bringing to the North.

9

At the national level, these developments were reflected in the rise to power of radical right-wing governments – exemplified by the march of Thatcherism in the UK and Reaganomics in the USA – both committed to rolling back the frontiers of the state. This was not all-encompassing – within the UK, for example, resistance came from a 'new urban left', with its power base in the major urban municipalities. As part of its strategy to seize back the initiative from Margaret Thatcher's government, it continued to fund and promote community practice. But the scope for resistance was increasingly curtailed as the 1980s progressed. This was due to trends which were reflected in many countries across the globe: a combination of public expenditure cuts, the privatisation (or contracting-out) of services and the devolution of state functions to an increasing number of non-elected quangos (quasi-autonomous non-governmental organisations) at national and local level, the latter used in the UK in particular to circumvent the power of democratically elected local authorities.

Interest in 'community' did not die away completely, but it was increasingly subordinated to other agendas. In the neo-liberal lexicon, 'community' was reinterpreted predominantly in terms of self-help, with the potential to substitute for what leading right-wing thinkers saw as excessive dependency on the state. Community organisations also had the potential to offer alternatives to state service provision, and could be more responsive to consumer needs.

This new pluralism in the delivery of welfare was one for which many in the voluntary non-profit sector had been arguing for years. It also had the potential to give people in communities the opportunity to take control of their own services. However, many commentators took a more critical view of such developments. In a climate of increased pressure on public expenditure, with an emphasis on the responsibilities of individual citizens rather than their rights, critics argued that communities were being used to cut costs and free the state from its own responsibilities. Under the guise of self-help, they argued, communities were being asked to pick up the pieces of structural adjustment and new market policies. Where welfare service delivery was being 'contracted out' to non-state providers, many were concerned that voluntary and community organisations would become either tools of or substitutes for the state. This was a concern that spanned North and South:

> NGOs have a long history of providing welfare services to poor people in countries where governments lacked the resources to ensure universal coverage in health and education; the difference is that now they are seen as the *preferred channel* for service-provision in *deliberate substitution* for the state. (M. Edwards and Hulme 1995b, p. 6 [original emphasis])

Furthermore, as the focus moved more and more to the individual as a *consumer* in the marketplace, the importance of *citizenship* and *collective action* was sidelined. The needs of those who did not have the resources to choose scarcely featured at all, except when they drew attention to themselves through rioting and urban unrest. Structural adjustment, meanwhile, bound many countries in the global South to policies which impoverished the public sector and public welfare programmes.

By the end of the 1980s, the 'economic hegemony of the market ... appeared ... to be complete' (Craig, Mayo and Taylor 2000, p. 325). But this brought with it an increasing polarisation between rich and poor. If wealth was being created by the move to market policies, there was little evidence to suggest that it was trickling down to the most disadvantaged in society as it was supposed to do. Thus in 1996, the UN Research Institute for Social Development reported that 'As government services have crumbled and more and more ground in the so-called social sectors is left to market forces, there has been an explosion in the numbers and categories of marginalised and excluded people' (Dey and Westendorff 1996, p. 8). This was not just a polarisation between nations or between South and North, hugely significant though this was; it was a polarisation within nations, with richer nations such as the UK and the USA among those with the highest rates of inequality and the fastest growing inequalities (Hills 1998). Indeed Northern non-governmental organisations (NGOs) that had previously focused solely on the global South – Oxfam, for example – began to turn their attention to those who lived on their own doorsteps, to what John Gaventa (1999, p. 22) called 'the South within the North'. Gross inequalities were becoming acceptable, while cultures of poverty, unemployment and backwardness were explained away as part of the natural order of inherent inequalities in enterprise and ability (Dey and Westendorff 1996, p. 9).

These trends continue to the present day. A study in the latter years of the New Labour government in the UK found that, despite that government's commitment to reducing child poverty, the numbers of low-income households were rising and that the country was moving back towards levels of inequality in health and poverty last seen more than 40 years ago (Dorling *et al.* 2007). It also found that rich and poor were living further apart – a spatial segregation common in many parts of the world. Similar trends have been noted elsewhere, with the top 1 per cent in the USA accounting for 21.2 percent of the national income in 2005 (Judt 2010) and capturing half of the country's overall income growth between 1993 and 2007 (Saez 2005).

Critics of the market also comment on the way that public goods – from health and education to leisure – are being 'commodified', putting them out of the reach of those who cannot afford to pay for them. Offe and Heinze (1992) cite the disappearance of institutions in which time can be passed in a useful, satisfying and socially recognised way without the possession of additional disposable income. Public space has been privatised. The privately owned shopping mall, subject to continuous surveillance, has become the new 'town centre'. Some have argued that as the public sphere is abandoned, the whole concept of civilization is under threat (Hutton 2002). Neo-conservatism, Mouffe argues (1992), thus reduces the common good to a question of wealth creation, taxpayers' freedom and efficiency – and we might add, consumer choice. Even the alternative public spaces of the Internet are not immune to being commercialised and bought up by media barons.

Public space is also being evacuated by fear. As more intrusive surveillance and impersonal CCTV cameras replace the municipal park warden, this becomes a self-fulfilling prophecy. The case for increased surveillance has been compounded by major terrorist incidents in Bali, London, Madrid, Moscow, Mumbai, New York and other target cities. But Zygmunt Bauman (1999, pp. 5–6) comments that 'Most measures undertaken under the banner of safety are divisive. ... They sow mutual suspicion, set people apart, prompt them to sniff enemies and conspirators behind every contention or dissent, and in the end make the loners yet more lonely than before'. He laments the loss of the *agora*, a space that is the province neither of the public nor the private, but of both at the same time. This is 'the place where private problems meet in a meaningful way', he argues, where private troubles can be re-forged into public issues and which can thus provide collective levers for the alleviation of private misery and uncertainty (pp. 3, 7).

The impoverishment of the 'public' has extended to politics. In the 1990s, Manuel Castells (1996) described the way in which the 'information society' allows capital to flow beyond the reach of political institutions. With key decisions in the hands of multinational corporations, the power of the nation state has been 'hollowed out'. The state has also been under sustained ideological attack from international economic institutions and neoliberal commentators. The power of the ballot box, according to Naomi Klein (2000) is being replaced by corporate power.

Community regained

At the end of the 1980s, I was involved with colleagues in editing a special issue of the international *Community Development Journal* (Craig, Mayo and Taylor 1990) that looked back at the fortunes of community development over the *Journal*'s 25-year life. At that time it was easy to be pessimistic about the prospects for a policy and practice that would give recognition to communities. In the UK, we were into our eleventh year of Thatcherism, with Margaret Thatcher's celebrated observation that 'there is no such thing as society – only individuals and their families'. Elsewhere, structural adjustment policies were biting and privatisation policies were beginning to creep into the social democratic heartland of mainland Europe (Ascoli and Ranci 2002).

Ten years later, as Chapter 1 has already remarked, the picture seems very different. The 'marketisation' of welfare continues but, as the costs of the globalisation of the economy become more apparent, and neither government nor the market seem equipped to address the challenges facing society, 'community' has been brought back in from the cold. What have been the triggers for this?

A rapidly increasing demand for welfare

In 1997, the then editor of the UN newsletter *Habitat Debate* argued that rising levels of need were outstripping the state's capacity to provide:

> It is now widely recognised that government alone cannot bear the entire responsibility of providing housing, infrastructure and other basic services to the poor. Scarce public funds and increasing populations are straining government's capacity to deal with the problems brought on by rapid urbanisation. Many governments and local authorities are, therefore, enlisting the support of the private sector, nongovernmental organisations (NGOs) and community-based groups. (Warah 1997, p. 1)

The informal care and support provided by families, neighbours and communities has always been a major source of welfare provision, both financial and social. In some countries in the South, for example, where a weak state cannot or will not provide, community provision and/or remittances from family and community members abroad are essential. Elsewhere, states that over the years have taken an increasing responsibility for welfare have come under increasing criticism from the right of the political spectrum for sapping people's initiative and encouraging dependency. There are therefore both economic and moral arguments being made for communities themselves to take on more responsibility. Community-based provision is also seen as more sensitive to consumer needs and preferences than more professionalised and formalised state systems.

A breakdown of moral cohesion and responsibility

Some argue that the market has produced an individualistic culture, dominated by self-interest. But a number of other trends have led to increasing fragmentation and the loss, some believe, of a moral compass. One is the displacement of populations across the globe, along with the flare-up of racial and inter-community tensions, some ancient in origin, some linked to patterns of immigration. Another relates to the geographical concentration of low income, unemployment, dependency on state benefits, poor health and a range of associated social problems in pockets of deprivation, as a result of economic restructuring. In the 1980s and early 1990s, this latter trend led some critics to suggest that state welfare has encouraged the emergence of an underclass, detached from the morality of mainstream society (Murray 1990). Whether it is the state or the economy that is seen to be at fault, reinstating a sense of community is seen as essential to the development of greater cohesion and mutual responsibility, based on shared meanings and moralities.

A breakdown of democracy and political legitimacy

Some of the defining images towards the end of the twentieth century were those of South African citizens and citizens from post-Soviet countries flocking to the polling booths for the first time in decades. But at the same time that those images were published, citizens in the more established democracies seemed increasingly disenchanted with the quality of their democracy, with falling voting figures in many countries (Dalton and Wattenberg 2000) and a decline in the membership of mass political parties (Durose, Greasley and Richardson 2009). In the Netherlands, Klijn and Koppenjan (2000, p. 384) noted that

> The Dutch Social Cultural Planning Bureau, which has done survey research on the political and societal opinions in the Netherlands, concluded that individualisation is one of the major trends in society and that political participation becomes an option rather than something 'natural'. Support of politicians has to be earned and is not given 'naturally' any more. Individuals no longer support values because they are members of societal or political groups or because political actors tell them to do so.

Related to this is a loss of trust in public institutions, especially among the most disadvantaged. Narayan et al.'s World Bank study (2000, p. 117), for example, reports the belief amongst poor people that 'State institutions – whether delivering services, providing police protection or justice, or as political decision makers – are either not accountable to anyone or accountable only to the rich and powerful'.

Fukuyama (1989) lists a number of factors that have been blamed for this loss of faith in democratic institutions: privatisation, decentralisation, professionalisation, the increasing importance of information technologies, the decline of ideologies and the advance of individualism among them. Shore and Wright (1997b) lay the blame at the door of an increasingly remote and commercialised policy-making process, with its corporate influence, spin and preoccupation with the media. Indeed, it is increasingly difficult to know what it is precisely that citizens are voting for, as the public sphere is steadily eroded by privatisation and the globalised economy eats into the powers of the nation state. In the global South, meanwhile, the story is less one of democratic decline than of concern over the suitability of established models of democracy in countries with very different historical conditions and different challenges (Gaventa 2004).

In the face of apparent public apathy and the loss of democratic legitimacy that this implies, the response of the state in many established democracies has been an expansion of the participatory sphere (Cornwall 2008a). Communities and third-sector organisations have been supported to re-engage their members in public life, powers have been devolved to the local level and new forms of participatory or deliberative democracy have been introduced, which can bring decision making closer to the citizen.

Increasing uncertainty
In the post-modern world, uncertainty is a fact of life. Bauman uses the German word *Unsicherheit* to convey the mix of insecurity and unsafety that he considers the 'most sinister and painful of contemporary troubles' (Bauman 1999, p. 5). Peter Marris (1996, pp. 103, 104) describes how the restructuring of industry has robbed people of security, throwing 'the burden of their uncertain future back on local communities, with fewer and fewer resources to turn to'. The consequences are particularly severe for those where, as he puts it, the 'hierarchical displacement of uncertainty comes to rest': 'The competitive management of uncertainty, as it thrusts the burdens of insecurity progressively onto the less and less powerful, provokes a profound social alienation'. Networks of trust, social capital and community are all seen as offering routes to 'the reconstruction of the coherence and orderliness of widely divergent worlds', which Barbara Misztal (2000, p. 232) describes as 'a battle for the quality of life'.

Climate change and sustainable development
The Brundtland Commission, convened by the UN in 1983, defined sustainable development as: 'development that meets the needs of the present without compromising the ability of future generations to meet their own needs' (Brundtland Commission 1987). Since then, evidence of accelerating climate change has added urgency to this agenda.

There are many who see a fundamental contradiction between the demands of the capitalist economy for growth and the sustainability of the environment. But there is disagreement about what can be done at individual and local level. Ledwith (2005) argues that environmental crisis impacts disproportionately on those at the bottom of the income ladder. But, in keeping with the mantra 'Think Global, Act Local', Carley and Smith (2001, p. 192) see communities as key actors in the stewardship of the future and in the development of sustainable production. They deplore the advance of the consumerist lifestyle that capitalism promotes and which fuels 'excessive, inefficient resource consumption' and see the potential for communities to develop alternatives as producers in the informal and social economies, mobilising human creativity rather than seeking economic growth for its own sake. In this, their interests combine with critics of mainstream economic models, who are searching for alternative economic forms which combat alienation and exclusion from the production process (Offe and Heinze 1992) and create a 'more democratic, locally embedded, people-centred and ecologically sustainable economic system' (Robertson 1998; see also Held 1996; Carnegie UK 2010).

In summary, therefore, 'community' and the ideas that surround it offer resources, social glue, alternative ideas and knowledge that are now seen as essential to society. They are seen to contribute to the reform of welfare services, the revitalisation of democracy and the reintroduction of a moral compass and sense of purpose where this is seen to be lacking. They are potential weapons in the march towards development and sustainability. Involving the 'community' is now seen as a particularly formidable weapon in tackling the social exclusion that disfigures the progress of globalisation.

However, communities have not waited for an invitation to participate. Earlier I referred to the social movements that swept many countries in the 1960s. Since then, disabled people in many countries have taken to the streets to improve services and demand their rights as both consumers and citizens. The power of collective citizen action has been felt by governments from the communist regimes in the Soviet bloc at the end of the 1980s, through the Philippines and South Africa to Thailand, Tunisia and Egypt in more recent years. Environmental activists have scored notable victories across a number of fronts, although there is clearly a long way to go. There are, of course, thousands of examples where local communities have taken less visible initiatives to improve their own circumstances at local level.

In this context, it is essential to remember that globalisation has positive as well as negative consequences for communities. The information society may allow capital to flow beyond the reach of political institutions but, at the same time, it provides the means through which citizens can act. The communications revolution and the possibilities that the Internet has opened up for linking action by citizens in different parts of the world have fuelled a 'globalisation from below' (Della Porta 2006) which has challenged the economic hegemony of international capitalism at successive meetings of the G20 and, most recently, the failure of governments across the globe to respond to climate change. International grass roots campaigns have challenged major multinational companies on their employment and environmental practices and brought the issue of debt cancellation to the top of international agendas. They have also allowed less high-profile (but potentially powerful) connections to be made that link the concerns of the North to the South, share learning and ideas and allow local action to 'think global' (Gaventa 1999).

Can community deliver?

The problems of the twenty-first century demand imaginative solutions and the release of new resources. The commitment to participation suggests that the 'tacit' knowledge, resources and skills that lie in the most marginalised communities are at least being acknowledged as part of the solution to some of these problems. But how robust is this commitment to 'community' and can 'communities' deliver what is expected of them? It is possible to imagine three different responses to these questions: optimistic, pessimistic and pragmatic.

The optimistic scenario

An optimistic scenario might argue that the current vogue for 'community' provides the opportunity to create a new settlement. In this analysis, it offers real opportunities for communities to be equal partners at the policy-making table, while the search for new forms of governance offers communities and those who work with them an opportunity to be at the cutting edge of change. Optimists would point to such examples as the participatory planning and budgeting initiatives that have spread from Brazil across the globe or the commitment to community empowerment in countries like the UK. They would also see real potential for change from below in 'bottom up' citizens' organising initiatives in the US and elsewhere. Optimists would see civil society as holding the key to a third way, which would balance the shortcomings of state and market and open up a new political space. They would also remind us that many communities do want to take more control over their lives (Powell and Geoghegan 2004, p. 154).

Two trends discussed earlier offer hope that there can be real change. One is the apparent commitment to participation and empowerment from organisations such as the World Bank and an increasing number of national governments, backed up by real incentives. This gives those who have been excluded a powerful lever for change. It also strengthens allies across the system and helps to persuade the doubters. The second is the sweep of action from below, as people question whether the costs of globalisation and economic growth are really so inevitable and necessary as the advance of capitalism suggests.

The pessimistic scenario

Pessimists, on the other hand, might question how deep-seated the commitment to 'community' is. They might argue that government commitment to community participation remains vulnerable to political fashion and political change and is very dependent on the regime in power.

They could also argue that local and even national initiatives are small-scale in comparison to the structural factors that lead to financial, political and social exclusion – equivalent to 're-arranging the deck chairs on the *Titanic*'. A pessimistic analysis would see the new-found interest in community participation as a cost-cutting and legitimising strategy on the part of the state, giving structural adjustment and market-based policies a 'human face' but ultimately making the most disadvantaged and marginalised people in society responsible for dealing with the consequences of capitalism and structural economic change.

In this scenario, communities are being bought off and co-opted into an agenda that remains relentlessly top-down and which primarily serves the interests of capital. Critics of community-based intervention strategies argue that the logic of the global economy is inescapable and the problems it creates are far too massive to be 'solved through the patchwork of community regeneration' (McCulloch 2000, p. 418). The power of global capital, in this scenario, is not only overt but also covert, shaping the way we see things and what we think is possible. Indeed with the increasing individualisation that has come with the market economy and the neo-liberal agenda, it is difficult to see where an effective resistance would come from. Empowerment is interpreted as consumerism, with the quality of life 'equated increasingly with the consumption of more and more goods' (Carley 2001, p. 5). This makes it increasingly difficult to argue for public goods and public investment, let alone any kind of redistribution.

An alternative, but equally pessimistic approach, could be drawn from post-modernist theories where, instead of everything being controlled by international capital, everything is relative. The evidence of increasing fragmentation and racial/ethnic/religious tension world-wide would, in this scenario, confirm that, instead of offering the cohesion that the advocates of 'community' urge, community and identity are defined increasingly in terms that divide.

The pragmatic scenario

A pragmatic scenario would find the optimists too romantic about the prospects for community, but the pessimists too deterministic. It would accept that power flows through privileged pathways (Clegg 1989; see Chapter 7). But it would also

argue that the flow of power in society is not as rigid, as predetermined or as immune to human agency as the pessimist might
argue. Policymaking, in this view, is a process of paradoxes, balancing acts, irresolvable tensions and contradictions that can be
exploited in favour of those who have been marginalised. More
wary than the optimists, the pragmatists might see the future in
terms of equipping communities to make the most of the windows of opportunity and cracks in the system, and to open up
new opportunities and new accommodations on an incremental
basis. At the very least, this offers possibilities for small-scale
influence, even if the fundamentals of power are not addressed.
At the most, these small starting points can provide the foundation for more fundamental change (Cornwall 2004; Healey
2006).

So, which of these scenarios is most realistic? What is it that
international institutions and national governments seek to
achieve through the mobilisation of this nexus of ideas? And
what prospect is there that this new language will have more
than symbolic value, that it will change the balance of power
in society, reduce exclusion and polarisation and/or deliver sustainable improvements in the quality of life of the world's poorest citizens? Can communities, social capital and civil society
achieve what states and markets have failed to do? In the next
few chapters, I explore the way in which concepts of community
and empowerment have been applied in policy and debate before
turning later in the book to the opportunities for change.

Chapter 3

Community in Policy and Practice

Community policies have undergone several metamorphoses over recent decades. They are also shaped by the socio-political context and history of the particular country in which they are based. It is, however, possible to identify several distinct themes that cut across time and space – each with its own definition of the problem, its own ideologies and assumptions, and its associated solutions. One theme focuses on the *community* as the target for change. Approaches of this kind may assume that there is something lacking in the community itself, whether it be capacity, confidence, cohesion or moral integrity. Or they may want to build on and maximise community assets so that they can be used more effectively for community benefit. A second theme sees the *system* as the focus for change. Approaches of this kind seek to make services work more effectively together and make them more responsive to community needs.

A third theme focuses on *structural* causes of exclusion. Some approaches in this theme target the capitalist economy, mobilising communities to demand fundamental structural change. Others seek to improve employment and economic opportunities, or develop radically new forms of enterprise and employment. Finally, a fourth theme focuses on the state as the arena for change. Some approaches in this theme promote the market instead and focus on communities as consumers. Others seek to introduce new forms of partnership, which include communities alongside the state and other partners in developing and implementing strategies for change.

Table 3.1 summarises these themes according to the definition of the problem that they imply, ideological underpinnings, policy solutions, and relevant strategies or forms of intervention. In doing so, it draws on a number of classifications developed in the North and South (Glen 1992 (UK); Rothman and Tropman 1993 (US); Abbott 1996 (South Africa); Smock 2003 (US) and De Filippis 2007 (US)).

TABLE 3.1 *Recurring themes in community policy and practice*

Source of the problem/ Target for intervention	*Ideological foundation*	*The policy solution*	*Relevant strategies*
Community failure Skills and knowledge deficit Technological incapacity	Social democracy	**Capacity building** Skills, training and technical support	Locality development Community development Community education
Lack of resources, confidence or recognition		**Capacity development**	Asset-based community development Women-centred development
Loss of community Community pathology	Communitarianism	**Restoring community** Civil renewal Re-engineering community Restoring social order Support for self-help	Community development Community building
Fragmentation and racial tension	Pluralism	**Community cohesion**	Community building

→

TABLE 3.1 *(continued)*

Source of the problem/ Target for intervention	Ideological foundation	The policy solution	Relevant strategies
System failure Poor co-ordination Unresponsiveness	Social democracy	**Making the state work better** Community planning Co-ordination Consultation Managerial and technical solutions	Social planning Community services approach
	Communitarianism	**Community management** Contracting out state services Decentralisation Transferring assets	Asset-based community development Community management
Structural and economic failure	Marxism	**Structural change** Building power Building a broad-based movement for change	Power-based/ transformative models Community action and campaigning Coalition building Conscientisation (Freire) Community organising (Alinsky)

→

Structural and economic failure	Neo-liberalism	**Economic development** Physical development and attracting business investment Deregulation	Social enterprise development Asset development
	New economics Co-operativism	Asset transfer Social enterprise	Community development corporations Community economic development
Government failure	Neo-liberalism Market consumerism	**Moving to the market** Privatisation Consumer charters and targets User participation Community management	Consumer empowerment Asset development Community management
	'Third Way' discourse Social democracy	**Governance/ Partnership** Localism Partnership	Negotiated development Community building

Community failure

This theme covers all those approaches that seek to address a deficit within communities themselves, whether in skills, networks, moral cohesion, confidence or responsibility. Originating in the post-war colonial administrations, it underpinned some of the earliest approaches to community policy and community practice in the post-1945 era, but continues to be relevant in the twenty-first century in many parts of the world.

Developing skills and capacity

The first sub-theme under this heading sees disadvantaged communities as lacking the skills they need to participate effectively in social, political and economic life. Its origins lie in the British, French and Belgian colonies, where administrators sought to encourage self-reliance and stave off unrest among their 'charges' (Mayo 1975; Parsons 1995, p. 503) and also in post-war reconstruction and foreign-aid programmes. During the 1950s, for example, community development was a central element in imperial strategies to prepare the colonies for independence, both economically and politically, and to drive off the threat of communism.

Rothman and Tropman (1993) see this approach, which they define as 'locality development', as encompassing not only self-help but also education and the development of indigenous leadership. Glen calls it 'community development' (1993, p. 24) citing the 1979 UN definition of community development as: 'The participation of the people themselves in efforts to improve their level of living with as much reliance as possible on their own initiative, and the provision of technical and other services in ways which encourage initiative, self help and mutual help and make them more effective'.

This theme and, in particular, its commitment to skills development, technical support and training, has re-emerged in recent years in the form of 'capacity building' – a central strategy in community policies across the globe. However, the deficit model that it assumes has been roundly criticised by advocates of asset-based approaches (see, for example, Kretzmann and McKnight 1993), who seek instead to recognise the assets that such communities already have and build on these. Thus, while

Rothman's 'locality development' defined approaches that saw communities as 'apathetic, lacking in fruitful human relationships and problem-solving skills' (Rothman and Tropman 1987, p. 9), subsequent approaches have framed their interventions in terms of enabling, encouraging and educating (Glen 1993), 'capacity development' or 'women-centred development' (Smock 2003). Recent use of the term 'community resilience' also seeks to identify and build on the characteristics that equip communities to respond to crisis (see Chapter 14).

Restoring community

As applied to developing countries in the 1950s and 1960s, the 'problem' that community policies sought to address was seen as technological backwardness. This, as Daniel Moynihan (1969, p. 63) suggested, could be 'the result of *too much* community cohesion' (my italics), resulting in isolation and resistance to change. By contrast, the problem in the developed world was seen as too little 'community cohesion', whether for reasons of physical displacement, institutional change or, in the eyes of some commentators, the rejection of mainstream moral values.

After the Second World War in the UK, intensive efforts went into 'slum clearance', creating homes 'fit for heroes' by clearing poor quality and overcrowded housing and rehousing whole communities in new towns and new housing estates outside the inner cities. But, here and elsewhere, the transfer of significant populations to new neighbourhoods with few facilities and away from their traditional social networks led to isolation (Marris 1998) and created a new set of problems. In the UK, George Goetschius (1969) describes how, in the 1950s, tenants' associations were formed to tackle social, adult education and housing management issues. The ethos was very localised, based on encouraging community self-help and local support networks. Residents were encouraged to help themselves, by developing community ties and local activities, and supported in acquiring the individual and organisational skills to help them address their problems.

Initially, therefore, community work approaches were applied to restore ties broken by physical displacement. But, first in the US and then elsewhere, the 1960s brought with them urban unrest, racial tension and rising crime in the inner cities, all of which demanded a government response (Edwards and Batley 1978). Various explanations were offered for this apparent community breakdown. Some blamed the collapse of traditional social ties and the fragmentation of society. This line of argument drew on the work of Robert Nisbet (1953), who saw the loss of community as an outcome of social and economic progress. His theme was that the erosion of the institutions that formerly mediated between the individual and the state – family, community and other traditional associations – had led to alienation and insecurity. In part, he placed the responsibility with Protestantism and capitalism, which had 'gradually stripped off the historically grown layers of custom and social membership, leaving only levelled masses of individuals' (Nisbet, cited in Moynihan 1969, p. 10). Nonetheless, Nisbet saw the restoration of community as an alternative to what he saw as increasing dependence on the state.

A second explanation also sought to address the problems of increasing dependence on the state, but blamed communities themselves, arguing that some suffered from a moral failure to take responsibility that was passed on through the generations. In the UK in the 1990s, a prominent politician (who is seen by many as the architect of Margaret Thatcher's rise to power), Sir Keith Joseph, popularised the concept of a self-perpetuating 'cycle of deprivation'. A targeted social work approach was needed to change the behaviour of those dysfunctional people who were to be found in particular spatial locations (Atkinson 2000b).

The concept of a poverty cycle, which assumed an inherited inability to respond to opportunity, had already taken root in the US. According to Marris and Rein (1967, p. 39), this was a concept that seemed to 'leave the responsibility for their poverty with the poor themselves, and even to echo the harsh moral strictures of the nineteenth-century poor law reforms'. Such attitudes, they argued (*ibid*. p. 53), arose from 'a self-protective hardening of middle-class American society, which at once neglected and condemned those it excluded'. This 'moral underclass discourse' (Levitas 1998) never quite went away and was to reach a new peak some 20 years later in the writings of neo-liberals such as Charles Murray (1990), who characterised those living in excluded areas as being divorced from the morality of the rest of society.

Whether or not 'the poor' are blamed for their own exclusion, what these different approaches have in common is the assumption that the 'problem', however caused, is one of deficiencies within the community and can be addressed by and within the community. The solution lies in community development and self-help, which will help people to manage their lives better, restore 'community spirit', reduce tension and develop community networks and/or new mediating institutions. However, in the past, critics have seen this approach as a cynical move by government to forestall and manage dissent in the face of industrial restructuring (Craig 1989) and also to defuse growing racial tensions, as immigrants, brought in or encouraged by governments as part of economic expansion, began to mobilise against the widespread discrimination, exploitation and racism which they found in their adopted countries (Popple and Shaw 1997).

The 'restoring community' theme was given a new lease of life in the 1990s by a communitarian movement that drew support from across the political spectrum. For communitarians, the solution to urban decline was to reinstil a sense of responsibility as well as rights, and to make communities rather than the state the primary institutions of decision-making and service provision. It remains potent today, for example, in the UK government's 'Big Society' policies (see Box 1.2). The revival of this theme also owes a great deal to the popularisation of the concept of 'social capital' and concern about its decline in society more generally (Putnam 1993; 2000), prompting interventions to rebuild community ties thought to have been lost and to promote 'community cohesion' within and across communities.

Approaches to the need to 'restore community' have also over the years included initiatives to improve the physical environment and thereby to improve the physical image and sense of safety in disadvantaged neighbourhoods. More recent initiatives have focused on the need to re-engineer 'community', by diversifying tenure within neighbourhoods in order to break up large and easily stigmatised blocks of social housing and bring in a more mixed population. The intention is that this will combat the association of particular areas with low income and socially excluded populations but also, in echoes of the communitarian approach, bring in new sets of values and 'role models'.

The ideal of a homogeneous, morally coherent community, which underpins much communitarian thinking, feels increasingly outmoded in the post-modern world. Struggles around race, gender, disability and sexuality, with identities forged around communities of identity and interest as well as place, have over the past 30 years forced policymakers to engage with diversity, to recognise multiple forms of exclusion and to confront prejudice and discrimination. The racial landscape meanwhile has changed considerably since racial tensions triggered the urban renewal initiatives of the 1960s in the UK and the US. On the one hand, black and minority ethnic (BME) communities continue to be over-represented in disadvantaged neighbourhoods in many OECD countries and racial tensions continue to flare, demanding a policy response. Concern for community cohesion has been further intensified – and further complicated – in the wake of the threat from Al Qaeda and allied movements as well as the rise of the far right. On the other hand, in many countries, the demographics of ethnicity have changed with many second, third and fourth generation BME citizens as well as a much wider ethnic diversity. A growing awareness of the complexity of the issues involved has, in a number of countries, led to a move away from easy assumptions about assimilation and prompted debates about diversity, multiculturalism and their relation to community, identity and citizenship, to which I shall return later in the book.

System failure

Making the state work better

The concern to 'restore community' has commonly been accompanied by strategies to correct the shortcomings of systems of administration and service delivery in disadvantaged or 'deprived' areas. The need to co-ordinate the work of professionals and make them more sensitive to local communities was a key theme in the US War on Poverty in the 1960s but, as Box 3.1 demonstrates, its concerns still sound remarkably contemporary.

There have been two strands aimed at making the system work better over the years. One has been better co-ordination between services; the second has been more community participation in services.

System failure was initially seen as one consequence of the rapid growth of the welfare state and of a public sector that was characterised by complex, professionally based public institutions, with all their attendant failings. As well as being a key

---

BOX 3.1 The need for reform

Moynihan (1969, pp. 69–70) highlights seven issues that the Presidents' Committee on Juvenile Delinquency, set up in the early 1960s, sought to address:

'1. Many voluntary welfare programs were not reaching the poor
2. If they were reaching the poor, the services offered were often inappropriate
3. Services aimed at meeting the needs of disadvantaged people were typically fragmented and unrelated
4. Realistic understanding by professionals and community leaders of the problems faced by the poor was limited
5. Each speciality field was typically working in encapsulated fashion on a particular kind of problem, without awareness of the other fields or of efforts toward interlock
6. There was little political leadership involvement in the decision-making processes of voluntary social welfare
7. There was little or no serious participation of program beneficiaries in programs being planned and implemented by professionals and elite community leadership.'

---

feature of the US War on Poverty, therefore, co-ordination of local services and between central and local government was also a significant theme of the subsequent wave of initiatives introduced by the UK government in the 1960s: Education Priority Areas, the National Community Development Project, the Urban Programme and the short-lived Comprehensive Community Programme among them. Participation was also seen as a remedy for some of the previous failures of the system. In the UK, as elsewhere, reconstruction after the Second World War – which included large-scale developments in public housing, road building and urban renewal (and the attendant issues of displacement) – made planning and redevelopment issues the obvious focus for participation initiatives (Gyford 1976).

The push to improve services came from below as well as above. The new social movements of the 1960s spawned a range of demands and inspired others to fight for their rights.

The growth of welfare rights movements in the 1960s and 1970s addressed the complexity of access and process associated with state welfare as well as the issue of basic rights to income. In the wake of the Vietnam War, disabled people's organisations in the US demanded better services, a movement which rapidly spread into other countries. BME groups demanded an end to discrimination while women's organisations took on the health establishment. From above, the state felt the need to re-establish its legitimacy and participation became an important strategy for sustaining administrative stability and incorporating potentially troublesome elements. Some in the US saw this as a cynical move to increase the power of the bureaucracy (Moynihan 1969) or to win the Black vote. Policies to co-ordinate service delivery and to encourage participation were, they argued, geared more to social engineering than to encouraging local democracy. Nonetheless, others saw it as a genuine recognition of the need to seek the views of those who were the objects of redevelopment and urban policy, at a time when the economy was still growing.

For community practice, this suggested an approach that was variously described as 'social planning' and a 'community services approach' (Thomas 1983; Glen 1993; Rothman and Tropman 1993; Smock 2003). This emphasised the need to work with service providers to encourage the delivery of more responsive services that would maximise community involvement and community participation.

The system failure theme has reappeared on the community agenda in various guises over the past 30–40 years. One incarnation has been through initiatives in many countries to decentralise government. In Europe, this has been consistent with the doctrine of subsidiarity; in the US, it has been a feature of the withdrawal of federal government from the welfare arena; internationally – as we have seen – it has been a requirement of structural adjustment programmes. In the UK, decentralisation initiatives were led in the 1980s by local authorities keen to re-establish their credentials as providers in the face of the privatisation agenda of the Thatcher government (Burns, Hambleton and Hoggett 1994). Most of these initiatives were designed to decentralise service delivery and locate services closer to their users, but some also devolved decision making. Localism has an appeal across the ideological divide. It resurfaced again in UK policy in the 2000s under New Labour and is now a central platform of the Conservative-LibDem coalition government elected in 2010, seeking to devolve powers both to local government and to local communities themselves (see Box 1.2).

The need to co-ordinate between the different arms of government at local level was a feature of the New Labour government's National Strategy for Neighbourhood Renewal (Social Exclusion Unit or SEU 2000) in England. Arguing that 'the poorest neighbourhoods get the poorest services' (Social Exclusion Unit 2000, p. 24) and that services and policies had been working at cross purposes (Social Exclusion Unit 2001, p. 7), its neighbourhood management initiative aimed to put local services under the charge of a single person, team or organisation at neighbourhood level, and to bring local service providers, budgets and accountability systems together. Neighbourhood management was also a central theme in the influential *Regies de Quartiers* in France, which were developed in the early 1980s and which brought public authorities, professionals and residents together to manage neighbourhood services and development as well as to engage residents as employees (Clark and Southern 2006). Both models aimed to harness the knowledge and energy of local people and give them more say in local services. Indeed, participation was fast becoming the 'new orthodoxy' in Western Europe (Atkinson and Eckardt 2004; Grimshaw and Lever 2009).

Community management

A second set of initiatives to address system failure that has been developed across different countries aims to empower local people not only through giving them more opportunities to participate in the planning and development of services but also by devolving the management of services and public assets down to communities themselves. Community management has long been part of development policy in the global South, where the absence of state provision places a premium on local knowledge and resources in the delivery of services and the management of water and other amenities. In the North, governments have seen community management as a way of putting communities at the heart of neighbourhood renewal initiatives and giving them a sense of ownership. As we have seen, critics warn of the dangers of governments devolving responsibility without adequate resources. Nonetheless, from below, too, residents have demanded more control over local services that government has failed to provide effectively or taken over services that were threatened with closure. With government subsidies, for example, community development corporations (CDCs) in the US have successfully developed and managed low-income housing, while in the UK government subsidies have encouraged tenant management of housing and are now promoting asset transfer and community-based social enterprise.

Structural and economic failure

Structural transformation

Shaw and Martin (2000, p. 402) place both the themes discussed so far within a social democratic ideology:

> Essentially, the problem was defined in two ways: there was something deficient in individuals or groups (social pathology) or in the ways institutions responded to their needs (institutional deficiency). ... The solution was two-fold: first, to integrate deficit/disaffected individuals and groups into the mainstream; second, to make providers of services more sensitive to their needs.

Policies to restore community and make services work better thus went arm in arm. But the oil crisis in the mid-1970s exposed the shortcomings of both approaches. Until then it had been possible to conceive of a society with no losers, if only the 'disadvantaged' could be given assistance in making their case. But with the recession that followed the oil crisis, the economic growth and optimism which had fostered these policies receded and, with them, the capacity of government (in the view of some of its critics) to 'buy off' the discontented. By the mid-1970s, two of the major social democratic programmes of the 1960s and 1970s – the War on Poverty and the UK's National Community Development Programme – were unravelling, caught on the contradictions between a reformist agenda, the resistance of the bureaucracy and the aspirations of the people whose participation the programmes had sought (see, for example, Marris and Rein 1967; Piven and Cloward 1977; Loney 1983; O'Connor 2007).

The state's agenda might have been institutional co-ordination, but the agenda on the ground was institutional change.

Some of those who introduced these programmes may have had a genuine desire to enfranchise the poor and create such institutional change, but this desire was frustrated by 'the intransigent autonomy of public and private agencies, at any level of government' (Marris and Rein 1967, p. 222). The intention of the War on Poverty, as Gaventa (1998, p. 52) points out, was to encourage citizen participation, not to turn control of the programme over to citizens or, indeed, to bypass local political structures. When the political impacts of enhanced participation became apparent (Lawrence 2007), empowerment was redefined in ways that served the status quo.

Moynihan (1969, p. 185) describes a potent mixture of political rhetoric, high expectations, bottled-up frustration and professional idealism (or even manipulation):

> The blunt reality is that sponsors of community action programmes who expected to adopt the conflict strategy of Saul Alinsky and at the same time expected to be the recipients of large sums of public money, looked for, to paraphrase Jefferson 'what never was and never will be'.

This mismatch of aspirations was reflected in the UK. Atkinson (2000b) argues that the policies and programmes of the late 1960s failed to link the problems of inner-city deprivation to a wider societal analysis. However, these links were made by those who were working on the programmes. A trenchant critique of government policy at this time was presented in a series of publications by the UK National Community Development Project (CDP 1977). These challenged explanations of urban deprivation rooted in community pathology or even system failure, drawing attention instead to the structural causes of deprivation that CDP workers saw as being inherent in the pursuit of capitalism. The state (national and local) was targeted as the defender of capitalist interests. Urban decline in this analysis could not be reversed by action at local level alone. The problems faced by disadvantaged communities had their roots in wider economic forces. The appropriate response, for many of these critics, was not participation but protest.

This resonated with the 'community organising' approach advocated by Saul Alinsky and others in the US (Alinsky 1971). This 'power-based approach' (Smock 2003) encouraged large group mobilisation and confrontational tactics to demand change – stirring up non-violent conflict to agitate, antagonise, educate and organise (Ledwith 2005, p. 89). It looked to coalition politics – alliances with the social movements and trade unions – to strengthen the community voice. In the UK alliances were also developed with the more radical elements of local government, which themselves were engaged in a rearguard action against a Thatcherite neo-liberal agenda.

Rothman and Tropman (1993, p. 9) note that what they call the 'social action' approach may 'lean in the direction of either task or process goals'. Civil rights and cause-oriented organisations were task-oriented: they aimed for specific legislative outcomes or sought to change practice and procedure. But the Alinsky model was concerned with the process of empowerment as an end in itself: 'This objective of building local-based power and decision-making transcends the solution of any given problem situation. Goals are often viewed in terms of changing power relationships rather than tinkering with small-scale or short-range problem situations' (Rothman and Tropman 1993, p. 9; see also Chapter 11 this volume). For change to occur, Moynihan (1969, p. 186) argued, the lack of organisational power among the poor had to be addressed.

Also concerned with the process of empowerment was a parallel practice of critical popular education, drawing on the work of Paolo Freire (1972) with impoverished agricultural workers in Latin America. Freire's model of 'problem-posing' adult learning has since been widely adopted by practitioners in the North and the South, using 'dialogical methods ... as a vehicle for raising critical awareness about the way disadvantage and oppression ... was maintained through dominant social institutions and ideologies' (Butcher 2007a, p. 53; see also Ledwith 2005 and Chapter 10, this volume). Both Alinsky and Freire aimed to be transformational in their approaches, encouraging an alternative vision for society (Smock 2003).

In developing countries, where communities are struggling against authoritarian states, John Abbott (1996, p. 20) argues that political empowerment strategies are often the only realistic option. He describes these as confrontational but suggests that the South African experience demonstrates how these types of struggle – while essentially transitory in nature – can form the basis for more permanent change (1996, p. 194) – a process which has also been demonstrated in Latin America. However, as Viviene Taylor (1995), also writing from South Africa, points out, the legacy of violence and divide and rule tactics can be difficult to overcome. The transition from oppositional politics to engagement once battles are won and opportunities open up can be difficult to achieve.

Shaw and Martin (2000) argue that the structuralist critique was often reductionist and over-deterministic and too dismissive of the possibilities for social democratic reform, although they believe that feminist critiques and subsequent literature in the fields of race and disability have moved the agenda on significantly. Certainly the critique, as framed in the 1970s, left many community workers on the ground uncertain about the legitimacy of their work – indeed, critics argue that it conceptualised communities in largely passive terms (Waddington 1979; Marris 1982).

Nonetheless, the community organising tradition is still vibrant today. In the US, Alinsky-style organising has informed Barack Obama's election campaign and perhaps also the ideologically opposed Tea Party movement. It is also gaining in strength in England and has attracted the attention of high-profile national politicians, although it remains to be seen whether the transformational aspirations espoused by Alinsky are quite what advocates of the Big Society have in mind. It informs development practice in the South, driven by international NGOs like INTRAC and Civic Driven Change, which take a more radical view of capacity building than that described earlier. At a global level, the Internet has opened up new repertoires of action in order to challenge the wider economic forces behind poverty, injustice and environmental degradation.

Making the economy work better

Both the US War on Poverty and the UK CDP came to an end in the 1970s. However, a structural analysis was accepted, although in a different form and with a radically different outcome from the one that the activists in both programmes would have urged. The neo-liberal response to the flight of capital from the inner cities and to the economic exclusion of disadvantaged communities was one of economic development, physical renewal and wealth creation. Governments of the 1980s moved away from community-based approaches to property-led regeneration schemes. Access to jobs and the improvement of the urban fabric to make it more attractive to investors were seen as the route to urban renewal. The idea was that the wealth created would 'trickle down' to all levels of society. In the UK, it was the business world that was encouraged to take the lead. Local authorities – as the predominant providers of public services – were seen by the Thatcher government to be a significant part of the problem. Instead the government set up non-elected quangos, which bypassed the local state, to attract investment and jobs at local level, such as Urban Development Corporations, Task Forces and City Action Teams.

Community organisations were peripheral to these developments. Existing regeneration and poverty programmes, such as the Urban Programme in the UK, successors to the War on Poverty in the US and the European Structural Funds were rebalanced away from social and towards economic objectives. Nonetheless special employment measures introduced to tackle rising unemployment provided some opportunities for communities. Job creation schemes, for example, which were introduced in the UK in the 1970s, provided funds for many community-based organisations, often for the first time. However, they were a mixed blessing. Many organisations were unprepared for the management of significant resources and critics argued that these organisations were being co-opted into delivering a government agenda on subsistence wages (Addy and Scott 1988). By the end of the 1980s, anti-poverty programmes initiated by the European Union and a number of local authorities were beginning to offer a wider perspective from which to address economic failure (Alcock *et al.* 1995).

Most evaluations of the economic development programmes of the 1980s were lukewarm about their achievements. These programmes led to a decrease in the number of unskilled and semi-skilled jobs, an increase in part-time and casual jobs which did not provide a living wage, and a benefit system that provided the most minimal income but discouraged claimants from increasing this through casual work (MacFarlane 1997). Notably, economically driven urban regeneration initiatives failed to deliver jobs or housing to the indigenous population (Hausner *et al.* 1991). Wealth did not trickle down. Jobs went to outsiders and new housing brought in a more affluent population, which either displaced the indigenous population or, through a process of gentrification, pushed it to the margins. As the slogan of US protests in the 1960s put it, 'urban renewal equals black people's removal' (Mayo 1997b, p. 16).

This economic development agenda is one that has continued to the present day, although with some attempts to soften the more aggressive edges of 'trickle-down' and apply a more targeted approach. Thus Ruth Levitas (1998) argued in the late 1990s that the 'social inclusion discourse' at the time focused too strongly on getting individuals back into the labour market and too little on other aspects of exclusion. The objectives of the National Strategy for Neighbourhood Renewal in England, launched in 2001, were much more comprehensive, covering health, education, community safety, environment and housing alongside worklessness. But by the end of the decade, its main legacy was the Working Neighbourhoods Fund, which once again focused on the labour market at the expense of other, more social, objectives.

Governments in England and the other UK countries have, however, become interested in social enterprise, with its potential to combine economic and social goals by encouraging co-production, mutuality and collective ownership. In the US, Zdenek (1998, p. 43) describes how CDCs emerged in the late 1960s, mainly from minority ethnic and rural communities. He describes three phases of their development: the first engaged mainly in business development and was funded by federal government; the second wave in the 1970s emerged from organisations with an advocacy or housing background; and a third generation has emerged since the 1980s in response to cutbacks in federal funding for low income areas. Social and community-based enterprise also has a strong tradition in mainland Europe where it resonates with the language of *l'économie sociale* and co-operative traditions based on solidarity and mutuality. In the UK, however, community enterprise flourished mainly in Scotland, Wales and Northern Ireland. In England, despite a tradition of mutuality stretching back into the nineteenth century, the big money in the 1980s and 1990s went into top-down economic development initiatives (Twelvetrees 1998d). Until recently, the funding streams and infrastructure that supported the growth of CDCs in the US and the social economy in Europe were largely absent.

Advocates of social enterprise argue that it challenges the capitalist forms of production that have created exclusion, that it offers an alternative to forms of economic restructuring which continue to benefit the 'haves' at the expense of the 'have nots', and that it provides 'local work for local needs' (Birkholzer 1998). It also fosters alternative forms of production. The promotion of community management, where this involves the promotion of sustainable and independent enterprise, resonates with this agenda. These ideas have an appeal across the political spectrum and there are significant success stories. But they have yet to offer a substantial and sustainable alternative to other approaches. Indeed, as we shall see in Chapter 11, opinion remains divided over the achievements of the CDC movement. Some critics argue that far from achieving political and economic independence and self-sufficiency, CDCs are at best a plaster on the casualties of capitalism and at worst represent the co-option of a social movement (Stoecker 2007).

Government failure

Moving towards the market

I suggested earlier that the advance of the market in welfare has been a significant factor in the marginalisation of low-income populations. In the UK, the government's own reports acknowledged the extent to which social housing policies contributed to social exclusion by concentrating those with least choice in the most undesirable areas (Social Exclusion Unit 1998). Choice in schools has had similar perverse effects. But the introduction of the market into welfare has also offered some routes to empowerment, particularly through increasing and promoting the rights of individual service users. The combination of market policies with increasingly confident and vocal user movements has forced mainstream service providers and professionals from public, private and voluntary, non-profit organisations to re-examine their structures and practices, and service users have been more centrally involved, individually and collectively, in service planning (for example, in social care). These policies have created an environment in which an increasingly confident service user movement has been able to make its voice heard.

The new welfare market has also offered communities the chance to take more control over the production of their own services, as we have already seen. The introduction of social care markets in many countries offers opportunities in principle for community-based organisations to provide services on contract from local authorities. Although the main beneficiaries of these policies are likely to be national non-profit organisations and private care firms, community-based organisations and social co-operatives have found particular niches in the market, especially where governments are sympathetic to their development. However, the reality of market-based policies for many excluded communities has been the loss of local public services (Forrest and Kearns 1999; Page 2000), while a shift in funding from grants to contracts has led to increasing uncertainty and risks co-opting community organisations into delivering a government agenda (Russell, Scott and Wilding 1995).

From government to governance

An alternative response to the failure of government to meet the needs of its citizens in the past is not to replace it or strip it of its powers but to 'reinvent' it (Osborne and Gaebler 1992). This does not signal a retreat from the market but, in a local institutional environment where they are no longer (or have never been) the only player, government institutions are instead being encouraged into an 'enabling' role, working in partnership with others to release a range of resources for change. One part of the reinvention agenda has been a new managerialism borrowed from the private sector, which seeks to improve systems within government by introducing market principles, with the implications discussed above. A second, and sometimes contradictory, part of the agenda is the move from government to 'governance'. Recurring themes in this discourse are the need for collaborative, 'partnership' approaches to exclusion, crime and other persistent problems, and the need to revive the democratic process through democratic renewal or democratisation.

The theme of partnership has resonated across the globe, whether the partners are different levels of government, business, international NGOs, indigenous groups or community organisations. Government institutions are being encouraged to devolve decision making and promote participation through new forms of deliberative democracy and participatory planning, which recognise the limitations of relying solely on the electoral process. For communities, this offers the potential to work in partnership with outside agencies to achieve community goals, or to set up their own structures into which government and other actors can be invited – Abbott (1996) describes this as 'negotiated development'. These initiatives are discussed further in Chapters 8 and 11.

Area-based policies

Many of the approaches described above have been targeted on neighbourhoods or other spatially defined communities. But there have been strong criticisms of area-based social exclusion policies. These fall into three categories. The first is that low income and exclusion are not confined to particular targeted areas. In the UK in 1999, Glennerster *et al.* argued that area-based policies still excluded around two-thirds of disadvantaged households. There are systematic forms of exclusion based on race, disability, gender, sexuality and faith that area-based policies do not address (see, for example, Tilly 1999). A focus on place can ignore these forms, even within the very neighbourhoods they target.

A further dimension to this critique is that, often, the distinction between the most excluded neighbourhoods – which get targeted – and the only slightly less excluded is difficult to make. Chatterton and Bradley (2000, p. 101) suggest that there are 'overlaps and leakages' either side of physical boundaries, which mean that people just outside the area may suffer as much from exclusion as those within. Peter Ambrose (2000) has shown that, while policies targeted at specific areas may improve conditions there, they do not make any difference beyond the targeted neighbourhood. As such, they are 'a drop in the ocean'. And where neighbourhoods do manage to improve their position, they often do so by 'exporting' their problems (that is, their most disadvantaged people).

A second set of criticisms relates to the tendency of area-based policies to 'cream off' the most able in the locality, leaving such areas more impoverished than before. The problem, especially when area-based policies are based on employment generation, is that once their personal situation improves and they have the ability to make choices, achievers may well leave. If so, their place is taken by the most vulnerable in the housing market, increasing the pressure that these areas face.

This relates to a third set of criticisms, which derive from the structural analysis discussed earlier. This critique argues that social inclusion policies often focus their efforts at the neighbourhood level, rather than tackling the structural issues which are responsible for exclusion and which neighbourhood action cannot affect. Carley (2001) cites research in the US, which suggests that structural factors at the level of the regional economy explain about four-fifths of neighbourhood deprivation. Structural explanations of exclusion describe how the processes of urbanisation under capitalism have led to a reorganisation of space and created processes of urban marginalisation which will be discussed in more detail in Chapter 6 (Chatterton and Bradley 2000; O'Connor 2007). People working and living within the neighbourhoods created by exclusion cannot reverse this process on their own.

These are not arguments for abandoning an area-based approach. Friedmann (1998, p. 26) argues that 'the extension of the meaning of citizenship to the local ... has much to recommend it in an era that is marked by the hollowing out of the national state'. There are particular processes at work that concentrate poverty in particular places and these do need to be addressed. But they must be addressed in a context that recognises the other ways in which exclusion is manifested and the wider causes of that exclusion. There is increasing interest now in policies that relate to communities of identity and interest (Rothman 2000).

Summary

This chapter has described a number of different themes, which underlie community approaches over the past 40 years. It has explored the way the 'problem' is defined in each approach, the assumptions and ideologies behind them and the strategies adopted. Different themes have come to the fore at different times: community self-help and system co-ordination were central to community strategies from the 1950s to the 1970s, while economic development and consumer choice prevailed in the 1980s. Partnership and governance approaches have come to the fore since the 1990s. Self-help and community organising are now back in the spotlight. In fact all the themes described in this chapter can be found in current policies. The approaches that flow from these themes are not mutually exclusive; on the contrary, while it can be argued that they all have limitations as isolated approaches, each has a contribution to make to a comprehensive strategy. Later chapters will return to the question of how they can be integrated and the strengths and weaknesses of each; but first it is necessary to explore further the concepts of community and empowerment that lie at the centre of community policy and practice agendas.

Chapter 4

Ideas of Community

In Chapter 2, I set out some of the reasons why politicians and the media might be looking to 'community' and the set of ideas associated with it. I also suggested that these ideas were being used so freely and imprecisely by their advocates that they ran the risk of becoming almost meaningless. In a much-cited text, George Hillery (1955) found over 94 meanings of community. 'Civil society', meanwhile, is a term that has undergone several metamorphoses over the centuries while, in its briefer life, 'social capital' has been used by its advocates in many different ways. A bewildering array of other concepts and ideas also pop up from time to time under the community umbrella. So can these terms be more than a 'call to arms'? Do they have the potential to guide policy, especially policies which aim to tackle the intractable problems of poverty and social exclusion?

In this chapter, I will simply describe the way the terms have been used in public and scholarly debate, along with the claims made for them. The following two chapters will then assess the criticisms that can and have been levelled at these terms and the tensions and dilemmas that can arise when they are applied to issues of poverty and social exclusion.

Community

'Community' is a term that is used both as a description and as a prescription. Thus, drawing on Butcher (1993) and Purdue *et al.* (2000), it is possible to identify at least three general senses in which 'community' – and other terms discussed here – are used.

1. Descriptive: A group or network of people who share something in common or interact with each other;
2. Normative: A place where solidarity, participation and coherence are found;

3. Instrumental: (a) An agent acting to maintain or change its circumstances; (b) The location or orientation of services and policy interventions.

Descriptive

Communities may be defined (Taylor, Barr and West 2000) in terms of the common characteristics their members share. These may be personal characteristics (age, gender, ethnic origin, sexuality, colour of hair); common beliefs (political, ideological, religious); activities (leisure, arts, sport); use or provision of services and goods (commuters, patients; parents; carers, providers); or where members live or work. But just because people have characteristics in common, this does not mean they identify themselves as a community; this requires that they have *common interests*. These might include the following:

- A common cultural heritage (a common tradition or identity, a sense of continuity, of belonging and loyalty, perhaps in faith communities or ethnic communities)
- Social relationships (the mutual support and social interaction derived from kinship, a common residential base or common experience)
- Common economic interests (class; common or potential use of a product or service by home-owners, service users or customers; provision of goods or services by businesses, traders, service providers or workers)
- Common experiences of power or oppression (for instance, the 'old school tie'; refugees and asylum seekers; class; ethnic minorities).

These meanings of community overlap. An ethnic minority community may have meaning for its members because of its common traditions and history, the social relationships between its members, a common religious heritage, or a common experience of discrimination or powerlessness. Class appears twice in the above list, because it can denote both common economic interests and common experiences of power.

These common interests provide the glue that can turn community from a simple description to an active agent. But individuals may belong to many different communities at the same time: residential, work-based, kinship, religious, recreational and so on. For any individual, different allegiances and identities may come to the fore at different times or may pull in different directions at the same time. Similarly, communities themselves will be diverse and their members may have different interests, some of which overlap while others do not.

Butcher (1993, p. 13) points out that 'commentators, policy makers, and others are apt to assume that *because* a certain population segment live together in the same place or have some other characteristic in common they *therefore* can be referred to as a "community"'. To constitute a community, most commentators would expect living in the same place to be enhanced in some way through social or instrumental ties (Dale and Newman 2010).

In an age of increased mobility and the Internet, commentators increasingly question the extent to which people feel a sense of affinity with place. However, a recent UK study suggests that 71 per cent of the population felt either strongly or very strongly that they *did* belong to their neighbourhood, that they saw their neighbourhoods as places where people looked out for one another and that they valued their place-based relationships (Home Office 2003; Richardson 2008). Sampson (2007) also refers to research findings in the US that suggest that community ties are stronger than we might expect in contemporary society, especially in poor urban neighbourhoods. In the same volume, De Filippis (2007, p. 3) argues that 'even in their post-modern and mutating form', contemporary neighbourhoods 'are commonly traversed spaces where people meet face-to-face, sometimes co-ordinate their actions and purposes and, on occasion, act collectively to change the way these spaces and relations enable or constrain collective purpose'. It seems that, despite the changes in contemporary living, place still matters to a lot of people. However, significant places may not fit in with administrative boundaries defined by outsiders – heritage and social relationships may create territories that mean much more to residents. And, I have already suggested that allegiance to a community of interest may take precedence over territorial loyalties for some members.

Al Hunter (1974) captures the interlocking nature of different aspects of community in his conceptualisation of community as a 'variable' rather than a given. He identifies three dimensions along which communities vary: *ecological*, in terms of the space and time they occupy; *social structural*, in terms of the inter-personal networks and institutional density within them; and *symbolic/cultural*, in terms of the extent to which they confer a common identity and culture. When all three are combined, he argues, they characterise a strong community.

Normative

'Community' is not a word that is used solely in its descriptive sense, however. More often than not it carries with it assumptions about the way we should live. There are two particular judgments that are implied in its use. One of these contrasts 'community' with the impersonality of mass society and the state. Thus as we saw in Chapter 3, Nisbet (1960, p. 82) is among a number of authors who have argued for the need for mediating institutions between the state and the individual: 'The state can enlist popular enthusiasm, can conduct crusades, can mobilise on behalf of great "causes" such as wars, but as a regular and normal means of meeting human needs for recognition, fellow-ship, security and membership, it is inadequate'. He sees medi-ating structures, such as the family and small informal social groups, as spreading power in society and checking the modern tendency to concentrate power in the hands of the state.

The other normative judgment that debates about community make is to contrast the organic ties of community with the mech-anistic ties of the more contractual relationships, which charac-terise industrial and post-industrial societies. Most scholars track concern with community and 'loss of community' back to Ger-man sociological thought in the late eighteenth and nineteenth centuries (Plant 1974) and particularly to the work of Tönnies (1995) and the distinction that he makes between *Gemeinschaft* and *Gesellschaft*, contrasting traditional holistic, territorial communities (usually seen as rural) with the newer fragmented, contractual relationships of industrialised society (usually seen as urban: see Table 4.1). Often this distinction has been treated in a normative way, with the positive attributes of *Gemeinschaft* contrasted with the negative attributes of *Gesellschaft*.

Normative ideas of community emphasise dense overlapping social ties; the only thing that Hillery's definitions (or at least 69 of them) could agree on was that community involves social

TABLE 4.1 *Characteristics of Gemeinschaft and Gesellschaft*

Gemeinschaft	Gesellschaft
Place	Interest
Organic	Functional
Primary groups	Secondary groups
Shared values and world view – given	Shared values as a result of functional co-operation
Identity of interests	Differentiation of interests
Fixed	Mobile
Conservative	Progressive
Holistic/total	Fragmented; specialist
Co-operative	Contractual
End	Means
Traditional	Modern
Oral communication	Written communication

Source: Plant (1974); and others.

interaction and some ties or bonds in common. Philip Abrams's work on neighbours (Bulmer 1988) describes neighbourhoods as a densely woven world of kin, neighbours, friends and co-workers, highly localised and strongly caring within the confines of quite tightly defined relationships. In working-class communities, such as those studied by Pahl (1970), these distinctions are overlaid by the ties of work and religion. The overlapping at local level of a number of these different social relationships and, above all, the relationships of kinship provided the basis for local and moral control. It is these dense overlapping ties that tend to be contrasted favourably with the fragmented and contractual ties of industrialised society.

Others, however, argue that community has been transformed rather than lost. Sampson (2007, p. 165) argues that 'city dwellers have not lost the capacity for deep, long-lasting relationships, rather they have gained the capacity for surface, fleeting relationships that are restricted'. Instead of needing communities to satisfy our private and personal needs, he argues, local community 'remains essential as a site for the realisation of common values in support of social goods'. Still others – in contrast to the conservative values of *Gemeinschaft* – emphasise the value of community as 'the matrix through which new, more democratic and inclusive forms of democracy can emerge ... a space for contesting the social costs of capitalism to working class and marginalised people' (De Filippis and Saegert 2007, p. 2).

Instrumental

Politicians and policymakers – in seeking ways to work with a particular set of people identified as living in the same place or having characteristics/interests in common – often mix together descriptive and normative meanings of community. They tend to assume that common location or interests bring with them social and moral cohesion, a sense of security, and mutual trust. But they also tend to go a step further and assume that norms will be turned into action: that is, that community can be turned into agency, with people who live in the same place caring for each other, getting involved in collective enterprises and activities and acting together to change their circumstances.

Thus adding 'community' to a service may simply describe its location – siting it in a neighbourhood rather than a centralised office, designating staff to work in a particular locality or caring for people at home rather in an institution. But it may also imply any of the following descriptions of the way in which a service is provided (Taylor, Barr and West 2000):

- **Contact** with the public – a way of describing front-line staff
- **Support** – providing financial or other resources to organisations in the community
- **Outreach** – going into people's homes or local meeting places
- **Co-ordination** – bringing together the different agencies working in a locality; liaison with community organisations
- **Consultation** – consulting with people and organisations in a community
- **Devolution** – involving people from the community in managing local services.

These uses can be simply descriptive, but some also imply normative beliefs that the best way of providing services is in a way that is local and involves the people who use them. Community may also be applied to interventions in a symbolic sense, to lend an aura of trust, cohesion and security to a particular policy or intervention, regardless of whether or not these actually underpin or characterise the policy in practice.

Communitarianism

The normative promotion of community solutions has been most strongly associated with the communitarian school. This criticises both the individualism of the market, with its 'cancerous effects on community life' (Tam 1998, p. 3), and also the dependency produced by the state:

> A communitarian perspective recognises that the preservation of individual liberty depends on the active maintenance of the institutions of civil society where citizens learn respect for others as well as self-respect; where we acquire a lively sense of our personal and civic responsibilities, along with an appreciation of our own rights and those of others; where we develop the skills of self-government as well as the habit of governing ourselves, and learn to serve others, not just self.
> (Communitarian Network 1991, cited in Etzioni 1998, p. 43)

As the above suggests, communitarianism is in part a reaction against a perceived preoccupation with rights at the expense of responsibilities. It seeks to restore the balance by promoting the family first and then the community as the site of moral norms and obligations. It also seeks to revive the institutions that mediate between the individual and the state – in particular, communitarians see the school as an important source of moral education (Henderson and Salmon 1999).

Communitarianism is based on reciprocity and has been described as 'a morally charged concept because it is about the obligations and expectations one has to those people one lives closest to' (Revill 1993). Thus Frazer (2000, p. 181) writes that communitarians dispute the liberal contention that there are wholly rational foundations for ethics, politics and knowledge, arguing that what counts as justice can only be rooted in human ways of life.

Communitarians recognise that not all communities offer the opportunity for human fulfilment. Henry Tam (1998, p. 8) – who, since publishing his book on communitarianism became a senior civil servant in the government department responsible for community empowerment in the UK – argues that 'inclusive communities are to be distinguished from other forms of community by their operative power relations, which enable all their members to participate in collective processes affecting their lives'. He sees common values as emerging out of co-operative enquiry and open exchange, which is a much stronger basis for democracy than electoral democracy. However, he does argue that there are overarching values, which are maintained across different cultures. He defines these as the values of love, wisdom, justice and fulfilment, and sees mutual responsibility, based on these values, as central to the communitarian ethos.

John Gray (1996, p. 55) endorses this, emphasising the communitarian belief that localised collective choice is much better placed to resolve the competing claims of justice than market individualism. In fact, he sees the key insight of the communitarian liberal perspective as the belief that 'human lives conducted within a public culture that is desolated and fractured are impoverished, no matter how many individual choices they contain'.

Driver and Martell (1997, p. 33) stress the attraction of this creed to those who, while disenamoured of the excess of market individualism, still want to move away from state-based systems of welfare (advocates of the 'third way', for example). To these interests, communitarianism offers: 'a political vocabulary which eschews market individualism, but not capitalism; and which embraces collective action, but not class or the state'. But Driver and Martell do not see communitarianism as a single homogeneous approach. They identify six dimensions on which communitarianisms can differ. These are:

- Conformist (building an overarching morality) versus pluralist (recognising difference)
- More versus less conditional (responsibility arises from duties; responsibility arises from fellowship and solidarity)
- Conservative versus progressive
- Prescriptive versus voluntary
- Moral versus socio-economic (social cohesion due to shared morals; social cohesion due to socio-economic equality and shared rights)
- Individual versus corporate (that is, the responsibilities of business and institutions).

They argue that the New Labour government in the UK, and others of a similar persuasion, tended towards the former of each pair rather than the latter: a conditional, morally prescriptive, conservative and individual communitarianism at the expense of less conditional and redistributional, socio-economic, progressive and corporate communitarianisms. On some dimensions, they argue that proponents of this approach are torn, wanting institutional pluralism, which would devolve decision and delivery outwards and downwards on a subsidiarity basis, but also wanting ethical conformity to ensure that this is done within an overarching moral framework.

Social capital

The concept of social capital is most commonly associated with Robert Putnam, who defined it as: 'features of social life – networks, norms and trust – that enable participants to act together more effectively to pursue shared objectives' (Putnam 1993, pp. 664–5), the norms including reciprocity, co-operation and tolerance. He sees these norms as being produced through 'horizontally ordered' associations, particularly those involving face-to-face relations (such as choral societies and sports clubs). Like the communitarians, Putnam describes social capital as a 'moral resource' and he links the presence of social capital – built up over centuries – with the formation of the capacity for civic engagement that he sees as essential for modern democracy. Norms of trust and reciprocity created through face-to-face association, he argues, 'spill over' into society at large; a capacity is created for collective action in pursuit of shared goals; citizens expect, and representatives provide, competent and responsive government. He is concerned, however, with the decline of this resource in the US, due, he suggests, to a number of factors, including two-career families, urban sprawl and the growth of commuting (Putnam 2000).

Coleman (1990), whose work on social capital in organisations preceded that of Putnam, identifies social capital as a fourth and previously neglected form of capital in the production process, alongside financial, physical and human capital. He conceptualises it as a relational good, produced as a by-product of other activities. He describes how individual actors, in the process of pursuing their individual self-interest, produce social norms of trust and co-operation, which reduce the costs of monitoring and sanctioning activities and help to achieve effectiveness and efficiency.

The concept of relational capital bears some similarity to Coleman's ideas. Defining relational capital as 'the level of mutual trust, respect and friendship that arises out of close interaction at the individual level between alliance partners' Kale, Singh and Perlmutter (2000, p. 218) describe how firms create alliances as a strategic device to facilitate learning and access to new technologies and ideas, to exploit economies of scale and to share risk or uncertainty with their partners. Relational capital, they argue, helps to enhance the opportunities for learning and minimise the risks of opportunistic behaviour. It creates a mutual confidence that no party to an exchange will exploit others' vulnerabilities even if there is an opportunity to do so. Kale, Singh and Perlmutter also note that relational capital gains in value over time – prior alliances are a good predictor of the likelihood of building relational capital.

As conceptualised by Putnam and Coleman, social capital is a collective good, inherent in the relations between actors. As such it is 'a resource that is drawn upon to facilitate collaborative activities' (Maloney, Smith and Stoker 2000, p. 823). But Kale and his colleagues see relational capital as the property of individuals. Others, too, define social capital as an individual resource based on social ties or membership of networks (Bourdieu 1986; Portes 1995) – the social connections through which people can gain access to scarce economic and cultural resources.

The literature generally differentiates between three forms of social capital. The UK Office of National Statistics (ONS 2003) describes these as:

- Bonding social capital – describes closer connections between people and is characterised by strong bonds, for example, among family members or among members of the same ethnic group; it is good for 'getting by' in life.
- Bridging social capital – describes more distant connections between people and is characterised by weaker, but more cross-cutting ties, for example, with business associates, acquaintances, friends from different ethnic groups, friends of friends, etc; it is good for 'getting ahead' in life.

- Linking social capital – describes connections with people in positions of power and is characterised by relations between those within a hierarchy where there are differing levels of power; it is good for accessing support from formal institutions. It is different from bonding and bridging in that it is concerned with relations between people who are not on an equal footing. An example would be a social services agency dealing with an individual.

Bridging social capital is particularly important in addressing issues of social cohesion and I shall return to this in Chapter 5, while linking social capital is important in addressing issues of power, which will be discussed in Chapters 7 and 8.

There is a growing body of evidence that links the presence of social capital to a wide variety of positive outcomes, including better government, lower levels of crime, economic growth (Halpern 2005), improved health (see, for example, Wilkinson 1996; Cattell 2001), innovation in industry (Giddens 2000b). No wonder it has sparked considerable interest at national and international level (see Box 4.1). Peter Hall (1997, p. 35) spells out the attractions of Putnam's argument:

Formal and informal networks constitute a kind of 'social capital', with members more likely to participate in politics and more able to use their social connections to improve their own lives and their community. An organised citizenry can alleviate many social problems and ease the implementation of various kinds of public policy, for instance, by using neighbourhood watch groups to minimise crime. As a result, nations as a whole lose a resource when the ties between individuals erode.

Internationally, the World Bank has carried out a significant body of research to assist the application of the theory of social capital in community-driven development.

The concept of social capital is also closely linked to more recent concepts of 'collective efficacy' and 'community resilience', which examine the factors that enable communities to respond to social problems like crime or humanitarian disasters. Thus Sampson links collective efficacy, which he defines as a community's shared belief in its ability to realise the common values of

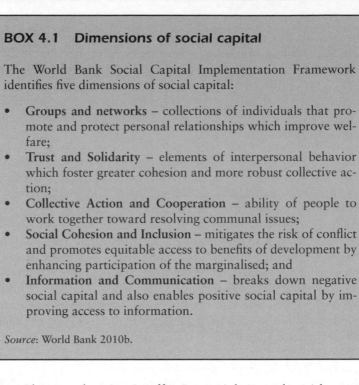

BOX 4.1   Dimensions of social capital

The World Bank Social Capital Implementation Framework identifies five dimensions of social capital:

- **Groups and networks** – collections of individuals that promote and protect personal relationships which improve welfare;
- **Trust and Solidarity** – elements of interpersonal behavior which foster greater cohesion and more robust collective action;
- **Collective Action and Cooperation** – ability of people to work together toward resolving communal issues;
- **Social Cohesion and Inclusion** – mitigates the risk of conflict and promotes equitable access to benefits of development by enhancing participation of the marginalised; and
- **Information and Communication** – breaks down negative social capital and also enables positive social capital by improving access to information.

Source: World Bank 2010b.

its residents and maintain effective social controls, with mutual trust, organisational participation, friendship and kinship ties (Ohmer and Beck 2006; Sampson 2007).

Civil society

Civil society, as popularly used, emphasises the direct collective engagement of citizens and consumers in economic, social and political development. Walzer (1995, p. 7) defines it as 'the sphere of uncoerced human association and also the set of relational networks – formed for the sake of family, faith, interest and ideology – that fill this space'. Tester similarly (1992, p. 8) defines modern civil society as applying to 'all those relationships which involve the voluntary association and participation of individuals acting in their private capacities'.

The concept has a long and distinguished history and its meaning has undergone several metamorphoses over the centuries. Drawing on Hegel and Marx, Tester (1992) argues that it emerged out of the separation of the realm of the state (public life) and the realm of the private. Feudal society's 'natural order' did not conceive of an independent private realm because what we define as personal matters (questions of birth, family, property, occupation and so forth) were all implicated in an overarching system, which determined the place of the monarch's subject in his kingdom (Tester 1992, p. 14). But as property relations extricated themselves from the ancient and medieval communal society, reciprocity between strangers, based on trust, became essential to the creation of wealth (Seligman 1992, p. 27): 'With society no longer conceived in the hierarchic and holistic terms of medieval orders but of discrete individuals, a new bond between its particulars must be found'.

In the eighteenth century, the Scottish Enlightenment tradition saw civil society as a new foundation for reciprocity, mutuality and co-operation beyond the calculus of pure exchange. It was a means of protecting moral and communal ties against corrupting influences (Seligman 1992, p. 206). It also represented an attempt to find 'a synthesis' between a number of emerging tensions: 'the individual and the social, the private and the public, egoism and altruism, as well as between a life governed by reason and one governed by the passions' (Seligman 1992, p. 25). A highly articulated civil society with overlapping membership was seen as the foundation of a stable democratic polity and a defence against domination by any one group (Edwards 2004). But critics suggest that civil society at this time was very much the preserve of the white, male, property-owning elite (Howell and Pearce 2002).

Moving into the twentieth century, the civil society discourse took a more radical turn in the work of Antonio Gramsci. Gramsci characterised civil society as the arena in which the struggle for cultural and ideological hegemony unfolds, highlighting the role of the institutions of civil society – the family, schools, universities and the media – in shaping the political dispositions of citizens. His analysis was concerned with the struggle for domination in civil society and stressed the potential of its institutions to entrench the dominant ideas of the ruling class.

Gramsci apart, for a long time before the fall of the Iron Curtain, Alexander (1998, p. 1) argues, civil society had been considered 'a quaint and conservative notion, thoroughly obsolete'.

But, with the overthrow of the Soviet regime, civil society was rediscovered and celebrated in academic and policy circles as a counterbalance to the power of the state, echoing Nisbet's earlier interest in community. For some at this time, drawing on a tradition that goes back to John Locke, civil society encompassed private enterprise and the market and thus had a considerable appeal for right-wing politicians and entrepreneurs committed to the free market. Conversely, it was also associated with leftist critiques of the capitalist state, especially in Latin America, and this meant that it was also taken up widely by those who saw civil society as a site of opposition to capitalism.

For many, however, it has come to mean a way of operating or a territory untainted by either state *or* market. Thus Gaventa (2004, p. xiii) sees it as an additional check and balance on government behaviour, through mobilising claims, advocating for special interests, playing a watchdog role and generally exercising countervailing power against the state, while De Filippis and Saegert (p. 2) describe it as a space for contesting the social costs of capitalism to working-class and marginalised people.

Michael Edwards (2004, p. vii–viii) identifies three common usages of civil society. The first is a descriptive use, defining it as associational life, distinct from market and state, although the above discussion suggests it might be bound up with strong critiques of either. In this sense, it has also been deployed in contemporary debate about 'where lines of responsibility fall between people and the state and mainstream institutions' (Richardson (2008, p. 240) – and is often regarded as synonymous with the non-governmental, non-profit or third sector. As such, it has been used as a peg on which to advance the claims of this sector in a mixed economy of welfare and as an important contributor to democratic life. Thus

> [c]ivil society, understood as the realm of private voluntary association, from neighbourhood committees to interest groups to philanthropic enterprises of all sorts, has come to be seen as an essential ingredient in both democratisation and the health of established democracies. (Foley and Edwards 1996, p. 38)

The second use that Edwards identifies is normative: civil society as the 'good society' – the realm of service rather than self-interest and a breeding ground for the 'habits of the heart' (Bellah *et al.* 1955). This usage is demonstrated in Nicholas Deakin's exploration of the concept (2001), which takes him to the land of Utopia, the characteristics of which have much in common with the aspirations many commentators have for civil society, including, for example, rotating and accountable leadership, new forms of association, equality and civic virtue. The latter concept – civic virtue – is defined by Brennan (1997, p. 259) as 'the capacity to discern the true public interest and a motivation to act in the public interest' (cited in Anheier and Kendall 2002) and reflects also a renewed interest in the concept of 'civility', which embodies ideas of respect, courtesy or politeness, tolerance, care for others, self-restraint and moderation (Dekker 2009).

The third usage sees civil society as an arena for public deliberation and rational dialogue in pursuit of the common interest. This is descriptive, but again has assumed normative overtones. Thus Howell and Pearce (2002, pp. 2, 8) describe it as

> an intellectual space, where people in a myriad of different groups and associations can freely debate and discuss how to build the kind of world in which they want to live ... a realm of emancipations, of alternative imaginations of economic and social relations and of ideological contest.

Mutuality

A fourth concept in the community stable is the idea of mutuality. In mainland European countries, mutuals are an integral part of the social economy, while in the global South, the principles of mutuality inform a wide range of initiatives, including micro-credit schemes. In Anglo-Saxon countries despite a long and influential history, the fortunes of mutuals have fluctuated. Nonetheless, recent years have seen signs of a recovery (Burns and Taylor 1998; Leadbeater and Christie 1999) and the promotion of co-operatives and employee-owned enterprises is part of the new UK coalition government's prospectus for the Big Society (see Box 1.2).

Leadbeater and Christie (1999, pp. 18–19) define mutuals as creating a relationship between owners, workers and consumers that is very different from an investor-owned company.

Members are consumers, employees or suppliers. In a consumer mutual, members are co-producers of the service they consume. They have a regular and reasonably close relationship with the organisation and are involved in its day-to-day running. This, Leadbeater and Christie argue, means that they have a competitive advantage over both traditional investor-owned companies and public sector organisations – through access to 'deeper reservoirs of *trust* and *knowhow* among their members' (p. 18; see also Ben Ner and Van Hoomissen 1993). As such, mutuals can be seen as an alternative to competitive market individualism. They are not just economic entities, however. Leadbeater and Christie (p. 18) argue that: 'What stands out about mutuals is their capacity to gather people around a common sense of purpose'.

It could be said that the mutual principle was the foundation for the associations that Alexis de Tocqueville found and celebrated in the US; mutuals have long played a significant role in the farming community there and in insurance, for example. In the UK, Black (1984) argues that mutual organisations were crucial to establishing the identity of the middle classes in the late eighteenth century (through, for example, the corresponding societies and the anti-Corn Law League). They later became a crucial factor in the establishment of working-class identity and politics (Black 1984).

The working-class tradition of mutuality in the UK and elsewhere was characterised by self-help initiatives coming from within communities themselves to insure against ill-health and poverty and to provide the education that would provide a route out of poverty. Friendly societies and the host of working-class organisations that grew up alongside them – building societies, housing associations, consumer and producer co-operatives, burial societies, trade unions and so on – became an increasingly important component of working-class culture in the late eighteenth and nineteenth century.

Mutuals provided not only the opportunity to pool economic risk, but also opportunities for social and political interaction. Some had elaborate initiation ceremonies, most set as much store by their social as by their financial purposes, and many generated significant benefits in terms of self-improvement and education. The co-operative trading association in Rochdale, for example (often seen as the birthplace of the co-operative movement), included a library and a newsroom, and adult education became an integral part of working-class mutuality.

The significance of mutualism for this book is that it had aspirations to transform society, defining membership in ways which were not confined to the upper or aspiring middle classes, and offering an alternative to the emergent private capitalism: 'The project was for such forms of association to become the norm, to set the rules of economy and society; to define in action a commonwealth, a state of the unions, free association, a new moral world' (Yeo 2001, p. 10). Co-operatives and mutuals thus had a deep political significance. They drew on a long tradition of political dissent. In the UK, for example, their organising principles and values owed much to Nonconformist religion, particularly the Methodist revival. Their power base was in the North of England, away from (and in opposition to) London, the established church and central government. In contemporary Spain, the Mondragon network, now a highly successful and well-known example of co-operative enterprise, is rooted in Basque nationalism and has been highly successful in drawing in funds from the Basque community.

In the UK, the mutual tradition has declined since its heyday in the late nineteenth to early twentieth century. Many of the original mutuals became formalised (housing associations), institutionalised into the state (health and national insurance) or incorporated as private companies (building societies and insurance mutuals). Mark Lyons (2001) charts a similar process in Australia. The mutual tradition has always remained strong in parts of Europe, however – particularly Spain, Italy and France – where solidarity and/or fraternity remain part of the political tradition (Black 1984). In the late 1990s, mutual banks account for about a third of retail deposits in France, Germany and the Netherlands (Leadbeater and Christie 1999). Nonetheless, co-operatives still have an income in the UK nearly equal to that of charities (Kane *et al.* 2009) and Leadbeater and Christie describe how new forms of mutual enterprise have emerged in recent years here, a trend which is being encouraged by the new coalition government. Even in the more individualistic US, community foundations and community development corporations provide further examples of a thriving social economy based in neighbourhoods and mutual traditions.

Networks

All these 'ideas of community' are underpinned by organising principles of networks, trust and reciprocity. Networks as a way of organising and co-ordinating human efforts have attracted increasing attention in both academic and policy circles in recent years. Challenging a view of the world that has tended to be framed in terms of a two-fold distinction between markets (based on prices and contracts and often associated with business) and hierarchies (based on rules and procedures and often associated with governments), a range of authors have defined networks (or in the case of Ouchi, clans) as a distinctive third organising principle (Ouchi 1980; Powell 1990; Nohria and Eccles 1992). Thompson *et al.* (1991, p. 5) define the essentials of this distinction as follows: 'If it is price competition that is the central co-ordinating mechanism of the market and administrative orders that of the hierarchy, then it is trust and co-operation that centrally articulates networks'.

However, although these principles correspond broadly to the three spheres of market, state and community, they are not specific to each one. Businesses can operate like hierarchies and government can operate through markets. Networks are significant not only for associations and communities, but are also found in both business and the public sector, mobilising trust and reciprocity as means of co-ordinating activity and interests alongside rules and price competition (Dore 1983; Clegg, 1990).

Among the characteristics that Powell (1990) ascribes to the network are complementarity, reciprocity, mutuality and *inter*dependence (as opposed to the dependence of a hierarchy and the independence of the market). In a business context, he argues that networks may be most apt where 'tacit' knowledge, speed and trust are required. Baker (1992) sees network forms of organisation as therefore being especially suited to products or projects which are unique, require input from various experts and must be solved creatively.

Networks are particularly important for contemporary, 'postmodern' society and the challenges it poses. Gilchrist (2009, p. 49) describes them as 'a complex system for storing, processing and disseminating information'. She argues that they are especially useful in situations where information is ambiguous or risky, since contradictions can be clarified by turning to alternative sources for comparison and checking. Citing complexity theory, she likens networks to an extended 'brain', processing information intelligently to construct a resilient body of knowledge and generating a collective consciousness (Rose 1998 cited in Gilchrist 2009, p. 50). Network configurations are said to reduce transaction costs, primarily through bonds of trust that minimise risk and enhance mutual commitment (Perrow 1992). Social networks also distribute risk across a larger group and over time, mitigating periods of scarcity and reducing uncertainty (Monbiot 1994).

One of the key characteristics in Powell's list is that of reciprocity. Gouldner (1960, p. 175) suggests that, in its universal form, the norm of reciprocity makes two interrelated demands: first, that 'people should help those who have helped them', and second, that 'people should not injure those who have helped them' (p. 171). As such, it resembles 'a kind of plastic filler, capable of being poured into the shifting crevices of social structures and serving as a kind of all-purpose moral cement' (p. 17). The 'return' that reciprocity implies is based on 'rough equivalents' and need not be immediate. However, it requires judgments to be made by one partner about the capacity of the other (or their proxy) to reciprocate.

Trust and informality

Norms of reciprocity and networks of civic engagement are also identified as the primary sources of social trust (Putnam 2000; Misztal 2005). A thorough analysis of trust is beyond the scope of this book but, as it is implicit in all the terms discussed in this chapter, it is useful to pay a brief visit to some of the different forms of trust that have been identified in the literature on networks and community.

Fukuyama (1995, p. 26) has defined trust as: 'the expectation that arises within a community of regular, honest and co-operative behaviour, based on commonly shared norms on the part of other members of that community'. This expectation takes different forms (Anheier and Kendall 2002; Zucker 1986): it may arise from traditional, deferential or fatalistic forms of trust associated with *Gemeinschaft*; it may be generated through reflexive processes produced through interaction in groups and networks; or it may be institutionalised, through legal constraints, certification, rules and structures, associated perhaps with *Gesellschaft*. Networks are particularly important to the *process* of developing trust, whether it be the utilitarian trust of Coleman's social capital or the moral trust associated with Putnam's formulation.

Misztal (2000, p. 2) introduces another underlying principle of networks – which itself contributes to the development of trust – and that is informality (see also Burns and Taylor 1998):

> In a world where so many issues look so complex and unpredictable, to recreate the condition of trust often requires to overstep the frontiers of formal divisions, boundaries and rules since, as Unger (1987:139) convincingly argues, the possibility of change and improvement of societal conditions depends on 'the replacement of the impersonal by the personal'.

Informality, she argues (p. 127), relies on implicit codes of civility and sociability and provides a basis for

> systems, where people are free to govern themselves, this means where civility allows them to preserve mutual respect, where they can use social networks (sociability) to limit the power of formalised structures, where there is enough space for individual autonomy and the development of intimacy, can secure voluntary compliance with the rules of co-operation.

An optimal balance between informality, which generates trust, and formality, which institutionalises trust, is, she argues, essential to an enhanced quality of social and personal life.

Summary

There are a number of common themes which underpin the ideas discussed in this chapter. Part of a language or discourse that has acquired considerable authority in recent years, these concepts of community, communitarianism, social capital, mutuality, networks and informality are frequently associated in the literature with integration and social cohesion, trust and reciprocity, autonomy and plurality, and with the flexibility to negotiate the enormously complex tensions of post-modern society. In a world where public space is devalued and disappearing, community and civil society can also offer important spaces for co-operative enquiry and debate.

Community and civil society are seen as alternatives to both state and market, while social capital is defined as a much-neglected resource that can bring with it access to other resources, as well as strengthening democratic life. Politicians in particular look to these ideas to import moral cohesion, to combat dependency, to provide a sense of safety and to balance rights and responsibilities through the promotion of reciprocity. But can community and the ideas associated with it deliver on this agenda? In the next chapter I shall introduce some more critical perspectives.

Chapter 5

Contradictions of Community

'The notion of a tight-knit affective community' Antony Black (1984, p. 1) argues, 'is notoriously alluring to modern western man; we tend to associate it with an ideal past, and to see in its restoration a focus for our hopes for a better society'. However, while the 'community' discourse has much to offer, it has also been much criticised for its oversimplification of complex ideas, its romanticism and its avoidance of the tensions inherent in many of its terms. It is to these that I now turn.

Community and communitarianism

There are three main reasons why policymakers need to avoid idealising community and its stable mates. The first is that the ties of community have a 'dark side' that is often ignored by those who promote them – their very strengths can also be their weaknesses. The second is that the notion of community that is promoted is, frankly, not the way most of us live now. The third is that the expectations placed on this set of ideas are simply unrealistic.

The dark side

Community is defined as much by Them as by Us. It can thus be both oppressive and exclusive. Suttles (1972, p. 13) argues that: 'It is in their foreign relations that communities come into existence and have to settle on an identity and a set of boundaries which oversimplify their reality. Keith Tester (1992, p. 47) goes so far as to say that 'it is precisely the identification of an abhorrent "them" which makes "us" possible'. In an uncertain and unstable world, strangers – or those who behave differently – become a receptacle for 'diverse and scattered fears' (Bauman 2001, p. 145) and we look to the safety of a known and trusted 'community'. The development of gated communities in many countries testifies to this, as do racism and tribal or gang warfare. The Not in My Back Yard (NIMBY) syndrome is well documented and even the most fragmented communities can be mobilised – at least temporarily – by the existence of a common enemy. This means that the communitarian perspective can be 'a recipe for parochialism and privilege' (Wolfe 1992, p. 311). More benignly, strong communities are often characterised by the fact that those who move in may still feel – and be treated – like newcomers years after their arrival.

In order to reap the benefits of being one of Us, community members often have to conform. The notion of *Gemeinschaft* that was described in Chapter 4 has been roundly criticised by scholars as being hierarchical, fixed and conservative. Many nineteenth-century novels testify to the way that people who went outside the norms of their communities – especially women – were ostracised and excluded. More recently critics of communitarianism have argued both that it is particularly vulnerable with regard to the rights of women (Lowndes, 2000) and that its responses to crime can be extremely illiberal (Henderson and Salmon 1999, pp. 29, 48). Leadbeater (1999, p. 15) further argues that 'settled, stable communities' are the 'enemies of innovation, talent, creativity, diversity and experimentation' as well as 'knowledge creation, which is the wellspring of economic growth'.

Philip Abrams saw the community networks of the past as unnatural rather than the normal state of things. Significantly for this book he argued that the reality behind the rhetoric of close-knit working-class communities was often characterised by 'chronic collective deprivation, class consciousness and powerful and extensive kinship attachment', which could be extremely oppressive (Bulmer 1988, p. 9). Rosenvallon (1995, p. 207) defends the concept of *Gesellschaft*, reminding us that far from transforming traditions of 'generous social support into widespread egotism', it evolved as a tool for emancipation from the rigid ties of feudalism, a view supported by Max Weber, who viewed citizenship as the antithesis of traditional community loyalty: the liberation of individuals from ancient ties of locality and tradition (Lowndes 1995, p. 163).

Politicians, pundits and policymakers like to talk about 'the community'. As well as sounding warm and positive, 'community' is a word that conjures up agreement on basic values. But critics warn against the use of 'community' as a moral voice 'to shore up the social, moral and political foundations of society' (Walker 1995, cited in Warburton, 1998, pp. 16–17). Not everyone, Warburton argues, is happy shoring up these traditional foundations, with their hierarchical and sexist implications. In the twenty-first century, amidst the rise of various forms of fundamentalism, the long-held assumption that there is one overarching morality to which all can sign up is, at the very least, open to debate, while Driver and Martell (1997, p. 41) are critical of the assumption amongst many politicians that 'moralism alone can deliver social cohesion'. Guijt and Shah (1998b, p. 1) warn that too strong a belief in the community cohesion myth can mean that many voices are not heard at all: 'This mythical cohesion', they argue, 'continues to permeate much participatory work, hiding a bias that favours the opinions and priorities [*and we might argue, morality*] of those with more power and the ability to voice themselves publicly'. In many cultures, it is the voices of women and young people that are silenced.

Communitarians do acknowledge that different communities may want to run their affairs differently (Etzioni 1998). There tends nonetheless to be an assumption that these differences will not clash with each other. This is an assumption shared by those who have advocated a new 'associational democracy' (Hirst 1994), with a 'light-touch' state mediating between a wide variety of associational interests. Both appear to underestimate the task of mediation across the spaces of civil society, assuming perhaps some kind of natural homeostasis along pluralist lines, rather than a scenario that is somewhat redder in tooth and claw and, if left to itself, ends up in the survival of the fittest.

Mowbray (2000, p. 308) is also dismissive of the assumption, still too common in community development and third-sector writing, that non-government or community-based agencies are more progressive than government agencies, reminding us that 'communities dominated by rednecks' are all too common. Conflicts across the world have shown how villages where people of different faiths or ethnic origins have apparently co-existed peacefully for years can easily and terminally be split down the middle. The extent of tribal and religious warfare (between Hindu and Muslim, Jew and Arab, Catholic and Protestant, Hutu and Tutsi, Croat and Serb, for example) only drives the message home more forcefully.

Rather than talking about 'community', therefore, it is essential to talk about 'communities' and to recognise the diversity that exists within any community – of place, identity or interest. The demands of different communities will not necessarily be compatible and may well conflict. A realistic assessment of community will need to acknowledge the politics of difference and focus attention on the ways in which links can be made across and between communities (see Chapter 10).

The way we live now

My second point is that the kind of close-knit community that seems to be implied in much of the discourse of community is simply not the way most of us live now. Many writers argue that this 'tight-knit affective community' is inappropriate to modern and post-modern societies. As early as 1970, Ray Pahl (1970, p. 105) was arguing that, 'with greater affluence and more choice, there has been a steady move from community to social network as the meaningful arena for social relationships'. This move to a *Gesellschaft* type of community allows the recognition of the plurality both of communities, and of the rules and authorities that should govern them.

A tradition of writing that is associated with Mark Granovetter (1973) questions the value of the strong ties that are associated with traditional notions of community. Granovetter, writing about access to employment, argued that strong ties were less effective than a large and more diverse network of weaker ties. Burt (1992) applied a similar concept to management, writing about the need for managers to bridge the 'structural holes' in their organisations and across their boundaries through weak ties. There is a parallel here with the distinction that is made between bonding and bridging social capital and I will return to this later in the chapter.

In the contemporary world, most of us have a variety of communities, perhaps through work, leisure interests, residence, children's friendship networks or even fellow commuters, and this creates different kinds of relationships:

> Community ties are negotiable commodities for the middle class. This wider experience and the ability to choose may make them more critical of the local situation, more confident

in taking part in local activities and less afraid of offending those more committed, perhaps for life, to the locality. Also they can always move on, leaving their mistakes behind them. (Pahl 1970, p. 103)

Wellman (1979, p. 1215) argues that, in today's 'liberated' networks, people are 'not encapsulated within the bounds of one solitary group, but are linked through their intimates to multiple, not strongly connected, social networks'. These weaker ties might have limits in terms of the claims that can be made on them, but they can also provide indirect access to a greater diversity of resources than can stronger, more socially homogeneous ties (*ibid.*, pp. 1, 226). For, as Granovetter (1973, p. 1371) points out, 'those to whom we are weakly tied are more likely to move in circles different from our own and will thus have access to information different from that which we receive'. In other words, diversity represents strength because it provides access to a wider variety of opportunities and perspectives on issues and problems. This might not always be the case. Perri 6 (1997a) argues that strong ties may still be of critical importance to older people in need of care or for young people seeking to establish their identity. They may also be important for the most vulnerable in our society.

Unrealistic expectations

There are limits to what can be expected of communities. Abrams (Bulmer 1988), for example, unpacked the relationships within geographical communities by distinguishing between neighbours, friends and kin, according to what sort of support can be expected from each. He argued that intimate caring could only be expected of the latter (partly perhaps because kinship provides a setting where 'serial reciprocity' can take place: that is, where the giver can expect to receive a return at a later date even if it is from a different family member). Neighbours would be involved in crisis response and practical tasks, but to expect more of them revealed a misunderstanding of the importance of maintaining a balance in neighbouring relationships between co-operation and privacy, helpfulness and non-interference, friendliness and distance (as summarised by Allan 1983). Research in Scotland (Burns *et al.* 2001) reinforced these findings: neighbourliness was mainly limited to interactions involving a low level of intimacy, such as borrowing tools or looking out for each others' houses while the occupants were away. Neighbours were less often used for more intimate interactions such as childminding or borrowing money.

If we expect too much of 'caring' communities, we may also expect too much in terms of political engagement. Those who see communities as the basis for a new political order might find their goal difficult to achieve. This is not so much because of the possible conflict between communities as the fact that many community members are not that interested in what goes on beyond their boundaries. Describing an example of successful action in New York, Michael Storper (1998, p. 241) argued that

> The East Village Activists ... might be strong on content, but ... they can't tell us how their local needs fit into a society which has all kinds of other needs, like those of mobility, openness, cosmopolitanism. These are values that fit problematically with localness, preservation of community and so on.

Many in both the North and South have acknowledged the difficulties of scaling neighbourhood activity up to a broader city or regional level – an issue to which I return in Chapter 12.

Social capital

Like many concepts that capture the popular imagination, 'social capital' is a term whose meaning is more widely contested than its popularity suggests. Nonetheless, it is a concept that has the capacity to overcome the pitfalls of a communitarian analysis. It allows for a looser and more flexible understanding of ties and relationships between people. It encompasses relationships across boundaries more easily. Used as a descriptive and analytic rather than normative concept, it is an important complement to other kinds of capital. It is also a concept with immense potential for filling in the vacuum that capitalist analyses of society have left. The distinction between bonding and bridging social capital in particular echoes the distinction between strong and weak ties discussed in the previous section and provides some tools to develop a more sophisticated analysis.

However, as a concept 'in use', the advantages of this idea have been blurred. There has been criticism of the way social capital has been conceived, of its normative use and of the links made between social capital and governance.

Imprecision

Forrest and Kearns (1999, p. 20) argue that social capital is a word that tends to 'lose precision' with its 'increasing use in a variety of contexts'. Scholars dispute whether social capital is a characteristic of individuals or of collectivities. They also disagree over whether it is a product of relationships or something that makes relationships possible – the 'infrastructure or the content of social relations' (Woolcock 1998, p. 156). Critics detect a tendency to define social capital in terms of its consequences, while Barbara Misztal (2005, p. 186) finds no explanation in Putnam's work of how interpersonal trust translates into generalised trust. In an earlier publication, she also comments on the absence of any theory as to the production, maintenance and growth of social capital, which means that he presents a rather circular argument:

> [T]he key condition for overcoming dilemmas of collective action is the existence of a stock of social capital, but at the same time, the fostering of norms of reciprocity and networks of civic engagement requires pre-existing solidarity and collaboration. (Misztal 2000, p. 121)

Similarly, Anheier and Kendall (2002, p. 354) argue that Putnam fails to specify how the micro and macro aspects of social capital are linked together. In their view, his argument relies on an indirect relationship between the creation of trust and the creation of social capital, which is highly dependent on the structure of civil society and the legitimacy of the political system in any given country. In this they echo James Coleman's earlier argument (1990, p. 302) that the utility of social capital is contingent on the specific setting, with the result that: 'A given form of social capital that is valuable in facilitating certain actions may be useless in or even harmful for others'. 'Context counts', as Foley and Edwards (1999, p. 151) put it, 'and counts crucially'.

Social capital as a normative concept

In a comprehensive review of empirical work on social capital in the 1990s, Foley and Edwards (1999) are critical of attempts to associate this concept with moral, ethical or cultural value on the one hand, or with civic engagement on the other. They come to the conclusion that 'neither resources in general, attitudes and norms, such as trust and reciprocity, nor social infrastructures such as networks and associations can be understood as social capital by themselves' (p. 146). They are highly critical of Putnam's normative use of the term and, with others, of the neglect in social capital discourse of the more negative potential of social capital (although Putnam's work does recognise that this 'dark side' exists).

Exclusivity is inherent in the concept of social capital. If everyone is connected, then nobody has any competitive advantage. Maloney, Smith and Stoker (2000, p. 832) argue that closure increases the potential for the effective sanctions, norms and expectations that generate trustworthy relations between participants. But closure also means 'that these social capital resources are not available for "outsider" voluntary and community associations. A familiar pattern of insider and outsider groups is likely to be observed'. Indeed, the very exclusiveness of these resources can increase their currency (hence the 'old school tie'). Using the example of the US construction industry, Portes and Landolt (1996) discuss the way in which, in industries with strong social ties, newcomers – in that case African Americans – find it almost impossible to compete. Indeed, if we see social capital as an individual resource, it can be as inequitable as any other form of capital, allowing those who are members of the right networks to gain access to scarce economic and cultural resources and thus reinforcing existing divisions and privileges in society (Bourdieu 1986). Those who go into the system with most will tend to come out with most.

Closure can also lead to secrecy. Misztal warns (2000, p. 91) that 'we need always to look beyond trust and check the accountability, transparency and goals of reciprocal networks'. Networks are essentially private and opaque rather than public and transparent. They can create their own norms, at odds with the outside world; illegal activities 'can take on the aura of normality' and members are protected from external sanctions.

The corruption scandals of governments across the globe testify to the negative potential of networks, while in the market, De Filippis (2001), echoing Portes and Landolt's earlier critique of social capital (1996), warns that too much trust is a recipe for economy-stifling cartels and monopolies. A number of writers argue further that some types of social capital facilitate social stagnation and resistance to change, limiting individual freedom and undermining competitiveness and innovation (see for example Misztal 2005, p. 185).

This means that social capital, with its emphasis on networks, comes with a health warning. Hence Fukuyama's comment (1995, p. 158) that 'Since social groups in any society overlap and cross cut each other, what looks like a strong sense of social solidarity from one perspective can seem to be atomisation, divisiveness and stratification from another'.

Does social capital improve governance?

Another set of criticisms questions the links Putnam has made between social capital and governance. Firstly, his claim that engagement is decreasing (Putnam 2000) is disputed both in the US and the UK. In the UK, John (2009, p. 17) argues that some of the key measures of social capital, such as social trust, have stayed at a constant level over several decades. Although Putnam's data are drawn from a variety of sources, critics accuse him of relying too much on traditional forms of membership and engagement, of failing to take account of gender or cultural differences (Morrow 1999; Lowndes 2000) and of failing to allow for the fact that people may choose to engage in different ways in the twenty-first century. He is also criticised for underestimating the role of large-scale economic changes in undermining civic engagement in the US and elsewhere (Skocpol 1996; Tarrow 1996). Social capital cannot do the job of cohesion in an economic environment that divides and fragments.

Putnam famously argues that social capital is the foundation for civic engagement and good governance but critics question the precise nature of this link. Thus Evers (2003, p. 15) comments that Putnam 'does not make any clear statement as to how social bonds get a civic quality', while Dekker (2009, p. 229) finds little evidence of a causal relationship between voluntary associations – in Putnam's analysis a strong indicator of social capital – and political involvement. Indeed, Maloney, Smith and Stoker (2000) provide empirical evidence to challenge the direction that is claimed for this relationship. While good governance and social capital interact, they argue, the latter does not cause the former. Rather, drawing on their own empirical research, they argue that the production of social capital *depends* on the political opportunity structure rather than *creating* this structure. Government can create the conditions in which social capital can thrive or not, as the case may be. Maloney, Smith and Stoker challenge Putnam's link between social capital and governance further by arguing that *low* levels of trust may sometimes promote the effective functioning of democracy by discouraging complacency and demanding accountability.

Foweraker and Landman (1997, p. 243) extend the political critique by dismissing as simplistic the centrality given in Putnam's account to small associations, sports clubs and choral societies. They argue that the democratic qualities of civil society have as much to do with social mobilisation and political contestation as with 'civicness'. 'Democracy' they argue, 'is not the comfortable result of righteous conduct, but the result of prolonged struggle in often dangerous and difficult circumstances'. Foley and Edwards (1996, p. 49) agree: 'We are likely to find that social movement organisations, grassroots interest groups and grassroots political associations of all kinds are more likely to generate Putnam's activated citizenry than the choral societies, birdwatching clubs and bowling leagues he is so fond of citing'. Evers (2003) is one of a number of authors to criticise the absence of politics in Putnam's work and its failure to engage with power and inequality – a critique to which we shall return in Chapter 6.

Many of these criticisms relate to the work of Putnam and the way his work has been interpreted by policymakers worldwide. Putnam has responded vigorously, pointing out that in his Italian study he clearly distinguished between the 'horizontal' social capital of northern Italy and the 'vertical' social capital of the south. This relates to the distinction between bonding and bridging social capital (see Chapter 4). Thus strong ties (bonding social capital) are associated with organisations that are vertically or hierarchically organised and, as such, are not associated with civic engagement. Weak ties (and bridging social capital) are associated with horizontally ordered organisations, which cut across social cleavages and, as such, are associated with civic engagement. He argues in his 2000 book that bonding social capital is preferable to no social capital at all, but that a mixture of bonding and bridging is necessary to address some of the 'dark side' issues (Putnam 2000, p. 413), as indeed do many of his critics. But bonding social capital still has an important role to play. Research in Northern Ireland suggests that high stocks of bonding social capital can sometimes promote bridging capital (Campbell *et al.* 2010) and Edwards (2004, p. 33) suggests that bonding social capital may be an essential underpinning of attempts to operate across community boundaries: 'Without the security provided by strong in-group ties', he argues, 'bridging may expose those on the margins to environments in which they cannot compete on equal terms, or benefit the few who can prosper at the expense of the many who are left behind'. Again I will return to this debate in Chapter 6.

Civil society

In his 2004 book on civil society, Edwards urges the need to rescue 'this powerful set of ideas from the conceptual confusion that threatens to submerge them' (Edwards 2004, p. vii). For civil society, as with the other terms in the 'community' stable, problems arise when an essentially descriptive and analytical term is charged with normative values. For example, in positioning civil society as something different from the state and market, its protagonists seek to free it from the failings of both. But, as Alexander argues (1998, pp. 14, 16), civil society is a concept that in popular usage conceals 'intense struggles for legitimacy and legitimation': 'The complex, decoupled nature of the subsystems of contemporary society', he argues, 'make archaic any notion of civility as a seamless, overarching principle of social integration and coherence ... [It is a] shell behind which privatising and fragmenting institutional processes and interactional practices are played out'. Civil society is the forum in which individuals establish identities. Because of this, its ultimate political impact on society may be insular and regressive rather than it acting as a springboard for fundamental social change (Whaites 2000, p. 138).

The fact that civil society is a forum for the expression of diverse and conflicting voices is one of its strengths. But the fact that it contains so many versions of the good life can lead to what Cohen and Rogers (1992) have called the 'mischief of factions'. Civil society is highly fragmented – a place of conflict and competition as much as of resolution. Its networks and organisations can be particularist, defensive and conflictual. It is also inherently unstable, prey to schism and faction, as the organisations within it seek to advance their own particular set of values. Friedmann (1998, p. 29) warns of the consequences of civil society turning in on itself, referring to: 'the tragic litany of racism, intolerance, terrorism and persecution of those who are judged to be different from us by some arbitrary distinguishing mark, whether of birthplace, language, skin colour, sexual practice, or religious belief'.

The stronger the values held, the greater the dangers of sectarianism, as members of associations and networks discover that their various versions of the good society do not match and break instead into acrimonious divisions. Paul Hoggett, in a paper which we wrote together in 1994 (Taylor and Hoggett 1994, p. 136), described the way in which 'the world of military modelling was torn apart in the UK in the late 1970s and early 1980s', with the result that two separate national federations were set up. We went on to argue (p. 137): 'The danger is that in certain contexts ... the process of mutual aid may be replaced by an escalating process of mutual injury leading to protracted feuding, the scale and duration of which may be such as to severely damage the material interests of the participants involved'. Conversely, the organisations of civil society can also ruthlessly suppress dissension in their ranks. Both Gosden's study of friendly societies (1973) and Black's study of guilds (1984) provide many examples of the development of rigid codes and rules which, when combined with solidarity and secrecy, could be an oppressive brew.

The 'motherhood and apple pie' image of civil society brushes all this firmly under the carpet. Foley and Edwards (1996, p. 46) argue, for example, that Putnam:

> clearly wants an activated and engaged populace, and he argues that the socialisation performed by civil associations is vital to the creation of such an engaged citizenry. Yet in the end only those associations qualify that invoke a civic transcendency whose spirit claims to 'rise above' the divisiveness of protracted socio-political and cultural conflict.

Cornwall and Coelho (2004, p. 6) question the assumptions that are commonly made about the inherently democratising potential of civil society. Antonio Gramsci, as we have seen, saw civil society as the medium for the dissemination and internalisation of the dominant ideologies of the ruling class (see, for example, Ledwith 2005, p. 22). Others too highlight the unequal distribution of power within civil society. As Schattschneider (1960, p. 35) has famously reminded us, 'The flaw in the pluralist heaven is that the heavenly choir sings with a strong upper class accent'. The more powerful and better-resourced organisations in civil society and those that are better networked are likely to carry the day. It cannot even be assumed that organisations within civil society are inherently democratic. They are as prone as any other to Michels' 'iron law of oligarchy' and, as Alexander points out (1988), their relationship with service users is often unequal – a patron-client relationship.

There is, argues Edwards (2004, p. 27), a strong strain of anti-politics among civil society enthusiasts. This neglects the role of the state in creating the conditions within which civil society and its claimed virtues can thrive. Thus, while neo-liberals seek to privilege civil society over the state and to popularise a distorted interpretation of the virtues appropriate to civil society, Keane (1988a) argues that civil society and the state are the condition of each other's democratisation; both are needed. Indeed, he blames increasing marginalisation and pauperisation directly on the withdrawal of the state from its responsibilities (1988b, p. 9). A similar argument is made by Zygmunt Bauman (1999, p. 156):

> Civil society ... has its splendours and its less prepossessing proclivities. ... The political indifference and apathy of the citizens and the state retreating on its obligation to promote the common good are civil society's unpleasant, yet legitimate children.

Civil society is an arena in which many tensions are played out (see for example, Tester 1992; Alexander 1998; Misztal 2000): between universalism and particularism, individuals and the collective, public and private, heterogeneity and equality, democracy and agency, formality and informality, reflexivity and order, enthusiasm and rules. As such, instead of seeing civil society as a third and separate sector – which is often the case nowadays – it is perhaps better understood as an ecosystem, in which the boundaries between civil society (especially when conceived of as voluntary associations) and the state or the market, are blurred, especially at global level (Edwards 2004). This resonates with European concepts of the third sector as a field of tension between the market, the state and informal communities, which again dispenses with the notion of clearly demarcated sectors (Evers and Laville 2004). Indeed, Cornwall and Coelho (2004, pp. 6–7) argue that, in a context where the role of civil society organisations as providers and intermediaries blurs the state-civil society boundary, we need to understand the state and civil society as 'heterogeneous and mutually constitutive terrains of contestation', constantly interacting and overlapping with each other.

Developing this theme, Evers (2009) rejects a narrow definition of civil society which equates civicness and civility with the third sector, while Dekker (2009) emphasises the importance of the hybrids at the margins of the civil society sphere, arguing that there is a 'dissolution of civil society', as the principles of the different sectors blend into one another. Both turn their focus away from civil society as such to focus on how concepts of civility are realised across sectors (see Chapter 4). They equate civility, citing Shils (1997, pp. 337–8, 345), with the readiness to moderate particular, individual or parochial interest and to give precedence to the common good. Edwards (2004, p. 67) takes us a step further:

> One of the legacies of the civil society revivalists has been a particular understanding of 'civility' as politeness, and the conflation of civil society with 'consensus', not debate or disagreement ... but this is a distortion of what civility originally meant. Civility ... assumes that we will disagree, often profoundly, but calls on us to resolve our disagreements peacefully.

Much of the debate reflected here is based in the global North. Although Cornwall and Coelho (2004) demonstrate that similar issues are raised in other parts of the globe, Edwards reminds us that definitions of civil society may have very different meanings in the global South, where the state may be either weak or authoritarian and where the market economy has only a fragile hold. Dekker (2009, p. 224), drawing on citizenship research worldwide suggests that understandings of what constitutes 'civility', may also be quite different.

Mutuality, informality and networks

Principles of mutuality and informality underpin many of the concepts in the 'community' stable. But as with these other concepts, the main strengths of these principles and the networks that sustain them are also their weaknesses. Thus, back in the 1970s, Jo Freeman (1973) coined the term the 'tyranny of structurelessness' to describe the way in which the apparent absence of rules and hierarchy in informal groups can mask the uneven way in which power relations are, in fact, played out. The very looseness of networks also means that they can fall prey to divided loyalties or lose member commitment to higher loyalties. Mutuals, for example, thrive when their members have a common purpose, but, as Leadbeater and Christie (1999) point out, the more dispersed their membership and the more diverse their interests, the more difficult it is to sustain a shared sense of belonging, let alone a mutual form of governance. Studying moneyless exchange systems, Offe and Heinze (1992, p. 167) found that the most successful examples were small and based on the 'solidarity capital' possessed by people who belonged to more or less tightly knit social groups: 'Once the limits of that particular frame have been reached, the very factor that was such a potent help at the beginning turns into a barrier to further growth'. Indeed Gilchrist (2009) argues that there is an optimal size for networks. Computer simulations of networked systems indicate that excessive connectivity can be a problem, reducing the adaptability of the whole system (p. 156).

Like the social ties we discussed earlier, networks can be unaccountable, opaque, inward looking and exclusive. Mutuals and other organisations based on network principles can thus lose their capacity to be flexible and innovative. Mutuals also need a sympathetic environment in which to thrive. The relative success of co-operatives in Spain, France, Italy, or even Scotland, reflects a culture and approach to social investment that is less common in Anglo-Saxon countries, although recent interest in social enterprise in these countries may change this.

In work carried out for the Joseph Rowntree Foundation, Danny Burns and I explored the potential for mutual aid and informal networks to address problems of social exclusion (Burns and Taylor 1998). We suggested there were three possible contributions: that informality could provide a more 'natural' way of meeting needs that are not met by more formal organisations; that they could provide a route into individual empowerment and engagement; or that they could be an alternative and preferred way of meeting needs. But the research we reviewed – in the South as well as the North – suggested that the very volatility and transience of informal networks limited their capacity to act as a dependable solution to exclusion (see, for example, Tungaranza 1993 and Dhesi 2000, who both offer a perspective from the South). Dhesi argues that, with excess demand, social networks are likely to become overwhelmed and the social system may break down. This raises questions about the capacity of associations to step up to the service delivery responsibilities that policymakers would like them to take on. The formalisation of informal systems can destroy them – trust in one situation does not necessarily translate into trust in another and formalisation – although often necessary to get things done – often alienates people.

In some cases, informality can only survive because of the existence of parallel formal systems, which act as a safety net or backstop. Foster (1995) suggested that informal systems of surveillance and crime prevention depended on the back-up of more formal intervention. In others, assumptions about a seamless web between informal and formal help can be misguided and attempts to co-opt informal care and self-help can damage its integrity (Hoch and Hemmens 1987; Wilson 1995). Finally, official systems and increasingly litigious cultures can put formidable barriers in the way of informal mutual support. In research I carried out with colleagues (Taylor, Langan and Hoggett 1995), a manager of a community facility bemoaned the fact that women volunteers who had been cooking all their lives were now required to have qualifications and submit to safety standards designed for more formal circumstances in order to continue as volunteers, because they were providing lunch for older people. Similar problems have been reported in relation to women helping each other with childcare.

Discussion

In the first edition of this book, I quoted the sixteenth-century English writer Sir Francis Bacon on the importance of doubt. 'The registration of doubts', he argued, 'has a double use: guarding against errors, but also broadening investigation. Issues that would have been passed by lightly without intervention end up being attentively and carefully observed precisely because of the intervention of doubts' (Sen 2000, p. 29). To subject community concepts to critical scrutiny is not therefore to deny their considerable value, but to encourage a realistic appraisal of how they can be applied. Pierre Bourdieu (1990, p. 52) is one of many who warn against simple 'common sense' solutions that mask the complexity of problems and are open to manipulation. So while these are concepts that have considerable potential to illuminate policy and debate, they need to be treated with caution.

I have argued that communities and networks are as likely to create exclusion as to resolve it; that too much trust can lead to corruption and abuse; that the moralities produced by communities can be oppressive; and that civil society is riven with conflicts and inequalities. The words that go missing from much of this discourse in popular use – and this may be what makes it so attractive – are 'power' and 'conflict'. The assumption is that communities, social capital and civil society will somehow and autonomously generate a morality which we can all in some way buy into, or at least that different versions of morality produced from within communities will somehow be compatible. This is illustrated by the way that much of the discourse ignores gender (Pateman 1988; Guijt and Shah 1998b; Henderson and Salmon 1998; Lowndes 2000), a surprising and rather telling omission in the light of the prevalence of women in community-based activities. Too often, in the past, it has also failed to engage constructively with race, disability and other forms of difference, although each has its own distinctive contribution to make to widening the 'community' debate. Alternative voices are now more likely to be heard, but in ways that too often 'paper over' the challenges each perspective poses, as we shall see in Chapter 12 (see, for example, Edwards 2004, p. 68 or Bauman 2001, Chapter 9).

The sections in this chapter tell a common story: of the imprecision surrounding each of the terms addressed, the failure to distinguish between normative and descriptive uses, and unrealistic expectations of their usefulness in addressing major societal tensions and dilemmas. But while this chapter may have drawn together a number of the criticisms associated with the community 'discourse', it certainly does not follow that we should abandon the language of community, civil society, networks and social capital. The increasing prevalence of this discourse represents a tremendous advance on the dualistic notion of state and market and recognises a huge territory of relationships that have previously been ignored in political and economic debate. This chapter has also reflected some of the ways in which concepts are being developed and refined so as to address some of the earlier critiques. In Chapter 4, however, I cited Hunter's conception of community as a 'variable' rather than a given. In a similar vein, Warburton (2009, p. 18) describes community as an 'aspiration' rather than a reality to be discovered or returned to. Such an approach helps to reclaim the power of this set of ideas, to unpack the assumptions behind their use and consider more carefully how they might be used in policy.

With this in mind, this critique aims to draw attention to the contested nature of these terms, to their complexity and to the fact that their strengths have a 'darker' side, which is too often ignored in the rhetoric of those who are espouse 'community' solutions. But these complexities and tensions are only part of the picture: they are one possible outcome only of relying on networks, on ties of trust, co-operation and reciprocity – in the same way that sclerosis is a possible but not inevitable outcome of hierarchy. The weaknesses that have been identified in these concepts are often the other side of their strengths and may indeed be strengths or weaknesses depending on the context in which they are applied. Thus particularism can be seen to be a virtue insofar as the spread of networks allows for diverse needs to be met in diverse ways, but a flaw if society relies on informal networks to meet need, because there will be many who will fall outside the net. Schism and conflict may be appropriate insofar as they ensure that outdated alliances and organisations wither and die, but destructive if they destroy the solidarity that is needed to achieve social change.

If change is to happen, then, it needs commitment from governments across the world, from the major global financial institutions and from business to work in partnership with communities and civil society, rather than ignoring or abandoning them as has been the case in the past. However, this commitment needs to be a realistic one. If community policies are to play to the strengths of the ideas discussed in these two chapters and to avoid the pitfalls, then what is needed is a better understanding of how communities, social capital, network and civil society actually work. Nowhere is this more true than in the case of policies to tackle social exclusion: community is overwhelmingly prescribed to 'the poor'. This chapter has taken a broad view of the community discourse, but how far can ideas of community be applied to tackle the persistent challenge of poverty and social exclusion? Can they provide a new platform for change and inclusion, or are they based on too simplistic and outmoded an analysis? In the next chapter, I shall first explore in more detail the significance of the concept of social exclusion and then how far ideas of community can be applied to its resolution.

Chapter 6

Prescribing Community to the Poor

In his nineteenth century novel, *Sybil*, Benjamin Disraeli, a politician who was to become one of the most famous prime ministers in Victorian Britain, spoke of Britain at that time as 'two nations'

> between whom there is no intercourse and no sympathy; who are as ignorant of each other's habits, thoughts and feelings, as if they were dwellers in different zones, or inhabitants of different planets; who are formed by a different breeding, are fed by a different food, are ordered by different manners, and are not governed by the same laws. (Benjamin Disraeli, *Sybil*, Book II, Ch. 5)

Along with Charles Dickens, Disraeli helped to awaken the Victorian social conscience to the evils of industrial life and of the gulf existing between rich and poor. Despite all the policies that have been introduced in the intervening years to combat poverty and social exclusion, this gulf is still very much with us; indeed, it is growing – within and between countries (see Chapter 2). The problems of alienation and disenfranchisement that this creates have been recognised by the concept of 'social exclusion', familiar in Europe and some other parts of the world, which highlights the multidimensional nature of poverty. In this chapter, I first explore the language of social exclusion, why it has been adopted and how it relates to the poverty debate. I then come back to the question raised at the end of Chapter 5 and ask how far a focus on 'community' and 'community participation' can address the persistent problems caused by poverty and social exclusion.

Poverty and social exclusion

Regeneration policies in the UK and elsewhere, especially those targeted at disadvantaged neighbourhoods, have over the years used a range of terms to define the 'problem' they seek to address: poverty, disadvantage, deprivation, decline and underprivilege among them. When I was writing the first edition, UK policymakers had begun to talk about 'social exclusion', adopting the terminology of mainland Europe. How significant was this shift in language? Was it merely a matter of semantics, was it just a new fashion or did it represent a significant change in the understanding of poverty and its consequences?

The concept of social exclusion

When Disraeli wrote *Sybil*, poverty was a moral issue. From medieval times, the Poor Law in England had divided poor people into the 'deserving' and 'undeserving' poor. The former – poor because of misfortune or frailty – were the subject of charity; the latter – poor because of moral turpitude – were subject to the workhouse, a destination designed on the 'less eligibility principle' to act as a deterrent by being worse than any other option.

The workhouse is long gone and the growth of state welfare in many Northern countries has brought with it an acceptance of the rights of all citizens to basic standards of welfare through universal entitlements. But the distinction between the 'deserving' and 'undeserving' poor lingers in many Anglo-Saxon countries today. Chapter 3 referred to the neo-liberal argument in the 1980s that state welfare encouraged the development of an underclass, divorced from the rest of society and rejecting its morality (Murray 1990; Levitas 1998). This return to the notion of the 'undeserving poor' was coupled with a belief, in some quarters, that absolute poverty was no longer an issue, instead poverty was seen as a relative term which centred around the question of whether the people concerned had access to 'luxuries' (new technology and cars, for example) that the rest of society could afford.

This view of poverty contrasts with the concept of social exclusion, which Mingione (1997, p. 10) defines as follows: 'The concept of exclusion is not a new way of defining the poor; rather it draws attention to a combination of economic hardship and institutional discrimination, both of which help to create unfavourable life chances and chronic exclusion from normal citizenship'. Bhalla and Lapeyre (1997, pp. 414–15) trace the evolution of this concept back to republican France, where it described a breakdown of the relationship between society and the individual and was deeply rooted in the republican tradition of solidarity, in which the state was expected to play a major role. They contrast this with the individualistic approach of Anglo-Saxon thinking, where exclusion is seen to reflect voluntary individual choices.

The language of social exclusion allows us to consider the interrelationships between social, economic and political exclusion and brings a number of new dimensions to bear on debates about poverty and deprivation.

First, it suggests that poverty is not just a question of low income. In his work on durable inequality, Charles Tilly argues (1999, p. 24):

> Recent students of inequality under capitalism have ... focused on wages, a topic that lends itself both to measurement and explanation in individual terms. They have neglected wealth, health, nutrition, power, deference, privilege, security and other critical zones of inequality that in the long run matter more to well-being than wages do.

There are two aspects to this. On the one hand, even where people have low incomes, this alone does not explain their social exclusion. What the concept of social exclusion draws our attention to is the fact that low income brings with it a number of associated problems, focusing attention on the way in which: 'significant minorities are excluded from participating in the mainstream life of society: from jobs, education, homes, leisure, civic organisations, and even voting, and on how this disconnection tends to coincide with vulnerability to poverty, crime and family breakdown' (6 1997b, p. 3). On the other hand, people can be excluded without being poor in absolute terms, because of other characteristics (race, gender, class, citizenship, disability, sexuality and so on); indeed, low income may be the result rather than the cause of these other kinds of exclusion.

The second important dimension that social exclusion adds to the poverty debate is that it takes the emphasis away from the individual (who can be blamed for being poor) and focuses instead on the relationship between individuals, groups and the wider society. It highlights the processes that create and maintain poverty and disadvantage. Thus exclusion, Murray Stewart (1999, p. 11) argues, is 'both the state of being shut out and the processes by which the shutting out occurs'. Graham Room (1995, p. 5), who traced the idea of social exclusion back to the European Poverty Programme, distinguished between poverty and social exclusion as follows:

> The notion of poverty is primarily focused upon distributional issues, the lack of resources at the disposal of an individual or household. In contrast, notions such as social exclusion focus primarily on relational issues, in other words inadequate social participation, lack of social integration and lack of power.

These processes include the restructuring of industry and the workforce, the operation of the market, and the nature and operation of professional and political power. By highlighting the relational nature of poverty, the concept of social exclusion focuses our attention on society's responsibility for exclusion and therefore also for inclusion.

The third dimension that the concept of social exclusion brings into focus is the civil, social and political rights of citizenship (Marshall 1950). The European tradition in which the concept of social exclusion is based 'emphasises the semi-contractual nature of relationships between classes and groups and the interdependence between such classes. There is thus a basic adherence to the notion of a cohesive society within which there are mutual rights and obligations' (Stewart 1999, p. 10). The state's responsibility is to guarantee these rights and exclusion is the denial of such rights (Atkinson 1999).

The concept of social exclusion has been criticised as a foundation for policy. It can impose 'an artificial top down homogeneity' on those it defines (O'Brien *et al.* 1997) and set conditions for inclusion, which may be unacceptably conformist. Atkinson (2000a, p. 1039) warns that too rigid a definition fails to recognise the legitimacy of difference and can impose a simplistic distinction between insiders and outsiders. The term can also be used in a very narrow sense, defining social exclusion primarily as exclusion from the labour market (see, for example, Levitas 1998; Marsh and Mullins 1998). This diverts attention from other causes and outcomes of poverty, especially for those who are on the fringes of, or even outside, the labour market.

The language of social exclusion will not be familiar to all readers. While it is common in Europe and some Anglo-Saxon countries like Australia, it has less purchase, for example, in the US. It is not generally used in the global South, although commentators suggest that it has much in common with the evolving poverty discourse there (O'Brien *et al.* 1997). Both discourses stress the fact that deprivation has multiple layers and emphasise social as well as economic components. Both stress the adverse impact of low income on civil rights and participation and, conversely, both stress the importance of participation and a sense of 'agency' in the lives of people on low incomes. However, there may be a difference of emphasis. Bhalla and Lapeyre (1997, p. 430) argue that notions such as exclusion cannot be divorced from their social and political context and that, in the South, low income still remains at the heart of exclusion. This, they say, has to be addressed before other aspects of exclusion can be dealt with.

How social exclusion works

The effects of global economic restructuring have always been a major factor in social exclusion, but the structure of the housing market within nations and the promotion of individual choice over other considerations have also made their contribution. In the US, a number of authors have described the way in which federal zoning policies in the 1960s and 1970s subsidised the exodus of middle-class and ordinary working-class people from the inner cities there (see, for example Wilson 1996; Fairbanks 2007; O'Connor 2007). In this 'federally paved march to the suburbs' (O'Connor 2007, p. 18), the middle classes took their spending power, their jobs and crucially their tax dollars with them. This led to the loss of facilities, institutions and social stability in the neighbourhoods they left behind, creating inner-city ghettos, usually along racial lines, increasingly divorced from mainstream America (Kubisch *et al.* 2007). The local taxation system in the US also means that state administrations cannot afford to improve conditions and public services in the areas the middle classes have left behind.

In the UK, the introduction of the market into welfare triggered a parallel process. One of the flagship policies of Margaret Thatcher's first administration was to offer tenants of public sector housing the 'right to buy'. This policy allowed a greater proportion of the population to become owner-occupiers; but the increase in choice for some, while commendable in itself, perversely reduced choice for others, especially since it was combined with policies which restricted the capacity for replacing and maintaining the social housing stock. This meant that, on the one hand, the stock of housing for social renting was diminished and increasingly confined to particular localities and, on the other, the housing that remained was of low quality and (because of pressure on public sector budgets) poorly maintained. Social housing increasingly became the option of last resort.

As Figure 6.1 illustrates, lack of choice in housing has come to be associated with lack of choice in other respects (Taylor 1995). Thus the lack of income that leads to lack of choice in housing in turn leads to a lack of choice in services and goods. Areas of

FIGURE 6.1   *Choice and exclusion*

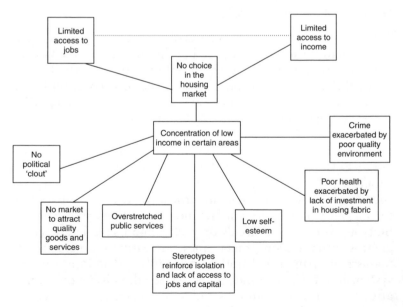

Source: Taylor (1995b), p. 9.

poor housing are not attractive to the market. They find it difficult to attract shops that sell at competitive prices, while vandalism means that many shops end up abandoned and boarded up. These are areas where people are highly dependent on public services since they cannot afford private alternatives; but, in today's policy environment, public services themselves are devalued and increasingly starved of funds. Nor do they provide an attractive market for other services. Mainstream financial services rarely serve them, leaving local people at the mercy of loan sharks. They are the failures of the market or, more accurately, the product of market failure.

Public housing remains a majority tenure in some parts of the world. But in others — the UK, the US and France, for example — public housing estates are increasingly the places where some of the most vulnerable people in society live. In the UK, areas of social housing contain rising proportions of single-parent families, without the support networks that they need. They also support high proportions of children and young people. One of the most telling features in this spiral of decline is that the skewed age balance in the population turns these young people into problems rather than the assets they are considered to be in more affluent areas.

Educational attainment is typically low and truancy high. Parents do not choose to send their children to the schools in these neighbourhoods, which therefore end up at the bottom of educational 'league tables', with falling rolls, falling investment and high exclusion levels, failing to attract the quality staff they need. Unemployment levels are also high: some families may have three generations without work. As real jobs disappear, those who are unemployed drop out of the primary economy. Some rely on the shadow economy, which makes re-entry into the mainstream more difficult. For others, crime and drugs offer a more dependable route to prestige and, for the lucky ones who survive, money. These countercultures fragment communities and engender fear, reinforcing the isolation and exclusion of many of the most vulnerable inhabitants (see Box 6.1).

We should add ill health to this catalogue of exclusion. Richard Wilkinson and colleagues (Wilkinson 1997; Wilkinson and Picket 2009) have demonstrated that differences in mortality in developed countries are explained not by the level of income, but by the level of income inequality. They argue that

---

BOX 6.1   The experience of exclusion

'If you don't have carpets or heating or video games, no one wants to come to your flat to play with you ... The other children call us names and say bad things about our parents. We want people to be our friends, we want to be able to join in things.'

'Poverty is isolating. You do not want anyone to know what you are feeling, what you need, because of the indignity of the situation, so you put on a brave face and do not let anyone into your private life.'

Source: UK Coalition Against Poverty (1998), Section 1, Leaflet 1, p. 4.

---

psychosocial factors – having no control over work, material insecurity, lack of social support, low participation in community life and low self-esteem – all impact negatively on health and that these are more effective indicators of health inequalities than behavioural or environmental factors such as diet, smoking or poor housing.

In many countries, the segregation of areas by ethnic origin, the spatial marginalisation of the poor and the association of poverty with particular ethnic groups mean that poverty is racially marked. In the US, Sampson (2007) and Lawrence (2007) both describe how urban renewal and forced migration in the 1950s devastated previously stable and well-organised black communities, concentrating minorities in public housing with disastrous consequences. The racial unrest in and between communities fragmented and ghettoised in this way has often been a trigger for policy interventions, as we saw in Chapter 3.

A spiral of exclusion

The combination of factors described above creates a spiral of exclusion from which it is difficult to escape. But, in describing the factors which create spatial and tenure-related patterns of disadvantage, there is a risk that we label everyone who lives in disadvantaged neighbourhoods as vulnerable or as 'a problem', adding issues of stereotyping and stigmatisation to the stresses that residents face (Taylor, Kestenbaum and Symons 1976; Dean and Hastings 2000). Media coverage certainly falls into this trap. As one resident graphically put it in a 1995 study (Power and Tunstall 1995, p. 62): 'We've been vandalised by the media'. These neighbourhoods then acquire a reputation from which it is difficult to escape. If the neighbourhood is known at all outside its boundaries it is because it features so heavily in the crime pages of the local newspapers. Relationships become strained as family members from other areas reduce their level of contact because of fear of crime. Colleagues from other areas make derogatory remarks: '"Where do you live" is a common early question on meeting new people, but for residents of stigmatised estates there is fear that they will be judged and found wanting' (Dean and Hastings 2000, p. 17).

As with most stereotypes, the image and the reality are often at odds. Ian Cole and Yvonne Smith (1993, p. 16) found in one estate that: 'The stereotypical image of the estate has made it difficult … to distinguish between the real and imaginary problems [the estate] faces'. They went on to argue that: 'The degree of stability on the estate, the positive views of most residents, and the low level of recorded crime all appear as quite remarkable, rather than exceptionally problematic'. But it is the image that counts and it is readily internalised (see Box 6.2). Deficit models (such as disadvantage, deprivation and exclusion), the need to 'parade' needs and problems in order to get funding, and policies based on community and individual pathology only reinforce exclusion by focusing on the failure of the estate and those who live in it.

This is unlikely to encourage people to engage. Talking about young people in a study of a European regeneration programme, a respondent in my own research remarked: 'They are expected somehow to be involved when the whole thing is based around them having a problem … and oppressing them in a stereotype which is really disrespectful and then everyone wonders why they don't get involved' (professional working in a neighbourhood renewal initiative).

Peter Marris (1996, p. 105) argues that people make sense of their exclusion by 'disengaging and disparaging their own abilities': 'By resignation, by living only for the moment, by other-worldliness or incantations of invulnerability, a psychological space can be protected in which some sense of agency

BOX 6.2   Stigma

'I've lost a few girlfriends because I live in the Valley. Once you've got a reputation, it sticks.'

'You wouldn't get credit down there ... As far as magistrates, probation officers and the police are concerned the place retains its problem aura. They don't understand the place. They find out that someone is from the Valley and then he's bound to be guilty ... [The police] always swoop on the Valley if something happens.'

'They've put the least satisfactory tenants into one area over the years. The Valley turned into a kind of ghetto, a self-contained area into which to put possible problem cases, which wouldn't be seen by the rest of the town. ... When people apply to the Council for a house, they say "as long as it's not in the Valley."'

Source: Taylor, Kestenbaum and Symons (1976).

can survive'. This is the bravado of the young people on the street corner and helps to explain the development of countercultures: a rejection of the values of a society in which they cannot win. Then, Marris goes on to argue (1996, p. 108): 'The rest of society ... blames them for trying to make sense of their situation in the only terms they can'. This is, he argues, one of the 'cruellest consequences of unequal protection against uncertainty'; the excluded 'collaborate in the crippling of their life chances'. For Tilly, this 'adaptation' is a critical factor in the maintenance of what he calls 'durable inequality' (1999).

Meanwhile, local public services are themselves stigmatised as low status and dependency-creating. Staff become ever more difficult to recruit and turnover is high. Indeed John Gray (1996, p. 43) argues that welfare institutions reinforce poverty: 'Because neo-liberal thought conceives of welfare institutions primarily as devices of poverty relief, it cannot avoid remodelling them in ways that institutionalise poverty itself'. Contact with the state in these circumstances consists of being told you are inadequate (Mathers, Parry and Jones 2008, p. 598), and 'subject to the often arbitrary and invasive authority of social service providers and other public and private administrators' (Young 2007, p. 280). This, and the erosion of public services, reinforces people's negative self-image on the estate. People in disadvantaged neighbourhoods expect to be treated badly because of where they live and their image of themselves.

In previous work, colleagues and I drew on the early work of Jock Young in the field of drug addiction (Young 1971) to describe this process as a 'cycle of exclusion' which is depicted in Figure 6.2 (Taylor, Kestenbaum and Symons 1976; Stewart and Taylor 1995; Taylor 1998). Overwhelmingly negative images in the press and elsewhere, combined with a policy focus on their 'needs' and their 'problems', strip people of their dignity. Labelled as failures and marginalised by the rest of society, people accept and internalise this negative definition. Outsiders – professionals, politicians, people from other parts of town and the press – reflect, reinforce and magnify this image. Residents suffer from postcode discrimination: employers lose interest once they know the address; financial institutions are reluctant to lend; taxis, buses and delivery vans avoid the most notorious areas. Outsiders have little reason to visit the estate or test the popular image against reality – they are more likely to avoid it.

FIGURE 6.2   *A cycle of exclusion*

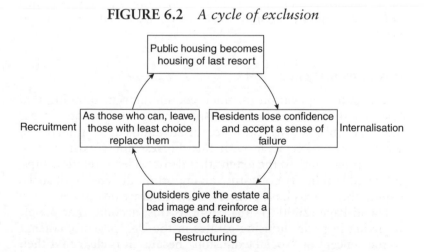

Source: Taylor (1998), reproduced by permission of Taylor and Francis (www.informaworld.com)

Moving further round the cycle, once an estate gets labelled, those who have any choice leave. As they move out, so those with least choice (who are often on the margins of the economy) are moved in and the cycle is repeated. Thus one of the limitations of policies that simply focus on getting people back into the labour market is that, while they may help individuals out of exclusion, they will not bring power into excluded areas.

This section suggests that social exclusion is a complex and self-reinforcing phenomenon. 'Community' is seen as one part of the solution. The second part of this chapter identifies some of the reasons why it might be difficult to address social exclusion with the tools of 'community' alone.

Prescribing community to the poor

Since social exclusion is a relational concept, ideas of community, social capital and civil society, which emphasise networks, ties and reciprocity, should be able to make an important contribution to its reversal. However, there are a number of assumptions in the community discourse that need to be addressed before this can be achieved. One set of assumptions is that community has somehow been lost in excluded areas; another is that communities themselves can turn around the spiral of exclusion described above; a third is that 'community' is what excluded communities need.

Has community been lost?

There is an implication in much communitarian thinking that 'community' has been 'lost' in disadvantaged and excluded areas and that this is why they are disadvantaged. A number of writers have taken issue with this. Forrest and Kearns (1999, p. 22) argue that 'To the extent that dense webs of relationships, trust and familiarity constitute an important dimension of social capital these areas have rich resources to draw on'.

David Page (2000, p. 46) confirms this, arguing that people on living in social housing estates in the UK 'pose a challenge to the concept of "social exclusion" because it is clear that their members are mostly well integrated with their local community'. Most people in his research saw their community as a friendly place (p. 21). Moreover, his research found that jobless people seemed as well connected as those in work to others in their own communities. Page also challenges the notion that people in declining neighbourhoods are less 'moral'. Even when they appear so, he argues, there are clear moral codes that prevail, although they may at times be at odds with the rest of society. Forrest and Kearns confirm this (1999, p. 11): 'While theft from businesses, cars and shoplifting might be seen as acceptable coping strategies, thieving from locals, the community centre or the local school was not'. More bleakly, Hoggett (1997a) has argued that strong norms and networks can exist on the most beleaguered estates, but that these are as likely to be those of gang law and the drugs cartel as those conjured up by the communitarians.

There is a body of evidence to suggest that middle-class people are more inclined to volunteer and to belong to formal organisations than working-class people or people living in disadvantaged neighbourhoods. In the US, for example, research shows that political activity is highly correlated with income, whether that activity takes place online or offline (Smith *et al.* 2009). In the UK, formal volunteering is related to levels of education and socio-economic status (CLG 2010). Research earlier in the decade confirmed that, by conventional measures at least, people living in more disadvantaged areas did indeed participate less (Prime, Zimmeck and Zurawan 2002) – the level of informal volunteering then was 71 per cent in less disadvantaged areas compared with only 59 per cent in the most disadvantaged areas; the level of participation in local community and voluntary activity 73 per cent in the least disadvantaged areas compared with 57 per cent in the most disadvantaged.

However, to conclude from this that people in these areas have no sense of community depends on what is being measured. Studies which measure participation through formal activity do not allow for the fact that informality may be preferred by working-class, poor or excluded communities or by particular ethnic groups. Membership of formal voluntary organisations tends to be associated with the middle classes but, for many people, especially in excluded communities, joining a formal organisation is not a natural thing to do (Burns and Taylor 1998). Thus in 1970, Pahl reported that while formal organisations and formal leadership were common in middle-class communities, working-class communities were more suspicious of formalisation and the emergence of leaders. Citing Broady (1956), he reported that many working-class people avoided formality and frequently pointed out that 'theirs was not a "proper" nor a recognised committee'. 'Committees', Broady reported, only 'start little differences' and thus were seen to undermine solidarity, which, for working-class communities, was the greater value. This account may not take sufficient account of trade unions and labour-related organisations but, since the 1970s, membership of these formal organisations has fallen sharply; they have become increasingly centralised and for neighbourhoods with high levels of unemployment they may have limited relevance.

The evidence suggests that informal mutual activity is an important source of support in excluded communities, helping to reconstruct and reinforce identity and to create and define 'safe' environments (Suttles 1972; Foster 1995). It also provides access to the goods and services that others might buy. Pahl (1970, p. 76) argues that, in the past, kinship ties were to the traditional working classes what property is to the middle class: namely, an important source of economic security and support. Similarly, writing from the South, Tungaranza (1993) stated that: 'social networks are important institutions for the urban poor – for money exchange, for pooling resources and for pooling labour'. But Williams and Windebank (2000, p. 147) deplore the way in which 'the perception that deprived populations can rely on kin and non-kin support networks has been used as a rationale for cutbacks, especially in the US'. This has been a particular issue for minority ethnic populations, where it is still often assumed that 'they look after their own'. Williams and Windebank (2000) argue that the poorest are further excluded by policies that encourage reliance on community exchange, because they engage in less activity of this kind than the relatively affluent.

Overall, there is still insufficient research evidence to test hypotheses about levels of activity, informal networks and participation between different types of area. However, Forrest and Kearns (1999, p. 22) report a high degree of mutual and voluntary activity in some neighbourhoods that lack key economic resources. So even if it were true on the broad scale that the most disadvantaged communities were less active and organised than others, there are certainly examples of neighbourhoods where levels of engagement and informal activity have been high and sustained over time. The informal economies that allow people to survive also demonstrate that excluded areas do not necessarily lack social and economic ties. Indeed, the level of resident commitment to many of the neighbourhoods that have been excluded is astonishing, given the difficulties they face.

However, the nature of this activity poses another problem for policymakers. In Chapter 5, I discussed the fragility of informal networks and the danger that formalising them might destroy them. Informal solutions may operate in a grey area between legality and illegality or in a counterculture. The favoured government solution to social exclusion – getting people back into work – faces the challenge of providing people with a way out of informal and semi-legal economies in a way that will compensate them adequately for making that move.

That apart, there are a number of reasons why 'community' on its own is unlikely to be the answer to social exclusion and the main one is resources. After their positive comment on the levels of social capital in excluded areas, Forrest and Kearns (1999, p. 22) go on to say that what is missing is 'the other elements that can be mobilised to positive effect', by which they mean the material resources of jobs and income. Frazer (2000, p. 185) argues that communitarianism is most likely to work where it is least needed. People in excluded communities, she argues, can organise, but they lack the cash resources to effect change.

Barriers to engagement

Poverty
Sampson (2004, p. 108) argues that 'inequality of resources matters greatly in explaining the production of collective efficacy'. One factor that makes it difficult for many people in disadvantaged communities to engage is the basic struggle for survival that they face. Hampden-Turner (1996, p. 11) argues in response to the communitarian agenda that 'those stakeholders disenfranchised by unemployment and persistent poverty cannot discharge their communitarian responsibilities to look after themselves, their families, neighbours and communities'. Many readers will be familiar with Maslow's hierarchy of needs (Maslow 1943), ranging from physiological (food and clothing), through safety and security, social factors and self-esteem to self-actualisation. There are many people in marginalised communities whose main preoccupation is physical survival, so

self-actualisation is a long way up their hierarchy of needs. And survival takes time and energy away from social engagement:

> The less free time individuals enjoy, the greater are the demands they make on the state and the more they are dependent on the market. They can involve themselves in mutual support activities, extend their network ties and establish various kinds of *ad hoc* solidarity only if they have the time to do so. (Rosenvallon 1995, p. 209)

Albert Bandura's work on self-efficacy provides another way of looking at this. He defines self-efficacy as an individual's belief that he or she has the capability to 'exercise influence over events that affect their lives' (1994, p. 1). This belief, he argues, is a product of social learning and he identifies four sources of self-efficacy:

- Experience (success increases self-efficacy; failure lowers it)
- Social modelling (if s/he can do it, so can I)
- Social persuasion (encouragement and positive feedback)
- Physical and emotional factors and how they are perceived.

It is clear that those who already have little power in society will find these hard to achieve. Their life experience is less likely to instil confidence in their ability to succeed, they may have few models of success around them, they may rarely be encouraged or put in a situation where they can succeed and, in the absence of these conditions, engaging in any kind of public action is likely to make them feel anxious, angry or insecure reinforcing their sense of failure (Gilchrist and Taylor 2011). Indeed, Bandura comments that it is easier to undermine a sense of self-efficacy than to instil it. People who have been persuaded that they lack capabilities, he argues, tend to avoid challenging activities that cultivate potentialities and give up quickly in the face of difficulties.

Thus everything that disadvantages people in the first place will prevent them from developing social networks or participating in collective activities: lack of money, poor transport, lack of childcare, an unsafe or depressing environment, the daily grind of having to manage on very limited financial resources, low self-esteem and little positive reinforcement. In addition, the withdrawal of the state and of public services is gradually depriving them of whatever official safety nets they might have had. Forrest and Kearns (1999, p. 20) report that children are a pivotal element in local networks and women are key actors. But lack of childcare and creche facilities and the struggle involved in coping with very limited financial resources inhibit more formal participation. As Portes and Landolt (1996, p. 20) put it: 'There is considerable social capital in ghetto areas, but the assets obtainable through it seldom allow participants to rise above their poverty'.

Structural change

A second factor that makes it difficult for people to engage is that there are many forces in society that are undermining the foundations on which communities are built. Today's labour markets often break up family and friendship networks (one frequent demand from the UK government in the Thatcherite 1980s was that unemployed people should 'get on their bikes' to find work). Even where people are not split up in this way, the residual nature of social housing makes it more and more difficult to house families close to each other: as social housing becomes more scarce it is increasingly allocated to those in greatest need. The institutions that underpinned community relations in the past have also disappeared. The industries around which many neighbourhoods grew have gone and, with them, the union branches, the social clubs, chapels and the smaller enterprises, leaving behind the shells of buildings and little access to jobs further afield. It is somewhat ironic, therefore, that, while the language of the market exalts individual choice and liberty, those whom the market has failed and who are thus increasingly excluded from the wider society are prescribed 'community'.

Their plight is intensified by the erosion of society and its communal responsibility for all its members. Citing Wacquant (1993), Bauman (2001, p. 120) describes these disadvantaged communities as a 'dumping ground for those for whom the surrounding community has no economic or social use'. Some early capitalists, he reminds us – Robert Owen, Titus Salt, the Cadbury family and others – sought to revive the natural understanding of bygone community that had been eroded by capitalism through developing model villages (p. 35). But today's global rich have opted out of the 'fraternal obligation to share benefits among their members' through communal insurance against individual misfortune (p. 58), leaving the casualties of capitalism without any support other than charity. Lawrence reiterates this point, arguing that the contemporary emphasis on non-profit solutions 'has pushed the obligations of the larger society toward poor communities too far into the background (2007, p. 291). In such circumstances, Fairbanks argues (2007, pp. 108–9), community becomes a 'burdensome cost' on poor neighbourhoods, 'as residents are expected to compensate for the disparities and assaults created by macrostructural forces of disinvestment'. Indeed, several authors have warned that the contemporary fashion for decentralisation and localism can have highly regressive effects, reinforcing the exclusion of the most marginalised (Evers 2003; Fairbanks 2007).

Exclusion breeds exclusion

Misfortune is commonly celebrated as bringing people together, but poverty is as likely to breed conflict and suspicion as community spirit. Both Page (2000) and Forrest and Kearns (1999) suggest that newcomers are often blamed for decline in marginalised areas of social housing in the UK: as the more successful move on, their places are filled by more vulnerable people. Hostility to immigrants is all too easily whipped up when access to social housing is limited and people see strangers rather than their sons and daughters moving in next door. Of course, it is not only (and not always) the poorest neighbourhoods that are hostile to newcomers – far from it. But in the most transient communities, high turnover, as Forrest and Kearns (1999, p. 12) argue, can breed suspicion and accentuate difference: 'Too many people simply pass through on their way from one precarious set of circumstances to another'.

It seems almost bizarre to expect communities excluded by the rest of society to be inclusive themselves, especially in a society that celebrates individualism so strongly. As Marris (1998, p. 14) argues: 'The more uncertainty we generate, the more we provoke a politics of defensive exclusion, scapegoating and cynicism'. Communities, as Lloyd and Gilchrist (1994, p. 135) point out, can be 'alienating places ... riven with incompatibilities and contrasts, which emerge as rivalries, prejudice and intercommunal conflicts. Within a neighbourhood, several communities may co-exist, whose members may have little to do with one another and who may bitterly resent the others' presence'.

Ralf Dahrendorf (1995) reminds us of the fragmentation that can be born of exclusion, pointing out that 'borders, especially social boundaries, are always particularly noticeable to those closest to them'. The stereotyping process I described earlier makes it difficult to develop links and networks across communities; instead, the stereotypes that are applied to a locality are deflected onto neighbours, people who look different or the kids hanging around on the street corner. People define their oppression in terms of each other rather than the wider forces that dictate their lives. The community thus becomes the site of fear rather than security. Identities *can* be created by exclusion, but the attraction of fundamentalist ideologies to the dispossessed, the horrors of terrorist shootings within as well as across factions in Northern Ireland, the persistence of racial harassment and the success of far-right parties in disadvantaged communities across the world should warn us of the dangers of seeing tight-knit communities or bonding social capital as a solution to social exclusion.

Safe havens?
Atkinson (2000a, p. 1048) stresses the need to differentiate between excluded spaces. Some, he argues, contain relatively stable populations who have a very distinct sense of community but also a very sharp sense of their exclusion from the rest of society. As we have seen, Page (2000) describes such areas as being difficult for newcomers to penetrate, but he also argues that, in these communities, it is not unusual to find people who have moved out moving back in again. Atkinson's argument contrasts this kind of community with those where residents are there as a result of powerlessness rather than choice. This powerlessness, he claims, is the only common experience they share with one another. In addition, the gradual withdrawal of the state and of public services means that there is less public presence than there used to be. Liz Richardson refers to the phenomenon of 'civic absence' on many social housing estates, where services may have little or no visible presence on the estate, are difficult to communicate with and have poor response times (2007, p. 264). Or they may be so heavily protected as to feel more like a garrison fending off the enemy, thus reinforcing the sense of siege in the neighbourhoods where they are based.

Brower has suggested that there are three dimensions to neighbourhoods: the physical environment (ambience); social interaction (engagement); and what he calls 'choicefulness' (Brower 1996; Forrest and Kearns 1999, p. 25). Choicefulness means the diversity of lifestyles present in the neighbourhood. It also means that people feel they have a choice about where they live and that their neighbourhood would be chosen by others. In 1972, Suttles argued that two of the most important considerations when choosing a neighbourhood to live in were status and safety. He argued that there were two main ways in which people could satisfy these requirements: one was to buy into an area where the character of fellow residents is assured by the costs of living there (and buy out again if the area declines); the other was to cultivate one's neighbours. People in the most excluded communities do not have the former choice – and the stereotyping attached to their environment makes it a place where it might not be seen as safe to cultivate the neighbours. Their communities might accord with what Suttles calls *a defeated community*. Fiona Williams (1993) captures this distinction between chosen and imposed communities when she contrasts community as 'space' (that is, territory and opportunity) with community as 'place', where people are put and/or constrained.

The defeated community is one where residents have no choice; Suttles (1972) describes three other kinds of community where they do. One is the community of *limited liability*, where it is the relationships and ties that lie outside the area that are most significant to residents. A second is the 'contrived community', put together by public and private developers, who in his account attempt to mix different populations, with varying results. The third type is the *defended neighbourhood*, which segregates people in order to avoid danger and reinforce status claims. Suttles characterises communities ruled by gang law and vigilantism as defended communities, but we might equally apply this term to the 'voluntary ghettoes' created by the rich (Bauman 2001) – the burgeoning number of 'gated' communities in many countries over recent years, fortified in order to keep out any potential for trouble. In an interesting take on this phenomenon, J. G. Ballard's novel, *Cocaine Nights* (1991) is set in a group of gated communities in Spain, which seem to have lost their soul – with everyone living their private lives behind their own front doors, no signs of communal life or sense of community – nowadays we might say no social capital. The only way to reinstil that soul and get people connecting with each other, according to his protagonist, was to rediscover a common enemy – by bringing the crime back in!

Safety comes at a price to the whole of society. Tajfel's theory of social identity (Tajfel 1981) describes a process of individual social mobility where individuals, from their own or others' perceptions of attributions of groups, decide to respond to dissatisfaction with existing group membership by moving to another group that is perceived as more highly valued. He argues that the less personal contact there is between groups, the greater the likelihood of rivalry and a belief in the superiority of one's group. Apartheid is one example where separation breeds exclusion, but commentators on residential patterns over the centuries have remarked on the problems caused as the rich have less and less physical contact with the poor. Pat Thane (1982, p. 63) observed that the 'suburbanisation' of towns in the UK, with the growth of access to transport in the late nineteenth century, reduced 'geographical and social contact between local business and professional elites and the poor of their towns', as the extract from *Sybil* at the beginning of this chapter described. This separation of rich and poor also meant that the interests that different classes had in common were reduced. Both factors were to put pressure on traditional philanthropy from rich to poor. Similar trends have been observed in the twentieth century, with the flight of the rich from inner-city areas referred to earlier in this chapter.

Are community ties what poor people need?
We could argue that it is the wealthiest people in the world who have lost community, insulated from the rest of the world, transferring from their gated mansion in their gated neighbourhood to their bullet-proofed car, their private plane, and to the five-star hotel in some other anonymous town, which is pretty much the same hotel as in any other country. No one is prescribing them community. But if their separation from the lives of the many affected by their decisions is a significant part of the problem, as I suggest above, one of the answers to exclusion may be not only to focus attention on the need for community among the poor, but also to reconnect the rich. We certainly need to be more careful about imposing outmoded or artificial notions of community on the most marginalised in our society (Hunter 2007).

Earlier in this chapter, I argued that community ties or bonding social capital remain strong in many excluded areas. However, increasingly, people are asking whether strong community ties are, in fact, the answer to exclusion. In Chapter 3, I referred to Daniel Moynihan's remark that some of the problems of disadvantaged communities could be blamed on 'too much community cohesion'. If, as Chapter 6 suggested, it is weak ties, or bridging social capital, that characterise the way we live now, it may be the lack of these ties – what Perri 6 has called 'network poverty' – that characterises and disadvantages such communities:

> Most people get jobs through people they know. ... The best kind of social network for finding work is rich in 'weak ties' to a wide range of people who are unlike oneself. Those people whose networks are dominated by strong ties to family, neighbours, old school friends and people like themselves have fewer chances to find work and fewer chances for mobility; many long-term unemployed people only know other long-term unemployed people. (1997, p. 6)

Forrest and Kearns (1999, p. 9) extend this analysis:

> The 'successful' suburb may have few of the features of community or neighbourliness ... but will contain people with rich and diverse relational webs. Conversely the poor neighbourhood may have weak and inward-looking networks which nevertheless offer strong support in adversity. The very strength and introverted nature of these networks may be a disadvantaging factor.

This is not a new phenomenon. As Pahl argued some 30 years earlier, the looser networks that made communities negotiable commodities at that time were predominantly a middle-class phenomenon. A study by Fischer in 1982 found that, in the US, more educated people had larger and more dispersed social networks, while Willmott (1986) cited the 1986 British Crime Survey as showing that, at that time, only 15 per cent of the friends of professional and managerial people lived locally compared to 34 per cent among unskilled people. It is in the nature of social

exclusion that most activity and networks in excluded neighbourhoods are centred on the neighbourhood, and often only a
small part of that neighbourhood. This gives people few alternative ties and few alternative role models, reinforcing values and
patterns of behaviour that in turn reinforce exclusion, such as
truancy. Carrying out research on child abuse in the US (which
is not, of course, confined to disadvantaged areas), Vinson and
colleagues came to the conclusion that 'because the limited social
contact the abusive mothers had was confined primarily to their
immediate families, who shared many of the same values, their
patterns of behaviour were probably resistant to change and
lacked the more varied input afforded by more distant parts of
their network' (Vinson, Baldry and Hargreaves 1996, p. 527).

Studying social housing estates in the UK in 2000, Page found
that activity there was more likely to be centred on the estate than
in other kinds of neighbourhood, where people moved across
the boundaries far more frequently. The least connected people
in his study (and that of Forrest and Kearns 1999) were white
younger people who grew up on the estate and who, as adults,
had little or no contact with the labour market. The most connected were older residents who could remember better times on
the estate and who had maintained contacts elsewhere. In Forrest and Kearns' study it was minority ethnic residents who were
the most connected, tapping into wider ethnic networks across
the city. They argued that successful entrepreneurs from minority ethnic communities were less likely to leave the neighbourhood because of these wider support mechanisms, once again
supporting the argument for weak ties.

There is another way in which weak ties are denied to excluded communities. In many cities in the UK, public housing estates
in the 1960s to 1980s were built on the peripheries of cities,
with poor transport links and few facilities. Often this problem
was exacerbated by the physical design of estates, which had
one way in and one way out, with a bewildering array of closes
and culs-de-sac inside. As public transport has given way to the
market, the absence of affordable transport has been a further
constraint on people's mobility and ability to make either strong
or weak ties. There is little reason for outsiders to visit these
peripheral areas or to move through them and they are easily
forgotten.

Discussion

The recognition that poverty and exclusion are the product of relationships within society has been significant in social policy and ideas of community and social capital are likely to be important in addressing these relationships. However, the complexities and paradoxes that I have discussed in this and the previous chapter mean that they are not easy concepts to apply. We cannot assume that people who happen to live adjacent to each other have common values and are willing to act in concert, especially when these are people who have been excluded by the rest of society. In the most disadvantaged neighbourhoods, people have no choice about where they live or who their neighbours are. Their exclusion by the rest of society persistently reinforces their problems and feeds internal instability, and can make community a source of fear rather than of cohesion, thus reducing the changes of developing collective efficacy.

This means that there are several issues that policymakers need to address before prescribing community to 'the poor'. First, Henderson and Salmon (1998, pp. 27–8) criticise the communitarians for their failure to address: 'the social responsibilities of governments, public agencies and private corporations. ... As a key principle of communitarianism, social responsibility should be applied not only to people, families and communities, but also to all those bodies which affect the lives of ordinary people'. Scholars have highlighted the way in which state policies have helped to create the concentrations of disadvantage that lead to social exclusion. Many therefore underline the need for sustained state action if spatial disadvantage is to be addressed (see, for example, Evers 2003; Sampson 2007). Successful policies will need to pay at least as much attention to the structural factors that reinforce exclusion and the stereotyped approaches of outsiders towards these communities, as to the responsibilities of these communities themselves.

Second, we need to consider the kinds of community that policy is prescribing to 'the poor'. More and more people are suggesting that the supposed tight-knit community of the past, with its clear moral order, is no longer relevant today (if indeed it ever was). Successful communities are characterised as much by weak as strong ties and people relate to many overlapping communities, each of which may take precedence at different times. Weak ties and overlapping networks give people choices within and beyond their locality. Successful policies will need to create the conditions under which these weak ties can be built in localities, turning them into 'permeable places' (Forrest and Kearns 1999). Attention needs to be given to the practical design and transport issues that isolate communities, as well as the relationships that are built with outsiders and professionals.

This means that focusing on the development of bonding social capital – strong ties – as the solution to the problems of excluded neighbourhoods, while important, may in itself be problematic. On the other hand, the rejection of these neighbourhoods by wider society makes it difficult to build the all-important bridging social capital, whether between different communities in excluded neighbourhoods, or between these neighbourhoods and wider society. Similar arguments could be applied to communities of identity and interest, which can themselves be excluded by too strong a focus in policy on area-based initiatives.

Anthony Giddens (2000) has coined the term 'shell institutions' to describe the way that institutions such as the nation state, the family, nature and work have lost their familiar meaning as a result of globalisation. He does not include community in that list, but it should be there. These two chapters have suggested that a call for 'community' needs to be informed by a better understanding of how community works in different settings and for different people. What we need for the twenty-first century is a concept of community that reflects the way we live and the way we want to live now rather than trying, as Offe and Heinze remarked in 1992, to dispatch those marginalised by globalisation 'to conjure up the charms of pre-capitalist ways of life' (p. 41).

Chapter 7

Power and Empowerment

In the early 1990s, the UN Development Programme's Human Development Report defined participation as giving people constant 'access to decision-making and power' (UNDP 1993, p. 21). A decade later, the idea of 'community empowerment' emerged as one of the central themes of policy in England and other parts of the UK. But if the language of community is contested, so too is the language of 'power': what it is, how it is created and how it is sustained and reproduced. Some people argue, as we shall see, that power is finite – a 'zero-sum' good – which means that if communities are going to be empowered, someone else is going to have to give up power. Others see it as a more fluid, positive-sum good that can grow as it is shared. Either way, the idea of empowerment can seem something of a paradox. If A can empower B, surely this assumes that A holds a position of superior power and could take that power away again? Or it could imply that the power that is given to B is somehow of an inferior kind compared to that held by A. Can power be 'granted' or must it be taken?

Chapter 3 described four decades of 'community' policies. Whether these policies have empowered people is a question that I will address in Chapter 9. Broadly speaking, however, research suggests that disadvantaged communities have remained on the margins of power. The pessimist from Chapter 2 would argue that this is because moves towards partnership are driven by the need to incorporate dissent and provide symbolic legitimacy for an essentially divisive capitalist system. Policies to tackle social exclusion would be, at best, a 'sticking plaster' for the casualties of the march of capital and an effort to stop them infecting the wider world. In this analysis, power is both a zero-sum game and one where the dice are loaded in favour of the existing power structure. The processes that produce 'durable inequalities' (Tilly 1999) have the capacity to resist most attempts to dislodge them. Power is woven into cultures and discourses that enshrine particular ways of seeing things and assumptions that we never even question. In such a scenario, community participation risks incorporation and resistance is the only feasible option.

A more optimistic analysis would reject this zero-sum and adversarial view of power, seeing power as an energy that flows rather than being possessed. It would argue that, while dominant forms of power are woven into our taken-for-granted assumptions about how things work and what is possible, power is nonetheless dynamic rather than static. Our 'ways of seeing' are thus constantly adjusted and reproduced through our day-to-day activities and interactions. In this view, individuals are not necessarily the pawns of capitalism, but are capable of redefining the rules of the game. Such an analysis would highlight the diversity of interests within government and see policy-making as a complex and contradictory process, with fault lines to be exploited and alliances to be made.

This chapter and the next explore these different views in more detail, both in general and in relation to the policy process.

Understanding power

Who has power?

One set of theories about power – Marxism, elite domination, patriarchy and structural feminism are examples – argues that it is held by certain groups or forces in society. The power of these forces – capital, privileged groups, men – is perpetuated through wealth, cultural conditioning and education. While later developments of Marxism have softened its historical determinism and refined its assumptions about how change is achieved, it is still associated with an essentially predetermined, zero-sum view of power, as are other theories in this group. Power, and hence policy, is determined by capitalist, elitist or patriarchal ruling ideas and interests.

Another set of theories, while still arguing that there is a finite stock of power, challenges the class domination of Marxism, the hierarchical domination of elite theory and the patriarchy of structural feminism. Instead, pluralists argue that there is no pre-determined dominant group. They argue that power is likely to be spread among the many rather than the few, and to be bargained for competitively rather than being inherent in existing structures (Clegg 1989, p. 9). In the first set of theories, whether you have power is defined by who you are (reputation); in the second, a pluralist approach defines power in terms of the outcome of decision making processes (achievement). Pluralist elites are also more scattered, more specialised and less co-ordinated than the early elite theorists such as Mosca suggested (1939); they are not always the same people. A pluralist analysis assumes, to quote Keith Popple (1995, pp. 40–1), that 'it is possible to achieve change through rational discourse, the fostering of collective values and moral persuasion'. Although power is still seen as a finite good for which different interests compete, it therefore has the potential to be more widely distributed. Since, in a pluralist analysis, those who are powerful in one arena are not necessarily powerful in another, all groups have a chance of being heard at some point.

How does power operate?

Peter Marris defines power as the 'power to command' (1996, p. 87). Piven and Cloward argue, as did Gramsci, that it is upheld by force, and also wealth (1977, p. 1):

> Common sense and historical experience combine to suggest a simple but compelling view of the roots of power in any society. Crudely but clearly stated, those who control the means of physical coercion, and those who control the means of producing wealth, have power over those who do not.

They might also have added the power to control information and communications.

In pluralist theory, competing interests challenge for these forms of power. However, critics take issue with the implication that everyone is equally equipped to compete. Pluralism, they argue, fails to recognise the unequal distribution of power in society or the role that powerful interests within society have in the creation and sustenance of ideas. The dice are loaded.

Gramsci developed the concept of hegemony to understand the way that power is perpetuated and reproduced. More subtle than the use of overt force, hegemony occurs 'when the intellectual, moral and philosophical leadership provided by the class ... which is ruling, successfully achieves its objective of providing the fundamental outlook for the whole society' (Bocock 1986, p. 63, cited in Clegg 1989). This ideological and cultural control serves to support the status quo and justify existing class and power relations (Butcher 2007b, p. 24).

These ideas have been developed in a number of ways. In 1962, Bachrach and Baratz argued that power could be traced through an understanding not only of the domination of one group by another, but also of what gets excluded from the policy agenda. They called this 'the mobilisation of bias'. In 1974, Stephen Lukes extended this into three dimensions of power:

1. In the first dimension, the overt resolution of conflict between two or more conflicting positions, A has power over B (the power to command).
2. In the second dimension, A dictates the agenda and excludes B's issues from consideration (power holders act as gatekeepers and filters).
3. In the third dimension, B internalises A's conception of power; power holders mould the way the rest of us think about what is and is not possible. Structures of power are accepted and internalised without question or even recognition.

The third dimension, which echoes the concept of hegemony, can be tracked though studying social myths, language and symbols and the ways in which they are manipulated both in power processes and in the communication of information (Gaventa 1980).

This set of ideas shows how, in Healey's words (2006, p. 29), 'relations of power have the potential to oppress and dominate not merely through the distribution of material resources, but through the fine-grain of taken-for-granted assumptions and practices'. As an example, she cites the dominance of rational scientific approaches to knowledge, planning and management which have fed policy analysis and planning by objectives for many years and more recently the new public management and the drive for evidence-based practice (see also Chapter 8). Charles Tilly (1999, p. 36) provides another example: the power of individualism in Western liberal thought. 'At least in Western countries', he argues, 'people learn early in life to tell stories in which self-motivating actors firmly located in space and time produce all significant changes in the situation through their own efforts'.

While Lukes' theories represent something of a breakthrough, they still focus on power as domination, adopting a 'zero-sum' analysis with the assumption that power is finite. He was later to acknowledge that this neglected 'the manifold ways in which power over others can be productive, authoritative and compatible with dignity' (Lukes 2005, p. 109). Stewart Clegg (1989) contrasts these approaches with a more 'positive-sum' analysis, which sees power as flowing through systems rather than being held by individuals and elite groups. With others, he contrasts 'power over' (the power of one group or individual to control another, or the subordination of others' preferences) with 'power to', which releases people's potential to act. The first set of ideas he associates with Hobbes' *Leviathan*, the second with Machiavelli. Table 7.1 summarises the distinctions between the two.

Michel Foucault develops these ideas further. He abandons the idea that structural positions have ascribed and objective interests fixed by the relations of production, as in Marxist analysis. He conceives power instead as a set of techniques and disciplinary practices whereby people are persuaded or 'recruited' to take a view of their own interests that matches those that the power holders want them to assume. In this analysis, dominant forms of power are still deeply engrained in society and perpetually recreated through 'disciplines' and 'surveillance' (Foucault),

TABLE 7.1   *Approaches to power*

Hobbesian (Leviathan)	*Machiavellian*
Grand narrative about the way things are	Rules of the game which can be negotiated
Intentional	Contingent
Power is held	Power flows
Zero sum	Positive sum
'power over'	'power to'
What power *is*	What power *does*
Modern, rational, scientific	Post-modern, fragmented

Source: Adapted from Clegg (1989).

'thoughtworlds' (Habermas), 'cultural and symbolic capital' (Bourdieu) and 'circuits of power' (Clegg). These processes are not easy to challenge, because power does not just privilege some people over others; it also legitimates certain kinds of knowledge, privileging certain ways of discussing, particular forms of organising and certain ways of knowing (Healey, 2006, p. 60). As Stone argues (1989, p. 22), the narratives it creates attempt to make it seem 'as though they are simply describing fact'.

Foucault sees power as being present in all social relationships. Knowledge is intimately linked to power, as bodies of ideas become established and put into operation as powerful discourses or 'gazes'. The dominant 'gaze' is expressed through disciplinary practices and power is exercised through the dominance of particular forms of knowledge (including professional knowledge): the medical 'gaze' is an obvious example and one that has been challenged in the past 20 years by disabled people, among others. Thus, Foucault argues that 'rationality ... is a tool of governance that legitimates political systems and power structures, through encouraging a belief that such systems have a scientific and hence correct basis' (Servian 1996, p. 12). Dreyfus and Rabinow (1982, p. 16) describe how this depoliticises discourse: 'political technologies advance by taking what is essentially a political problem, removing it from the realm of political discourse and recasting it in the neutral realm of science'. This is a theme that will be picked up at several points in this volume.

Foucault emphasised the 'capillary' nature of power', operating *through* rather than *on* its subjects. Central to his analysis is his argument that 'the exercise of power requires the compliance of willing subjects'. The perfection of power should thus render its *actual* exercise unnecessary, because external surveillance is replaced by self-surveillance. As Lukes (2005, p. 106) explains:

> Foucault-inspired work [begins] to explore subtle forms of the securing of willing compliance, in which human beings are enlisted into wider patterns of normative control, often acting as their own overseers, while believing themselves ... to be free of power, making their own choices, pursuing their own interests, assessing arguments rationally and coming to their own conclusions'

Bourdieu develops this through the concept of 'habitus'. Crossley (2003, p. 44) summarises his key ideas as follows:

> Practice for Bourdieu is an effect of actions and interactions which are shaped ... by the habitus and capital of agents, as well as the context and dynamism constituted by their shared participation in a common 'game' or 'market' (field).

Habitus can be defined as a set of dispositions that govern the way in which actors think and behave. It operates 'below the level of consciousness in a way that is resistant to articulation, critical reflection and conscious manipulation' (Lukes 2005, p. 140). Agents operate in a series of markets or *fields* (social, political, cultural) that operate in a similar way to the economic market. Each field has its own dominant institutions, operating logics, means of production, and profit and loss accounts determined by the rules specific to it (Taylor, Howard and Lever 2010, p. 149). Within these fields there are struggles over resources and status (power), to which agents bring varying amounts of different kinds of capital – economic, social (relationships) and cultural, depending on their background, education, wealth and other attributes. Bourdieu argues that habitus is only realised in relation to a field, and the same habitus can lead to very different practices and stances depending on the state of the field (Bourdieu 1990, p. 116). He also added a fourth type of capital – symbolic capital – which is consecrated by those agents and institutions that already have power within the field and allows them to influence the terms on which participation in a given field rests.

Habitus thus represents the point of crystallisation of the structure of domination and the play of power (Peillon 1998). It is through habitus that agents in a field respond meaningfully as a situation develops. As the mediating concept between the structure of the field and the practices within it, habitus translates relations of domination into power and into access to those resources that are at stake in the field. And it is in this way, as Bourdieu (1984) demonstrates, that aesthetic, political and lifestyle differences allow some groups symbolically to define their own habitus as superior to that of others (Taylor, Howard and Lever 2010, p. 149).

Both Foucault and Bourdieu emphasise the importance of discourse and classification. 'The social world', argues Bourdieu (1990, pp. 54–5), 'is the locus of struggles over words which owe their seriousness – and sometimes their violence – to the fact that words to a great extent make things and that changing words, and more generally representations ... is already a way of changing things'. Naming things, he argues, brings them into being. Thus, in the 'community' field, Nikolas Rose describes how the 'community discourse' has hijacked a 'language of resistance and transformed it into an expert discourse and professional vocation' (Rose 1999, p. 175), turning communities, into 'zones to be investigated, mapped, classified, documented and interpreted'. Similarly Fairbanks (2007, p. 114) argues that community is used to denote a 'third space of governance' and as a 'diagram for the reorganisation of publicly provided services'. More generally, Rappaport (1998, p. 231) highlights the significance of the mass media and other institutions in communicating dominant cultural narratives which stereotype and subjugate particular classes of people. He and others illustrate the way in which these narratives are perpetuated in racial profiling (Rappaport 1998; Lawrence 2007), in the construction of anti-social behaviour, or in the demonisation of young people (Barnes, Newman and Sullivan 2007, pp. 34, 39).

Institutional theory casts further light on the way in which dominant forms of power are perpetuated. It seeks to explain the ways in which human actions and interactions produce rules that regulate activity and norms that set out expectations of appropriate behaviour (Barnes, Newman and Sullivan 2007, p. 59). Once established, it argues, institutions and the rules that sustain them operate independently of individual actors. They are sustained by culture, role systems, routinised practices and objects, which communicate beliefs and practices to new actors: 'Confronted with a new situation, actors draw on their existing resources to interpret and respond to it, based on pre-existing rules and pre-existing logics of appropriate behaviour (Barnes, Newman and Sullivan 2007, p. 61). Through institutional isomorphism (DiMaggio and Powell 1983) or 'emulation' (Tilly 1999), preferred institutional patterns and systems of social relations are spread from one setting to another (see Box 7.1). There are clear parallels with Bourdieu's concepts of habitus and field here.

BOX 7.1   How systems are institutionalised

DiMaggio and Powell (1983) coined the term 'institutional iso-morphism' to describe how organisational practices become en-trenched. They identified three forms of isomorphism:

- Coercive isomorphism occurs when organisations are forced to behave in certain way (for example, by funders or by legal requirements)
- Mimetic isomorphism occurs when organisations copy what they see as successful ways of working in other organisations
- Normative isomorphism occurs when organisations assume that certain ways of organising are 'the norm' or particular standards are established by professionals.

Source: DiMaggio and Powell (1983).

The potential for empowerment

The previous section describes forms of power that serve domi-nant interests in society. But although Foucault and other writers trace the ways in which dominant interests maintain existing power relations in more or less subtle ways, their analyses also open up a range of possibilities for empowerment. Implicit in power, Foucault argues, is the notion of resistance. Furthermore, if power is embedded through language and ideas then it can also be reshaped. The fluidity of power allows for the creation of alternative circuits of meaning and significance. Indeed, Clegg argues (1989, pp. 17–18) that:

> This view of power is of a far less massive, oppressive and prohibitive apparatus than it is often imagined to be. Cer-tainly such effects can be secured by power, but nowhere as easily as some 'dominant ideology', 'hegemonic' or 'third di-mensional' views would suggest. Power is better regarded as not having two faces or three layers, but as a process which may pass through distinct circuits of power and resistance.

Both Giddens and Habermas have highlighted the possibilities for reconstructing power relations and 'ways of seeing'. Thus

Giddens (1990) emphasises the role of active agency in the creation and maintenance of structures and meanings, and the possibility of 'transformative power' through reflexivity. Healey (2006, p. 49) develops this idea to argue that:

We make structural forces as well as being shaped by them. So we 'have power' and, if sufficiently aware of the structuring constraints bearing in on us, can work to make changes by changing the rules, changing the flow of resources and, most significantly, changing the way we think about things.

She draws on Habermas's concept of 'communicative action' (Habermas 1984), which emphasises the potential for collective dialogue to confront the distortion of reality by the powerful. Communicative action represents a shift from bargaining and interest aggregation to the common reason of equal citizens as a dominant force in democratic life (Cohen and Fung 2004; Gaventa 2004) and while Healey acknowledges that the way we think is still culturally constrained, she argues that there are possibilities within such dialogue for learning, development and transformative action (Healey 2006, p. 53). Drawing on the work of Innes *et al.* (1994), she links these possibilities for transformation with ideas about social capital. The driving forces of social change, she argues, can be mobilised through networks, through which alternative systems of meaning, ways of acting and valuing can be learned, transmitted and sometimes transformed. Others have coined the term 'power with' or 'integrative power' to describe power acquired through solidarity or developing through the process of working together (Butcher *et al.* 2007, p. 26).

We start out in different places on the power map. Clegg (1989) draws an analogy with chess, where some pieces have more moves than others and some are in a better position than others (he writes of 'privileged pathways'). But he and others are critical of those who see Foucault's analysis purely in terms of power as dominance. Thus Rose (1999, p. 278) argues that 'our present arises as much out of ... moments of [radical] critique as out of some relentless logic of regulation'. Similarly, Barnes, Newman and Sullivan (2007) argue that the concept of 'capture' is too blunt and that the power of discourse can be overemphasised. In their research, they document the capacity of publics to refuse to conform to the identities offered to them and their willingness to challenge official rules and norms. Indeed, Foucault distanced himself from his earlier views – arguing that while discourse could be an instrument and effect of power, it could also be a hindrance, 'a stumbling block, a point of resistance and a starting point for an opposing strategy' (1991, p. 101). Applying his ideas to governing and politics, he acknowledged that 'the forms of totalisation offered by politics are always ... very limited' and promoted the idea of 'problematisation – developing a given into a question' (1984, p. 389). Thus, according to Morison (1990, pp. 119, 120), Foucault's later work replaces the notion of 'docile bodies' upon which power is inscribed with the possibility that self-steering actors outside the state can become 'active subjects', not only collaborating in the exercise of government but also shaping and influencing it.

Bourdieu's analysis also allows for agency, but only at points of extreme crisis, when accepted ways of seeing the world have to be suspended, giving way to more critical forms of praxis and new rationalities. For Crossley (2003, p. 49), however, this underestimates the 'capacity of social agents to reflect upon, criticise and protest against the social structures which disadvantage them in various ways'. He describes how a history of contentious politics and the cultural capital it creates can create a 'radical habitus' which encompasses: a durable disposition to question and criticise elites; the political know-how to transform this critique into action; and an ethos that gives participation a sense of individual meaning and worth. Crossley highlights the interplay between habitus, cultural capital and field, the latter including support networks, social events and 'pedagogic agents' through whom knowledge, commitment and reflexivity are conveyed, reproducing radical culture across historical time.

A post-modern approach to power might be expected to dispense with hegemonic analyses altogether, arguing that power is so fragmented that there are no longer any general principles or commonly understood 'thoughtworlds' through which to secure social co-ordination or control. Individuals can now develop a 'pick and mix' identity: they can step in and out of any definition (Jacob 2002). But while this analysis appears to break down centrally located power, it can equally disguise the interests and actions of the powerful.

Clearly these different conceptions of power have different implications for empowerment. *Structuralist* interpretations imply confrontational strategies which can overthrow the power holders; *pluralism* implies a strategy that helps excluded groups to compete; *transformative* and *post-modern interpretations* imply more subtle understandings of the policy process and the windows of opportunity that can be found within it. How these might be applied is a question I will return to in Chapter 10.

Routes to empowerment

The personal is political

This chapter has focused so far on structural analyses of power, looking at how collective power is defined and distributed. In these analyses, the individual is a manipulated element rather than necessarily the important part of the process (Servian 1996, p. 1). But the feminist movement in the 1960s and 1970s famously put the 'personal' back into 'political', introducing a multi-dimensional view of empowerment, which recognised, but was not confined to, a structural analysis. To understand how people in excluded communities can be empowered it is necessary, therefore, not only to examine structures of domination but also the factors which encourage or stand in the way of individual agency. What is it that determines whether individuals engage in these processes and how they use them?

I suggested in Chapter 6 that we could not expect individuals who were struggling to survive to carry out their communitarian duties. Before people can be empowered politically, they need access to the material basics of survival and to the psychological resources to engage in society. Using behaviourist experiments with dogs, Seligman (1975) demonstrated a tendency to 'give up' when faced with continued disappointment. Marris develops this, demonstrating how the more powerful forces in society force the weaker to bear the burden of uncertainty in a chain of displacement (from central to local government; from employer to employee; from richer to poorer) that constantly shifts the burden of adjustment onto the most marginalised. He argues (1996, pp. 103–4) that people in this situation can only defend themselves by psychological withdrawal: 'If they have no control over their work or assurance of its continuity, they will be less vulnerable if they do not invest it with any personal meaning'.

Chapter 6 described how defences against uncertainty can be self-defeating. Duncombe (2007) argues that apathy is the new form of resistance. In this he echoes Marris' view that, for the excluded, resistance can take the form of 'a kind of irresponsibility, which the rest of society condemns, but which is closely related to self-respect, because it is the only kind of self-assertion left to them' (Marris 1996, p. 107). Marris cites the schoolboy who stops paying attention or plays up and thereby confirms his own failure because it has become too stressful to keep trying to succeed. Victims, he argues (p. 108), make sense of their situation in a way that makes it stable and predictable, but which reinforces their exclusion.

In Chapter 6, I also introduced Albert Bandura's concept of self-efficacy to identify the barriers to engagement in disadvantaged neighbourhoods and among disadvantaged communities (Bandura 1994). Turning that analysis on its head, his sources of self-efficacy suggest the ways in which individuals *can* realise a sense of their own power. One factor is experience of success, although he stresses that 'easy success' doesn't work – it has to be success in overcoming obstacles through perseverance. A second is the existence of successful role models among people who are similar enough for an individual to identify with them. A third is social persuasion, which not only involves encouragement and positive feedback but also – and importantly – putting people in situations where they are likely to succeed. The final source he describes as physical and emotional factors, although the impact of these will depend on how these are interpreted. In this sense the sources of self-efficacy are likely to be cumulative and interdependent. They also vary over the life cycle and in different situations. A similar concept is that of 'power from within', which has been used to describe personal self-confidence, often linked to culture, religion or other aspects of identity and influences the thoughts and action that are seen to be legitimate. As Butcher points out (2007), this kind of power is positive sum and need not be gained at the expense of anyone else.

Chris Warren (1996) analyses the relationship between the personal and the political in terms of 'an empowerment journey'. People need to be empowered as individuals, he argues, before they cannot be empowered politically. From Warren's work, it is possible to identify four stages of the empowerment journey: engagement and individual support; support/care from peer group and critical reflection within a peer group; taking action; and citizenship through participation. He contrasts the different group work agendas of the social worker and the community worker: the former sees groups as having an expressive function, concerned primarily with members' emotional support and the group's capacity to nurture and support individual members; the latter sees groups as instrumental, with the group's main concerns as external to the group itself, with matters of nurture and support only important insofar as they serve these external goals. He sees the empowerment journey as bringing care and counselling perspectives in the early stages together with collective and political perspectives in the later stages.

The market or democracy?

Neo-liberal approaches to welfare have sought to empower people as consumers, by giving them what Hirschman calls the power of 'exit' (1970). If consumers do not like a good or service that they receive, they can 'exit' to another provider. This acts as a market regulator: if goods and services are not chosen, they will go to the wall.

Hirschman has famously distinguished between exit, voice and loyalty. This distinction recognises that not all services or goods are amenable to exit. If dissatisfied consumers do not wish to (or are not able to) exit elsewhere, they can exercise voice instead (see Table 7.2). This means they can change the existing service or situation rather than having to change to another one. Alternatively, they can opt for Hirschman's third dimension (loyalty), making the calculation that they are better off where they are.

A number of writers have been critical of the exit option, arguing that it oversimplifies the relationship between consumer and provider. While 'exit' may be straightforward when applied to simple products in the market, it becomes complicated once products or services become more complex, and more complicated still when consumers' ability to exit is constrained by their need or their buying power in the market. Applying the analysis to a product such as social care, we can see that there are a number of situations where it is simply not feasible to exit.

First, there are those who cannot afford to pay, which includes many who are excluded and many who are using public welfare services. In the public service field, consumers who cannot

TABLE 7.2   *Arguments for voice*

Individual	Collective
Loyalty	Equity
Access	Overall choice
Continuity	Public good
Confidentiality	Infrastructure
Complexity	
Crisis	
No control	

Source: Taylor *et al.* (1992).

afford to buy their way into better services often have to take what they can get. There is no other choice on offer. Second, social welfare is a product that requires continuity. How many times do people want to retell their story to a new set of professionals; how many professionals do they want trooping through their lives? Linked to this, of course, are issues about confidentiality.

Fourth, the complexity of many public services means that, while individuals may improve on one element by moving to another provider, they may lose out on other elements, which were better with the original provider. In the field of social care, for example, a new establishment might provide more choice in meals for someone whose faith requires a particular diet or it might be more sensitive to ethnic preferences. But it might also provide fewer opportunities for activities or smaller rooms. This means that exit is a blunt tool for regulating performance. It also means that people will sometimes put up with unsatisfactory and disempowering practice because other aspects of the product meet their needs: in home care, for example, they might not find the hours convenient, but the service may provide more choices or they simply like their carer.

A fifth complicating factor is that many people have to make care and welfare choices in a crisis situation, which limits their ability to amass all the information they need to access the full range of services or to make the rational choices that the market requires. Finally, some of the most excluded in our society have no control over exit: for example, many mental health service users are under compulsory treatment orders. In addition, many welfare choices are made by proxy: they may be made by professionals, including care managers, general medical practitioners, housing managers; they may be made on the recommendation of such practitioners; or they may be shaped by service planners through the rationing of funds.

Moving to the second column of Table 7.2, the market itself structures the choices that can be made. It does this in two ways. First, as the exponential growth of the marketing industry demonstrates, the market can manipulate information and structure the choices individuals make. Second, those who enter the market with least are likely to leave it with least – Chapter 6 described how the better-off purchaser is always able to dictate the choices that are available and push the less well off to the sidelines. In this way, as I argued in that chapter, the choices that many make to exit from areas vulnerable to crime or with poor facilities mean that those who have no choice are increasingly concentrated there. The choices of those with most money about where they live or where they want their children to go to school put those choices out of the reach of those with less; indeed, this is precisely their intention. Choice in some aspects of life is essentially inequitable.

However, the sum of individual choices can also work against everyone's interests. In the UK, where home ownership is at a premium, house prices in the most desirable localities have now become so high that it is getting more difficult to recruit teachers, nurses, social workers, carers or other public service workers. They simply cannot afford to live there. Village shops and schools have disappeared from many UK villages; because people choose to drive elsewhere to buy most of their goods most of the time, they have lost the facility to shop closer to home, as have those who do not have this choice. Public transport is unavailable for similar reasons: it is not viable because most people use their cars but this leaves those without cars stranded. Schools are non-viable because villages are full of second homes and local families cannot afford rural house prices. Similar trends apply to urban areas. As leisure and shopping facilities increasingly move out of town, the choices available to those who live in towns and cities but do not have transport are increasingly restricted.

For all these reasons we need to exercise voice. The limitations of an exit approach have been recognised in public services by more emphasis on customer charters or quality assurance, ideas borrowed from industry. In many countries, service users are being involved in the planning, delivery and co-production of services. However, access to 'voice' may be as limited as access to exit: the more powerful interest groups are still likely to gain at the expense of the less powerful. 'Voice' can mean many different things, according to whether it is exercised through representative or participatory democracy, whether it is backed up by . information and advocacy (just as choice in a market must be) and what rights the individual has. It can also be manipulated by service providers who want to legitimate their own choices rather than listen to those of their users.

The exit and voice approach to individual consumer empowerment has been applied both to group identity and to locality. Thus Tajfel (1981), in the research on social identity that I referred to in Chapter 6, argued that, for many people in low-status groups, exit from that group and entry to a higher valued group was not viable. But, he went on to argue, individuals could decide to join with others to improve their lot or at least to make the perception of membership of a particular group more positive. He cited three ways of increasing the value of a low-status group: to change the beliefs and interpretation of attributes of one's own group; to justify and make acceptable initially unwelcome features (adaptation); or to engage in social action to lead to desirable changes in the situation (Tajfel 1981, p. 24).

Lowery, de Hoog and Lyons (1992) apply the Hirschman model to geographical communities. Thus, if people do not like where they live, they can 'exit' to another area or they can exercise voice to improve the place where they live. They can also choose loyalty and choose to stay because the 'good' elements outweigh the 'bad'. Lowery, de Hoog and Lyons also add a fourth dimension, neglect, by which they mean disengaging from interaction with the locality (a dimension that is often left out in discussions of Hirschman's model). In an earlier publication, Murray Stewart and I called this 'alienation'.

People in communities can adopt these different strategies collectively or individually (Stewart and Taylor 1995). Rioting may be seen as collective 'neglect' or alienation but so would the apathy or withdrawal described earlier in this section; policies which have encouraged community management of public services or social co-operatives in Europe could be seen as giving service users the opportunity for collective exit; complaints procedures could be seen as individual voice, and so on (see Figure 7.1).

Rights, responsibilities and citizenship

While the market is rightly concerned with choice and efficiency, the above discussion suggests that it is less able to meet the

FIGURE 7.1 *Processes of empowerment*

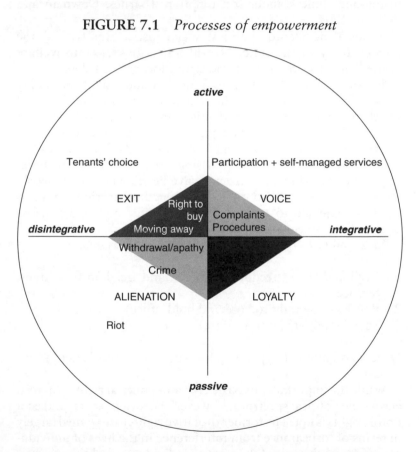

Note: Individual responses are shown in the diamond; collective responses are shown outside the diamond.
Source: Adapted from Lowery, de Hoog and Lyons (1992); Stewart and Taylor (1995), p. 15.

demands of social justice and equity. Back in the eighteenth century, even Adam Smith, that foremost advocate of the market, saw dangers in the narrow self-interest associated with the advance of capitalism. The advance of neo-liberalism in the 1980s and since has prompted similar concerns. Thus, Lawrence (2007, p. 288) describes how, under Ronald Reagan in the 1980s, empowerment in the US came to be reinterpreted as simply the enhanced potential to make one's own way in life. In the neo-liberal ethic, citizenship 'risks being reduced to an exercise in making choices about consumption' (Barnes, Newman and Sullivan 2007, p. 70).

In social democratic politics, social justice was seen as the responsibility of the state. Neo-liberal critics of state welfare argued that its attempts at redistribution created dependency. They sought instead a return to notions of individual and family responsibility. However, without a foundation of basic social entitlements on which to build, it is difficult to see, as I argued in Chapter 7, how people can exercise those responsibilities. I have referred earlier to Maslow's hierarchy of needs (Maslow, 1943). If self-actualisation is only possible once the basic material requirements of human existence have been met – shelter, work, income, services, and so on – then basic human rights have to be a prerequisite to empowerment, giving individuals access to the means to ensure survival and a basic quality of life.

Marshall (1950) distinguishes three types of rights:

1. Civil and legal (freedom of speech and freedom from interference)
2. Political (the right to vote and hold office)
3. Social (entitlement to welfare).

Others add a fourth type, which is economic (entitlement to income).

While the importance of basic civil and political rights is agreed across the political spectrum, however, the idea of social and economic rights is not. The former (negative rights) are framed largely in terms of forbearance from interference in the lives of individual citizens on the part of the state or individuals, and as such their enforcement is seen to be costless. Social and economic rights (positive rights) are seen by their critics to offer an open-ended commitment to provision which the state can simply not afford and which is in any case difficult to guarantee. However, policing, defence, data protection and security at airports suggest that negative rights are not as costless or as evenly distributed as their proponents suggest. In addition, many writers on citizenship deplore the struggle for the social and economic rights that they see as essential to human flourishing and argue that, without these rights, civil and political rights cannot be exercised.

It is important, in discussing rights, to acknowledge the very different ways in which rights and citizenship are understood in different cultures. When challenged about their human rights records, some Asian countries have argued that Northern concepts of rights are distorted and individualistic, whereas their concepts embrace social and economic rights for families and communities. This debate does not fit neatly into traditional right/left dichotomies (Mayo, personal communication).

Criticism of the open-ended nature of social and economic rights has given rise to the idea of conditional rights (Mead 1985), which test the individual's commitment to society. This reflects ongoing debates about the balance between rights and responsibility and sees rights as part of the 'social contract' between state and citizen. At one end of the spectrum, conditionality is applied mainly to those who are dependent on welfare benefits and raises the spectre of the old distinction between the 'deserving' and 'undeserving' poor. It is based on a belief that only those who subscribe to the dominant values of a society have the right to expect anything out of it and resonates with the moral underclass discourse. But, from the middle ground, Friedmann (1998, p. 27) cites an Australian Parliamentary enquiry on citizenship to argue that the idea of civic duty is crucial in all walks of life: 'Without individuals and organisations prepared to participate and take responsibility, without a concept of public interest, without the values of tolerance and compassion and some sense of solidarity and belonging, citizenship would become impossible and democracies difficult to govern, even unstable' (Parliament of the Commonwealth of Australia 1995, p. 67).

Advocates of conditionality argue that, rather than being a burden, responsibility can provide ladders out of dependency for people who have become trapped, if it is based on realistic expectations and accompanied by adequate support. Indeed this is the basis of social inclusion contracts in France. In this analysis, people need status and self-belief if they are to realise their potential and be freed from unnecessary and demeaning dependency. Conditionality can thus be a recipe for dignity amongst people who feel disabled and undervalued by society, but it would have to be realistic, accessible and patient about what people are able to give in return.

A further approach focuses on consumer rights, introduced into public services through charters setting out what citizen consumers can expect of public services as part of the market agenda. Most advocates of state intervention in welfare argue that, to have any real power, a service user must have a substantive right or entitlement to services as a member of society – this is listed as the first of the consumer rights adopted by the UN in 1985 (see Box 7.2). However, approaches based on the contract between producer and consumer rather than state and citizen tend to focus on more limited procedural rights to redress and information, for example, rather than issues of exclusion, control, accountability and quality of service. Disability movements argue further that empowering people solely as service users still confines them within someone else's definition of their reality, which can have the effect of defining them solely in terms of a particular need or impairment. The rights of citizenship are, they would argue, the context within which empowerment in the use of particular services must take place. If their participation is not understood as the practice of their broader citizenship rights, then this participation is 'effectively depoliticised' (Jones and Gaventa 2002, p. 7).

The distinction between *procedural* and *substantive* rights also relates to wider debates about democratic citizenship. The former define citizenship only in terms of basic rights, such as the right to vote, characterising citizens as relatively passive individuals choosing between different elites (John 2009, p. 13); the latter emphasise the participation of citizens in shaping the common purposes of the society to which they belong. This latter understanding is closer to the civic republican philosophy associated with the Greek polity and comes to us via the political philosophies of such thinkers as Machiavelli and Rousseau. It takes us beyond the narrow, litigious view of rights which prevails under neo-liberalism, a view which increasingly paralyses risk-taking in public service, increases regulation and largely favours those

> ## BOX 7.2 Consumer rights as defined by the UN
>
> **The right to satisfaction of basic needs** – To have access to basic, essential goods and services: adequate food, clothing, shelter, health care, education, public utilities, water and sanitation.
> **The right to safety** – To be protected against products, production processes and services which are hazardous to health or life.
> **The right to be informed** – To be given the facts needed to make an informed choice, and to be protected against dishonest or mis-leading advertising and labelling.
> **The right to choose** – To be able to select from a range of products and services, offered at competitive prices with an assurance of satisfactory quality.
> **The right to be heard** – To have consumer interests represented in the making and execution of government policy, and in the development of products and services.
> **The right to redress** – To receive a fair settlement of just claims, including compensation for misrepresentation, shoddy goods or unsatisfactory services.
> **The right to consumer education** – To acquire knowledge and skills needed to make informed, confident choices about goods and services, while being aware of basic consumer rights and res-ponsibilities and how to act on them.
> **The right to a healthy environment** – To live and work in an environment which is non-threatening to the well-being of present and future generations.
>
> *Source*: www.consumerinternational.org

who have the resources to pursue litigation, whichever side of the fence they are on. Instead it emphasises the participation of citizens in determining priorities within society, the balance between different interests and the definition of the common good.

This section began by underlining the importance of fundamental rights to income and access to the basic material goods and services as the basis on which participation and agency as citizens must be built. Bauman argues (1999) that by freeing citizens from uncertainty and transforming the polity from its role as an agency of law and order and crisis management, such basic rights should allow for the kind of civic engagement and solidarity that is the basis of citizenship. But he is pessimistic about the likelihood of such rights being accepted. That, he argues (1999, p. 184), would require a fundamental shift from the values of the market, substituting the principle of sharing for that of competitiveness and establishing the principle of rights grounded neither in competitiveness and consumption nor in the circumstance of 'needing it most' and hence grounded in a divisive and disqualifying means test.

But John Gray (1996) takes a different approach. He is sceptical of arguments that place too much emphasis on rights. Rights, he argues, cannot replace the need for recurrent political renegotiation to balance competing interests in society. In fact there is an iterative relationship between rights and political struggle. Rights are claimed and created through group struggle but, as Jones and Gaventa (2002, p. 12) argue in their synthesis of a range of citizenship literature, the outcome of such struggles is still likely to favour those who are better off and further exclude the marginalised unless action is taken to address the imbalance of power. This is yet another arena where those who go in with most are likely to come out with most.

Into this debate has come recent interest in the notion of capabilities, most closely associated with Amartya Sen and Martha Nussbaum. Advocates claim that this is a concept that can transcend some of the limitations associated with Marshall's social citizenship approach (Carpenter 2009, p. 351).

Carpenter (2009, pp. 355–6) outlines some of the key elements of this approach. It is based on the view that certain capabilities are essential to human functioning. It recognises, however, that 'people are not equally placed to realise their human capabilities, owing to barriers arising from structural inequalities of class, race, disability, gender and sexual oppression. ... It thus takes account of the fact that the playing field is bumpier for some groups than others, and offers ways of reconciling principles of equality and diversity in social justice'. It defines the goal of economic and public policy as 'a process of expanding the substantive freedoms that people have' (Sen 1999, p. 297), challenging the view that economic growth or consumption are the prime makers of progress, since they may or may not expand these freedoms. Sen's emphasis is on 'freedom' rather than just choice and is also on substantive rather than just negative freedoms.

BOX 7.3   The capabilities approach

The following list was assembled by the Equalities Review in the UK as the evaluative framework for the Equalities and Human Rights Commission in this country and is described by Carpenter as 'by far the most ambitious application of the capabilities approach in the UK' (2009, p. 364):

- To be alive
- To live in physical security
- To be healthy
- To be knowledgeable, to understand and reason, and to have the skills to participate in society
- To enjoy a comfortable standard of living, with independence and security
- To engage in productive and valued activities
- To enjoy individual, family and social life.
- To participate in decision-making, have a voice and influence
- Of being and expressing yourself, and having self-respect
- Of knowing you will be protected and treated fairly by the law.

Source: Adapted by Carpenter from the Equalities Review 2007, pp. 127–30.

The capabilities approach (see Box 7.3) offers an alternative to what Carpenter calls 'postmodern deconstructionism', providing a 'grand narrative that connects to other critical discourses but avoiding negative resistance' (Carpenter 2009, p. 369). It also helps us to think about power, since 'domination is said to occur when the power of some affects the interests of others by affecting their capabilities for truly human functioning' (Lukes 2005, p. 118). Advocates argue that it is more inclusive than the concept of rights. However, Carpenter (2009), while an advocate, remains critical of the gulf between the aims of this approach and the limited means proposed for meeting them. And while it addresses some of the dilemmas of the rights debate, it remains to be seen whether it could address the long-standing debate about the balance between rights and responsibilities let alone the tensions between such an approach and the demands of the globalised economy.

Summary

Previous chapters have described how people in excluded communities are disempowered personally, economically, culturally and politically. They have also shown how exclusion and powerlessness can be self-reinforcing. This chapter has discussed different views of power and empowerment and compared the merits of zero-sum and positive-sum approaches. It has underlined the force of structural analyses of power: our pessimists from Chapter 2 still have a persuasive argument. But, at the same time, it has promoted a more positive message: that power is not fixed and immutable and that it is possible to seize opportunities to redefine assumptions and divert the flow of power into new directions. It has also considered some different models of empowerment, individual and collective, exit and voice, rights and citizenship, introducing the concept of capabilities as an alternative approach. How, then, do these play out in the policy arena? In the next chapter, I will explore theories about the policy process and frameworks that assess the levels of power that participants are given within the decision-making process. I will then describe some of the opportunities that are opening up for policy influence and empowerment in today's political environment.

Chapter 8

Power in the Policy Process

Who makes policy?

Zero-sum explanations of power tend to see policymaking as the domain of particular elites or classes in society. Pluralist explanations provide more dispersed models. At one end of the scale, corporatist models formalise the involvement of potentially fragmented and conflicting interests – capital and labour, for example, or different ethnic or religious groupings – by incorporating them into the policymaking process through representative or 'peak' organisations (Schmitter 1974). At the other end, associational models of democracy promote a system based on self-regulating voluntary associations with the state taking a secondary, co-ordinating role (Hirst 1994). In pluralist models, the state is not controlled by any interest or group, but plays an independent though still dominant role. Power is still zero sum and policymaking still tends to be confined to certain groups. Nonetheless it is possible in a pluralist approach to argue that different groups will have power in different policy arenas.

Pluralist approaches recognise that various parties are involved in decision making. They see the policy arena as a marketplace to which players can bring resources that give them the potential to exert influence (Maginn 2002). Rod Rhodes (1988) develops this theme. He differentiates between *policy communities* and *issue networks*. The former are tight-knit relationships between actors who share central values and attitudes towards issues and policies and are highly integrated within the policymaking process. They have stable and restricted memberships, a high frequency of interaction and are 'more likely to develop where their members have important resources and the state is dependent on their members for implementation' (Smith 1993, p. 10). Each member will have resources to trade and the capacity to 'deliver' its constituency. Marsh and Rhodes (1992) have argued that policy communities act to ride out change, to constrain, contain and redirect it. There are echoes here of Clegg's argument (Clegg 1989) that, in an uncertain world, agents develop control by imposing their own circuits of power, through the construction of relatively stable networks with only a limited number of ways or conduits through them: the 'privileged pathways' of Chapter 6. Issue networks, by contrast, are larger, more diverse and more loosely linked, with unequal power and variable resources within the network. They are less important to government and more likely to develop in new issue areas where interests have not yet been institutionalised.

Regime theory has some similarities with Rhodes' analysis, especially with his concept of policy communities. It recognises the limits that complexity and fragmentation place on the capacity of the state as an agency of authority or control, and sees the state rather as a mobiliser and co-ordinator of resources. It contrasts power as 'social control', with power as 'social production' and defines a regime as 'an informal yet relatively stable group with access to institutional resources that enable it to have a sustained role in making governing decisions' (Stone 1989, p. 4). But, as with policy communities, not everyone can join the club. The structure of society still privileges the participation of certain actors who control resources or possess strategic knowledge and the capacity to act on that knowledge (Stoker 1995). And there are actors, such as businesses, which, because of their systemic power do not even have to act to have their interests taken into account. Finally, once assembled, regimes can be very difficult to challenge. As Stoker argues (1995), putting together an alternative regime is a daunting task, so existing regimes can assume 'a near decision making monopoly over the cutting edge choices facing their locality'.

Maloney, Jordan and McLaughlin (1994) are critical of simplistic distinctions between insiders and outsiders in policymaking. They see the key boundary as lying not between insiders and outsiders, but between groups who choose to stay outside, peripheral insiders (who may be similar to Rhodes' issue networks) and specialist or core insiders. Getting a ringside seat as a peripheral insider is relatively simple: 'In most cases, it would cause the official more problems to ignore the failed insiders than it would to accord them polite recognition' (p. 32). However, they argue that there is more scope for influence than the confines of policy communities or regimes would allow. First, while they acknowledge

that access (as a peripheral insider) is considerably more likely than influence, they argue that influence *can* be achieved if
groups have enough to trade: 'government offers groups the opportunity to shape public policy, while groups provide government with certain resources (e.g. knowledge, technical advice or
expertise, membership compliance or consent, credibility, information, implementation guarantees)'. Secondly, while they acknowledge that government 'is likely to grant status to groups
which share the bias, instincts, priorities and culture of the department' (1994, p. 29), Stoker elsewhere (1995, p. 67) describes
how: 'The position of some groups ... may be enhanced by the
dominance of policy ideas and a definition of the "problem" that
suggests that their participation and the kinds of solution they
offer are particularly appropriate or apt'.

If this is the case, there is potential for communities to gain
influence even if they are not dominant power holders, providing local knowledge and adding legitimacy to government interventions, as we shall see in Chapter 11. But if they want to
exploit opportunities to trade and thus gain access to policymaking, they need to understand the processes and games that
characterise the policymaking process. Where and how can they
gain entry?

How is policy made?

The policy process is often explained as a rational, scientific or
technical exercise, based on fact and objective evidence and un-
touched by values (Onyx and Dovey 1999). In this view, policy
goes through a cyclical process, where the assessment of needs is
followed by the identification of objectives, by the development
and implementation of plans to meet these objectives and by
systematic monitoring and evaluation, which feeds back into the
development of future plans.

Successive authors have challenged the view that policy works
in this linear and rational way, however. Some see the policy
process as being subverted by the actors within the system. From
the public choice tradition, for example, we learn how public officials are seeking to maximise their own power and self-interest
through maximising their budgets and the size of their bureaux
(Buchanan and Tullock 1962). From Lipsky's work on street-level

bureaucrats (1979), we learn how front-line workers make policy as well as implementing it. Other scholars use chaos and complexity theory to argue that the rational planning methodologies adopted by government assume that government is more in control of its environment that it really is (Haynes 1999, p. 67). Reflecting the complexity of the environments within which decision making takes place, March and Olsen (1976) conceptualise organisational decision making as a 'garbage can'. What the garbage can contains, they argue, depends on the labels on the bin, what garbage is currently being produced, the mix of cans available and the speed at which garbage is collected and removed. Hill (1997, p. 228) is inclined to see this garbage can as 'capitalist ... biased against the interests of ordinary people', yet he acknowledges that nonetheless it is impossible to keep it under control as it operates in 'incoherent and unpredictable ways'.

John Kingdon (1984) builds on this to try and make sense of the way policy agendas are set. He identifies three streams in the policy process:

- A 'problem' stream which puts issues onto the agenda and defines their nature
- A 'policy' stream that identifies and brings to the surface a range of ideas and potential solutions
- A 'political' stream which then mediates the policy process and decides what actually comes to fruition.

His policy stream is described as a kind of 'primeval soup', with its own rationale of natural selection, survival, demise and recombination (see also Parsons 1995, pp. 192–3). Within this 'soup', ideas float to the top or sink to the bottom, and swimming in this soup are policy entrepreneurs who act as brokers and are essential to the survival or demise of an idea. We can see this in the activity of think tanks, for example, in contemporary society.

Kingdon defines his streams as essentially separate processes that come together only at particular points when the opportunity for change occurs. Sabatier (1988) takes issue with this analysis. He argues that the relationship between agenda setting and the wider policymaking process is much more complex and dynamic than this suggests. In his view, the policy subsystem is composed of a number of 'advocacy coalitions' (composed of interest groups, agencies, and some legislators and researchers) based around particular sets of beliefs. Changes in core beliefs are rare, but changes in secondary aspects (the detail of how to achieve these core beliefs, the seriousness of the problem, the importance of different causal factors) come about as the result of 'policy oriented learning' within and between advocacy coalitions. Advocacy coalitions compete for influence and 'policy brokers' – civil servants, elected officials, commissions of enquiry and so on – find reasonable compromises between the different positions that they advocate. Policy change, according to Sabatier, is a function of this competition, of the actions of brokers, of events outside the subsystem and of turnover in personnel.

There are, of course, other theories and models, but what this brief review demonstrates is that the operation of power is not entirely predictable, that policymaking is a complex process, that it is concerned with the negotiation of competing and conflicting interests and that there can be many points of engagement. Models differ in the extent to which it is possible to change the views of policy elites. Most suggest that it is easier to change policy at the margins than at the centre of government's core beliefs. Thus Marsh and Rhodes argued in 1992 that the degree of change that is possible will depend on the salience of the issue. If the issue is peripheral (or secondary, *pace* Sabatier 1988), there will be more room to manoeuvre. Nonetheless, even with more central issues, they suggest that the journey from intention to implementation is far from straightforward.

From government to governance

Another take on this question, which consolidates and builds on these ideas, is provided by the governance discourse. Like community, governance is a term used in a number of ways: as theory, as a normative model and as a description of practice. As a theory, it goes beyond those described above to describe a significant shift in the way that governing happens, in response to the increasing fragmentation and complexity of society. At one level, the shift to governance is seen as a response to the process of globalisation that, commentators argue, has reduced the capacity of nation states to manage their own economies. At another, it refers to 'the emergence of 'negotiated self-governance' in communities, cities and regions, based on new practices of co-ordinating activities through networks and partnerships (Newman, 2001, p. 24). This involves a 'reconfiguration of relationships and responsibilities, encompassing complex alliances of actors and networks across permeable institutional boundaries and an expanded vision of the public domain' (Cornwall 2004a, p. 1).

Governance theory moves us away from fixed ideas about power as a commodity rooted in particular institutions to more fluid ideas of power developed and negotiated between partners. It involves propositions about an enabling state, 'steering not rowing' (Osborne and Gaebler 1992); new combinations of markets, hierarchies and networks; the opening up of decision making to greater participation; rescaling and multi-level governance; decentralisation and devolution; and new sets of relationships between citizens, policymakers and agencies responsible for policy implementation (Taylor 2007a, pp. 299–300). Some governance theorists hail its self-organised interorganisational networks as 'the ultimate in hands-off government' (Rhodes 1997, p. 110), offering participants the opportunity not only to influence policy but also to take over the business of government (Stoker 1998). But others are critical of the failure of governance advocates and theorists to address issues of power, agency and accountability (Newman 2001; Jones 2003) or to address the contradictory tensions in which most forms of governance are embedded (Swyngedouw 2005).

Following Foucault, governmentality theorists explore further the ways in which power has become decoupled from the state as' government' and the implications of this. Nikolas Rose thus defines governing as 'all endeavours to shape, guide, direct the conduct of others – and ways in which one might be persuaded to govern oneself' (1999, p. 3). Although Foucault did not locate power within the state, he did argue that forms of power at a distance from or beyond the state could often sustain the state more effectively than its own institutions (Foucault 1980, p. 73). As Chapter 7 argued, this is not achieved through coercive control, but through a more complex and subtle diffusion of techniques through which a society is rendered governable and individuals come to govern themselves (Rose 1999, p. 176). Thus, 'to govern is to presuppose the freedom of the governed ... not to crush their capacity to act, but to acknowledge it and utilise it for one's own objectives' (Rose 1999, p. 4). Governmentality theory thus concerns itself with the technologies and practices through which a society is rendered governable and individuals come to govern themselves.

This affects both the 'what' and 'how' of policy. In relation to the 'what' Swyngedouw (2005, p. 1993) describes how new decentralised arrangements of governing beyond the state are situated within a neo-liberal economic discourse, both globally and nationally, that determines the context within which local solutions have to be found. In relation to the how, Healey (2006) describes a constant tension between the more fluid systems of governing implied by governance and the technologies of central control that seek to control uncertainty and complexity or maintain dominant interests. Citing the work of Fischer (1990), she summarises this contradiction as follows (2006, p. 241):

> There is a pervasive struggle in the terrain of governance at the present time between pluralistic democratic tendencies, which seek to acknowledge a wider range of stakeholders, forms of knowledge and value bases, and techno-corporate ones, which seek to keep control over the management of our societies, using the tools of technical analysis and management, or the knowledge and interests of key corporate interests.

The growth in uncertainty and the complexity of decision making means that: 'Never before has it been so necessary to regulate complexity by means of decisions, choices and "policies", the frequency and diffusion of which must be ensured if the uncertainty of systems subject to exceptionally rapid change is to be reduced' (Melucci 1988, p. 251). In relation to the 'how' therefore, one response has been the spread of what has become known as the 'new public management' to governments across the globe (McLaughlin, Osborne and Ferlie 2002) and by current preoccupations with 'best' or 'evidence-based' practice.

In this respect, Michael Power (1994) describes what he calls an 'audit explosion'. He expresses concern about the 'institutional foothold that audit now has in the public imagination' (p. 8) and argues that audit has 'assumed the status of an all-purpose solution to administrative control'. Over the 1990s, he argues that

> Political demands for greater accountability of public services became tightly coupled to a neo-liberal preference for

exercising control at a distance through the managerial instruments of accounting, budgetary control, auditing and quality assurance. (Power 2003, p. 191)

The dominance of the audit culture illustrates the way in which dominant assumptions become internalised and taken for granted (see Chapter 7). But it limits considerably 'the scope for participation to contribute to a more open and reflexive form of governance' (Newman 2001, p. 163).

Power's concern in shared by others. Parsons (1995) describes how the rational, positivist approach which is in the ascendant today has put power into the hands of the professionals, experts, technocrats and bureaucrats who are doing the measurements and evaluations that now underpin policy implementation. Indeed, Perkin argues (1989) that auditors and accountants have become the dominant professions of the current age. Healey (2006) explains that while, in theory, production targets are to be informed by scientific research and technical understanding, in practice building up an adequate knowledge base at the centre can prove rather more difficult; the logic of efficient and effective production quickly gets replaced by a 'politics of meeting targets'.

The use of 'expert' knowledge is central to the process of 'governing at a distance'. This gives consultants, especially those preferred by government, considerable power, since they are often the means by which dominant discourses are transmitted, communicating meanings down the system to local authorities and communities, and then back up the system to central government. In both North and South, this growing industry is advising on how to shape funding bids, how to design governance structures, how to measure achievements, in ways that risk encouraging a 'normative isomorphism' which spreads the new managerialism through all sectors.

Parsons (1995) extends this argument to show how public policy has come to be dominated by the creation of meanings through the manipulation of symbols, becoming the property of markets, managers, moralists and media. So, while the ideas of communicative action and reflexivity discussed in Chapter 7 suggest that the potential exists to reinterpret dominant discourses and the meanings that they impose on the policy process, it could be argued that there is a more powerful industry, which is still reinforcing and 'consecrating' those dominant discourses and systems of meaning, as Bourdieu's 'symbolic' capital, also discussed in Chapter 7, suggests. This is particularly evident in the extent to which policy, and consultation about policy, has become the province of marketing and public relations departments. A common cry of politicians today is not that the policies may be inappropriate or misguided, but that they have not explained them properly or got the message across. Public opinion is manipulated in this battle for control of the policy 'consumer' through constant repackaging of opinions and through market research techniques, while, as Parsons again argues, policies are now being sold like products in a marketplace for ideas by a new breed of policy entrepreneurs.

There is plenty of scope for Chapter 2's pessimist in the above analysis. At the same time, however, we have seen that powerful institutions all over the world are encouraging community participation and putting their weight behind participatory pluralism, with all the messiness and risk that this involves. This provides scope for the kind of dialogue and mutual learning that those who advocate 'power to' and communicative action approaches are arguing for. Complexity theorists also offer the prospect of developing footloose and highly adaptable connections across the policy universe that would operate across boundaries. They argue that disorder and instability is needed in order to allow for new and more functional forms of order (Haynes 1999; Gilchrist 2009). In addition, the very complexity and ambiguity of the policymaking process, in these analyses, offers windows of opportunity for Morison's 'active subjects' (see Chapter 7) to exercise agency, shaping and influencing policy from 'below'.

O'Donovan (2000, pp. 226–7) summarises some of the characteristics of new theories that attempt to conceptualise an 'interactive state'. In her view, there is an emphasis on agency rather than automatic co-option into state agendas, policy is negotiated rather than predetermined and the state is not seen as monolithic but as internally differentiated. However, she warns against the assumption that these processes are fed by egalitarian power relations. There are new ways into the policy process but these still have varying degrees of influence and generally all depend on entry being granted by the state. In addition, as Chapter 7 argued, all forms of knowledge – including beliefs about what is and is not possible – are socially constructed.

John Abbott (1996) is critical of analyses of community participation that see the interests of the community as necessarily
opposed to those of the state and community participation as a
struggle for control between those governed and those governing. He argues against the dominant view of government in the
1980s that 'saw government as either manipulating communities or controlling communities to meet the ends of a minority'
(Abbott 1996, pp. 113–14). The relationship between governments and people is, he argues, much more complex than this.
He bases his model of different community policies on the extent
to which government is open or closed to community involvement, and the degree of systems complexity that govern the issues on which decisions are to be made (see Figure 8.1).

Where government is closed and decisions complex, communities are excluded and oppositional tactics may be the only
option. Where government is open and decisions simple, communities are included through community development and
community management schemes, which organise people around

FIGURE 8.1   *John Abbott's community participation surround*

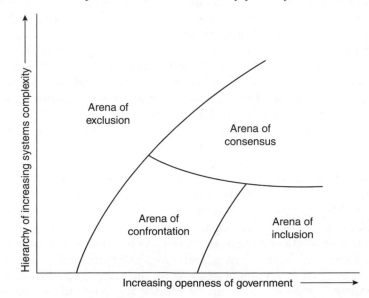

Source: Abbott (1996), p. 124.

focused programmes with clearly defined outputs. But where issues are complex and government is open, a more complex interrelationship is necessary, and this Abbott calls 'negotiated development'.

In the rest of this chapter I want to identify some of the new opportunities that exist for citizen influence and power, then explore some tools for assessing how far they actually change the balance of power in the policy process – how far in fact they may constitute a new approach to governing based on Abbott's negotiated development.

The interactive state

The current interest in participation is offering unprecedented opportunities for citizens to engage in the decision-making process. With the transformation of the state from controlling to 'enabling', from 'rowing' to 'steering', Klijn and Koppenjan (2000, p. 386) argue that

> The political primacy of politicians should be based not on the right to define the substance of governmental policy based on an ex ante interpretation of the general interest, but the capacity to initiate and guide societal discourses aimed at the exploration of interests, the creative invention of solutions and thus, the gradual *discovery* of the common interest.

To use the language of the social movement theorists, this creates a new political opportunity structure which has the potential to provide new openings, new alliances and maybe even to fashion new policy communities. In the new forms of interactive decision making that are emerging, Klijn and Koppenjan argue, participants are no longer confined to institutionalised forms of interest representation, as they were in the corporatist model, discussed at the beginning of this chapter. Potential partners are brought into the process at an earlier stage, before agendas are set or solutions formulated. New processes are used, including workshops, role play, simulation games, future search and opinion surveys. This has encouraged innovative new forms of consultation and partnership. Two overlapping manifestations of this new style of decision making – consultative and deliberative forms of democracy, on the one hand and partnership working, on the other – are of particular concern to us here.

Consultative democracy

A range of consultation techniques has been introduced to give the public a greater say in policymaking. These include user satisfaction surveys, opinion polls, interactive websites, citizens' panels, question and answer sessions with the public, citizens' juries, focus groups, visioning exercises and so on. Market research techniques have been extensively used to develop forms of consultation and imaginative ways have been found of encouraging people who had never engaged in the policy process before. The Oregon experiment in the US is an early and widely disseminated example where citizens were given the opportunity to generate ideas on how to solve the city's financial problems. This was an opportunity for them not only to give their views but also to engage in complex decisions over a period of time in a way that allowed for deliberation and reflection (Goetz and Gaventa 2001, p. 30). This was encouraged through a series of deliberative forums and the city council also used a series of surveys, which attracted high response rates, to ask where it should be spending money.

However, while these techniques have undoubtedly given some measure of voice to many citizens, they also have a number of shortcomings. Thus the Oregon experiment was criticised for its tendency to reflect the majority view and sideline the interests of minorities (the needs of disabled people, for example). Surveys might give people a measure of voice but the questions that are asked and the analysis of the results are not usually in the control of the people who respond, and they do not necessarily have the information on which to make a considered response. Zygmunt Bauman has coined the term 'command economy of thought' to describe the process whereby information is gathered together at the centre, processed at the centre and then used as the basis for directives from the centre (Hillier 1997). Many of these techniques also prioritise the involvement of individuals rather than organised groups (Lowndes and Wilson 2001, p. 635).

'Consumerist' forms of consultation seem far from the ideas of 'communicative action' and dialogue discussed in Chapter 7. But more deliberative techniques do bring us closer to this ideal, offering the possibility of a discursive, educational democracy instead of interest aggregation and bargaining (Dryzek 1990; Gaventa 2006). Citizens' juries, for example, give people from communities the resources and information to come up with their own solutions to a defined problem, and Chapter 11 will discuss the role community arts initiatives can play in opening up community issues for debate with professionals and other communities. Deliberation has the potential to move us away from populist politics too, by encouraging informed reflection on complex issues that do not lend themselves to instant responses.

However, deliberative techniques may still be a technology of control if they do not lead to action. Goetz and Gaventa (2001, p. 48) warn that citizens' juries have had little impact on public policy in the US and the UK, for example. They contrast this with Germany where, at the time of writing, central government commissioned the juries, which involved more than 50 members, and the public authority had to agree to take their recommendations into account.

Chandler (2002, pp. 10, 11) dismisses this range of developments as 'therapeutic politics' because, he argues, they do not give participants 'any greater control over policy making'. He argues that 'the aim of "giving voice" to people is primarily to give individuals a feeling of inclusion and sense of community'. He is also critical of the frequent failure to connect participation and consultation with representative forms of democracy. Nonetheless, while these are clear dangers, there has been considerable experience of their use over the past decade and Chapter 11 will discuss in more detail what we have learnt about their potential to make a positive contribution to community and citizen empowerment.

Partnership

With the change of language from 'government' to 'governance', partnership has become the currency of policymaking in many countries. In today's complex and globalised world, government depends on the co-operation of other actors. It is no longer possible to concentrate the knowledge and expertise needed to solve social problems in one central point. As regime theory suggests, other actors are needed for their resources, knowledge, mechanisms for consultation and so on, as well as the legitimacy they can confer. And, if they are not on board, these same resources give them the capacity to frustrate and block the decision-making process. Thus, Peters and Pierre (2001, p. 131) describe how

> we are moving from a model of the state in a liberal-democratic perspective towards a state model characterised by complex patterns of contingencies and dependencies on external actors. ... Political power and institutional capability is less and less derived from formal constitutional powers accorded to the state but more from a capacity to wield and co-ordinate resources from public and private actors and interests.

On p. 140, I referred to 'the complex alliances of actors', the 'networks across institutional boundaries' and the 'expanded vision of the public domain' that governance involves (Cornwall 2004a, p. 1). Commentators also refer to a process of 'multi-stakeholder involvement, of multiple interest resolution, of compromise rather than confrontation, of negotiation rather than administrative fiat' (Hambleton, Savitch and Stewart 2002, p. 12). This offers the opportunity to move from fixed ideas of power being rooted in the institution of the state to more fluid ideas of power that is shared, developed and negotiated between partners, with the potential for dynamic, interactive social learning amongst autonomous but interdependent agencies (Jessop 2003).

There are other forces driving towards partnership. One is the 'multiplication and fragmentation' of government functions which has resulted from market and privatisation policies. This has created a new institutional environment, particularly at local level. At the same time, challenges from below – the 'fragmentation of class politics, growing diversity and the clamour for recognition of different interests' (Daly 2003, p. 119) – have weakened government's political legitimacy and integrity (Newman 2001, pp. 18–19).

Klijn and Koppenjan (2000) suggest another driver, which is concern about the growing gap between citizens on the one hand, and elected politicians and the civil service on the other (Klijn and Koppenjan 2000). Goetz and Gaventa (2001) also add the dimension of political parties, noting that in many countries parties need to demonstrate responsiveness to win votes.

Benington and Geddes (2001) argue that partnership is particularly salient in the European Union, where they describe it as a response to four key challenges: political legitimation, economic innovation, social problem solving and organisational complexity. Deriving from the European principle of subsidiarity, which requires the involvement of those closest to the problems for which solutions are being sought, it offers a 'homogenising concept' (p. 2) to support the notion of European integration. It was enshrined as a principle in the 1988 Reform of the Structural Funds and, although it dropped down the agenda in the late 1990s, Benington and Geddes argue that the new millennium saw signs of a revival. Atkinson, too (2001, pp. 395–6), cites European documentation that promotes the engagement of residents in partnerships to counteract trends towards increased alienation from the political process. However, Benington and Geddes argue that partnership is still an exotic species in some European countries.

Further afield, partnership has been described by Alan Fowler (2000) as the 'only type of relationship that seems to count' in the official international aid system, while in Australia, Onyx and Dovey (1999, p. 187) have defined 'collaboration' – the favoured word in that setting – as the 'buzzword of state sector policy'. Partnership and collaborative working have also long been a feature of Canadian policy development (O'Neill 1992) and of comprehensive community initiatives in the US (Connell *et al.* 1995). These latter include the Empowerment Zones and Enterprise Communities programme set up by the Clinton administration in 1993 (Gaventa 1998; Morrissey 2000; O'Connor, 2007), with the aims of developing economic opportunities and a strategic vision for change, based on sustainable community development and community based partnerships that engaged representatives from all parts of the community. Box 8.1 provides further examples from the South.

The understanding of what partnership entails, the definition of key partners and the role of the state within partnership may differ from country to country. But, as we saw in Chapter 2, it seems that everywhere communities are being invited into these partnerships. They are valued both for the new knowledge and expertise they can bring to bear and also for their resources – tangible and intangible. They have the potential to contribute to the reform of public services, both through being involved in service planning and meeting local needs directly; their involvement addresses concerns about the democratic deficit and they

---

**BOX 8.1   Strengthening participatory
approaches to local governance
in the global South**

In Porte Alegre every year thousands of citizens gather in neigh-bourhood meetings to debate and deliberate on local priorities, and to elect representatives to negotiate with other neighbour-hoods and local officials to approve the annual budget.

In Indonesia, following decades of authoritarian rule, hundreds of 'forum wargas' (citizens forums) have emerged as a new space where citizens, local officials, business and other sec-tors can meet, discuss local issues openly and identify solutions.

In the Philippines, local government legislation has created spaces for local community organisations and NGOs to sit at the same table with local elected officials to draw up development places. Through a national coalition, NGOs, community groups and local officials are working together in new ways, and creat-ing changes in how services are delivered.

In Uganda, villagers across the country are involved in par-ticipatory approaches to developing priorities for the national budget through a programme involving the finance ministry, na-tional NGOs, and district and local governments.

Source: Gaventa (2004b).

---

can build social capital and community cohesion (Taylor 2007a, p. 300). Incentives for governments and large-scale institutions at all levels to involve communities in decision making include the realisation that:

- Shared ownership of initiatives makes it more likely that they will be sustained
- The tacit knowledge of residents is an asset in developing solutions to the 'wicked issues' of policy
- Residents are in a critical position to monitor outcomes and can act as an important check on poorly defined and targeted services
- Community involvement also has an intrinsic value in devel-oping skills, confidence and vision at community level.

As Jackson (2001, pp. 135–6) argues in relation to planning: 'Planners and decision makers have acknowledged that involving affected people can identify alternative values and solutions, resolve inequities in land allocation, increase ownership in decision-making, reduce conflict and lead ultimately to better decisions and more sustainable environmental management'.

As a result, innovative new models have developed in many countries across the globe, new 'hybrid democratic spaces situated at the interface between state and society', with the potential to act as 'crucibles for a new politics of public policy' (Cornwall and Coelho 2004, p. 5).

The use of the governance language is not, however, without its critics. Jessop (2003, p. 101) argues that it gives a fashionable new legitimacy to old practices, like corporatism. In its practical application, critics question the commitment of partners and highlight the danger that partnership will be used simply to offload areas of government responsibility onto citizens (Healey *et al.* 2002; Atkinson 2003, p. 102).

Partnership is a complex process. Partners bring very different expectations, goals, cultures, worldviews, skills, powers and resources to the process. While the complexity of policymaking may, as I have suggested earlier, create windows of opportunity for communities, it might also exclude them further. So how can we assess the extent to which the balance of power is shifting?

Frameworks for empowerment

Dryzek (2000, p. 29) distinguishes three further dimensions that need to be considered/in assessing how much power communities have. These are:

- Franchise, the number of people capable of participating effectively in collective decision
- Scope, the issues and areas of life that are brought under democratic control
- Authenticity, whether control is real or symbolic, involving the effective participation of autonomous and competent actors.

The first two address the 'who' and 'what' of empowerment, the third raises the question of how much. Sherry Arnstein's 'ladder of citizen participation' (1969) still dominates writing about the extent of community power. Her famous and much-cited eight-rung ladder takes us from non-participation (manipulation and therapy) at the base of the ladder, through degrees of tokenism (informing, consultation, placation) in the middle, to degrees of citizen power in the higher rungs, moving through partnership and delegated power to citizen control at the top.

A number of authors have used a similar approach, moving from less to more community control. Two – one from the North, one from the South – are reproduced in ladder form in Figure 8.2.

Guijt and Shah (1998b, pp. 9–10) identify four problems with these models: they are static and do not consider how power relations change over time; they oversimplify the distinction between participants and outsiders; they assume an ideal form of participation in which everyone participates; they treat communities as a homogeneous whole, ignoring their diversity. They observe that 100 per cent participation is, in any case, a myth and that participation will ebb and flow depending on the stage in the policy process and the particular aspect of decision making that is being considered. In all these models, too, there is an assumption that the top of the ladder is the place to strive for. This assumes that control is what participants want, that this is

FIGURE 8.2   *Types of partnership*

Hall 2000	White 1996
Autonomous – mechanisms to ensure sustained involvement.	**Transformative** – to facilitate empowerment of communities
Participatory – equal access and frequently shaped policy priorities	**Representative (voice)** – to build sustainable organisational capacity, communities may join to gain leverage
Consultative – other partners can make changes at the margins	**Instrumental (means)** – to tap community resources and knowledge against a background of cuts in public spending
Shell – nominal and tokenistic	**Nominal (display)** – legitimating, communities may join to 'get in the loop'

always appropriate and, indeed, that those participants who win control will then empower others.

It may be preferable to conceive of participation as a cycle or wheel, in which participants engage at the point and for the purposes they choose. Laurie Skuba Jackson develops an alternative model (see Figure 8.3), which is based on her belief that 'the ultimate level of stakeholder involvement is collaborative, shared decision-making' and not, as in Arnstein's model, community control. Her model (2001, p. 140) is conceived not as a ladder in which higher rungs are superior, but as a spectrum of involvement. She argues that different kinds of involvement might be appropriate at different stages and for different stakeholders.

The frameworks discussed so far could be seen as cumulative, in the sense that in assessing the extent to which power has shifted, we are looking for higher levels within each framework.

FIGURE 8.3 *Jackson's stages of public involvement*

	SET OBJECTIVES	FOR WHOM?	CHARACTERISTICS
	Informing	For those who are uninformed about an issue	One-way communication
	Public education	For those who are aware of the issue but not of its technicalities or implications	
	Testing reactions		Two-way communication, consultation
	Seeking ideas and alternative solutions	For those who are progressively more informed	
	Seeking consensus		Shared decision-making

Degree of involvement (vertical axis, arrow pointing down)

Source: Adapted from Jackson (2001).

Others focus on: *who* is engaged – levels of knowledge within 'the community' and the way 'the public' or 'the community' is constituted, relating to both the first and third of Dryzek's dimensions; and *where* citizens and communities are engaged – the stage in the policy process, and the types of decision-making space.

Firstly, w*ho* is engaged? The 'real' and authentic community – unbiased and uninvolved in collective activity – is often contrasted favourably with the 'usual suspects', who act as representatives and community leaders, or with those who have an 'axe to grind'. But the contribution that the 'real' community member can make will be different in quality from that of someone who has more involvement with decision making and policy development, as people have different capacities for engagement and different kinds of knowledge. Taylor and Lupton, writing about public involvement in health, distinguish between what they call the 'naive user' and the 'informed' user (Taylor and Lupton 1995; Lupton, Peckham and Taylor 1998). The first relies on anecdotal evidence and his or her own personal experience; the second relies on experience and knowledge gained from accumulating knowledge over a period of engagement with the process of decision making and a greater understanding of the nature of the decisions that need to be taken. Both contributions are valuable and many initiatives in deliberative democracy have tried to bridge the two. But keeping participation to the naive or uninformed participant will always privilege the centre, because this is where the gathered information will be processed and interpreted, allowing for Bauman's 'command economy of thought' to prevail. Allowing informed users to work with authorities in processing information and ideas from a wide variety of informants is more likely to allow citizens and communities to exercise power in governance than simply canvassing the views of 'naïve' users.

Still on the question of *who*, Barnes, Newman and Sullivan (2007) focus on the way in which the public is constituted in participative forums: as an 'empowered' public, a 'consuming' public, a 'stakeholder' public or a 'responsible' public. They explain that the empowered public discourse aims to shift the balance of power between state players and particular communities or groups; the consuming public discourse is concerned with the rights of consumers of public services; the stakeholder public discourse focuses on the public's right to a voice as service users, tax payers and those affected by policies directly and indirectly; the responsible public relates to the responsibilities of citizenship, with a reduced role for the state and little concern with power. Clearly these relate to different ideological assumptions about empowerment, the state and the market.

In assessing how far power is being shared, it is also important to consider the points in the process at which new players are allowed in – the *where* question. Consumerist policies, as we saw in Chapter 7, allow power in the selection and use of a service, but they do not allow the public to have power as citizens over the range of services that are available to them or in determining the rights that people should have to those services. Any analysis of participation needs to consider whether communities are involved only in implementation, however important this may be, or whether they are involved in agenda setting and policy development. It also needs to consider how far community partners are being allowed to inform the process of decision making – the rules of the game.

Another approach to the *where* question is provided by Gaventa and his colleagues at the Institute of Development Studies. They distinguish between three types of decision-making 'space' dependent on who controls them: 'closed' spaces which are closed to citizens and communities; invited spaces, into which citizens and communities are invited but which are owned and controlled by those who issue the invitation; and claimed or popular spaces, which are set up and controlled by citizens and communities. This distinction is one aspect of a three-dimensional model they use called the power cube, which is reproduced in Figure 8.4.

A second element of this framework is the level of policymaking involved: local, national or supranational. The third focuses on the type of power at issue and is based on Stephen Lukes' three dimensions of power described here in Chapter 7. These are defined in the power cube as: visible (observable decision making mechanisms); hidden (shaping or influencing the policy agenda); and invisible (shaping norms and beliefs).

Discussion

The fact that global power brokers and governments are making participation a condition of funding and debt relief programmes

FIGURE 8.4   *The power cube*

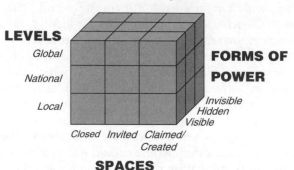

Source: the powercube.com

provides a powerful lever and incentive for change. It strengthens the position of allies within government systems and of communities that are knocking on the door, and it helps to provide incentives for those who may be more reluctant. But pressure from the top is not the only lever for change.

Social movement theorists have long seen political opportunity structures as a crucial factor in the growth and success of change from below. Tarrow (1994, p. 99) argues that: 'The opening of opportunities produces external resources for people who lack internal ones, openings where there were only walls before, alliances that did not previously seem possible and realignments that seem capable of bringing new groups to power'. For the optimist of my opening chapter, the move towards governance and partnership has the potential to open up new political spaces in which we can find new ways of addressing the persistent issues of exclusion, forge new forms of decision making, and develop alternative economic solutions. But the power analysis in Chapter 7 suggests that the new governance spaces may simply perpetuate old patterns of power in less visible ways. If partnership and deliberative forms of democracy are simply a bolt-on to existing systems, co-opting partners and communities into existing systems and frames of understanding, they will end up contributing to alienation and exclusion rather than offering a route to their resolution.

So is the momentum for change from above and below being harnessed into a creative dialogue and the 'negotiated development' that Abbott espoused earlier in this chapter, or is the reality more complicated than this? Will it be a demonstration of 'power over' or 'power to'? Will it discover new forms of policymaking or will it fall into tried and tested systems for playing safe? Chapter 8 unravels some of the paradoxes and tensions that arise when trying to put these new opportunities into practice.

Chapter 9

Experiencing Empowerment

Window dressing or window of opportunity?

Previous chapters have described how empowerment through community participation has become a central element of responses to poverty and exclusion across the world. Promoted within the context of a move from government to governance, community participation and partnership policies have the potential to open up a new public and political space. The partnership rhetoric implies a move from a fixed idea of power being rooted in the institution of the state to a more fluid idea of power shared, developed and negotiated between partners. Like all the other terms we have been examining, however, governance, partnership and participation are terms that can be overexposed and oversimplified. So are the new political opportunities that we have been discussing symbolic or are they real?

In Chapter 1, I referred to the review that Murray Stewart and I had carried out of the literature on empowerment to 1995. We concluded there that although there had been changes in the ideological, political and professional context for community participation over time, 'the same issues about lack of power and about the limited access for community interests to power structures' remained (Stewart and Taylor 1995, p. 63). We referred to the 'extensive reinvention of wheels' and the 'triumph of expedience over experience'. Have things changed since then?

The evidence of a growing body of UK research, both at that time and since, suggests that some real progress is being made at the level of implementation: residents have for some years been influencing small-scale decisions and managing projects determined by themselves (Mayo 1997b; Anastacio *et al.* 2000; Coaffee and Healey 2003; Richardson, 2008). Shifting the policymaking agenda (Lukes' second face of power) has proved more difficult (Burton *et al.* 2004). While gains have been made, therefore, there is still some way to go (Schofield 2002; Atkinson

2003; Jones 2003; Somerville 2005; Ingamells 2007; Barnes, Newman and Sullivan 2007).

Experience elsewhere in the world tells a similar story. In 1995, Fainstein and Hirst (p. 190) reported that, in the US, neighbourhood organisations were achieving specific victories 'but not challenging the broader forces that lead to deprivation in the first place', while Gittell (2001, p. 100) later described the Empowerment Zones, which were set up under the Clinton administration, as 'a familiar failed model' (see also De Filippis 2007, pp. 28–35). Atkinson and Carmichael are sceptical about what partnership and other forms of resident participation have achieved in France, Denmark and the UK (Atkinson and Carmichael 2007, pp. 59–60). In the global South, too, researchers have been highly critical of the many participation initiatives which, despite a rhetoric of decentralisation, are characterised by power imbalances between participants, explicit and implicit co-option, cost-shifting and continuing centralisation (Cooke and Kothari, 2001; Hickey and Mohan, 2004). In 1998, Blackburn and Holland (p. 3) commented that:

> It is one thing to direct resources to participatory planning in villages or poor urban districts. It is quite another to question and begin to change the often rigidly hierarchical and risk-averse management structures that exist within institutions and make participatory initiatives difficult to implement over the long term.

Ten years later, Cornwall (2008) argues that community participation still falls short of its democratic potential. With Coelho (Cornwall and Coelho 2004), she argues that new democratic spaces are not yet genuine spaces for change.

While any form of consultation may be a considerable improvement on whatever went before, therefore, it still fails to match the rhetoric of partnership and participation, let alone the expectations of communities. It often ranks fairly low down on Arnstein's ladder. Indeed Cornwall (2008, p. 270) describes how, for the World Bank, giving information and consultation are considered forms of participation and empowerment. Communities are now being consulted across the board, but consultation is too seldom followed by action. In the UK, for example, an Audit Commission report found that three-quarters of 'best practice' authorities failed to link the results of consultation with decision-making processes (Audit Commission 1999, p. 41). In these circumstances, the suspicion is that communities are simply being marginalised in a larger arena than before. This is not, of course, the whole story. There are also success stories, which we will return to later in this volume, but this chapter will explore some of the reasons why community participation and empowerment policies have yet to achieve their potential.

So, what are the factors that hold these policies back? Ideas about governance and partnership tend to assume a pluralist analysis of power. They assume that inviting all the stakeholders to the decision-making table will allow for a rational weighing up of different arguments and that this in turn will lead to consensus. But this fails to take into account differences in power, culture and resources between the different partners. Pluralism does not imply equality of access, let alone empowerment.

The rules of the game

Stewart Clegg argues that: 'Power will always be inscribed within contextual "rules of the game" which both enable and constrain action – with some players having not only play-moves but also the refereeing of these as power resources' (1989, pp. 200–1). The problem this creates for communities in the new 'invited spaces' of governance is that they do not decide the game that is being played; they do not determine the rules of play, the system of refereeing or, indeed, who plays; and the cards are stacked in favour of the more powerful players. In fact, many find they are in the wrong game altogether (Taylor 2001).

What game are we playing?

To date, Lukes' agenda-setting power has remained firmly in the hands of public authorities (often with private sector interests in the background). In many countries, it has been predominantly economic; community representatives have found it difficult to get social issues into the frame. Indeed, as I argued in Chapter 3, after introducing a more comprehensive approach to social exclusion in the English National Strategy for Neighbourhood Renewal, New Labour returned towards the end of its period in power to a primary focus on tackling worklessness. For Atkinson (2000b, p. 226) this traditional economic focus is 'tinkering at the margins' and reflects an assumption that globalisation is inevitable in its current form and that 'governments cannot buck the market'. Even where social aspects are built into these programmes, an 'overarching policy agenda that encourages footloose capital, low labour costs, reduced social spending and persistent wage equality' makes it very difficult to make any meaningful headway (O'Connor 2007, p. 25).

This economic agenda is dictated from the national and international level, but it is often reinforced at the local level, where agendas may be set by the need to attract in private investment (Anastacio *et al.* 2000; Fraser *et al.* 2007) or a particular public funding programme in competition with other areas. A preoccupation with economic competitiveness, for example, means that decisions about large-scale developments are often off limits to the communities they affect (Taylor 2007a, p. 304). And economic development objectives can come to dominate partnerships, overriding other concerns (Thekaekara 2000). Partnership workers and community representatives thus find that they have to spend their time explaining the external world to the community rather than driving community perspectives into programme design and planning (Diamond 2001).

Agendas are also determined by what will be counted as success. Even where communities are involved in programme planning and design, they have little say in the criteria by which these programmes are monitored and evaluated, that is, in the criteria by which they will be judged (see Box 9.1). An emphasis from politicians and funders on 'hard', quantifiable outputs' leads to a technical bias and institutionalises the rational scientific approach to programme design and management discussed in Chapter 8. This is an experience which has been reported from many parts of the globe (Uphoff 1995, p. 26): 'Accountability is commonly taken to require much advance specification of objectives and means, so that evaluation can be done in terms of the achievement of those objectives and the timely utilisation of predetermined means for achieving those ends'. As such, he argues, projects are isolated from the economic, social, cultural, physical and other contexts in which they operate.

Because what counts is what is done, this can exclude from consideration the less measurable work that communities consider to be important, or squeeze what they want to do into clothes that do not suit: 'It's about someone else's agenda. They just want you to tinker with this bit or that bit, you are never actually asked to set the priorities' (community participant in a neighbourhood renewal programme). It also leaves little room for flexibility as the programme evolves.

The two programmes in Box 9.1 were both long-term (seven and ten years respectively). But in the US, Gittell (2001) is critical of the replacement of comprehensive approaches to community development over the years with funding that is dependent on specific projects, despite research evidence that shows the value of broader, non-specific support. In this she echoes many others who are critical of short-term programmes and projects that seem continually to replicate, rather than learn from what has been done in the past (O'Connor 2007; Butcher and Robertson 2007, p. 98).

BOX 9.1   Deciding what counts

The Health Action Zones were introduced in the UK by the New Labour government in 1997 to tackle inequalities and deliver better services. But they turned out to be more top down than expected. Priorities were set centrally and more energy was expended in negotiating the place of the initiative in the context of the statutory system than in establishing community objectives and priorities (Barnes, Newman and Sullivan 2007, p. 29).

A similar thing happened with the flagship New Deal for Communities programme, which aimed to tackle urban deprivation. It took on board many of the lessons of past partnership programmes and committed itself to putting communities 'at the heart of renewal by allowing time and resources to ensure communities could get involved from the beginning (see below). However, the criteria against which success were to be judged were drawn up by a consultant according to a central government brief, with 67 mandatory indicators. Other locally determined criteria were not excluded; in fact, they continue to be encouraged by the rhetoric. But with time, resources and energy absorbed by meeting government's criteria, local or community criteria inevitably took a back seat.

Finally, in this section, Barnes, Newman and Sullivan (2007) comment on the propensity of local authorities to set up their own fora in response to calls for community participation, without considering what might already exist on the ground (p. 187). Naidu (2008) notes a similar phenomenon in South Africa where 'ward committees have displaced many vibrant community initiatives', describing this as 'a convenient vehicle for the administration to say they have satisfied public participation requirements'. This is common problem, too when there is a change of political administration. In Nicaragua, a citizen's initiative to create a municipal committee was swept away when the Sandinista government came back into power in 2006, replacing existing initiatives with its own committees (Taylor *et al.* 2009).

How to play

If setting the agenda reflects Lukes' second face of power, the third face of power is evident in the way that the 'rules of the game' are taken for granted. From a governmentality perspective (see Chapter 8), Atkinson (1999, p. 70) argues that

> Whilst processes of partnership creation and empowerment may be a way of ensuring that (some of) the benefits of regeneration reach the disadvantaged, they may also have the effect of reinforcing existing relations of domination and control, of legitimating a particular representation of reality which defines what is 'reasonable' and the language in which demands can be made.

There are three aspects of the rules of the game that exclude: structures and systems of decision making; codes of behaviour (particularly around conflict and consensus); and the system of refereeing.

Structures and systems

Many studies report on community frustration with impenetrable structures, hierarchies and procedures: 'The whole process seemed to be so unwieldy ... community reps had to grapple with this huge bureaucratic process' (Taylor and Seymour 2000). A preoccupation on getting the structures right too often takes precedence over establishing a shared vision and delays action.

This alienates potential participants, who want to address their more immediate and practical concerns. Administrative and procedural preoccupations can sap the energy and enthusiasm of the most committed resident.

Partnership has generally developed within existing structures, processes and frameworks of power: new rhetoric poured into old bottles. Public sector cultures are so deeply engrained that power holders are often unaware of the ways in which they perpetuate existing power relations through the use of language and procedures that outsiders find impenetrable. The conventions of public-sector meetings and processes dominate and there is still remarkably little consideration of whether procedures and language should be changed, or even whether community participants might need some explanation so that they understand what is going on. The problems that this creates for community participants are described in Box 9.2.

Stereotypes that are engrained within public sector cultures assume that communities will not understand the complexity of the decisions that have to be made, that they will not be willing to make the sacrifices that are dictated by limited budgets and the need for fairness, and that they will be ruled by self-interest. The concerns of many people in communities can be narrow, especially at the beginning of participation processes, but there is a growing body of evidence, as Chapter 11 will demonstrate, to suggest that people from excluded communities can and do understand the need to balance interests and budgets, and that they will make difficult choices. In doing so, they can bring significant new insights to bear on intractable problems.

Technical complexity can nonetheless be used to exclude communities. Thus O'Neill (1992, p. 291) cites research on participation in health in Montreal where participants from the community were put off by

> highly technical and complex issues and by a technoprofessional culture to which they did not belong. Running the health system was thus left in the hands of professionals and administrators, the population delegates being perceived as 'creating time losses, impeding the speed and efficacy of the decision-making process as well as generating sterile conflicts between various groups in the agency or the facility'.

BOX 9.2   Some comments from communities and service users

Who adapts?

'In all the work I've been involved in, it's us who have to put effort into reaching the council's level. ... They never come down to ours.'

Getting to grips with unfamiliar systems

'With so many men in suits, it was difficult to find the courage to speak up. Sometimes you went along determined to say something this time, but somehow the meeting would be over and you wouldn't have opened your mouth.'

A discouraging response

'Some never regained their confidence after making their initial comment, as they were "made to feel" they had "said something stupid" or "at an inappropriate time during the meeting" or "under the incorrect agenda item".'

Implicated in decisions you don't agree with

'It may be difficult to query or campaign against a decision or do anything like that if you've sat there and agreed with it, either proactively agreed with it or reactively agreed by the fact that you missed a meeting, you've actually passed some document through.'

'The Action Plan went through in the last twenty minutes of a crowded agenda.'

Dominated by professional agendas

'It is meant to be the Community Forum but we have to sit through reports by other people.'

Source: Hastings, McArthur and McGregor (1996); Skelcher *et al.* (1996); Kumar (1997); author's unpublished research.

In the UK the complexity and short timescales of bidding processes mean that community groups are often encouraged to employ consultants, whose assessment of what is likely to succeed reinforces top-down agendas (see Chapter 8) or they may feel they have to accommodate to alien rules and systems in order to play the game – a demonstration of the 'isomorphism' described in Box 7.1.

There are more subtle ways in which communities are recruited into adopting the rules of the game. Foucault's governmentality thesis, discussed in Chapter 7, suggests how technologies of government are used to secure willing compliance from citizens, even against their interests. Larner and Butler (2005, p. 38) illustrate how this works on the ground, citing the good practice guides, transferable models, visioning exercises and community action days that are being used to 'reconstitute individual citizens as community subjects'. Even where requirements are not written in stone, guidelines inevitably frame the ways in which those who are less powerful understand the tasks ahead of them. Such guidelines are offered with the intention of supporting those who have limited experience of the tasks that they are taking on. They also ensure that local developments can be understood within an overarching national policy framework. They can, where they emphasise community involvement, help to pull recalcitrant partners into line. But coming from the centre as they do, they are likely to enshrine pre-existing cultures of programme design and decision making, rather than taking the risk that communities, given time and resources, may do things differently. Such guidelines may not be mandatory, but they are taken seriously by lead partners, who are understandably reluctant to take risks with high-profile initiatives.

Community representatives in partnerships also learn how to adjust their language and behaviour in order to develop the technologies required of them by government programmes (Schofield 2002). But, to use Robert Sampson's words (1993, p. 1220):

> If, in order to be heard, I must speak in ways that you have proposed, then I can be heard only if I speak like you, not like me.

This assimilation goes beyond language. Atkinson describes how community organisations 'restructure themselves' as they are forced to 'demonstrate that they are capable of governing themselves, both collectively and individually, in ways that reflect these wider demands' (2003, p. 118). Meanwhile, policies that seek to construct community organisations as service providers and social enterprises risk driving out 'their specific social origins, ethos and goals, as if these are politically and socially irrelevant to their activities and role in relation to the state' (Carmel and Harlock 2008, pp. 156–7).

Acceptable behaviour

The above discussion highlights the unwritten codes behind the operation of the game. Prominent among these is the unwillingness of many partnerships and participation initiatives to engage with conflict. Annette Hastings and her colleagues reported, in their 1996 study of ten partnerships, that partnerships seemed to be overwhelmed by a consensus culture. Any failure by residents to bring a united view to the table was treated with impatience and residents' resistance to their partners' proposals was treated as obstruction. More recently, Barnes, Newman and Sullivan (2007, p. 204) have been critical of the preference for dispassionate argumentation over committed representation of a particular position or experience. 'Governments', they argue, 'want to exploit community but are deeply uncomfortable with community activism'. Cleaver (2004, p. 272) goes further, arguing that 'respectful attitudes, conflict avoidance and consensus decision-making can all serve to reinforce inequality despite securing functional outcomes'. This failure to accept and work with difference or disagreement is very disempowering to residents (Taylor, 2007a; Taylor *et al.* 2009), especially since conflicts are usually resolved in favour of more powerful partners:

> There is a flight from conflict which I don't think is helpful. A large percentage of the people who participate in this agenda see conflict as a negative dynamic and dysfunctional. I don't think it is. I think if there isn't conflict in a room or in a process, I'd worry about it. Because from my perspective, it's not in any way addressing the status quo if there isn't conflict. (professional in a neighbourhood renewal programme)

As Sarah White, writing from experience in the global South, puts it (White 1996, p. 155): 'the absence of conflict in many supposedly "participatory" programmes is something that should raise our suspicions. Change hurts'. Conflict can be a sign that partnership is working, as the less powerful partners gain the confidence to disagree rather than going along with the majority view. Some of the most successful initiatives in a regeneration programme that involved 33 different studies in the 1990s were plucked from the jaws of conflict and entrenched positions (Taylor 1995b). Indeed, Derrick Purdue and his colleagues came to the view in their research (Purdue *et al.* 2000) that, sometimes, trust can only emerge from periods of opposition and conflict.

The drive to consensus goes beyond partnership working. In Chapter 7, I quoted Nikolas Rose's comment about the way in which the community discourse had been turned from a language of resistance into a professional discourse. De Filippis, Fisher and Shragge (2009, p. 38) argue that the increased role played by community-based organisations in local development and social provision is mirrored by a diminishing of critical political perspectives. There seems also to be increasing discomfort with traditional forms of opposition and social activism such as demonstrations and strikes (Barnes, Newman and Sullivan 2007, p. 204; Cornwall 2008, p. 282; Bunyan 2010, p. 122) – an issue to which I shall return later in this volume.

The refereeing
I argued earlier that agendas are predetermined by 'what counts'. Research across the globe suggests that one of the major factors that stifles community engagement in partnership is the excessive monitoring and accountability that is often required of partnerships and community programmes, especially when they involve public money. Perversely, while the funding involved in partnership initiatives not only provides the incentive for partnership arrangements, it can also obstruct them – by focusing attention on the spending of money, rather than the need for a policy vision and by swamping the agenda with procedural (and upwards) accountability issues.

Michael Edwards and David Hulme (1995b, p. 13) describe how this approach has permeated the global South. Here, they argue, a heavy reliance on 'logical framework' approaches and bureaucratic reporting has fostered 'accountancy' rather than 'accountability', favouring hierarchical management structures, standardising indicators and discouraging learning. This serves neither communities nor a strategic approach: 'strategic accountability is nearly always weaker than functional accountability and downward accountability is nearly always weaker than upward accountability' (Edwards and Hulme 1995a, p. 219).

Few would dispute the need for appropriate monitoring and accountability. But it is the concern to spend the money properly that dictates the complex application forms, the emphasis on measurable, largely economic outputs and a preoccupation with structures and procedures – all of which get in the way of many promising initiatives. While New Labour government ministers in England, for example, were tying their colours to the mast of social entrepreneurialism, innovation and initiative, the system was still designing the impenetrable forms, the impossible deadlines, the rules, the regulations and the hoops to jump through: 'Every New Labour paean to local involvement and active communities ends with a rider that brings the state back in and institutionalises government regulation at an even greater level than before' (Chandler 2000, p. 10). The current government has set up a deregulation task force to reduce bureaucratic burdens on small voluntary and community organisations. Experience of similar initiatives in the past suggests that this will be a challenge.

Monitoring and accountability demands fall disproportionately on those at the bottom of the accountability chain (Taylor and Warburton 2003). The displacement of uncertainty that Chapter 6 described, whereby 'the most powerful departments and authorities maintain their balance by forcing the weaker to bear the burden of adjustment' (Marris 1996) is a process that goes down the line from the international and national through the local state to community organisations across the world. European Union experience suggests that the more layers of bureaucracy are involved, the more risk averse statutory partners are likely to be. Lower levels of government are likely to be particularly risk averse, protecting themselves against potential demands from above.

Communities are not unaware of the ironies in this. While they are being pursued for the bus ticket that will provide evidence that they have spent £1, €1 or $1, they read in the newspapers of problems with fraud at the highest levels of the European Commission or in politicians' expense claims. They also read about the millions of pounds that are routinely overspent on government flagship projects. Thus one resident involved in a European funding programme argued (Taylor and Parkes 2001):

> I think they take financial responsibility more seriously than they take the responsibility to the community and so there is this 'hand-me-down' responsibility that is being reflected in the

voluntary and community sector throughout the country. ... Government initiatives and projects ... can go millions and millions over budget and that's OK, whereas if a community organisation goes over budget or puts a step wrong they come down on us like a ton of bricks.

The recent banking crisis and the continuing resistance to regulation in this industry despite the huge bail outs at the taxpayer's expense have only reinforced this scepticism.

Over and above the irony and sense of unfairness attached to burdensome monitoring requirements is the fact that the complex application forms, appraisal processes and monitoring systems that partnership funding tends to require generate a mistrust that sours relationships between funders, public bodies and communities. As a voluntary sector representative in another study put it (Craig *et al.* 2002, p. 19): 'Too many statutory bodies still treat voluntary sector applications as if they have to avoid fraud – there are prejudices that need confronting'. And it has long been observed that regulation tends always to ratchet upwards, very rarely downwards (Bardach 1989, p. 224).

The hegemony of what Michael Power calls the 'audit society' (1997) has three major outcomes, which fly in the face of both good policy and community empowerment. First, it runs against current wisdom about innovatory practice. A UN cross-country study found that one of the critical features of a good community development programme was 'flexible rather than fixed procedures' (Rothman 2000, p. 101). This is endorsed in a study by Purdue and colleagues (2000), which argued that 'improvisation around minimal structure is the key to collaborative and flexible innovation' (p. 48). And yet, they go on to argue, 'the current practice is to tie all the details down in the bid, often before there has been any explicit community involvement'. If the persistent problems of social exclusion are to be addressed, risks will have to be taken.

Second, excessive monitoring requirements deter the very communities that development, empowerment and regeneration programmes are intended to engage. They erode motivation (Anheier and Kendall 2002) and also divert energies from front-line work. Third, the demands of monitoring professionalise the way that community-based organisations operate, thereby putting at risk their distinctive contribution. The emphasis on a narrow definition of performance measurement is also at odds with a developmental approach to empowerment. Shepherd (1998, p. 95), for example, describes a European Union funded initiative in Uttar Pradesh, where 'donor pressure severely constrained the potentially positive results of what was supposed to have been a participatory project'. And, as we also saw earlier, what gets counted rarely accords with what communities themselves feel is important:

> The numbers game just doesn't reflect how much time and work can go into just one contact, one young person.

> It's an awful lot of paperwork and it's a huge number crunching exercise. [In smaller projects], you're spending more time doing that than to get on with the work.

> One feels it's ticks in boxes on pieces of paper and that any kind of human reality has got lost somewhere. (Author's unpublished research)

Peter Marris (1996, p. 75) suggests that this is not a new problem:

> In the 1960s, for instance when applied social research became fashionable in American cities as an instrument of planning for disadvantaged communities, the people who lived there were often frustrated to discover that their own account of their needs was not assimilable as valid information until it had been codified, analysed and represented in a sociological form that was sometimes no longer intelligible to them.

The irony is that, while all this is based on a rational scientific approach to policymaking, it is extremely difficult to demonstrate conclusively what has been achieved by any single programme. Referring to the War on Poverty, Marris argued that

> In the event, the attempt to conduct policy as an authoritative science discredited most of the programmes, because such a relationship between intervention and desired outcome rarely appeared. ... This does not mean the interventions did no good; only that they cannot be shown conclusively to have caused the particular good they were designed to achieve. (Marris 1996, p. 75)

Many commentators have argued that effective policy is more likely be developed through long-term dialogue and learning, coupled with good but focused information, than punitive monitoring systems based on preconceptions of what works.

This discussion also illustrates the way in which discourses of power can secure the 'willing compliance' of subjects, as Foucault suggested, and silence alternatives. Thus Banks (2007 p. 92) argues that 'the very intensity of the gaze of all the agencies and their obsession with meeting targets can at the same time result in a co-option of these groups, with a resulting loss of "critical edge" as they too begin to work towards "shared" targets and outcomes'. Few people question the need for audit or the assumptions of the auditor; they just fill in the boxes. But, like the famed butterfly's wing of chaos theory, the seemingly insignificant demand that a certain box is ticked in a certain way or that a certain piece of evidence is required can reverberate back throughout entire systems in determining what is and is not possible. Decisions on policy implementation are taken out of the political sphere and into the technical sphere by the requirement that monitoring records need to be kept and presented in a particular way, or that organisations are constituted and managed in particular ways.

It would, of course, be foolish to deny that governments should be looking for evidence that outcomes are being achieved or that hard evidence is important. Communities want evidence of tangible changes as much as their government partners do. But an approach that transforms social problems into technical problems neutralises both their value base and debate about what has caused the problems in the first place (Onyx and Dovey 1999). Assumptions of objectivity and rationality favour particular worldviews and powerful interests. They obscure the values by which judgments are made and ignore the games through which elites hold on to power. Thus, as Sarah White (1996, p. 7) argues: 'What began as a political issue is translated into a technical problem which the development exercise can accommodate with barely a falter in its stride'. The new public management thus depoliticises both the problem of exclusion and the search for effective solutions.

Who plays

Chapter 8 described how policy communities create 'privileged pathways' through the policy process. Kendall and 6 (1994) argue that community organisations lack the resources and *locus standi* to be present in the intensive, regular contact points by which policy communities are knit together. In Maloney *et al.*'s distinction between outsiders, insiders and peripheral insiders (Maloney, Jordan and McLaughlin 1994), therefore, it is as peripheral insiders that communities appear to be most often involved. An evaluation of one regeneration initiative in the UK found that it was the larger non-profit organisations or intermediary bodies that were often consulted by partnerships – as a proxy for local communities (Clarke 1995); these larger organisations are in any case more likely to be embedded in the policy process through a 'complex interweaving of elected members and management boards' (Wistow *et al.* 1992, p. 33). Alternatively, a rhetoric of participation is simply not reflected in practice. Fraser *et al.* (2007, p. 317) describe how in one US city, which had a reputation for 'progressive politics and civic engagement', local residents had no seat on the board which redesigned their neighbourhoods. Similarly, De Zeeuw (2010) describes how significant parts of the community were excluded from the redevelopment programme she studied in the Netherlands, a finding echoed by Atkinson and Carmichael (2007) elsewhere in Europe. Scratching the surface of much feted 'best practice' examples suggests that practice on the ground does not always match up to the PR.

The definition of who plays is certainly expanding. The current emphasis on participation does give communities new opportunities to get into the game, with powerful backing from the top. There is more acknowledgement of diversity, particularly of the need to address issues of race and gender and to ensure that smaller organisations are included. Global institutions and national governments are emphasising the need to differentiate between NGOs and community-based organisations.

However, a strong emphasis on leadership in many approaches to community participation can sit uneasily alongside equally strong concern to get beyond organisations to the 'real people'. Policy emphasis on 'social entrepreneurs' and individual community leaders, for example, can result in too little attention being paid to the ways in which they are and can remain embedded in their communities. This begs questions about legitimacy and the capacity of leaders to reflect the views of their wider constituency. It also raises questions of sustainability. Many community representatives who have been through successive rounds of re-generation face the problem of burn out as increasing demands create too heavy a burden to be sustained. Not enough attention is given to the need to build their succession. Successful community leaders are feted, adopted and promoted by public authority partners in ways that make it very difficult to follow them.

A number of factors contribute to this. The first is that public-sector partners and other power holders too often select the 'expert citizens' (Bang 2005) with whom they want to work. Inevitably these are likely to be those whom they find the easiest to work with or the most easily approachable (the 'acceptable' face of community involvement) – those who 'share the bias, in-stincts, priorities and culture of the department' (Maloney, Jordon and McLaughlin 1994, p. 29). They are unlikely, therefore, to be 'typical' of the communities from which they come. Mayo (1997b) describes the tendency of some public authorities to set up ad hoc groups for consultation as a 'puppet show', which marginalises the very interests and organisations that should be the key to successful community partnerships. Meanwhile Purdue *et al.* (2000, p. 36), in their study of regeneration, argue that the qualities that partnership encourages in community leaders are the ability to cope with bureaucracy and finance. The compliance culture, in their view, fails to encourage dynamic, innovative leaders to get involved; the leaders that are valued by partners are rather those 'who are keen to learn the procedural aspects of regeneration programmes'.

By these means, the much maligned 'usual suspects' are often created by the partnership system itself. If they are not carefully selected by partners, they are created by the short timescales, the proliferation of partnerships, the complexity of the rules of many partnerships and the knowledge that is required, which mean that only those who can hit the ground running can realistically get involved. Too often agencies filter all their consultation and involvement through one formal mechanism, which acts as a bottleneck. And the pressures that partnership and participation initiatives put on community representatives can easily cut even the most accountable leaders off from their communities, especially when they do not have the resources to support effective accountability.

Mario Diani (1997, p. 140) asks how far it is possible for community representatives to be integrated into new elite networks and simultaneously continue their role in their former associational networks. Community representatives need a considerable amount of time at their disposal to meet all the demands of partnership, and this can entail huge costs. They need incredibly thick skins, caught between public-sector partners who are all too ready to accuse them of being unrepresentative if they say something unpalatable and communities that may well hold them responsible when the partnership does not deliver (see Box 9.3). Anastacio and her colleagues argue (2000) that 'community stars' easily become victims.

As Chapter 8 pointed out, the desire to get to the 'real people' can sometimes be a desire to get to those who are less likely to challenge, rather than the 'informed user'. Purdue *et al.* (2000, pp. 1–2) suggest that partners may also criticise communities for their lack of representativeness as a way of deflecting attention away from their own shortcomings. Community representatives are quick to point out that other partners (including those from

---

BOX 9.3   Catch 22: Can community representatives ever win?

The disturbing tendency of professionals and power holders to discount the views of knowledgeable communities and consumers is illustrated in the following two comments:

- Representatives for organisations of disabled people ... were sometimes dismissed by social and health officers as being unrepresentative of users because they appeared too articulate to be 'real' users (Bewley and Glendinning 1994, p. 165).
- Every time you keep hearing 'Oh we want the real people to be involved in this'. So we say OK, let's help you get the real people. They get the real people, they tell the real people you have to be organised ... and they become a group and then they say 'Oh no, we don't want groups, we want real people (Taylor and Warburton 2003, p. 334).

In a further study, a council officer bemoaned the fact that as community representatives learn the ropes of the partnership game, they risk becoming divorced from their constituencies and 'less useful' as a result (Author's unpublished research).

the private sector) are rarely questioned about their own legitimacy or representativeness. But there is always going to be a
tension between representation and widespread participation –
between depth and breadth. The chair of a local partnership in
a recent study explained the dilemma as the community representatives on her partnership came up for re-election:

> We need some consistency. We have spent ages building up
> capacity ... As they get more experienced and have greater
> ownership of the agenda, they [*the community representa-
> tives*] will have greater parity. If we get a whole new load, we
> will go back six months. (Author's unpublished research)

The community gatekeeper, who finds it difficult to share power
and prevents access to the wider community, is all too familiar
a figure. But this does not mean that all the people who give
up time to sit on committees should be tarred with this brush.
Indeed, Liz Richardson (2008, p. 235) warns against the stereotyping of the usual suspects, who, she claims, are like 'gold
dust'. As she points out, their accountability often operates in
informal ways, over tea and toast (or maybe over a beer in the
pub) and through informal relationships and chance encoun-
ters. What effective representation requires over and above this
is the infrastructural capacity to ensure that representation and
leadership are firmly embedded in the community. Representatives cannot be expected to reflect the diversity of community
views if they do not have the time and resources to relate to
their constituent communities or any forum in which to discuss these different views. I will return to this vexed issue in
Chapter 12.

The dice are loaded

Negotiating and learning to manipulate the 'rules of the game'
mean that communities need to be highly sophisticated if they
are to stand a chance of engaging on equal terms with partners
let alone maintaining their distinctive contribution. But they often come to the table with unequal resources. With very rare
exceptions, community participants do not have the officers,
technical resources and information back-up that other partners
take for granted. In addition, partners are rarely sensitive to the

demands they are making on communities and fail to appreciate the huge costs of participation, both personal and organisational, especially in stressed communities:

> There is no one to take up the slack if you stop work for your community to talk to a statutory body or work with them on an issue. You need to feel that something of real benefit to your community is going to happen in the foreseeable future to compensate your community for the loss of your skills. (Author's unpublished research)

Several studies have underlined the importance of community development support to assist communities in building up their skills, confidence and capacity. But partners rarely appreciate the scale of resources that is necessary if communities are to make a full and considered contribution. Too often, one community worker might be dispatched to a neighbourhood and expected to overcome decades of alienation.

In addition, the very popularity of the partnership idea is stretching participants – from all sectors – to their limits. In one study, a key player in the local voluntary (non-profit) sector told us that she was participating in 48 partnership bodies, while a respondent in another case study site counted 83 partnerships in the locality overall (Craig *et al.* 2002).

There is another resource issue. Power usually depends on the material assets that partners bring to the table or are expected to bring (in the case of potential employers, for example). Asset transfer has been an important part of policy in England and other UK countries for some time now and larger asset-based organisations like the Community Development Corporations in the US or some community development trusts in the UK (see Box 11.1, for example) can play this game. But smaller community groups often lack assets of this kind and the less tangible assets that they do bring – of local knowledge, for example – are consistently undervalued. Even where they do have material assets to bring, these are often dependent on government subsidy, which creates its own imbalance of power.

Money and officer support are not the only resources. Communities are rarely given the *time* they need to participate effectively. There are two aspects to this. The first is the stage at which communities are asked to make an input. Public authorities often seem reluctant to go out for consultation on any initiative until they have dotted all the 'i's and crossed all the 't's. By the time communities gain access to the agenda, powerful vested interests have been established and it is too late to take on board community priorities or new ideas about what needs to be done:

> Once something gets written, it gets very difficult, because people have obviously sweated blood and tears over it. You trust us to be a partner in lots of other ways, trust us to be a partner when it actually comes to sharing ideas before something starts'. (Author's unpublished research)

It is not so much that authorities are intentionally repressing community views, but by following traditional procedures and processes and by privileging their own needs over those of communities, they reinforce imbalances of power.

The second time issue relates to the time allowed for communities to make an effective input. In City Challenge – one of the earliest of the recent partnership initiatives in the UK – local government authorities were given only weeks to involve communities in their bids for central government funds and for a long time there was no consideration of the need to give any resources to communities to help them to engage in partnership bids. There were similar problems with its successor, the Single Regeneration Budget: few of the early partnership bids were community led or had even involved communities beyond an eleventh-hour signature from a local voluntary sector intermediary body.

Later initiatives have attempted to address these issues by building in a lead-in or development phase – this was the case with a number of the programmes launched as part of New Labour's National Strategy for Neighbourhood Renewal in England, for example. However, there are still too many examples where political imperatives for a high-profile launch of a new initiative frustrate the imperative to give communities the time they need to participate in any meaningful way. And the need to spend the funds according to Treasury or political timescales means that only those who are 'ready to go' can benefit or that partners short-circuit the need to spend time on developing an effective partnership and a strategy that is jointly owned. In a number of recent English initiatives, late release of funding and delays in decision making centrally, coupled with the imperative to spend all the money by the end of the relevant financial year, have meant that year-long programmes have been squeezed into a matter of a few months – another example of the way in which risk is passed down the line and hardly an efficient way of operating.

Are we in the right game?

Reid and Iqbal distinguished between two network 'cultures' in policy: entrepreneurial and collaborative. The more informal 'entrepreneurial' networks are flexible and opportunistic, and confer a lot of autonomy on members. They can be highly effective but they are also more exclusive, relying on 'organisations using their skills in managing inter-organisational relationships to secure their own entry' (Reid and Iqbal 1995, p. 31). The more formal 'collaborative' networks are less exclusive, concerned more with legitimacy, and appear to achieve a great deal less than the effort put in by participants.

This distinction may explain the lack of power felt by many community organisations. Their presence adds legitimacy to formal partnerships but they feel they are excluded from the more informal entrepreneurial networks where the 'real action' is. Community participation and community empowerment are not the same thing, and we saw in Chapter 3 that the expectations of government and citizens in relation to participation programmes can also be very different (Gaventa 1998). Research suggests that there is considerable variation in the way that partnerships and participation initiatives are implemented, within countries, across countries and at a very local level between different services. Commitment sometimes goes only skin deep, with agencies sending along junior staff to partnership meetings who do not have the authority to agree anything. Staff from one part of an authority often know little about partnerships led by other departments.

Even where leading politicians put their weight behind community empowerment, this intention can be frustrated further down the line by those who see their own power or freedom to manoeuvre threatened. In the UK, local government has long felt that it is under attack from central government (Lowndes and Sullivan 2004) and so it is not surprising that some officers and elected politicians view community participation with suspicion – as a device to bring them into line or bypass them completely. In one recent study, a respondent referred to elected politicians as 'wounded lions', wounded by central government policies but still dangerous (Taylor 2007a). Elected politicians find it difficult to give up control.

This capacity for resistance permeates the international literature too. Writing mainly about development experience in the global South, Cornwall and Coelho (2004, p. 3) point out that 'the micropolitics of engagement can subvert the best intentions of institutional design' (*ibid*. p. 3). In the US, it has undermined programmes from the War on Poverty onwards. Thus Gittell (2001, p. 91) describes how, in the Empowerment Zones, 'city officials and bureaucrats defended their turf to the exclusion of any change in process or participants' (see also Marris and Rein 1967; De Filippis 2007). For many in the local state, power is still seen as a zero-sum game.

In this context, non-participation may be entirely rational, as a respondent in research by Banks (2007, p. 94) commented:

> People know that when they're consulted, the chances are that what they say will not make a jot of difference because the regeneration of the estate will happen in the way that it's down in the appraisals anyway. As a result, I think it's been difficult to develop an active community.

There are other costs to being involved in partnerships. While communities are being awarded ringside seats in partnerships, they can find themselves at a battle for territory between public bodies or departments, as the rhetoric of partnership comes up against the competitive ethos that the market has introduced into the public sphere or more traditional forms of departmentalism. In the UK and elsewhere, governments have identified the need for 'joined up' services and policies and placed the blame for past failures on the failure of local government departments and other agencies to work together. But this is not just a problem at local level: the lack of co-ordination between the policies and practices of central government departments often leads to policies which flatly contradict each other in their intended outcomes by the time they get to local level. Even within one department, different programmes and initiatives can travel down separate silos leading to unco-ordinated action on the ground. As the policy and service environment gets more fragmented, it is local communities that are left picking up the pieces.

Should we be playing this game at all?

Being sidelined into the 'wrong game' is one issue, but being in the right game brings its own dilemmas. Can communities keep to their own agendas and maintain their distinctive contribution, or will they become co-opted into government agendas? Partnership without incorporation is a major challenge for communities. Getting involved in partnerships requires trade-offs to be made. Maloney, Jordan and McLaughlin (1994, p. 37) argue that communities may in the end be: 'interested in getting what they want most of the time, rather than the prospect of one big pay-day'. But there are many examples where, as a result, communities declare themselves satisfied with opportunities and achievements that in no way match up to the rhetoric of partnership, because they have adjusted their sights and modified their claims according to what they think they will get; an illustration, perhaps, of Lukes' third face of power (Stewart and Taylor 1995; Barnes, Newman and Sullivan 2007, p. 191).

There can be little doubt that, despite the reservations discussed in this chapter, community actors have more access to local decision making now in many countries than they have had in the past. However, to the extent that they have, the stability and continuity required of accepted network members, the shared assumptions and, indeed, the sheer time involved may distance community representatives further and further from their constituencies. There is also an ambiguity about partners' expectations. They want community participants to be representative and accountable to their communities, but there is a culture of delivery about partnerships and partners want representatives to 'deliver their communities', and to provide legitimacy for what the partnership is doing. This means they are often impatient with the need that community representatives have to check back with their constituencies and will put pressure on representatives to make decisions that are not grounded in wider consultation. While there is clearly a balance to be struck between the need for decisions and the need for a mandate, community representatives need more leeway than they are often given to judge how this balance should be managed. Rushing decisions through 'in the last twenty minutes of a crowded agenda' (Taylor and Seymour 2000) can leave communities feeling both short changed and ineffective.

The funding game magnifies most of these problems. The mechanics of managing a highly complex bidding and appraisal process may teach communities new skills, but it can suck communities into a game they did not really want to play. A respondent in Mayo's research (1997b, p. 20) describes the process through which community participation in partnerships becomes co-opted: 'City Challenge took away the debate, the struggle and forced people to focus on funding and imposed outputs, they can't, don't fight back any more'.

More destructively, it can set groups against each other, especially when the funding at stake is relatively small. As I have argued elsewhere: 'The high expectations that apparently large sums of money create can make disappointment inevitable when the millions are divided between different objectives – the drive for a piece of the action can seriously impair the development of trust and relationships' (Taylor 2000a, p. 1028).

In Chapter 8, I introduced the distinction that Cornwall and others have made between 'invited' spaces and 'popular' or 'claimed' spaces. As partnership working becomes increasingly prevalent, the danger is that it becomes 'the only game in town', that the energies of community activists are drawn more and more into the 'invited' spaces whose agendas and rules of engagement are determined by external actors and that there is no place else to go (see Box 9.4). In many Northern countries, this danger is increased by the disappearance of many of the alternative 'popular' spaces at local level where people – especially working-class people – used to find their voices, test out their opinions and learn the skills of negotiation. Trade unions and political parties have become increasingly centralised, while the chapels, the workers' education institutes and working men's clubs that used to be a feature of industrial towns and villages in the past have largely disappeared. This has left a huge vacuum – democracy needs these alternative spaces – and, in some European

BOX 9.4   Partnership: the only game in town?

A major neighbourhood renewal initiative was introduced into a Welsh town as part of the Welsh Assembly Government's Communities First programme. A previous programme had already set up a highly successful partnership and this was incorporated into the new initiative, with the local authority acting as the accountable body and providing staff support. A small group of residents from the original partnership continued to operate as a separate group, believing that it was important to continue to provide an independent voice for the residents to which the initiative could be accountable. The group was represented on the partnership and attempted to represent community views. But when these views were critical, the local authority staff became very defensive and the group eventually decided to withdraw because it felt that it was not being heard – a view endorsed by other third-sector participants. However, after some time, the group felt that it had no option but to return, since the partnership was the major route for the information it needed if it was to serve its constituents. There was simply nowhere else to go to get the information it needed to operate effectively and no other forum where the local community could find its voice.

communities, the danger now is that the most successful organisers may be far-right organisations, which target the most disadvantaged neighbourhoods and play on people's fears.

Discussion

In Chapter 8, I suggested that new political opportunities were opening up a new public space for communities and their allies to tackle social exclusion and achieve the changes they need. The experience reported in this chapter suggests, however, that there is a long way to go before this can be achieved. It has questioned how far communities are able to come to the policymaking table as equals and suggested that they are easily recruited into top-down views of how power should and can be shared. It has argued that partnership can exclude the very community groups it is supposed to benefit.

In these circumstances, it is easy to agree with John Gaventa's conclusion that:

> While such spaces offer some possibilities for influence and may allow social justice groups possibilities for organising, it is questionable whether these invited spaces actually create opportunities for any long-term social change on critical issues. The danger is that they may even serve to legitimise the status quo and actually divert civil society energies from working on more fundamental policy-related problems. (ESRC/NCVO 2007: 7)

Partnerships often generate high expectations – especially if major funding is involved – and their failure to deliver can leave communities feeling disillusioned and unwilling to try again. Community initiatives may even destroy the very cohesion and capital they seek to create. As we have just seen, funding-led initiatives can drive wedges between communities, if poorly designed and managed. Meanwhile, heavy monitoring and administration demands sap energies and deter the very communities that are intended to benefit. Indeed, the rules and regulations that surround such initiatives sometimes seem expressly designed to replace trust rather than to foster it. The emphasis on hard outputs ignores the social capital that sustains, uses and maintains the technology (Cernea 1994, p. 13). The pace and complexity of partnership working and the amount of information that has to be assimilated, coupled with the absence of resources, can easily pull those who engage in the process away from the rest of the communities they represent.

In their research on public participation in the UK, Barnes, Newman and Sullivan (2007, p. 184) admit to some pessimism about the potential of new initiatives to overcome entrenched institutional or political forms of power. This pessimism is echoed elsewhere (see, for example, Cornwall and Coelho 2004; De Filippis and Saegert 2007). Does this mean that participation and partnership have nothing to offer? Not necessarily. There are allies and champions within the system, there are chinks of light hidden amongst the critiques in this chapter and there is a demand from communities for more voice. Later chapters will explore the potential this offers in more detail. But the criticisms reviewed in this chapter do draw attention to the fact that the largely positive rhetoric of partnership conceals tensions that need to be understood if they are to be addressed: between public account-ability and flexibility; between leadership, representation and participation; between competition and collaboration; between consensus and conflict; between bringing a distinctive contribution into new forms of governance and co-option. Working through these tensions requires considerable skill and imagination. In the remaining chapters I will explore the ways in which different communities and their partners have addressed this challenge.

Chapter 10

Reclaiming Community

Chapter 6 described the cycle of exclusion that many of the most disadvantaged communities in our society experience. It described how their residents or members find themselves labelled as in some way inferior or abnormal, how they internalise this label and how it is further reinforced by the way in which outsiders and the media treat them. Community for them becomes a place to leave – if they can – rather than to stay. The cycle can be reversed, however. If people can develop confidence, skills and build on their assets, if they can build up networks both within and beyond their own neighbourhood or community, they can challenge the way in which outsiders treat them and the way they are portrayed. If they can develop organisations that can act on behalf of their residents or members, then they can work with other organisations to create change. A confident community which is respected by the outside world can then become a place where people want to live and work, which reinforces the self-esteem of those who live there and so on.

To set such a positive cycle in motion requires (Stewart and Taylor 1996; Taylor 1998, p. 825):

- Confidence and social capital in these communities and realising existing assets and strengths, so that their members no longer see themselves and their neighbours as failures
- New relationships with outsiders (service providers, business, the media) that empower people as service users, consumers and workers, as well as changing the image of the locality
- Jobs and assets that bring people and resources into these communities, creating stronger links between them and the mainstream economy and empower them as co-producers
- New forms of governance to empower people as citizens.

In this chapter and the next I will unpack this agenda and explore what it implies in practice. This chapter will discuss the starting points for change by exploring initiatives to release potential through building confidence, skills and capacity within communities. Second, it will briefly review more technical approaches to making neighbourhoods better places to live, through improving the physical environment, changing the population mix and creating the 'permeable places' that link people with the outside world (Forrest and Kearns 1999, p. 51).

Releasing community power

The work that is done with communities is often described nowadays as 'capacity building'. This is a 'top-down' term that has been criticised for implying that communities are empty vessels into which information and knowledge have to be poured. An activist quoted by Anastacio and her colleagues (2000) echo the feelings of many others by saying: 'communities are pretty bloody capable already'. For many, capacity *building* implies a deficit model, which focuses 'on a community's needs, deficiencies and problems' rather than 'a commitment to discovering a community's capacities and assets' (Kretzman and McKnight 1993, p. 1). Capacity *development,* however, can be understood in terms of drawing out potential that is already there but may be lying dormant or unrecognised. Many disadvantaged neighbourhoods are, after all, areas whose capacity has been undermined and undervalued for years. As Diane Warburton (2009, p. 27) argues: 'Any programmes of capacity building must recognise that what is needed is not a redressing of the inequalities of *abilities,* but a redressing of the inequalities of *resources* and *opportunities* to practice and develop those abilities in ways which others in society take for granted' (Warburton's italics).

Capacity has often been understood in terms of individual technical skills. But relational capacity is now recognised as equally important (Howard *et al.* 2009). Individual skills and knowledge can be seen as 'human capital', while the networks and norms built up through developing relational capacity can be seen as 'social capital'. Habits of organising and a willingness to take action might be seen as 'organisational capital'. Together, these forms of capital enhance the potential for communities to become active agents and to realise the power of community.

To develop this potential requires three interlocking processes:

- Learning – recognising, discovering and acquiring skills, finding out how to do things, acknowledging and sharing knowledge, developing awareness and ideas, engaging in *praxis* (learning by doing)
- Networking – engaging with others, building informal links across and between communities
- Organising – mobilising energies and knowledge, developing organisational skills, building organisations, nurturing leadership, taking action.

Each depends on the other: people learn by doing and they gain knowledge through mobilising to take action; but learning is what gives this action its transformational potential. Networking builds relationships and gives people confidence, ensuring that more formal activity is embedded and accountable at community level. It gives them a chance to learn from each other. Organising then helps to institutionalise and sustain informal relationships and collective learning. In community practice, action and learning are two sides of one coin (Horton and Freire 1990), helping people develop the confidence, relationships and skills to get activities going and to build the organisational capacity that will allow people to pool their energies and to take more effective action. At the same time, this three-dimensional approach encourages people to reflect on and learn from their action, and it can support them in developing their activities beyond their immediate concerns to tackle the wider social and economic forces that contribute to their exclusion.

Community learning

Chanan (1992, p. 43) argues that people in excluded areas experience exclusion as a personal thing and not as an objective problem. They internalise their experiences and blame themselves for their exclusion. It is difficult for people to change this perception on their own: 'No matter how strong or competent one is, sustaining changes in one's life is difficult in the absence of other people who share one's worldview' (Rappaport 1998, p. 237).

Spaces need to be created where people can share this experience and reforge 'private troubles into public issues' (Bauman 1999, p. 7), to forge 'power with' as well as 'power to' (see Chapter 7). The empowerment journey begins therefore when people who have been isolated in their exclusion discover that their experiences and feelings are shared. Rappaport (1998, pp. 226, 230) describes how, when people share their stories, they can create a new, shared narrative: 'Narratives create memory, meaning and identity among individuals. ... All communities have narratives about themselves and these narratives have powerful effects on their members. ... These narratives tell the members and others something about themselves, their history and their future'.

Chapter 7 described how we are drawn into 'dominant cultural narratives', which are disseminated by the media and our social institutions and tend to exclude or stereotype the least powerful in society. As people share their stories, however, through word of mouth (or, indeed, visual art), they discover that their experiences are shared and begin to frame problems in group rather than personal terms. Instead of blaming themselves or accepting the labels of personal inadequacy that are typically imposed by the outside world, people begin to frame what Woliver (1996) calls 'narratives of resistance'. Such narratives do not simply place the blame for injustice on the outside world, however; they appeal to people's sense of community in a way that shares the responsibility for change. They also provide a counter to the negative images that so often characterise excluded communities.

It is to the work of Paolo Freire (1972) that much of the community education tradition is indebted. Freire (1972, pp. 23–4) argued that: 'The oppressed, having internalised the image of the oppressor and adopted his guidelines are fearful of freedom'. He rejected traditional pedagogical approaches to education as a 'one way flow of facts to fill empty vessels' (Chambers 1997, p. 60). Through his work on literacy he developed the idea of *conscientisation* to describe an educative process that allows people to reflect on their experience and their situation. Through dialogue with each other, they begin to question ideas and situations which they previously took for granted or accepted as unproblematic; through *praxis* (ongoing critical reflection and action), they re-establish the personal and collective agency that has been denied them through dominant social institutions and ideologies 'putting values into practice on the basis of practical wisdom' (Banks 2007b, p. 143; see also Ledwith 2005; Butcher 2007b). In South Africa, Abbott (1996) contrasted the progress of an oppressive elite (conquest, divide and rule, manipulation and cultural invasion) with Freire's dialogical action (co-operation, organisation, cultural synthesis and unity for liberation). In a Northern context, we can perhaps contrast dialogical action with the more familiar top-down approach, which assumes that expertise lies outside communities and that communities need to be 'em'-powered.

Freire's approach resonates with Foucault's ideas about 'problematisation', which allow people to escape from 'willing compliance' and become 'active subjects'. It has been reflected in emancipatory and popular education movements across the globe, which work with people to understand the political and social context that shapes their lives. This tradition has deep roots. In the UK, Keith Jackson (1995) traced it back to Tawney, an eminent UK sociologist and adult educator:

> If you want flowers you must have flowers, roots and all, unless you are satisfied, as many people are satisfied, with flowers made of paper and tinsel. ... And if you want education you must not cut it off from the social interests in which it has its living and perennial sources. (Tawney 1926, pp. 20, 22)

But emancipatory education here can be traced back beyond Tawney to the battle for the vote in the nineteenth century and also to the battle for the emancipation of women (Thompson 1963). In the nineteenth century, education and action were interwoven in the mutual organisations of the working classes, in the settlements that took members of the upper classes into the poorer parts of the cities and in the trade unions. In the twentieth century, Freire's work has underpinned liberation struggles in Latin America, while institutes like the Highlander Research and Education Center founded in the US by Miles Horton in the 1930s helped to provide the foundation for civil rights movements across the globe.

Freire (1972) argued that liberation could not be handed down to communities; it needed to come from the people themselves.

The PAR (participatory action research) approach developed by Chambers and others has developed this approach:

> PAR ... has sought actively to involve people in generating knowledge about their own condition and how it can be changed, to stimulate social and economic change based on the awakening of the common people and to empower the oppressed. The techniques used in PAR include collective research through meetings and socio dramas, critical recovery of history, valuing and applying folk culture, and the production and diffusion of new knowledge through written, oral and visual forms. (Chambers 1997, p. 108)

Chambers argues that people who are marginalised should do much of their own investigation, analysis and planning. Conversely professionals should reflect critically on their own concepts, values, behaviour and methods, and be prepared to learn by engaging with the process of participatory research as catalysts and facilitators.

PAR has been used to develop people's own definitions of poverty and exclusion from the ground (Narayan *et al.* 2000). It has been widely adopted and used as a method of identifying local needs, assets and priorities rather than having these defined from above. It has also spawned a number of related approaches. One such technique is 'power mapping', in which participants create a map of the networks, organisations and individuals through which power flows or where power seems to be concentrated in their locality, in an organisation or in a partnership: 'Through drawing the map (using local materials, flip charts or even laptop computers) participants explore their varying perceptions of where power actually resides, in its different dimensions, setting the context within which to explore what needs to change' (Mayo and Taylor 2001, p. 51; see also Harris *et al.* 2009).

There are countless other examples of educational activity and awareness-raising techniques in the community development and wider development literature: education and literacy campaigns, community arts and community radio all feature heavily in reviews of community involvement and change policies across the globe (Dey and Westendorff 1996; Goetz and Gaventa 2001; Annette and Mayo 2010) and I will return to these later in this and the next chapter. However, Cooke and Kothari (2002) and the authors in their edited volume deliver a health warning about participatory appraisal techniques. Indiscriminately applied, these can become reductionist, manipulated, culturally inappropriate and methodologically parochial, masking difference and concealing the complexities of power and power relations. Waddington and Mohan (2004, p. 221) argue further that imported participatory exercises override existing and potentially legitimate forms of local decision making, assuming that communities do not have the capacity to develop these themselves.

This is not a reason for dismissing their use. It does suggest, however, that it is inappropriate to transfer methodologies and exercises from one situation to another without considering the power relations and context within which they are being introduced or how they are going to be used. This may simply set up expectations that are then not met and create a picture of local preferences and aspirations that is incomplete. It is essential in all these approaches to build analytical skills within communities that allow them to unpack accepted notions and envisage alternatives to what they are being offered, as Box 10.1 demonstrates. And these need to be set in a context of continuous learning and action – short-term initiatives are unlikely to be effective.

The focus on learning in community practice not only raises awareness but also redresses one of the major disadvantages that people in low-income and excluded communities experience: either lack of access to education or an experience of education that is overwhelmingly negative. A community worker in a South Wales project (*Unleashing the Potential*, video 1995) argued that one of the most important things for the people she was working with to understand was that 'It is not that they have failed in education; it's that education has failed them.'

Furthermore, while these forms of transformative education are central to community and individual change, it is important not to underestimate the potential of more 'elementary' forms of education to act as a springboard for engagement on a wider front. In research I carried out in Wales, for example, some local people first got involved in a European Union capacity-building project through attending language classes; young people were attracted in by a class on how to make a music video. The project itself had grown out of a local history project set up by a group of people attending a local evening class. Another example is given in Box 10.2.

BOX 10.1 Developing political literacy in West Africa

The experience of trying to apply conventional approaches to local development in West Africa led to the development of an approach called *Arizama*, designed and managed by the people themselves. This aimed to enhance political literacy, using the REFLECT paradigm (Regenerated Freirian Literacy through Empowering Community Techniques) – a paradigm which uses participants' own ideas and shared analysis of their problems to generate keywords and visual graphics which then form the basis for literacy development. *Arizama* brings people together in an open and flexible space, allows them to raise sensitive issues and 'get to know one another very well'. As applied in Ghana, it started by identifying how local communities actually communicated and then building on this. But the process also allowed communities to recognise and challenge potential inequalities in existing systems through dialogue and discussion. A key part of this is learning to appreciate other people's views and perceptions, bringing together peer groups who had first met separately.

Arizama fora on a community level have, for example, enabled men and women to explore their different information exchange networks, the former working through formal and traditional structures, the latter through more informal networks, which span different groups and interests. The fora have discussed how the two types of communication engage, where they conflict, and where they disempower. A chiefs' conference also addressed the exclusion of women, meeting with NGO representatives, women's chiefs and local opinion leaders to discuss the role of women in traditional society and the problems they face. These issues were taken back to the communities through village-based workshops to drive change. Concrete outcomes included the emergence of localised cartels as result of women being recognised as competent business people and more mobility across communities. One successful and mobile trader contributed to the building of a school because she had begun earning money.

Source: Adapted from Waddington and Mohan 2004, pp. 222–4.

BOX 10.2   Learning as a route to organising

The way in which informal activity can lead to further engagement is illustrated by the example of a quilters' group in Bristol. For years a local organisation, which carried out housing improvement work for older people, had been trying, without success, to involve local people and users on its management group. One year, money was raised to provide sessional support and material resources for about ten women to start up a quilting group. The women got very involved in quilting and established a strong network. It was through this activity that they became more interested in the organisation and some became members of the management committee.

Source: Adapted from Burns and Taylor (1998).

Conversely, there are many examples where people who have become involved in community initiatives have re-entered formal education and taken up new opportunities as a result. Becoming involved in community organisations gives people new skills, such as running and chairing meetings, organising finances, administration, research, information and communications technology. Accreditation schemes make these skills explicit, so that they are properly valued and also allow them to be transferred into employment and other settings.

An explicit focus on learning has further advantages insofar as it highlights a crucial asset that communities can bring to the search for solutions. to the 'wicked issues' of policy – making their tacit knowledge explicit. This, as we shall see in Chapter 11, is an important source of legitimacy and, along with the skills in negotiation and deliberation that the learning process gives them, increases their power when dealing with outsiders.

Networking and organising

Dalrymple and Burke (1995, cited in Jacob 2002) suggest that empowerment works at three levels:

- The level of feelings – discovering feelings are shared

- The level of ideas – developing self-knowledge, self-definition and self-efficacy leads to changed consciousness
- The level of action – moving from the personal to the political.

The previous section addressed the first two of these but, while raising awareness is important, it does not of itself create change. Hannah Arendt (1958) argues that power really emerges when people come together and act.

People join groups for a variety of reasons (Taylor, Barr and West 2000):

- To engage in shared activities (including education)
- To get a sense of belonging and identity
- To provide mutual support
- To provide services or support for others in the community or in another community
- To fight against a threat from outside or to defend rights and privileges that are under attack
- To try to get a better deal for themselves and their community
- To gain influence with external actors.

Groups may have more than one objective: for example, a number of women may meet in each other's houses as friends and to provide mutual support, but they may go on to set up an after-school play group and apply for funds for childcare. As the group becomes more formalised, it may develop an educational angle as the women seek to learn more about their own and their children's health, and it may become politically active as the women lobby for better childcare facilities in the neighbourhood.

These activities can happen spontaneously but, while some communities may already have within them people with the experience, confidence and skills to set up successful organisations, many do not. A middle-class neighbourhood that wants to stop an unwanted new development locally may well contain within it a solicitor, an architect, an accountant, perhaps also a local councillor. But the communities with the least confidence and resources are unlikely to boast these professional skills or, indeed, the contacts to help their cause along. They are likely to need the catalyst and support that a community worker provides.

Community practice often begins through making contact with people in their homes and about their day-to-day business. In Northern countries, this might include: knocking on doors;

mixing with parents picking up their children at the school gates; going to the launderette or the pub; offering drop-in, leisure and educational opportunities; finding out how people feel about living in their area and what they want to do (or to be done) about it (for an example, see Box 10.3). Playgroups, environmental clear-ups, youth activities, mums and toddlers groups and self-help groups may not hit the headlines, but it is here that community engagement often starts. Small-scale activities give people the opportunity to engage with others that they feel they can trust as a first step towards wider involvement.

If we borrow the 'circuits of power' metaphor from Stewart Clegg (1989), the challenge for community policy is to (re)connect and activate circuits that have been dormant or in disrepair or, following Melucci (1988, p. 248), 'to activate the web of networks submerged in everyday life' along with the alternative 'frameworks of sense' that they generate. Without such circuits, activities and events are unlikely to have any sustained significance (much as appliances which are not 'plugged in'). Circuits that are in disrepair, moreover, are vulnerable to the 'short circuits' of conflict and division.

Alison Gilchrist emphasises the importance of informal networking in reclaiming and empowering communities. 'The capacity

---

BOX 10.3   Malvern's front-room meetings

In a small estate in Malvern in England, the existing community group had become moribund. So the community worker asked a number of her initial contacts whether they would be willing to host an informal meeting in their front rooms to talk about how local people felt about where they lived and what they thought should be happening there. Each meeting involved five to six people and they were invited by word of mouth. Careful preparation and expert facilitation helped to ensure that the meetings ran well and those who attended felt they were being treated as 'experts'. Each meeting produced at least one person who was willing to get involved in more formal structures that were being set up for participation on the estate.

Source: Taylor *et al.* 2007.

of a community to respond creatively to change and ambiguity', she argues, 'is to be found in its web of connections and relationships, rather than in the head of individuals or the formal structures of voluntary bodies' (p. 174). Informal networks are easier to access; they feel more natural to people. They require less explicit commitment than a formal organisation and offers easy escape routes. They allow people to opt in and out, which can be particularly important for people in stressful situations. Unlike their more formal counterparts, informal networks are able to mobilise quickly and adapt to emerging situations. Even where residents are not actively involved, Liz Richardson reports (2008), they still see informal groups as visible signs of community spirit. Informal networks are also an important component of social capital and the benefits that can flow from it (see Box 10.4).

Gilchrist (1995) defines the steps involved in networking as follows:

- Building overlapping networks in communities, of various kinds and offering a variety of access points
- Encouraging the organisation of events that make networks visible, reinforce links and give people a sense of common identity

---

BOX 10.4   The benefits of social capital

In a study of three neighbourhoods as part of the evaluation of the UK government's neighbourhood management pathfinders, respondents identified the following benefits of work to build social capital:

- Greater trust and civic engagement can discourage anti-social behaviour and encourage the reporting of crime
- A higher level of trust and confidence in the area is more likely to reduce fear of crime
- Participation, social support networks and a greater sense of belonging can contribute to better health
- More willingness to engage in learning can lead to greater civic engagement, thus creating a virtuous circle.

Source: Taylor 2007b.

- Linking local networks into more formal organisations and linking these into outside organisations with resources and power
- Ensuring that expertise acquired in formal organisations and specific actions flows back into the community at large and is translated into the capacity to respond to further needs and opportunities
- Ensuring that information flows in and out of networks and that more formal organisations are accountable to the wider community.

This may feel like common sense: networking skills have rarely been codified. But notions of network development make hidden processes visible and more effective through being recognised, consciously deployed and recorded (Gilchrist and Taylor 1997).

However, informal networks can, by their nature be transient, as can the learning and dialogue that takes place within them (Taylor 2006, p. 336). Their capacity to act can be limited. Too heavy a touch risks distorting them and it is essential to avoid smothering them with unrealistic and inappropriate demands (Burns and Taylor 1998). Gilchrist also reports that 'a lack of clarity over remits and responsibilities can cause problems when there is much work to be done or competition for scarce resources' (2009, pp. 153–4). They have a limited capacity to deal with conflict and are easily overloaded with information. Thus, although networks are an invaluable springboard for collective action, it is formal organisations that allow communities to take sustained action and to achieve longer-term goals, to become active agents, to relate to external actors and make changes. Writing from a social movement perspective, Caniglia and Carmin (2005, pp. 202–4) argue that formal organisations are needed for a number of reasons: to mobilise people, to provide stability, to develop talent, and to enable maturation. The formality of clear roles and structures can also help to reduce conflict and ambiguity. Sidney Tarrow (1994), too, cautions us against looking entirely to networks for a way forward. The power of unincorporated associations, he argues, is limited. If communities are to become active agents, they need to channel the energy that can be generated through the myriad potential networks within them and take more formal action.

Tarrow argues that formal organisations are needed to provide the ability to take action and to be accountable to the wider
community for that action. But formal organisations still need
to remain embedded in informal networks, if the expertise that
they generate is to flow back into the community at large and to
be translated into the capacity to respond to further needs and
opportunities (Gilchrist 2009). Describing a 'women-centred'
model of community development, Smock highlights the importance of providing 'safe, nurturing spaces where residents can
gather, provide mutual support and build shared leadership'
(Smock 2003, p. 25). These can help to lubricate more formal
structures, acting as the breeding ground for engagement building the trust and motivation for action. Often people will attend
a meeting in the first instance because someone else has asked
them to (see Box 10.3). And whether they come back is likely to
be influenced by the social networking opportunities they find
there as well as more instrumental and personal development
goals. Informal networks also provide channels of accountability. As Gilchrist explains, people use their networks to check
things out and explore where people stand (2009, p. 108).

A variety of ways in

The discussion so far underlines the importance of a variety of
ways into engagement – formal and informal. Those who wish
to promote change need to be wary of putting all their eggs into
one basket, unless this basket is woven from the many different
strands that exist in any locality. Carl Milofsky (1987, p. 280)
argues that: 'Communities are knitted together with cross-
cutting and mutually supporting memberships in small voluntary organisations'. He likens communities to markets, arguing
that the maintenance of a particular organisation matters less
than the growth of overlapping networks that can hold organisational intelligence and from which more formal organisations
can spring. 'The greater the density of social networks in a community', he writes, 'the more likely that bystanders will be recruited to participate' (Milofsky 1987, p. 283). With Al Hunter
(1994), he argues that community capacity is based in 'a rich
supply of neighbourhood-based organisations' or background
communities, which store organisational experience, generate
social entrepreneurs and act as a 'Greek chorus', commenting

on and holding more formal organisations to account. What is important is not to keep one organisation going against all the odds but to build a store of 'organisational intelligence' on which communities can draw.

There are echoes here of Gramsci's call for multiple levels of leadership and initiative in challenging dominant hegemonies. Milofsky also cites Alinsky's argument that people become politically effective when they become part of an active community and not when they act only on one issue (Milofsky 1987, p. 281).

People need many different ways of engaging if the different needs and preferences of different parts of the 'community' are to be recognised. Meetings and events organised by adults are not likely to be attractive to young people (see Box 10.5). Meetings during the day exclude those who work in the day and vice versa. In areas plagued by racism, it is not enough for existing organisations to say they are open to anybody: people from ethnic minorities may only feel safe among others of their own ethnic group, at least in the initial stages of engagement (see Box 12.1).

Diverse activities allow people to engage in the ways that suit them best and with the people they feel most comfortable with. They build the patchwork of overlapping communities and ties that are needed to build resilience and embed strong organisations. It is from these beginnings that the confidence can grow to engage more widely and to find common ground with others (see Chapter 12). Offering a variety of ways into engagement also recognises the different places that people themselves are coming from: the different points they may be at in their empowerment journey, the different stages in their lives. Earlier in this chapter, I described how adult education provided a way into further engagement for many people in a South Wales community centre. In fact, for some people there, the journey to empowerment started even earlier in their contact with the centre. The community café there gave people a place where they could just drop in without having to make any further commitment. From there, however, they got the confidence to join in other activities in the centre. A community worker commented:

> If it's about education, only the educated come. Here they come for a cup of coffee.

Involving children can be a particularly effective way to spread involvement across communities as this can get parents interested

BOX 10.5   Defending Da Hood: involving young people

The project developed as the result of the escalating and gang-related stabbings and shootings that were taking place on local estates in London.

A systematic analysis was carried out to find out which young people were most 'hard to reach' and why. The programme was particularly sensitive to historical conflicts based on territorial claims (notably inter-estate gang battles). Then the project set up a series of consultation events – eight have been staged since September 2004 – attracting as many as 500 people at a time. Texting has been one innovative and successful method for informing young people about these forthcoming events. The events have been jointly funded by the police, the social landlords and the local council (at an average of £14,000 a time) and have provided an opportunity for agencies to hear the views of young people.

These (events) have attracted young people through entertainment and music, but always with the requirement that serious issues are discussed first and that agencies and partners listen. (local councillor)

As a result, the project has laid on opportunities for young people to learn about music and video production and helped a group of young people to set up and operate a radio station – Street FM Community Radio Station. Initially developed as a project to provide a focus for local youth and an opportunity to undergo accredited training, the radio station is now providing opportunities to build inter-generational links. An event was held at the end of 2005, where older residents had a meal cooked and served by local young people. It has also attracted national coverage, thus – in principle at least – beginning to break down external stereotypes about the neighbourhood and its young people.

Source: Taylor 2007b.

as well. In Plymouth, a town in the south-west of England, children were involved in the redesign of a run-down housing estate when local schools were encouraged to get involved in designing the security gates and an entrance mosaic for the estate (Watson

1994). Elsewhere children have been involved in environmental audits, planning and maintaining school gardens, and designing community newspapers and notice boards (Taylor 1995b). This can be particularly important in engaging with minority groups within the community.

Community arts, community video and community theatre have been powerful ways of involving people of all ages. Matarasso (2007, pp. 456–7) describes how they allow groups to define themselves and their beliefs, starting from their own experience, forms of expression and traditions. Community arts, he argues, have the power to lift people out of resignation, focusing on assets rather than externally imposed goals and definitions. They are a vehicle for building skills, confidence and social capital, helping to create and value individual and community identities. They can also be a means for people to broach taboo issues without risking punishment (Abah 2007). Kinloch (2007) describes, a youth-based project in Harlem, for example, that responded to the challenges of gentrification by studying different forms of Harlem art over the decades. This helped to redefine the neighbourhood, to reconnect with its history and spark debate between generations.

Urban design exercises have long used techniques such as 'planning for real', which involves building a model of the locality in a way that engages all parts of local communities (see Box 10.6). The highly visible and practical nature of such exercises brings in the professional and the amateur, the young and the old, the articulate and those who find speaking in public difficult.

Short-term activities, such as urban design exercises, community festivals and so on, act as recruiting mechanisms for informal and formal networks. But, maintained over the longer term, they help to maintain a broad base and provide a kind of social 'glue'. Few of these activities are 'rocket science', and they might not be the stuff of social transformation, but they may be the acorns from which oak trees can grow: the point at which the empowerment journey can begin.

All these approaches have been enhanced by the possibilities that the Internet has opened up. We are still learning about how its potential can be harnessed – especially by young people who have grown up in the Internet culture. As it stands in 2011, however, there can be little doubt that it is a powerful information resource, especially for communities have limited access to other

---

BOX 10.6   Placemaking in the UK

Around 180 residents in East Brighton, including 40 young people, were trained in action-planning techniques as 'barefoot urban designers'. Placemaking events were organised in 14 localities and run by residents. Each area:

- Identified priorities for projects and service improvements
- Provided a comprehensive photographic survey of the physical state of their neighbourhood, with pictures mostly taken by young people
- Recorded views of residents in pictures and words on the standard of local housing and environmental management services
- Identified initial ideas for spending £1000 on making their area 'cleaner, safer and more attractive'.

The event finished with a celebratory party at the local racecourse attended by about 450 people, which included an exhibition of the photographic survey with prizes awarded for the best photographs. Young singers and musicians from the area performed as part of the entertainment. The event was covered extensively by local radio, which later helped in the production of a CD containing residents' views and music. This was distributed to every home with the Spring issue of the local community newsletter.

The exercise was significant in building a broad picture of local aspirations and priorities, as well as in engaging people who had not engaged before. It was particularly successful in involving young people.

Source: Adapted from Capital Action 2001.

---

information channels. Local websites can provide virtual hubs where people can share information and find out what is going on. The Internet can also enhance deliberative forms of democracy, although it is likely to be most powerful when combined with face-to-face contact, where it can amplify the potential of a single or infrequent encounter. It can also build bridges beyond face-to-face communities – its value has perhaps been demonstrated most powerfully at the global level where it has allowed communities to learn from each other across continents and to mobilise against global institutions (see Chapter 12).

But research to date suggests it has its drawbacks – like most magic bullets. Technology, like any other resource, is distributed inequitably. A study by the Pew Internet and American Life Project, for example, argues that on conventional measures, the well-off and better educated are more likely to engage politically on the Internet than their peers (Smith *et al.* 2009). However, its authors do see this changing into the future with the increased use of social networking – which could become the great leveller. Nonetheless, from a governmentality perspective, virtual spaces can be 'governable spaces' colonised just like any other space by government (O'Donnell and McCusker 2007; Morison 2008) or by media barons and commercial interests. State censorship in some parts of the world means that the Internet it is not available to all. And even as a popular 'uncolonised' space, it does not guarantee quality of informed dialogue – Navarria (2008) warns against the shallow demogoguery that can be found there, highlighting issues of accountability, representativeness and transparency.

Time, resources and support

Establishing a range of informal and formal networks, building these into viable and sustainable organisations, building links across different interests: all this takes time and resources. There are few short cuts. One of the most successful initiatives in the research carried out by Annette Hastings and her colleagues in 1996 – in Wester Hailes in Scotland –was based on more than 20 years of activity. The study concluded that it took five years for an active community even to develop community networks to a stage where they could engage effectively in partnership (Taylor 1995b).

Resources need to match the task in hand. But the resources that make the difference between inactivity and engagement can sometimes be relatively small: enough to pay a telephone bill, hire a meeting place or organise transport. Community buildings can also make a lot of difference to a neighbourhood and provide a focus for activities, services and local identity. Buildings are important for communities of interest, too, which may be isolated within a particular neighbourhood.

As I suggested earlier, sustained and organised activity is likely to require dedicated community work support, especially in initiatives where there is little history of activity. The Plymouth example given earlier, for example, comes from an estate where residents successfully fought for their homes to be rehabilitated, despite local authority resistance. That they were able to do so, to develop their own plans and to hold their own in negotiations with outsiders, owed much to the full-time support that they received from an independent technical aid worker (Taylor 1995b). But groups can also benefit from a 'lighter touch' approach. In the second example described in Box 10.7, a UK Foundation provided a package

---

BOX 10.7   *Small grants with no strings*

The Community Chests and Community Learning Chests funded as part of the English Single Community Programme provided small sums of money to local organisations, many of whom were new or working with marginalised populations. Groups were supported in applying for funds, and helped to become formally constituted where necessary. Once funds were allocated, there were celebratory events in some areas, which brought beneficiaries together to find out what else was going on in and beyond their neighbourhoods. Sometimes too beneficiaries were recruited onto subsequent grants panels, which gave them both recognition and new skills.

In another initiative, as part of a package of support, community groups were given a line of credit which they could spend as they wished over a period of four years. This was spent in many different ways: on room hire for events, equipment e.g. tents and marquees for a festival, children's activities, accredited training courses, a planning application for a community building, software for a bilingual newsletter, expenses for travelling to conferences. One project used it to buy the shutters they needed for their community centre. A local facilitator remarked:

'The groups have used credit with only the smallest amount of control, very largely to good effect and often with remarkable ingenuity and significant visible impact, contrary to what people might have expected in such a relaxed funding regime.'

Source: CLG 2005; Taylor *et al.* 2007.

of credit, networking events and facilitation over four years. Even though the facilitators only had a maximum of 30 days allocated to any one neighbourhood over four years, groups valued having someone who knew their organisation 'on the end of a phone' when they needed help (Taylor *et al.* 2007). The long-term nature of the relationship allowed for the development of trust and also addressed a perennial problem with capacity building – that of finding ways to get beyond an organisation's immediate 'presenting problem' and work with it to understand its real needs.

Support in kind is also important. Service providers and other outside agencies can make it easier for residents to engage by disseminating information, providing meeting places, play areas, workshops and other public spaces where people can interact, and setting up 'coffee mornings' and events.

Designing in community

So far this chapter has discussed the ways in which change can be effected from within communities themselves. But policymakers have also looked to solutions that 'redesign' the community (see Chapter 3). These can take three forms. The first, in which communities are often involved and which they also often initiate, is to improve the physical environment, which can improve their sense of belonging and safety. The second is to change the population mix: this is generally a top-down solution, but where it works, it can break down stereotyping and the cycle of seemingly inevitable decline. The third is to develop the infrastructure and local facilities in ways that make communities into 'permeable places' (Forrest and Kearns 1999, p. 51), linking them with the outside world. While not sufficient to achieve change on their own, these policies can make a significant contribution.

Physical improvements

Physical improvements are often high on the agenda in disadvantaged and low-income communities. Physical neglect is the most visible sign of neighbourhood decline and a major factor influencing the public image of social housing estates. Images of boarded-up buildings and litter-strewn stairwells are a familiar feature of television police dramas, for example. Visible improvements can therefore 'have a disproportionate impact on creating a mood of optimism and on generating a feeling that the area has a future' (Forrest and Kearns 1999, p. 50). They can build trust and confidence among residents by making the neighbourhood look and feel safer (Taylor 2007b). But they are only likely to be sustainable if they are designed in response to, and in full consultation with, residents.

We have already seen in this chapter how design and physical improvement initiatives, such as urban design or 'planning for real', can engage a broad cross section of local communities. Design and planning has also been a major element in approaches to community safety. The residents who wanted to redesign their estate in the Plymouth example above worked with a community architect to find ways of changing the layout of the estate so that public space could be made visible and could be supervised (Watson 1994). But there can be a tension between the requirements of security and the design of a welcoming and attractive environment. In Plymouth, involving children in the design of new security gates on the estates was important in softening the negative image that security gates inevitably carry, but too much of an emphasis on security can create a forbidding environment and increase the fear of crime. It risks creating a fortress mentality that can reinforce the sense of stigmatisation and the negative image of the estate, as well as increasing suspicion.

Changing the population mix

Chapter 3 described early attempts in the UK to rebuild communities through slum clearance and the development of new towns. These days, a more familiar approach in the UK is that of 'tenure diversification', which seeks to break up large and easily stigmatised blocks of social housing into more mixed communities. This would seem to make a lot of sense. It is a policy with the potential to bring more income, skills and self-esteem into marginalised areas, as well as keeping economically active and ambitious residents in the area. It can reduce turnover and the number of empty properties. It also has the potential to develop the weak ties that the most marginalised residents need and can sustain, even create a demand for, better public services.

However, there are also some reservations. In a number of localities over the years, tenants have fought against the break up of their existing communities for 'redesign' purposes. On one estate in the early 1990s, a redevelopment to diversify tenure left the original tenants very unhappy: 'The community they fought so hard to preserve has been broken up; they are surrounded by private homeowners whose territory is marked off from their own with high fences erected by developers' (Hyatt 1994). Reducing physical distance did not reduce social distance (Pahl 1970).

Nearly 30 years later, Forrest and Kearns (1999) remained unconvinced of the merits of tenure diversification and argued that it could set up new divisions, with imaginary or even real brick walls between tenure types. Jupp's study of mixed tenure housing estates in the UK at the same time (Jupp 1999) confirmed that the links between people in different tenures were limited, although he argued that street-level mixing was significantly more effective than separating tenures in different zones within the neighbourhood. He also acknowledged that links might increase over time, arguing that community-based staff could help to increase links by identifying the issues that people from different tenures have in common and by fostering informal links. Certainly more recent experience is positive and also suggests that mixed tenure initiatives can address the increasing social polarisation associated with public housing. Martin and Watkinson (2003) find that, contrary to earlier studies, initiatives that extend the mix of tenures and incomes on social housing estates have consistently led to an improvement in property prices, lower turnover and increased demand for vacated homes. They have also led to higher levels of tenant satisfaction.

Allen *et al.* (2005) suggest that the evidence on whether tenure diversification improves the reputation of stigmatised neighbourhoods is mixed, arguing that 'tenure mix by itself will not will not guarantee the success of a development' (p. 4). Their study suggests that a lot depends on other factors, including the quality of the local environment and local services. The process of change also needs to be sensitively managed if it is not to be divisive, and to give adequate consideration to those residents who are going to be displaced. Of course, tenants do not have to be moved out of housing estates in order to diversify tenure: diversification can be achieved through giving tenants the right to buy or through transferring stock to different landlords. However, residents in hard-to-let estates often do not or cannot exercise their right to buy (in Power and Tunstall's 1995 study of 20 estates, only 5 per cent had chosen to do so). The success or otherwise of such schemes is likely to depend on the local context.

Creating 'permeable places'

Another approach – either separately or in parallel – is to promote physical and other ways of linking disadvantaged neighbourhoods back into their surrounding areas, in order to facilitate the development of bridging social capital and break down stereotypes. As we saw in Chapter 6, twentieth-century public housing is often on the periphery of cities, cut off from the surrounding area and from employment opportunities. Transport links are often poor. Policies are needed that will 'help expand the worlds of such areas' and give people from other areas reasons to go to such places (Forrest and Kearns 1999, p. 51), putting them on the map from which they have disappeared, creating passages in and through them, and improving the corridors between them and their surroundings. But regeneration and neighbourhood renewal policies rarely address this issue. Dean and Hastings (2000) make the point also that linking these neighbourhoods to the city will take more than physical changes, and they recommend active marketing policies to reverse negative images and stereotyping.

Summary

At the beginning of this chapter, I argued that the first step in empowerment is to build the confidence of the people who live in excluded communities, to realise the assets that already exist in the area but which are undervalued, to energise the networks and potential circuits of power that are latent within them, and to provide opportunities for learning and dialogue within and between communities. There are many examples in the literature and on the web of this kind of community learning and action, which builds on the capacities of local people or groups to offer modest local empowerment through shared activity and learning, as well as building links between communities. The strengths of this activity are the acknowledgement of local assets, the ability to start from small beginnings, the potential for involvement and ownership, and the fact that relatively limited resources can release considerable energies. It creates the spaces in which people's private concerns can become public, to use Bauman's phrase, and can also offer safe spaces where differences can be debated. Such empowerment, as Murray Stewart and I argued in 1995, is a positive-sum game: there need be no real loss of power by others and, while the power gained by communities is valuable, it is not threatening to stronger and more entrenched power structures. However, that last sentence also highlights the limitations of this approach. It does not address the more fundamental economic and structural processes or the deeper power imbalances that marginalise and exclude people.

Perhaps this can best be illustrated by returning to Clegg's 'circuits of power'. Empowering communities is not just a question of reactivating dormant or disused circuits within communities or even between them; it is also a question of connecting those circuits into 'more privileged pathways', which supply more sustainable reserves of power. An isolated generator can only do so much. If power is to flow through the system, these local circuits have to be linked into the social, political and economic circuits from which they have been cut off. How this might be done is the subject of Chapter 11.

Reclaiming Power

Once the foundation described in Chapter 10 has been developed, the process of change and empowerment will take different and overlapping forms. Communities may be empowered as *consumers* by having a greater say in the quality and delivery of services provided by others. They may become *producers and co-producers*, taking over the running of local services or developing other kinds of social enterprise. They may become involved as *citizens* in governance or partnership initiatives, working on an equal basis with other players to set policy agendas and to develop and implement policy. Or they may decide to take independent action, creating their own 'claimed spaces' (Cornwall 2004) to campaign for change from below. This chapter describes some of the different initiatives that have emerged in each case.

Communities as producers and co-producers

All over the world, communities have taken responsibility for meeting their own needs. In the US, community development corporations have given communities control over low-income housing and other forms of enterprise (see Chapter 3). In France, *Régies de Quartiers* are resident-led companies, which employ local residents and provide services in neighbourhoods, with the aim of both providing better, more responsive services and creating local employment for excluded groups within the communities they serve, especially the long-term unemployed and unqualified young people (Clark and Southern 2006). In Scotland, community-based housing associations have shown how communities can manage and turn around the most degraded low-rental housing. Elsewhere in the UK, there are growing numbers of community development trusts managing assets and providing services. Government policies in the UK have encouraged tenants to take over the management of their housing (see Chapter 3) and have for some time been promoting the transfer of service delivery to third-sector organisations, including communities, co-operatives and social enterprises. Recent policies are also encouraging the transfer of public assets – buildings and land – to third-sector organisations.

There is, of course, a long tradition of such initiatives in the South. UN, Commonwealth Foundation and other commissioned studies (Dey and Westendorff 1996; Goetz and Gaventa 2001) provide ample examples of initiatives where local communities have taken control of schools, rural forestry, village water supplies, health insurance, community managed sanitation systems, and so on. Some of the best-known success stories in this field are the micro-credit schemes that have developed in many countries in the South, although Chari-Wagh (2009) is critical of the failure of many such programmes to displace patriarchal structures or address the non-economic issues that perpetuate poverty.

Community-run enterprises have flourished in different contexts. In the US and in many parts of the South they have grown in response to the failure or lack of capacity on the part of the state to invest in social welfare. Conversely, in parts of mainland Europe, social co-operatives have flourished with state funding, sometimes because of the lack of capacity in the state to provide but also because of a solidarity-based ethos which supports the social economy – a paradigm that Evers and Laville (2004) contrast with the charitable ethos of the UK or the philanthropic, non-profit ethos of the US.

In the UK, Stephen Thake (1995) identified a number of catalysts for such enterprises:

- *A response to invasion* – enterprises formed in response to the threat posed by a major redevelopment programme (see Box 11.1) or a motorway through a neighbourhood
- *A response to violence* – enterprises formed following civil disturbance or in response to the threat posed by escalating crime
- *A response to withdrawal* – enterprises formed following the closure of factories, schools and other local services
- *A response to outside intervention* – bodies set up in response to (or as successors to) special government funding initiatives.

These enterprises may provide childcare or other caring services, environmental services, workspace, training, cultural activities, housing, enterprise development opportunities and/or credit. They may provide alternative energy, organise bulk buying of goods (food co-operatives) or provide services to local businesses (farm co-operatives). The development of community buildings offers opportunities for locally accessible sports, arts, and so on as well as a hub for local services. They can provide an umbrella or holding company for community-based, short-term, grant-aided projects that would struggle to obtain funding or survive on their own. They can also provide an intermediate labour market for people within the neighbourhood who have been out of work for some time and need work experience and skills.

Their income stream may derive from: charges for services and goods, charges for space, service contracts or assets, such as housing, against which they can borrow. In the US, low-income housing for families has provided the most sustainable asset base for community development corporations over the years and some of the most successful community development trusts in the UK also have a strong financial base in low-income housing and land, as Box 11.1 illustrates. In sympathetic environments, as we have seen, community enterprises are often supported by the state, especially at the development stage. In the UK, while many community development trusts are autonomous, others – especially those that were set up as a result of government funding initiatives in neighbourhood renewal – are constituted as partnerships with government and other partners, which may provide funding.

In many disadvantaged localities, resources flow out of the area: to loan sharks who charge exorbitant interest rates; to professionals who go home to somewhere else; to agencies based elsewhere; to businesses owned by outsiders, and so on. Similarly, many social inclusion initiatives place local residents with external employers. But community enterprises have the capacity to transform local economies, valuing work that has not been valued, keeping ownership of assets and resources in local communities, providing locally based services, circulating wealth and generating job opportunities within local communities (See, for example, Box 11.2). Local ownership taps the tacit knowledge of local people and their understanding, both of the needs and capabilities of local people and of local resources. By its nature, it gives communities more power over those services.

BOX 11.1   Community enterprise in London: a response to invasion

Coin Street Community Builders (CSCB) was set up as the result of a decade-long campaign by local residents in the 1970s against proposals for excessive commercial development in their neighbourhood. Helped partly by the antagonism of local government to the policies of the Thatcher era, the community was successful in securing the land in question for its own use. The freehold of the land was sold to CSCB and covenants were imposed which confined land use to the approved community scheme. CSCB borrowed the money from the Greater London Enterprise Board and the Greater London Council. The loan was charged and repayments made out of income from temporary usage of the site, principally car parking. Subsequently, CSCB has refinanced using bank loans charged against its developed properties.

Since 1984 CSCB has transformed a largely derelict 13 acre site into a thriving mixed-use neighbourhood with new affordable homes, shops, galleries, restaurants, cafes and bars, with a riverside walkway and gardens, sports facilities, a neighbourhood centre with a nursery and a range of programmes for local residents. It is a company limited by guarantee under UK

→

Support for community-run assets and enterprise is only one part of the growing interest in the 'social economy'. Initiatives that support more informal community activities and informal helping can feed into and supplement the conventional 'cash' economy (Atkinson 2000a) and provide people with a stepping stone into conventional work or alternatives for those outside the labour market. Indeed, Atkinson argues that a social exclusion discourse – which has largely denied the value of these non-traditional forms of work – needs to recognise the contribution these can make to 'a renewed sense of citizenship and participation in the wider society' (2000a, p. 1050). Williams and Windebank (2001, p. 17) agree, arguing that micro-level exchange helps develop the social norms and networks from which trust may derive.

law, established to 'provide public service otherwise than for gain' and has worked in partnership with a range of other bodies including commercial organisations in the area (including multinational companies). All of its Board members are local residents.

'Homes rather than offices' was a core objective of the original campaign and promotion of the housing co-operatives, by helping to create a stable and viable residential community, has been an integral strategy for regenerating the local economy. Membership of the housing co-operatives is restricted to tenants of each estate and Coin Street Secondary Housing Co-operative provides advisory, training and management services. There is also a quarterly South Bank Forum, to which all residents get a personal invite from the local MPs and ward councillors.

CSCB has also set up a number of autonomous local charities for which it provides accommodation and administrative and financial services. These include Coin Street Centre Trust, which oversees a family and children's centre, and a community and sports centre. Further developments are currently being planned.

Source: Tuckett (1988), interviews and Coin Street Community Builders (2010). A booklet on *Coin Street Community Builders: Social Enterprise in Action* is available from CSCB, G2 Oxo Wharf, Bargehouse Street, South Bank, London SE1 9PH.

At a time when both state and market welfare systems have been proved inadequate, the appeal of social enterprise to government is obvious – with its concept of a double or even triple bottom line, encompassing social and environmental as well as financial benefits. Some, as John Abbott remarks (1996, p. 41), might see community control of services and assets as the objective of all community empowerment processes – the top of Sherry Arnstein's ladder (see Chapter 8). Twelvetrees (1998b, p. xxiv) sees community ownership and economic development as a means of filling the 'massive and growing gaps resulting from [capitalist] development'; others take this argument further, pursuing it as a critical element in the search for alternatives to the capitalist system and as a means, in the wake of the 2009 global economic crisis, of developing a more civil and sustainable

---

BOX 11.2　Applying Community Economic Development principles to advocacy: The Philippine Women's Centre in Vancouver

The Philippine Women's Centre (PWC) was set up in 1989 in response to the increasing social and economic marginalisation faced by Filipino women who came to Canada in the 1980s to seek employment. It was part of a government programme to facilitate the entry of foreign nationals into Canada as live-in care givers. Aside from providing a space for support, PWC has been active in educating, mobilising and organising around human rights issues for immigrants and migrant workers. In 1995, it embarked on a community economic development pilot, which established five CED ventures: these include cooperative housing, a savings circle or 'paluwagan', a loan guarantee fund, an in-house arts and crafts store, and a catering service (run mainly by volunteers). Through these ventures, Filipino women are given the opportunity for affordable housing, sharing their resources collectively for mutual benefit, receiving training, and developing new skills through the catering service and arts and crafts store. Revenue from the two income-generating projects is directed towards salaries, workshops for members and travel to conferences. Partnerships with academic and legal groups have highlighted the position of immigrant women and raised awareness.

Source: Adapted from Lo and Halseth 2009.

---

economy (Commission of Enquiry into the Future of Civil Society in the UK and Ireland 2010). Community management and ownership of services can also challenge the accepted 'rules of the game' in service delivery by demonstrating 'the extent to which alternative delivery patterns, information generation systems, or client self-organisation, can result in more accessible, appropriate services' (Goetz and Gaventa 2001, p. 23).

While community enterprise and co-production are an essential part of the jigsaw of social inclusion, however, they are not sufficient. Firstly, where problems are complex, giving communities control of implementation without involvement in the wider policymaking process can become simply a form of government manipulation, dumping communities with problems others cannot solve. As Geoff Mulgan has argued: 'It is hardly progressive to distribute responsibilities to the powerless' (Mulgan 1991, p. 45). This is a particular concern given the context of major public expenditure cuts in many countries. In addition, the confidence, energy, time, political knowhow and money to take on these services are not equally distributed in society (NEF 2010) which means that the people who have least are likely to benefit least from a wholesale transfer of power and responsibility.

Giving people more control over their services is a great idea in principle. But Goetz and Gaventa (2001, p. 63) make the point that communities will not always want to run their own services: 'It must not be assumed', they argue, 'that citizens prize direct participation over the notion of improved responsibility and trusteeship amongst public service providers'. Sarah White (1996) echoes the thoughts of many when she asks why people in excluded communities are expected to participate when most of the rest of society is not. Most of us do not want to run all our own services; what we do want is to ensure that those who do provide them reflect our needs and preferences and also provide quality and choice. Excluded communities should not have to 'participate' in order to have the same claim on service quality and provision as other members of society have. The danger is that externally driven initiatives to encourage community management are forcing communities to manage their own exclusion, with the responsibility but not the resources or power to tackle local needs effectively.

On the other hand, it is important to recognise that many communities have made conscious choices to take on responsibility for local programmes. What might feel like dumping to one community may be empowerment to another. Ownership of assets also increases a community's leverage in local partnerships as it has something to bring to the table. Liz Richardson (2008, p. 239) argues that residents often feel disempowered by too much dependency on outside bodies. They recognise the limits of self-help, she argues, but feel they can offer something the state cannot provide. A community group is not sustainable if there is little or no demand for its services, so it has to have good intelligence gathering and stay close to the 'customer' (p. 158). Indeed some of the groups in her study prided themselves on the cost savings they were able to make. Local communities may also take a more robust approach to the 'wicked issues' of policy than professionals dare: 'residents have fewer qualms than professionals about discussing controversial measures like vetting social housing tenants, being tough on anti-social behaviour' and so on (p. 94). But they still differentiate between choosing to take on services and 'having to take up the slack from poorly performing public agencies' (p. 129).

A second point is that it is important not to romanticise community-run services. Community management of services may simply shift the line between those who are in control and those who are not. Whole communities do not run services and assets, and those community members who do end up running them may offer no more control to their service users than state or market providers do. Thus, one review of the US literature concludes that many community development corporations in the US have lost contact with their roots and their ability to represent neighbourhood interests (Murphy and Cunningham 2003, p. 40).

A third argument against relying too heavily on community-based enterprise is that it is unlikely to be able to reverse the tide of economic decline on its own. In the US, many low-income communities remain on the margins of the economy despite community economic development initiatives. Murphy and Cunningham's review suggests (2003, pp. 38–43) that the advances made by CDCs here have been mainly at the micro-level and offset by continued disinvestment and decline on the macro-level. They may still offer benefits to local people but ultimately they cannot overcome the contradictions within capitalism. This is a point developed by Stoecker (2007, p. 305), who argues that they can be diversionary, set up to deflect blame, and thus to fail:

> CDCs are grotesquely underfunded organisations working in disinvested communities requiring massive capital infusion. ... The media celebrate a single small initiative in a sea of decay and the public sees small CDC accomplishments portrayed as big victories and come to believe there is little need for their taxes or donations. Then they blame the CDC and their associated communities when redevelopment fails.

This theme is developed by James De Filippis who argues that, in the 1950s, community control became black capitalism: 'The radical potential of demands for black economic power ... became coopted into a debate about how best to reproduce capitalist practices in black urban neighborhoods' (2007, p. 30). He goes on to argue that, as state funding was cut, CDCs became more and more part of the American tradition of individual entrepreneurship but also that they became a 'shadow state', providing the goods and services that had previously defined municipal governments.

A fourth challenge is that of viability. However attractive they find the idea of running their own services, some groups find themselves overwhelmed by taking on these responsibilities, having underestimated what it involves. Similarly, assets can quickly become liabilities if they are buildings in poor repair or have no revenue stream to keep them going. In addition, small businesses of any kind have a high failure rate. The scope for economically viable small businesses in areas where there is limited spending power will itself be limited. Trying to combine commercial concerns, high public visibility and the local concerns of marginalised estates is a tall order:

> The things that make CDCs community-based (their smallness and community roots) inhibit access to the capital and expertise that comprehensiveness demands, while the community-based ideology in the CDC model promotes amateurism and volunteerism, isolating CDCs from capital actors and experts. (Stoecker 2007, p. 305)

A fifth and related challenge for community economic development initiatives is sustainability. A comparison between the UK and the US highlights the importance of a social investment infrastructure, a strong philanthropic tradition, and policies, such as the US Community Reinvestment Act, which encourage financial institutions to put money back into local communities. However, as we have already seen, in the US it is the provision of low-income housing that has been the centrepiece of local economic development, and even that success has been threatened, according to Zdenek (1998), by cuts in federal funding. The restructuring of the banking industry meanwhile means that the infrastructure of local banks, which used to be major partners in US community development projects, is being significantly eroded (De Filippis 2007, p. 329).

This picture of the challenges needs to be balanced by the successes of small community-based enterprises in many parts of the world – in parts of Europe, for example, where the social economy culture is strongly embedded, or in the global South, where governments may be weak and where international NGOs offer an alternative source of investment. And this is an area of activity that is constantly developing with innovative new ideas on social investment and community finance. Despite his criticisms of the CDC movement, De Filippis (2007) concludes therefore that the tension between the market and community practice principles is something that we must learn to live with.

However, the earlier discussion in this chapter reminds us that successful community enterprises are often dependent on the provision of public money either directly, through subsidised housing or through benefit payments. So, while there are many who have aspirations for community-based enterprises either to replace state services or to offer an alternative to the capitalist economy that has failed these neighbourhoods, experience suggests that, if community economic development is to scale up to any significant level, it paradoxically needs the state. This may threaten the independence of a community initiative, or mean that community economic development is dependent on a sympathetic administration. But in the past, community-based enterprises have been able to exploit different levels of state funding. The European Union has been a particularly important investor in the UK, for example.

Arguing for state support in these straitened times may seem optimistic, especially where many states see community enterprise as a way of cutting costs. But there are other arguments for state support. Twelvetrees (1998c) argues that it allows community enterprise and management initiatives to be integrated with income maintenance policies, thus making it easier for people to move from income support (or survival on the informal economy) into paid work. A further argument relates to equity. Community-based services cannot commit to universal coverage in service delivery in the way that the state can; they need to be part of a wider strategy. Choices also have to be made in the public sphere between the needs and claims of different communities. This is one of the tasks that democratic governments are elected to perform. Ultimately, the resolution of society's problems is a task that requires all the resources and skills within society and not one that should be left to the casualties of change. So while community economic development and management initiatives have an important part to play, community policies will need to engage all those whose actions and decisions impinge on the locality or who have resources to offer. The next part of this chapter explores how this can be done.

Communities as policymakers

Maximising new opportunities

Chapter 9 painted a rather pessimistic view of the progress of partnership and empowerment policies to date. Rather than opening up spaces for the kinds of communicative action and transformative power advocated by scholars from Habermas to Healey, research across many parts of the globe suggested that the discourse of partnership has not significantly shifted power relationships and continues to enshrine 'power over' rather than 'power to'.

There are alternative and more optimistic perspectives and it is these that will be the focus of the remainder of this chapter. It is easy to forget how far we have come. Chapter 9 reviewed the past and focused on the tensions and pitfalls of partnership but, for many, partnership has offered a genuine window of opportunity. Even if it has not transformed the nature of decision making, let alone the distribution of power, it has increased the leverage which community organisations have in relation to other partners, as well as the resources they are able to bring with them. The windows and doors that it has opened will not easily be closed.

I wrote in Chapter 7 of the potential for citizens and communities to become 'active subjects'. In his later work, Foucault wrote of the scope for resistance or 'immanent critique'. Bourdieu, too, recognised that 'the agent is not a mere bearer of the structure' (1990, p. 20), an analysis developed by Crossley's discussion of 'radical habitus' (2003). More recent research has endorsed this. Jones (2003, p. 594), for example, argues that 'communities ... must not be seen as inevitably co-opted and incapable of (re) learning different ways of acting and knowing'. He finds in his research that 'community groups have shown themselves to be quite capable of manipulating prevailing discourse to their own advantage' (p. 595). Writing from an Australian perspective, Larner and Butler (2005) too are sceptical of claims that local partnerships are merely an ideological shell for neo-liberalism (p. 100). They argue that the partnerships they study are reconstituting the state itself and mobilising new forms of expertise, approaches to social auditing and so on. Gilchrist (2009), meanwhile, draws on complexity theory to illustrate how community players can influence what happens in unpredictable ways. The strategic and practical task of community practice might therefore be to support the sector in finding ways to 'play the game' successfully, to understand how power is working and manipulate it more effectively, giving 'local people power to read the dynamics occurring in their localities and to "play" these dynamics rather than get caught up in them' (Ingamells 2007, p. 246).

The deliberative democracy initiatives described in Chapter 8 provide further opportunities for citizens to make an informed and considered input into policy. Used intelligently and put at the disposal of the people they aim to empower, they have the potential to give a voice to people who have not been engaged before, to raise awareness within communities and public authorities, and to develop dialogue between community members and professionals.

Many techniques have been developed to encourage dialogue and mutual problem solving between residents and professionals. Simple and common examples include 'goldfish bowls', where professionals observe discussions between community members and are then invited to respond, and 'decision wheels', which give residents the opportunity to put their concerns to a series of individual professionals in rotation and then to comment on the solutions they are offered. What is crucial about these methods is that they engage community members and professionals face-to-face in a problem-solving situation. Job titles are given a face; knowledge is demystified; professionals are exposed to the tacit knowledge of communities, which is given an equal value to professional knowledge; new questions are asked; informal contacts are made which can be followed up. Community players can bring new forms of expertise into governance spaces – as service users and providers. They provide new solutions based on common-sense principles (Richardson 2008, p. 94). They also develop their own expertise in the way the system operates – sometimes bringing a more holistic view of the world than insiders, who can remain trapped in their particular silo. In this way, professionals can be involved in the work of residents rather than vice versa.

It is worth elaborating further on some of the ideas that have been developed to engage communities and policymakers together in needs assessment and policy development. Legislative theatre, for example, allows community members to present their experience to professionals and engage professionals in debate over how the problems they raise can be tackled (see Box 11.3).

Citizens' juries, which we briefly visited in Chapter 8, bring a random sample of citizens together over a three-day period to debate a particular policy issue. They are given the resources to pull together relevant information, to call witnesses and debate the issues that arise, in sharp contrast to the one-off surveys or consultation meetings that sometimes pass as community involvement. While citizens' juries typically take place over an intensive three-day period the principles can be adopted in longer-term exercises, which do not require such intensive involvement, to give residents the lead in coming up with solutions for persistent problems (see Box 11.4).

Most consultation and partnership initiatives address the question: 'How can existing services and opportunities work better?' But approaches that start from communities address a rather different question, which is: 'How are existing services and jobs produced and controlled?' Ideally the two approaches need to be combined. Residents need to become co-producers alongside professionals in services and enterprises that are valued and invested in by society at large, and not just seen as the last resort for 'the poor'. Talk about 'top-down' and 'bottom-up', as Wilkinson and Applebee (1999) argue, needs to become obsolete and we need to find new ways of working in the middle ground.

However imaginative some of the exercises described above are, they are not enough. Carley and Smith (2001, p. 196) argue that temporary initiatives 'can divert attention from a real need for innovation and to make steady, incremental improvements in mainstream policies and practices in local government, as well as to institutionalise the role of the community in that process'. It was the linking of citizens' juries into the decision-making system in Germany (see Chapter 8) that gave them the potential to trigger change, which can be jointly owned.

BOX 11.3   Legislative theatre

Legislative theatre originated in Brazil and has been piloted more recently in the US and Europe as a means of involving communities in problem solving and policymaking. Communities devise a play about issues they feel are important to them. The play is then toured to accessible venues in that community where the audience is encouraged to stop the play and suggest changes to policy or community-led initiatives that would have a positive impact on the issues presented. It is this process of interaction and proposals for change which is a particularly distinctive feature of the approach. It is also used to encourage dialogue with policymakers and professionals. One example I have seen, for example, was presented by the 'Amazing Graces', a group of older women. It was based on the everyday experiences of an older woman leaving work and trying to survive on her pension as her health deteriorated. It highlighted the perversities of the benefits system, the way in which older women can be patronised by care workers and the growing marginalisation experienced by women after they have left the workforce, when families move away and so on.

'It was a great confidence boost for me. When we performed ... I felt proud, like I was home and I belonged somewhere. It was really good to be doing something you knew was going to make a difference' (performer).

'I've been there. You just showed me my life. It was brilliant the way it was so believable and really interesting to watch at the same time' (spectator).

'I thought it was a brilliant way of engaging people, very real, visual and easy to understand. I loved the way people were doing it instead of writing or reading about it. We need to do more of this, the time and labour involved reaped good stuff' (professional).

With acknowledgements to Novas Scarman.

Carley and Smith are critical not only of one-off or temporary initiatives, but also of the prescription of participation *only* to disadvantaged communities. Participation will not give these communities power, they argue, unless it is applied across the board: 'Decentralisation of power to residents will only really work when it is not temporary or a special case, but when it is a uniform policy throughout the local authority, to rich and poor neighbourhoods alike, so that a "culture of decentralisation" takes hold' (p. 196).

The last 20 years have seen a great deal of institutional innovation in this respect, where governments have created the space and legitimacy for people to engage in the policymaking process and audit government performance. Some examples were given in Box 8.1. Others include the Vigilance Committees, which have been set up in parallel to local elected bodies in Bolivia, women's budget initiatives at provincial and local level in South Africa and Uganda (Goetz and Gaventa 2001), efforts to give women a greater voice in Indian local government and health-watch committees in Bangladesh (Cornwall 2008b), and Circles of Change in the US (Box 11.5).

Perhaps the most famous example is participatory budgeting (see Box 11.6), an initiative that began in Porto Alegre in Brazil, but has since spread both within Brazil and to many other countries.

So how far do these initiatives address the challenges posed by Chapter 9? Research in Europe suggested that applications of participatory budgeting here fall short of the Porto Alegre example, with politicians still having the major voice (Grimshaw and Lever 2009, p. 8), while in England a government minister's description of participatory budgeting as 'community kitties' reveals that the budgets involved have often been small and peripheral. However, even if change from these and other initiatives is not transformational, there are many examples in the literature of incremental improvements that have made a considerable difference to individuals and communities (Richardson 2008; Gilchrist 2009). Citizens – and their partners – gain new skills and knowledge (Butcher *et al.* 2007). The opportunities for face-to-face contact in these initiatives break down stereotypes and can build trust, even in the most difficult partnership arenas (Friedmann 1998, p. 32). Abers (1998, p. 60) writes of the participatory budgeting experience in Porto Alegre that: 'the longer groups work together, the more often co-operative attitudes will guide their decisions'. As it builds up a momentum, participation, she argues, 'can have a cascade effect' (p. 63). Even in the

---

BOX 11.4   Involving professionals in the work of residents: neighbourhood management in East Brighton, UK

When neighbourhood management was introduced into East Brighton, we looked for a way of demonstrating to residents how it could work and why they should be involved. We brought together some 20 residents for a morning to consider an issue that they defined as top of their agenda: abandoned cars. In their neighbourhood, cars were often dumped on the kerbside by people who could not afford to have them towed away or by kids who had taken them for a joyride. They stayed there for weeks, gradually being stripped of anything useful that could be removed and acting as a magnet for bored and disaffected young people; often they ended up being set on fire.

Residents worked in small groups to identify the problems that arose out of the simple fact of dumping a car on the street. They decided which agencies needed to be involved and worked on a series of recommendations for those agencies, thinking also about what local residents could contribute to a solution. Three professionals were on tap to answer questions and act as a sounding board to test out whether proposed solutions might work: a local police officer, a community safety officer, and a local manager from the environment and housing department.

→

---

least promising circumstances, respondents in research on an English participation initiative (CLG 2005) suggested that:

> The very fact of being in the same room talking has meant a slow development of trust between the council and the community sector.

Contacts made in formal settings build up valuable linking social capital, which can lead partners to engage with community players in other settings, creating more pathways through which power can be accessed (CLG 2005). As Hickey and Mohan have reminded us, 'not all local elites and power relations are inherently exclusive and subordinating' (2005, p. 15). There

There was a real buzz around the room and very positive feedback at the end. The day produced: a series of viable proposals to tackle this issue; a sense among residents that they had really been listened to, but also that they had found out a number of things they did not know before; and, crucially, a number of residents who felt they now understood more about neighbourhood management and who were interested in getting more involved. It also produced a set of proposals for training and support. As a result, the Community Safety Team took action on a number of the issues raised: running an unwanted car amnesty; removing abandoned vehicles within 24 hours; changing the way abandoned vehicles were notified of removal, in order to draw less attention to them; working with the vehicle licensing authority to take action on unlicensed vehicles. New links were made between agencies that could work together to address the problem (a recycling agency and the firm that tows the cars away, for example).

The key success factors were:

- Residents in the driving seat in the search for solutions, but with access to the relevant professional expertise
- Working in small groups so that everyone had a chance to have their say and with facilitators in each group who made sure that everyone was heard in the final plenary (those who came were by no means all known community leaders)
- A clear output, which residents could monitor in order to see if anything would change as a result, and on which service providers could make quick progress.

are allies within the system and the community discourse in policy has strengthened their hands (Taylor 2007a). Indeed, some share values, ideals, prejudices and social networks with community players – 'a far cry from the dull or instrusive bureaucrat' (Cornwall and Coelho 2004, p. 7). For some of these allies, support from communities gives them the leverage they need to create change in their own institutions.

The evidence thus endorses Cornwall's observation (2004a, p. 9) that:

New participation programmes acquaint people in government with the business of making accommodations, while

---

BOX 11.5   Dialogue and deliberation in Wisconsin

In Eau Clare, Wisconsin, US, the local government organised
Circles of Change, a series of community roundtable discussions
on racism and human rights. The focus was to provide ways
fordiverse groups of citizens to engage in public conversations
about perspectives and experiences of racism and to develop a
list of suggestions for community action. The planning group included the city manager and assistant manager, staff from the local university and schools, leaders from the Hmong Mutual Aid
Association, college students and interested citizens (recruited
through public advertisements). The Circles of Change initiative
trained 35 volunteer facilitators, recruited 135 economically and
racially diverse citizen participants, organised 15 separate discussion groups, prepared booklets to guide the discussions and
organised community-wide events to focus public attention on
racism and discrimination concerns in the community. The City
Manager said:

*Citizens needed safe public spaces where they could share personal
and sometimes searing experiences and perspectives in the context
of public policies and issues ... For me the key learning outcome
was the recognition of the power and impact of citizens participating in small group settings where everyone speaks. Traditional
government public hearings in large audiences cannot achieve
this.*

Source: Citizenship Development Research Centre and Logolink 2008.

---

people in the voluntary and community sector gain skills,
confidence and understanding of how to work with government, lessons that may stand them in good stead in other
arenas. The difference this may make ... may be incremental
but it is not inconsiderable. ... Even where institutionalised
participation has little or no policy efficacy, there are tactics
to be tried, alliances to be built.

But larger gains are possible too. Gaventa (1998, p. 52) argues
that in the 1970s, despite its early demise, the US War on Poverty left a significant legacy in the communities where it had

BOX 11.6 Participatory budgeting in Brazil

Participatory budgeting involves three parallel streams of meetings: neighbourhood assemblies, 'thematic' assemblies and meetings of delegates for city-wide co-ordinating sessions. These meetings continue throughout the year. The first stream discusses fund allocations among 16 districts or neighborhoods of the city for the usual departmental responsibilities, such as water supply and sewage, street paving, parks and schools. The district-based meetings begin with 16 'great assemblies' in public places, including union centers, gyms, churches, clubs and even a circus tent.

The city government's 'Presentation of Accounts' from the previous year marks the beginning of events every year. The government also presents its investment plan for the current year, as decided in the previous year's meetings. Then a debate starts for the next year. The debates continue for nine months and each district gives two sets of rankings, one set for requirements within the district (such as pavement, school construction or water lines), and the other set for efforts which affect the whole city (such as cleaning up the beaches). A public debate decides the criteria for allocating investment budget among districts. These criteria can be population, an index of poverty, a measure of shortages (such as a lack of pavement or the lack of a school), the assigned priorities and so on.

Source: World Bank 2010c.

been located: 'The policy intervention helped to galvanise the formation of new local groups and leaders, who would continue to organise self-help and other non-governmental efforts for the next two decades'. This is a view confirmed by Marris and Rein (1967, p. 223; see also Chapter 14) who argue also that the benefits went beyond particular communities, stimulating 'a realignment of resources and ideas which informed future programmes and reforms. O'Connor (2007, p. 23) adds that it was grass-roots organising that achieved legislative change which forced financial institutions to be more transparent about their practices in disadvantaged neighbourhoods through the Mortgage Disclosure Act and the Community Reinvestment Acts of the mid-1970s.

Alternative spaces

Dilemmas remain, however. One is that even the more success-ful initiatives run up against the 'paradox of empowerment' that I referred to earlier in this book. If one party can 'empower' another, does that imply that it has superior power and could equally take that power away again? A second dilemma is that partnership practice on the ground is patchy. In the UK, as in other countries, local authorities and government departments can vary quite markedly in their willingness and capacity to implement the rhetoric of participation and policy initiatives handed down from above. A third dilemma is that, by learning to play the game, communities may find themselves co-opted into agendas and ways of operating dictated by external actors.

It is for these reasons that partnerships and similar initiatives must build on the firm community foundation outlined in Chapter 10. In previous chapters I have referred to the distinction made by Cornwall and colleagues at the UK-based Institute for Devel-opment Studies between 'invited' spaces, shaped by external actors, and 'popular' or 'claimed' spaces, shaped by communi-ties themselves. Gaventa (2005, p. 38) argues the need for an effective countervailing power to hold those operating in invited spaces to account. Without popular, autonomous spaces, the new invited spaces of participatory governance 'might simply be captured by the already empowered elite' (p. 36). He goes on to suggest that it is at the interstices between 'popular' and 'invited' spaces that new possibilities for action, engagement and change reside. Fraser similarly argues that marginalised groups may find greater opportunities for exercising their voice through creating their own spaces, which she calls 'subaltern publics'. These spaces allow communities to withdraw and regroup, and can act as training bases for community action directed towards wider publics (Fraser 1992, p. 124, cited in Cornwall and Coelho 2004, p. 18). Indeed, Rose (1999, p. 279) sees these subaltern forces – those that, as he puts it, refuse to codify themselves – as offering the most hope for alternative futures.

There is much to be learnt from social movement theory in de-veloping strategies for change from below. Social movements can, after all, be seen as 'natural experiments in power, legitimation and democracy' (Crossley 2003, p. 9). They mobilise people; they reframe agendas and public debates; they push the boundaries of the do-able and say-able (Craig *et al.* 2004). Describing events in the 1980s in Hungary during the Soviet era, Ewa Kuti (1999, p. 4), explains that intellectuals and professionals found a way of working at the boundaries of the possible: 'They went beyond the actual legal and political bounds very rarely, but frequently reached and sometimes managed to broaden them'. Melucci (1988) describes how social movements challenge hegemonic power by advancing alternative frameworks and revealing the paradoxes within existing systems of power. They expose the shadowy zones of invisible power and silence that a system and its dominant interests tend to create. 'Power which is visible' he argues (1988, p. 250), is also negotiable, 'since it can be confronted and because it is forced to take differences into account'. Movements also carry cultural capital through their symbols, repertoires and images, and provide a political education – their fields of contention provide the support networks, social events and 'pedagogic agents' through which knowledge, commitment and reflexivity are conveyed, reproducing radical culture across historical time (Crossley 2003, p. 56).

Thus, at a local level, social movements create 'a space where members of local communities are given the opportunity to articulate their contradictory experiences and understandings of the world' (Popple and Shaw 1997, p. 194). They create change by identifying windows of opportunity in the system, by mobilising supporters and by reframing existing debates and agendas in a way that admits previously excluded issues into the decision-making arena. Merely placing such issues on the agenda 'in an expressive and challenging way – at least in liberal democratic states – enables coalitions to form around them' and allows these new issues 'to be aligned within general cultural frames' (Tarrow 1994, p. 185). As such they challenge dominant narratives and tackle the all-important issue of the management of meaning, which has been a theme of the discussion of power in this book.

The importance of discourse and narratives is emphasised by a number of other writers. Bourdieu (1990, pp. 54–5) draws attention to 'the power of naming, which by naming things brings them into being' (see Chapter 7). He cites as an example the way that people accept the frequent assertion by politicians that 'Public opinion is in favour of X or Y ... without any question as to whether there is such a thing as "public opinion"'. But he argues that 'words to a great extent make things and that changing words and, more generally representations ... is already a way of changing things'. Rappaport (1998, p. 237) illustrates the importance of developing a community narrative of change with an example of community-led action on health in Champaign-Urbana in the US. He describes how community activists succeeded in expanding the coverage of a local hospital, challenging policies on psychiatric patients' records, increasing the availability of prenatal care and improving services for older people. Crucial to the success of their action, he argues, was the way it provided: 'a powerful community narrative, available to many of the area's least powerful citizens as a story they could can personally join in'. The growth of the mental health service survivors' movement worldwide provides another powerful example.

It is also possible to resist existing systems by parody (for example, working to rule), or by refusing to acknowledge the games that more powerful players think they are playing and resisting the meanings that are implied by their moves. I referred in Chapter 10 to the role of the arts in freeing up people's voices. Branagan (2007) describes how humour can be used to subvert power. Nick Deakin (2001, p. 118) similarly describes how dissidents in Hungary in the 1980s resisted the system by engaging in what he calls 'sceptical manoeuvre' and refusing to play the game, for instance, by failing their examinations in the Russian language.

Social movement theorists emphasise the importance of networks in developing narratives of change. Citing Laguerre (1994), Gilchrist acknowledges that networks can be used to suppress views that question prevailing assumptions but she argues that they are also the mechanisms by which subversive ideas circulate, gather momentum and finally surface to challenge the status quo (2009, p. 63). But Sidney Tarrow (1994) laments the failure of social movements to turn the free spaces that they create into permanent places. He argues that a key element in the decline of movements is disputes over tactics, as some militants insist on radicalising their strategy, while others seek to consolidate their organisation and deliver concrete benefits to supporters.

Nonetheless, Jenkins (2001) argues that social movement activity provides a powerful counterweight to the dangers of co-option. He describes how civil society organisations in Costa Rica and South Africa avoided co-option during their transitional periods and developed their own momentum in the context of partnership and similar initiatives. What made this possible, he argues, was their ability to link into wider urban social movements, which could underpin more localised action. This has been a critical force in Latin America too, where research suggests that the sense of 'radical habitus' and the cultural capital that Crossley (2003) writes about is still strong (Pearce, Howard and Bronstein 2010; Taylor, Howard and Lever 2010; Pearce 2010).

I suggested in Chapter 9 that, in the UK at least, the traditional class-based movements, where community players could find their voices and develop their political skills at local level, are disappearing. However, it is not possible – or indeed wise – to try to reinvent the past. Carley and Smith (2001, p. 187) argue that these traditional movements cannot articulate the increasingly diverse interests in society and that new social movements have moved into the space they have vacated. So what are these alternatives and what is their potential to provide an alternative field where local communities can develop Crossley's more radical habitus?

One new arena that has attracted a lot of attention is the global anti-capitalism movement. Globalisation is often seen as the villain of the piece in tackling social justice issues. But Sending and Neumann (2006) argue that this is an arena where non-state actors play an increasingly powerful role, not least because there is no state as such – or at least the state is more fragmented. Globalisation from below has challenged globalisation from above not only through the high-profile demonstrations at meetings of world leaders, but also through the myriad less publicised but equally powerful connections made over the Internet between communities in North and South. Globalisation from below presents organisational challenges, but Michael Edwards (2004, p. 106) describes how 'the global justice movement has been particularly innovative in developing new and less hierarchical structures and organising techniques across borders', although he adds that 'it remains to be seen whether these innovations will generate any consensus at the level of specific policy alternatives'.

If there are new possibilities at global level, where are the alternative spaces to be found in local neighbourhoods? New social movements tend to be issue specific and operate on a larger scale, although transition towns and other environmental movements have taken to heart the mantra: Think Global, Act Local. I have mentioned the survivors' movement in mental health and disability movements, and there will be common ground between these and the wider community on some but not all of their issues. In the past, community development workers have played an important role in opening up spaces for independent learning, action and debate at neighbourhood level (see Chapter 3), but the scope for this has diminished with more instrumental job descriptions and target-driven programmes (Gilchrist and Taylor 2011). Some of the more radical approaches to capacity development offer an alternative. Value-based civil society organisations like PRIA in India, the Industrial Areas Foundation and the Center for Community Change in the US and Civic Driven Change in the Netherlands have country or world wide

---

BOX 11.7   Civic Driven Change in the Netherlands and beyond

The Civic Driven Change Initiative is a collective effort to explore and communicate a perspective of change in societies that stems from citizens rather than states or markets. It was initiated by a group of Dutch private aid agencies (Hivos, Cordaid, ICCO Oxfam-Novib, SNV, IKV-Pax Christi, Context) and is co-ordinated and hosted by the Institute of Social Studies (ISS) in The Hague (Netherlands). Its premise is that mainstream aid development interventions do not address the underlying systemic problems that keep the majority of people in poverty and unable to influence change. Civic Driven Change proposes concerted programmes of action that can generate new methods and a new language of civic action to help (re)claim citizen control of the institutions that influence their lives. The logic of capacity building in these terms is that of strengthening citizenship and civic agency to engage in local, national and global governance for the deepening of democracy.

Source: Howard *et al.* 2009.

programmes working with communities for change (Howard *et al.* 2009) (see Box 11.7). But their reach is still limited.

Faith organisations can be another focus for change, especially in minority ethnic communities. They have been key players in Saul Alinsky's model of citizen organising, for example, whose aim is to build power organisations that 'teach politics in action'. This is a model of citizen organising that builds agendas from within communities rather than responding to those from outside, forming alliances that can transcend parochial concerns. Its key players have been dismissive of partnership:

> Politics is strife, struggle, pain and angst. This model of citizenship that we are being offered through the government system and the paraphernalia of curriculum machinery never talks about struggle – it never talks about power either. The one word you won't find in any of the literature is power. We find the language of partnership instead. That is anathema to us because we've seen the partnerships, we've tried them. ... If you haven't got the same power, it's a fallacy. ... So we try to avoid partnership until we can get into an equal power relationship when maybe something can be done. (Author's unpublished research)

Nonetheless, this approach, the origins of which lie in 1930s Chicago, has gained momentum again over recent years, thanks in part to the role that citizen organising played in Barack Obama's rise to power in the US. In the UK, it has attracted the attention of the new coalition government, which – inspired by the success of London Citizens (see Box 11.8) – has stated its attention to train 5000 community organisers over the coming years. Critics suggest, however, that the intention behind this initiative is more to get communities to run services than to foster the kind of challenging voices Alinsky had in mind.

The Alinsky model has its limitations. One, according to De Filippis and Saegert (2007, p. 160) is that its principal organising base around faith groups can leave those who are not organised outside the loop. The basic community development is taken as read, in theory if not always in practice. Nonetheless, it can be a powerful anchor and a foundation, as we shall see in Chapter 12, for scaling action up from the very local onto the national and international stage.

BOX 11.8   Community organising in the Alinsky tradition

The **Industrial Areas Foundation** in the US is based on the writings of Saul Alinsky and emphasises the need to link intensive grass-roots support with national campaigns that can address the wider causes of exclusion. It is strongly linked with religious congregations and looks beyond the community to build coalitions with social movements, the labour movement and so on. It is 'proudly political' and works with power and social change to identify, recruit, train and develop leaders, through a foundational 10-day training programme plus tailored training as needed.

London Citizens is part of the IAF family. Its membership of some 150 organisations with some 50,000 members overall includes school groups, mosques, churches, students, university facilities and race-based organisations from across London. Its public meetings have been described as part Question Time, part civics lesson, part high-school talent show, all delivered in the style of a pentecostal sermon. Campaign goals are decided democratically over many months of one-to-one meetings and assemblies with members. Current campaigns focus on a 'living wage', affordable housing, making the 2012 Olympics work for citizens, an amnesty for long-term undocumented migrants, an anti-usury campaign, and immigration and asylum. It has a strong relationship with the Mayor's Office in London and considerable purchase with all three major political parties.

Source: Howard *et al.* 2009; Open Democracy 2010; London Citizens 2010.

So should communities 'play the game'? Or should they organise to confront the system from outside? I will return to this question in Chapter 12.

Discussion

Chapters 10 and 11 have outlined the potential for communities to take power as co-producers, citizens and consumers. Chapter 10 underlined the importance of building a foundation for change by releasing and building community capacity, whereas this chapter has described different approaches to community control. It has described how communities seek to take control of their own services and goods as an alternative to poor quality and under-provision by the state and the market, and also how communities engage with other players to achieve change, either in response to opportunities created from 'above' or by pushing for change from 'below'. In Figure 11.1, I represent this as an empowerment 'tree'. The roots of change at Level One are the learning, networking and organising opportunities described in

FIGURE 11.1 *An empowerment tree*

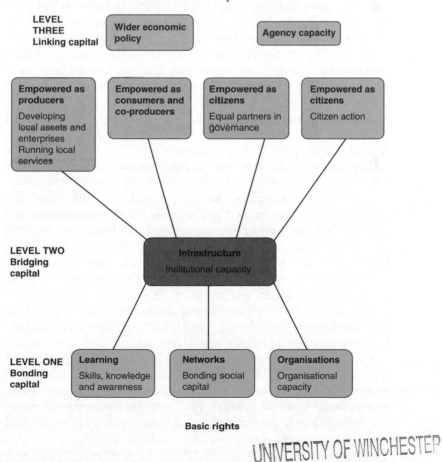

LEVEL THREE
Linking capital

Wider economic policy

Agency capacity

Empowered as producers

Developing local assets and enterprises
Running local services

Empowered as consumers and co-producers

Empowered as citizens

Equal partners in governance

Empowered as citizens

Citizen action

LEVEL TWO
Bridging capital

Infrastructure

Institutional capacity

LEVEL ONE
Bonding capital

Learning

Skills, knowledge and awareness

Networks

Bonding social capital

Organisations

Organisational capacity

Basic rights

Chapter 10, the variety of local facilities and activities that build social capital and encourage individuals and groups to set out on their various empowerment journeys. It is from these roots that communities develop their own collective stories or 'narratives' – a shared understanding from which they can either create their own solutions or engage with external actors on their own terms (A version of this tree, emphasising the relationship between the different forms of social capital appears in Taylor 2006).

Some groups will not wish to move beyond Level One, but their members will nonetheless improve the quality of their life by engaging at this level and will also benefit directly from activities at other levels. However, the individual and collective capacity – or human, social and organisational capital – that is created here feeds energy and knowledge up to Level Two – the trunk of the tree. It is here that bridging social capital is built and institutional capacity developed, creating an infrastructure that links the different activities and energies together to achieve common ends. This institutional capacity provides the basis on which community members can move through into Level Three – the branches of the tree – to take charge of their own futures, run their own services, develop their own economic enterprises, engage with outside agencies and other communities, whether of territory or locality, to achieve change, or develop radical alternatives, building from the community out.

The health of the tree will depend on its environment. The soil in which it grows needs to be favourable to its development. I have suggested several times in this book that individual empowerment must be rooted in the basic political, economic and social rights that underpin citizenship. It is also important that the roots are fed continuously or else the structure above them will die. The trunk needs to be firm and well embedded. The air around the tree must allow it to breathe and flourish. It is most likely to thrive in an environment that tackles the structural causes of exclusion and brings excluded communities back into the mainstream, and where professionals, agency and politicians have the capacity to engage effectively with it.

The progression through these levels is not a straightforward one. The contradictions of community and the paradoxes of power discussed in previous chapters mean that, although ideas of community, social capital, participation and empowerment are tremendously important in tackling social exclusion and disadvantage, they also contain within them tensions that are extremely difficult to resolve (see Chapter 9). If these tensions are to be addressed, communities and agencies need to develop not only individual and organisational capacity, they need to develop the infrastructure and the institutional capacity to grapple imaginatively with these tensions. The next two chapters will address these issues in more depth, unpacking some of the tensions and considering how to develop the infrastructural and institutional capacity within communities, agencies and institutions to make community policies and practice work effectively for change.

Chapter 12

The Challenge for Communities

In previous chapters, I have identified a number of tensions within community policy and practice: between cohesion and diversity, integration and difference; between leadership, representation and participation, inclusion and effectiveness; between negotiating on the inside with the danger of incorporation, or campaigning from the outside with the danger of irrelevance. This chapter discusses the challenges these tensions pose and considers how they can be addressed. It also considers a further challenge, which is that of 'scaling up'. By this I mean developing the links between different communities that will enable them to support each other and to address issues beyond the neighbourhood at different levels of government. Addressing the problems of disadvantage and social exclusion is something that needs action beyond the neighbourhood if change is to be achieved. Communities need therefore to engage with other communities, whether of locality, identity or interest, if they are to make a lasting difference. All this needs an effective infrastructure, which can mediate difference and channel a diversity of voices into the policy process.

Reconciling cohesion and diversity

Community action and organising has strong roots in difference. Chapter 3 described how racial tension had been a trigger for the development of community policies in both the US and the UK in the 1960s – a Conservative minister at the time in England acknowledged as much by giving a major urban policy paper the title: 'It Took a Riot'. I also described how community practice and community action drew inspiration from the civil rights and feminist movements. In the UK in the 1980s, traditional forms of community practice faced a strong challenge, first from feminists and then from BME groups. For these challengers, the assumption that there was an identity of interest within

240

communities institutionalised a white male view of the world. Later the disability movement and gay and lesbian organisations highlighted the exclusion within communities of place, identity and interest of people whose abilities and sexuality did not match the norm. Some UK local authorities channelled funds into these organisations both to promote equal opportunities and as a strategy to gain community support in their resistance to Margaret Thatcher's right-wing agenda.

It would have been difficult for community practice and policy in any country to ignore the racialised nature of exclusion or any of the other 'durable inequalities' that have persisted and been actively maintained through changing economic and political circumstances (Tilly 1999). But the rise of a politics of identity within community practice in the 1980s also reflected the emergence of 'new social movements' based on identity, along with the decline of older movements based on class. It was becoming clear that 'the emancipation of the "working class", even if it were achievable, would not, of itself bring an end to social divisions and conflicts' (Butcher and Mullard 1993, p. 228). There was no longer one narrative within excluded communities, if indeed there had ever been.

This new politics not only challenged the dominant pluralist paradigm in community practice and policy, with its social democratic vision of reality. Popple and Shaw (1997, p. 194) describe how it also challenged the structuralist paradigm for its class reductionism and its emphasis on the labour movement as the 'sole agent of revolutionary social change'. They describe how feminist critics focused attention on the personal and on the need to work with process as well as task, and how disabled people attacked dependency-creating models of disability. These critics forced community policy and practice to confront the diversity, conflict and contradictions within the 'myth of community' (Guijt and Shah 1998a).

In subsequent years, urban renewal policies have recognised the need to consider 'communities of identity' as well as 'communities of place'. Governments in many countries have introduced equalities policies, frequently based on rights. But the hysteria whipped up against refugees and asylum seekers in recent years, the rise of far-right political parties and the reprisals faced by Muslims in predominantly non-Muslim countries after the events of 11 September 2001 bear testament to the continued challenge of this agenda. As cities become 'superdiverse', racism is alive and well but also more multifaceted, as are many of the other forms of discrimination and prejudice that the movements discussed here were set up to confront. Communities already alienated from mainstream society can be a fertile breeding ground for myths and mutual suspicion.

Helen Meekosha (1993, p. 179) has drawn attention to the fundamental paradox in attempting to address an agenda of equality and social justice through collective action. She argues that any attempt to address commonalities undermines attempts to discuss difference and vice versa. Minority groups, she argues, have been attempting to work through these contradictions (often with considerable trauma) since the 1970s. Against a background of state withdrawal from welfare, the contradictions have become sharper as groups are set against each other in the competition for scarce resources, creating a situation in which: 'ever more tightly delineated minorities and sectors of society experiencing discrimination are channelled into organising the provision of specific, usually volunteer operated services' (Meekosha 1993, p. 185). In countries where the state has never been the main provider, Gilchrist observes a similar reluctance to network because of pressure to secure funding from international NGOs (2009, p. 154).

A consumerist model of competing interest groups reinforces divisions and the sense that power – even within communities – is a zero-sum game. An insistence on representing separate interests can also be highly vulnerable to manipulation or 'outflanking' (Clegg 1989, p. 122) by power holders wishing to 'divide and rule', thus dissipating community power. Richard Rorty (1998, p. 88) states this more graphically, claiming that the bottom 75 per cent of Americans and the bottom 95 per cent of the world's population are kept busy with ethnic and religious hostilities, while the elite claim to be impartial judges and promoters of equality between the clashing clans (cited in Bauman, p. 104).

In the 1990s, Meekosha welcomed the decisive challenge that identity politics threw down to an ethnocentric tradition within mainstream community work theory and practice both in the UK and elsewhere in the 1970s. Theorists within the feminist and civil rights tradition provided a new dynamism at the time. But, with Cockburn (1991, p. 212), she warned of the consequences of setting empowerment strategies 'adrift in a sea of relativity'. More recently, O'Connor stressed the need to recognise the complexity of this agenda. Solutions to racial tensions, she argued, 'need to move beyond the simplistic black-white dichotomy to investigate how racial barriers operate across ethnic, class and gender divides' (2007, p. 26).

Some share Meekosha's concerns about the fragmentation inherent in identity politics. In 1990, Miller and Bryant argued that this emphasis on difference, while it was promoted in the name of empowerment, may have 'led to increased levels of conflict, hostility and resentment between social groups who otherwise share a common material existence' (Miller and Bryant 1990). This is 'community' understood as Us and Not Them, with fears of identity loss in one community finding their expression through fear and hatred of other groups (Young 2007, p. 283) – an easy and tangible target and the more so the further down the pecking order they are. Thus, as we discussed in Chapter 5, insecurity translates multiculturalism into multicommunitarianism (Bauman 2001, p. 141) and exclusion breeds exclusion.

Several commentators – including Meekosha – warn that too much emphasis on difference and on separate individual and group rights also moves the spotlight away from the wider structural issues that cause economic, political and social exclusion and masks the need for fundamental economic reform. Diversity is essential to a healthy and sustainable ecology in human as well as in plant and animal life (Harman 1993) and also, as business interests in England have recently been arguing in response to a proposed immigration cap, to a healthy economy. So how can the tensions between cohesion and diversity, universalism and particularism be resolved?

There is no 'right' solution to the dilemmas expressed in this section; there is rather a balancing act to be negotiated. First, society needs to acknowledge and create space for difference. Flyvbjerg (1998, p. 209), for example, argues that 'the more democratic a society, the more it allows groups to define their own specific ways of life and legitimates the inevitable conflicts of interest that arise between them'. This means giving different groups an opportunity to find their own space. New communities need support to settle, different cultural groups need opportunities to celebrate their own culture and to share problems with those they know best and trust most. Only then are they likely to have the confidence to engage with others (see Box 12.1).

BOX 12.1   Working separately to work together: an example from the UK

In one London neighbourhood, where recent years had seen an influx of families from Bangladesh, the community development team faced the challenge of making contact with Bengali women. Few spoke English and their religion forbade them to mix with men. There was a women's group in the neighbourhood, but it was, inevitably, made up of white women. The local authority as funder encouraged the local neighbourhood council to employ a Sylheti-speaking woman as their community worker. She worked with the whole community but was able to win the trust of the Bengali men in particular, because she was able to provide them with advice and information (many of the men worked in the evenings in the catering trade and would not have been able to come to existing residents' meetings even if they wanted to). After going from door to door and talking to the women, she set up a sewing class. The white women did not see this as particularly empowering, but it was what the Bengali women wanted. It was a 'way in' that provided an opportunity for them to discuss other issues that concerned them and gain access to health workers and others who could provide information and support. After some months, an International Women's Day event was organised, which brought together the three women's groups in the area – there was also a Chinese women's group – and this was the first in a series of regular contacts between women in the neighbourhood.

Maalouf (cited in Bauman, p. 141) argues that: 'The more immigrants feel that their original cultural lore is respected in their new home and the less they feel that because of their different identity they are resented ... the more willingly they open up to the cultural offering of the new country and the less convulsively they hold onto their own separate ways'. The same may apply to 'host' communities, especially those who already feel marginalised and excluded, insofar as racial tension is caused by their own fear of identity loss.

To start from strength on all sides also requires ensuring that all groups have access to fundamental rights as the basis for empowerment, as Box 12.2 illustrates. Only then, is it likely to

BOX 12.2 Working with Gypsies and Travellers: from small beginnings

The Give Us a Voice project works with members of the Gypsy and Traveller community to empower them to work together and to have a voice that is heard and recognised. It also works with agencies to raise awareness and the profile of the community and to help them to adapt the way they deliver their services to ensure they are culturally appropriate. A project worker from the Gypsy and Traveller community has been working with community members to defend their rights and prevent evictions:

I start my job by going out and well let's be honest having a coffee with people. We talk through issues, we discuss life and we get some small things changed. At the same time I am getting to know influential people nationally and educating myself in the policies and issues. It's difficult at times. Gypsies and Travellers are very proud, self-sufficient people, to ask for help is to show weakness, so quite a bit of the work I do gets done without them actually asking for help but from conversations which highlight problems. This also makes it difficult to celebrate our achievements. It is also very difficult to get a few of them in a room together to talk about issues, because we are a very private people. One way I get over this is to have a consultation party. We invite members from all the different Traveller communities and we give them the opportunity to talk about small universal problems together. We also set up Forum meetings in people's homes – so that the meetings don't feel like meetings, just chats, but again we talk about what is comfortable and we get small things changed, like the council to come along and clean the entrance to one site.

As a result of gaining this trust, the worker was contacted when people from the community started getting eviction notices. She attended a course on Gypsy and Traveller law and, working with allies in the local council, was able to get the evictions overturned. Other gains followed and there is now a chance that the law will be revised.

Source: Give Us a Voice: Gypsies and Travellers make it real, *Voices from Experience*, Yorkshire and Humber Empowerment Partnership, March 2009.

be possible to find common ground and build the trunk of the empowerment tree.

Where there is conflict, Gilchrist argues that it is vital to create a 'safe space' for discussing contentious issues and for members of different groups to get to know one another personally (2009, p. 117). She and others see the way forward as lying in developing loose and overlapping networks – informal spaces to support learning and neutral spaces where different groups can work out when it is important to agree and when to disagree. As Sampson argues (2007, p. 167), 'Collective action does not rest on homogeneity. Diverse populations can and do agree on wanting safe streets'. But getting to this realisation may involve mediation – a skill that is often undervalued but likely to be increasingly important in the diverse societies of the twenty-first century.

It is particularly important to build links between neighbourhoods and communities of identity both to increase understanding across these divides and also to ensure that the most excluded within neighbourhoods can benefit from and contribute to area-based initiatives. Debates about whether action on exclusion should be targeted at territorial or identity communities should no longer be an 'either or' debate, but should explore ways in which the two approaches can be integrated. Gains made at neighbourhood level need to be rolled out beyond the area through communities of identity. Area-based initiatives also need to draw on the expertise of communities of identity to ensure that they reach seldom-heard groups that they have not yet been able to reach. This will be a challenge, especially in the aftermath of recession as public spending cuts in different countries bite and competition for resources gets fiercer. It will certainly require more than the short-term, isolated initiatives of the past.

There is, of course, a strong seam of experience to draw on from Northern Ireland and other conflict regions in the world – but part of what it tells us is that, however many good initiatives there are, unless they are pulled together in an incremental and multifaceted strategy, sustainable long-term change is unlikely to be achieved. Policy and practice also needs to draw on the experience over the decades. At a recent seminar I went to on the subject discussants lamented the lack of institutional memory in government, with frequent changes in personnel meaning that learning from past initiatives was lost and history was repeated.

Change also needs to take place at many different levels. Despite the progress that has been made, 98 per cent of social housing tenants in Northern Ireland still live in neighbourhoods dominated by one religious faith.

Acheson and Milofsky (2010) describe this as a process of 'sustained dialogue' (Saunders 1999). Although there is still a long way to go, they take a number of lessons from the case study in Box 12.3. The first is the need for *action at different levels*. At a macro-level, Derry's economic isolation and the segregated nature of social housing continue to frustrate progress towards lasting peace. But structural change alone will not change a culture of sectarian hostility or erase memories of the trauma inflicted on the different communities. This needs dialogue at a very local level. Second, they argue that dialogue also needs to be *long-term and resourced* – so the availability of EU resources, the emergence of a cross-sectoral policy community and the commitment of state actors to investing in community development were key factors in moving things along. Third, they argue that *leadership* was crucial. Community leaders were publicly modelling the possibility of negotiation over conflict, in a way that allowed more people to take the considerable personal risks involved in dialogue. The case study also demonstrates *the need for formal dialogue to be embedded in informal relationships*. Dialogue between key city leaders began as private gestures, on intimate terms, thus building trust and friendship on which more formal negotiations could be based. Finally, it demonstrates the important *role of civil society organisations* in embedding and institutionalising change.

Reconciling leadership, participation and representation

Recognising the importance of leadership takes us to our second tension. In its discussion of 'who plays', Chapter 9 began to discuss the challenges of representation and leadership. The phenomenon of the 'usual suspects' is well documented in the literature. Research suggests that there is rarely competition for places on community boards and partnerships, especially after an initial rush of enthusiasm. This may be because newcomers are nervous about taking over from acknowledged and experienced community leaders, or it may be because of exclusionary practices and

BOX 12.3   Peace and reconciliation in Northern Ireland

Derry is the second largest urban centre in Northern Ireland. During the height of 'the troubles' there, it was a hotspot of sectarian conflict. Public housing there was – and remains – segregated. There were few opportunities for cross-community social relationships and 'simply meeting people from the other side' was 'difficult, dangerous and unappetising'. But during the 1990s, a number of factors came together to produce a period of sustained dialogue that offered real hope for change.

At macro level, there was a de-escalation of the 'war' as both sides began to accept that there would be no military victory. This provided a context in which community leaders were able to emerge and begin dialogue. The coincidental availability of resources from the European Union, coupled with the growing commitment of state actors to investing in community development as a central strategy for combating social exclusion, helped to support a number of initiatives at city-wide and neighbourhood levels that created a framework for peace.

The rebuilding of the city centre and a political agreement over Protestant marches framed a range of more local activities: arts

→

the dominance of particular cliques. But a more mundane explanation in many cases is that the majority of people seem happy to let the leadership get on with things most of the time, as long as things are going in roughly the right direction:

> Federations and partnerships are about leaders. This is not necessarily bad – people who find direct participation risky may willingly hand over this right. (Hickey and Mohan 2005, p. 19)

As I have already argued in this volume, there is no reason why we should expect more participation from excluded communities than we expect elsewhere. The anger and frustration – or indeed enthusiasm – that can lead to high levels of involvement organisations that drew people from both communities by focusing on work that had no immediate sectarian focus; the Nerve Centre, which supported youthful rock musicians and developed community video projects; the Verbal Arts Centre, which teaches writing to young people from both Catholic and Protestant schools; a hospice supported by both communities; a programme involving developmentally disabled people in cooking and selling food. A group of Catholic and Protestant women defused potential flashpoints between teenagers on either side of the divide by taking them off for fishing trips or vacations and cutting off the leadership of civil disorders. Groups across the divide also calmed the rumours that are rife on both sides by providing accurate and trusted information.

Another significant initiative was concerned with storytelling, working with groups to remember past events and publicly tell their stories. This helped to surface and manage the emotions of conflict and to recognise the losses sustained by both sides. But it still requires a long-term commitment if people are to confront and give up their anger: 'The willingness of leaders from both sides to engage an enemy that they truly saw as evil required a challenging personal reflection process'.

Source: Adapted from Acheson and Milofsky (2010).

in strategic and programme planning decisions at the outset can be very draining and is rarely sustained. A respondent in a recent research study commented: 'The groups go in cycles – when you're meeting to form decisions at the beginning you get more people interested than when it gets to implementation and contracts – people aren't that interested'.

Participation – at least at the more formal end of the scale – is very much a 'minority sport'. Skidmore, Bound and Lownsbrough (2006) suggest that one per cent of the population is a reasonable aim. There are many reasons for this. First, engaging in partnership at this level absorbs an enormous amount of time and personal resources. For many people, day-to-day survival, looking after family, holding down a job (or more than one) may be their priority. Second, there are communities where taking action or speaking out is a high-risk strategy. Sometimes, putting your head above the parapet can have devastating results, unless community representatives can be protected. Challenging crime, drugs or sectarian conflicts gets people killed.

Even in less violent situations, there can be high costs. A community representative in research I carried out with colleagues said: 'Anyone who has gone in trying to promote any issue at all has been tarred. That's why some of them dropped out. ... Some of the public comment was extremely offensive and people were getting quite intimidated.' In Chapter 9, I commented on the way in which community representatives can be caught in an uncomfortable no man's land between their communities and their partners on decision-making bodies, in danger of being accused on the one hand of failing to deliver and on the other of being unrepresentative or of failing to sell partnership decisions back to their communities. The demands of the job are high and are likely to lead to burn out. And as I argued there, the resources to represent communities effectively are rarely available.

Third, the expectations of community representatives can be highly unrealistic. Trying to represent the diverse and often fragmented interests in many communities is an extremely difficult business, if not impossible. This has been a particularly difficult problem for BME communities, which tend to get lumped together in one tokenistic category (or, indeed, for disabled people).

Finally, Chapter 9 argued that the 'usual suspects' are often created by the systems, timescales and structures of partnership itself. And with a multiplicity of initiatives encouraging community involvement, Liz Richardson (2007, p. 255) warns against increasing competition over the small pool of active residents who are willing to be involved.

So, the 'usual suspects' may well be a group to be treasured and cosseted rather than maligned. On the other hand, Chapter 9 also acknowledged the existence of community gatekeepers. A community worker I spoke to in one study found that:

> One of the most difficult things about doing an enabling job is to get other people to learn how to enable. Once you've empowered somebody, to get them to empower other people is quite difficult. Power sticks to people and then the whole system gets clogged up.

It is not difficult, as a student once commented to me, to find examples of community leaders who have climbed up Arnstein's famous ladder of participation (see Figure 8.2) and then pulled it up after them.

Purdue *et al.* (2000, p. 3) argue that community leaders may self-select in ways that do not make them the best people for the job. Similarly, in one early case study of community development in the UK (Taylor, Kestenbaum and Symons 1976), the community members who initially came forward were people who wanted to get out of the locality; it was not until much later that the people who were central to community networks showed an interest. But then the power balance switched. Once key local families took over, there was little room for those on the periphery.

McCulloch (2000, p. 414) comments on the way in which representatives can become an 'inverse community', whose reference group is not in the community itself but in the politics and policymaking external to the community. Community leaders who have struggled against the odds to achieve a say in the decision-making process may not find it easy to cede control to others (Pitcoff 1997; Purdue 2001). There is nothing to be gained by expecting people from excluded communities to somehow avoid the traps that others regularly fall into or to reject the opportunities that their contribution has opened up. Leaders need support.

Often, it is community professionals rather than local people who get involved in partnerships, especially at the strategic level. Marris and Rein (1967, p. 186) suggest that: 'Community organisation falters because it cannot offer any future to the neighbourhood leaders it promotes but a lifetime of parochial effort. The real leaders are the professional community organisers, who alone have the incentive of a career with widening opportunities'. As opportunities have opened up for community members to be employed on local initiatives themselves, this may have changed, although, of course, once employed, they too can be dismissed as not being the 'real people' (see Chapter 9). But it is still likely to be those who have most resources and time and who are most confident and socially secure who engage. And this becomes self-reinforcing; the costs of participation decrease as people gain political and technical skills (Abers 1998), but remain high for those who do not.

Funding introduces another complicating factor. Groups are attracted into participation by the prospect of funding, and representatives may join partnerships in order to gain resources for their organisations and their causes. While some develop a broader perspective, this is not always the case. This may be self-interest; it may also be because they cannot devote their energies to both their own projects and a broader agenda. And of course, there are cases of maladministration. But whether or not it is justified, this can creates suspicion and resentment within the wider community, especially among those whose applications have been unsuccessful, and who are cynical about people feathering their own nests. This is confirmed by other recent UK studies (Anastacio *et al.* 2000; Purdue *et al.* 2000) and also by a case study in my own recent research. Here, local residents were impatient to see the fruits of the area's first major Lottery grant. However, managing expectations after the initial euphoria proved difficult. The first few months were taken up in setting up new systems and recruiting staff. In the absence of tangible returns, suspicion (unjustifiable in this case) fell on two leading community activists who had just bought a new car.

Where partnerships are dispensing money, conflicts of interest are bound to occur: 'I think it's inevitable with regeneration that someone along the line has a degree of involvement either as a user of a project or as a supporter' (Taylor and Parkes 2001). The agencies as well as the communities involved will have their own vested interest in how the money is distributed. Indeed, it is hard to conceive of a system that could produce good and committed community representatives who at the same time would have no vested interests at all in how funding is distributed. Nonetheless, roles can get very confused as committees turn from more strategic tasks to allocating funds. Transparency is crucial and structuring the partnership in ways which separate out different functions can help here (see below, pp. 259–60). Adequate support for all those who wish to apply for funding is also important along with accessible procedures that do not favour those who are already experienced in the programme. And institutional creativity is required to design frameworks for the allocation of funds that can address these tensions.

How else can these dilemmas be addressed? A government rhetoric that tends to celebrate the individual 'hero' entrepreneur neglects the basis on which leaders are given legitimacy to lead. Drawing on the discussion in Chapters 9 and 10, a number of lessons emerge.

First, spreading involvement helps. It is essential both for effective participation and sustainability that there is a diverse pool of potential leaders. Different leaders may be needed for different purposes – leaders who inspire and connect people are as important as those who take up formal positions (Gilchrist 2009, p. 102). This requires that people have, as I argued in Chapter 10, many different ways into engagement. The wider the spread of activities on the ground and the greater the variety of 'ways in', the larger will be the pool from which leaders can be drawn and the greater the chance that Milofsky and Hunter's 'Greek chorus' (1994) will emerge to hold leaders and representatives accountable (see Chapter 11). A wide range of activities allows diversity to be expressed; it provides the foundation from which people gain the confidence they need to come together and find common ground.

Second, the most successful participation initiatives – in terms of spread of involvement – are likely to be those where there is a history of investment in community development. This is the conclusion that Carley and Smith (2001) draw from their international study of sustainable change initiatives and it is confirmed in a recent systematic review of the evidence in the UK (Pratchett *et al.* 2009). Mentoring and similar schemes (see Box 12.4) can also spread involvement and leadership.

Third, it is important both that this investment is given the time to bear fruit. In the UN study cited in Chapter 9, Rothman (2000, p. 101) found that, 'a moderate pace, rather than accelerated action' was a key feature of successful community development programmes – a finding confirmed by Richardson in the UK (2008, p. 254). Similarly, Abers (1998) describes how, at the beginning of the participatory budgeting initiative in Porto Alegre, it was indeed the most organised neighbourhoods that took part. But, over time, participation spread and, by the time of her research (six years after the initiative began), over half of the participants at the big opening assemblies were participating for the first time.

This means it is also important to invest at an early stage in any partnership or participation initiative. Chapter 9 reported that, too frequently, the essential resources to provide community development are not invested in new programmes until *after*

BOX 12.4   Spreading leadership

In 2007, Bradford's Community Empowerment Network set up a community mentoring scheme. Mentors were recruited through a variety of channels and an introductory evening gave them a chance to find out more and sign up. This was followed by a training session. The scheme gives those who are mentored – often new or inexperienced workers – the chance to talk to someone who has 'been there', who can listen, provide encouragement and offer the benefit of their experience. It gives them an opportunity to develop their skills, knowledge and understanding for their own benefit and for the benefit of their community. The mentor also gains from a deeper understanding of other communities, develops additional skills and has the chance to gain qualifications

One person who was mentored was a woman who was having difficulty getting involved with her local community centre – the chair was gatekeeping and the committee was not working properly. This woman wanted to get on the committee to revitalise it but could not find a way to do it. She was put in touch with a mentor from a local voluntary organisation and they met four times to discuss how she might deal with the issue. The mentor made various suggestions, which she tried out and the two of them then discussed how these ideas had worked. Eventually the woman found a route through the barrier by becoming involved in healthy cook and eat sessions, encouraging friends to join and creating a strong group of people who went and talked to the chair together. The chair backed down and together the group formed a stronger committee and organised elections. The woman from the mentoring scheme is now chair of the community centre.

Source: Yorkshire and Humber Empowerment Partnership (2004) 'Community Mentoring – a gift relationship', Voices from Experience, May, pp. 1 and 4.

---

the systems have been agreed and the shape of the programme decided. It argued that, if communities are to be involved effectively, a development phase needs to be built into new initiatives, which gives communities the time and resources to develop the organisational capacity that is essential to effective representation. This could be readily addressed through a Year Zero, and probably, if the diversity within a community is to be adequately reflected, a Year Zero minus One. If everyone is to be kept on board, however, there may need to be some provision for 'quick wins', which can give all parties the assurance that the longer-term investment is worthwhile.

Fourth, people need incentives to participate. One simple incentive is that there is a return on their investment – that they can see or are told what has happened as a result. If action is not taken, they need to know why. In follow-up events to the exercise reported in Box 11.4, for example, the session always began with a report back on what had happened as the result of earlier consultations.

Next, we need to know more about what makes leadership work. In the wealth of research that exists about participation, most addresses imbalances of power between communities and power holders in government or NGOs. Relatively little addresses community leadership and the sources of power and accountability that back this up. If we are to cultivate effective leadership, we need to know much more than we do about how community leaders and representatives in different societies link into, and are supported by, social networks – how formal and informal leadership connects up. The question of how people in communities can spread involvement and accountability along these networks still remains a priority concern both for participants and other partners. We need more information, too, about how partnership affects the networks of those involved both within communities and beyond them; how can we ensure that partnership and participation initiatives promote rather than prejudice social capital?

Finally, policymakers and partners need to be realistic both about the levels of participation they can expect and the expectations they have of those who come forward as representatives and leaders. Since the number and range of people who can take this on is always going to be limited, Cornwall argues (2008, p. 276) that 'it makes more sense to think in terms of *optimum* participation: getting the balance between depth and inclusion right for the purpose at hand'. Those who are prepared to do so need learning opportunities, support and resources (see Box 12.4), if the information and accountability links between leaders and their communities are to be strong enough to sustain representative structures. The secret of effective leadership will partly lie in personal skills, political awareness, opportunities for personal development and training; but it will also depend on the infrastructure that supports it.

Scaling up

At various points in this volume, I have argued that communities cannot achieve sustainable change on their own. Government and other agencies have to tackle the structural causes of exclusion that keep communities swimming against the tide (O'Connor 2007). If this is to happen, communities will need to band together to drive change from below. Indeed, De Filippis, Fisher and Shragge (2009, p. 49) argue that 'going beyond the local is a central aspect in the struggle for social and economic justice' (see Box 12.5).

BOX 12.5   Moving beyond the local

Fifth Avenue Committee is one of the largest and most dynamic community organisations in New York City. A CDC that emerged in the 1970s, its major business is housing development, where it has encouraged the development of mutual or limited equity co-operative forms. But it believes that development alone will never change the larger political and economic contexts in which communities exist. So it has combined its development work with organising to address the long-term needs and interests of low-income people in its own and surrounding neighbourhoods.

A major campaign has been for a 'displacement free zone' to address issues of gentrification in its own and adjacent neighbourhoods. This involves negotiation, confrontation and also working with the state legislature to pass a bill that would give landlords an incentive to let at below-market rents to low- or moderate-income households. Even where its own campaigns, e.g. for rezoning, have not been successful in its own back yard, it has been able to support more successful efforts elsewhere by sharing the fruits of its experience.

→

There are other reasons why neighbourhoods need to look beyond their boundaries. Whether working in or outside the system, coalitions across neighbourhoods (and indeed with communities of interest) can:

*   Give neighbourhoods access to allies, knowledge and skills that they may not have
*   Share and build a common store of knowledge and best practice which is generated from the bottom up rather than the top down
*   Provide a space where different groups can come to a common view and thus help to ensure that power holders do not 'divide and rule', playing one neighbourhood off against another.

Interest in partnership has led to new opportunities for community representation at district- or city-wide and even regional level. Coalitions are needed to devise effective ways of feeding

Key to its success is its outward-looking ethos, for example, it has collaborated with the labour unions to protect wages in the construction of affordable housing. It also built a splinter organisation Families United for Racial and Economic Equality – a group of women on, or formerly on, public assistance – which has put pressure on the city government to improve the pay and working conditions of people with childcare responsibilities who are leaving welfare for employment. It is also playing a leading role in a long-term and city-wide effort to transform the way in which local economic development is understood and done in the city.

This is one case study in an article that argues the importance of combining an explicit social justice vision with concrete successes on the ground. The case studies begin with local work, which builds a base and membership. But they combine service provision with political education, advocacy and action as well as connecting with a range of organisations with similar interests. Moving beyond the local is an essential element in the struggle for social and economic justice.

Source: De Filippis, Fisher and Shragge 2009.

into these, if communities are not to have systems imposed or to be fighting with each other for places on partnerships at this level. Coalitions across localities can also compare local government practice across different localities and lobby on the basis of best practice elsewhere.

Gittell (2001), researching the Empowerment Zones in the US comments on the 'inherent parochialism' of most community-based organisations. If it is difficult to involve people within their immediate localities or communities of interest, as we have seen, it is even more difficult to interest them in issues beyond these boundaries (Storper 1998; see Chapter 5). All the tensions we have discussed in this section are magnified at this wider level and can be infinitely more difficult to negotiate. Representatives are separated further from their communities and a larger variety of interests needs to be reconciled. For all these reasons, an effective infrastructure is absolutely critical. This can develop bridging social capital and channel the skills, knowledge and capacities that have developed in local communities into effective and collaborative action and leadership; it is the trunk of the empowerment tree (see Figure 11.1).

A strong community infrastructure can serve as a focus for feeding the views of local communities to power holders and providing legitimacy. It can act as a channel for accounting back to those communities, and it can provide the information backup to community players that government partners take for granted. Such an infrastructure will also develop the capacity of others in communities, so that the tasks of leadership can be spread and succession be assured.

However, the task facing the community infrastructure is considerable. It is the familiar challenge, discussed earlier, of reconciling diversity within a coherent whole, identifying common ground that can unite people while providing channels for them to represent their different interests. Without this infrastructure, conflict and competition can erode scarce resources, community representation can become divorced from its constituency and activities can become very dependent on one or two individuals.

Rich, Giles and Stern (2007) warn of the danger in 'scaling up' of losing what small groups can offer. So, just as participation cannot be imposed from above, neither can community infrastructure, if it is to be owned and trusted by communities. It needs to be built up from below, and to be accountable and accessible. Infrastructure bodies may need to resist the expectations and demands of funders, or indeed the temptation to mimic traditional models, if they are to retain these qualities.

Structures need to be adaptable: different stages of development may require a different response. They need also to be adequately resourced. Goetz and Gaventa (2001) describe how, in the US Empowerment Zones, successful initiatives were those that invested heavily in staff whose primary function was to manage citizen contacts with the administration. Similarly, Abers underlines the importance of the community organisers who worked with community delegates in Porto Alegre (see Box 11.6). Chapter 10 referred to a successful community partnership in Wester Hailes, a large public housing estate near Edinburgh in Scotland. The Rep Council there – the community-based organisation which provided community development support and elected representatives onto city-wide decision-making structures – employed 15 workers to support its work (Taylor 1995b). This allowed representatives to keep in touch with community views and to build a wide pool of involvement: workers were charged, for example, with ensuring that at election time posts were contested and new candidates were supported.

In thinking about structures that can involve communities at different levels, Esman and Uphoff (1984) argue that an assembly model has worked well in developing countries. Writing about rural initiatives, they found:

> The decision making structure that is most often successful, a combination of committees and assembly, combines the advantages of both modes of deliberation: a smaller group working out details and a larger group for eliciting divergent views and building consensus through participation.

Coin Street Community Builders (see Box 11.1) has developed a 'nested' structure involving bodies with the main Board overseeing a range of different legal structures with different memberships to perform different functions. Such structures, which can also separate out executive from representative structures, help to address the conflicts of interest highlighted earlier in this chapter and provide opportunities for people to engage at different levels. Being part of an informal working group, for example, might give a newcomer the confidence to consider standing for the main Board at a future date.

However, it is important not to get too hung up on structure. In Chapter 10 I argued the need for both formal and informal ways of organising and this applies to the infrastructure too. Sidney Tarrow (1994) shows how social movements are mobilised and kept alive through their base in social networks, which can act as 'abeyance structures' (Rupp and Taylor 1987, pp. 138, 142) during periods of inactivity or repression. He argues that these do not need a permanent organisation but rather a set of 'social relays' (Ohlemacher 1992). This is particularly important in relation to infrastructure. 'Social relays' make connections between different communities, and find and promote the common interests beyond the diversity. They mediate difference, competition and conflict, and identify opportunities for wider action. They maintain networks and contacts through periods of relative inactivity so that the organisational intelligence is not lost. Doing this through loose rather than formal organisations can often help to build bridges between disparate and even conflicting communities in neighbourhoods. As Chris Skelcher and his colleagues suggest (1996), networks allow boundaries to be crossed without loss of identity. They also allow for overlapping links – if one relationship becomes overloaded, there are several other information routes or sources of support (Gilchrist 2009, p. 171).

Earlier I reported Milofsky's argument that what is needed in neighbourhoods is not so much a permanent organisation but 'organisational intelligence' that can be mobilised when needed. He embodies this in the idea of a 'social treasury' or 'transorganization' (see Box 12.6) – a loosely wired or virtual organisation, which can support networks, encourage entrepreneurs and leverage resources. The concept of a 'social treasury' was developed to counter dependence on outside professionals and instead build the capacity of individuals to identify problems, create movements, form mutual support networks to mobilise resources and build local assets. While it sets up a series of projects to build networks and link them together, for the most part these are not seen as an interconnected set of achievements by an organisation or a set of experts doing things FOR the community. It is the combination of relationships and resources that comprises the social treasury (Milofsky 2008, pp. 37, 189).

BOX 12.6   A social treasury

The Wild River Institute in the Eastern United States is a 'virtual' organisation, which connects activists and networks and channels resources that exist in one organisation or context into other settings where they can be used. It was incorporated in 1990 and covers a largely rural area some 50 miles across, a region which is both fragmented and isolated geographically. There are strong commitments within local communities but few networks across them and sometimes intense rivalries.

The Institute, which has no staff of its own, acts as a 'social treasury' to foster community action. When it needs administrative structure it borrows it from the organisations that are involved with it. When it is able to negotiate the resources for development workers, these are also employed by member organisations. It builds overlapping networks of mutually reinforcing organisations, which can come together around common issues. So it is a catalyst, which has supported and stimulated a range of development work locally. It is also the repository of organisational intelligence, which can be drawn on by new developments. It provides a legal framework for action and, through those involved, physical resources, using its formal incorporation to receive an occasional small grant, to process small payments to participants where necessary, to maintain an address and a post office box, and to give a public face to the work in the area. Among the issues where it has provided this networking and catalyst role are provision for recovering drug addicts, a programme working with men who batter women and a campaign of resistance to a hazardous waste incinerator.

Source: Adapted from Milofsky (2008).

Inside or outside?

Chapter 9 asked whether communities should be playing the partnership game at all. The final tension I want to discuss in this chapter, therefore, is the choice communities have to make about whether they fight for change from inside the system or from outside. This is always a difficult decision:

The dilemma is whether to become involved in the institutionalised political process and remain key agents of transformation within this, or assert autonomy and pressure from
without – which may permit under-represented sections of
society a voice not possible within the political process, but
may not effect fundamental change. (Carley and Smith 2001,
p. 186)

Communities do not have to enter new governance spaces.
There will always be organisations and communities that 'remain incompletely domesticated' (Morison 2000, p. 131). Such
organisations may have tried co-operation and persuasion without success; or they may have reached the limits of what they are
willing to compromise. For them, campaigning on the outside
may be the only route left.

Being on the outside is not always the most progressive place
to be, however. Religious fundamentalism – of whatever hue –
reminds us that not all movements seek progressive change and
that civil society can be extremely uncivil. Alternatively, the
outsider world can become very 'cosy' as protesters fall into
what a research respondent once called 'a lazy world of cau-
cuses' (Craig, Taylor and Parkes 2004). Paradoxically, respondents to this study argued, staying on the outside could be more
'comfortable' than engaging with the considerable challenges
of partnership. More than one BME respondent in this study
argued that years of staying determinedly on the outside and
independent had got them nowhere.

Communities can get 'stuck in opposition' (Taylor 2007a,
p. 312). Their scepticism towards systems that have let them
down before may be a principled stand; for others, however, it
may be an inability to change and can act as a barrier to others
in the community who want to test out the new possibilities:

There's often been key times in the partnership where I felt that
they ... need to learn to negotiate, they need to learn how to
make deals, they need to learn how to resolve conflict, because
they're still storming like even when they've won, they don't
know. (Author's unpublished research)

Long-term campaigners can find it difficult to change their ac-
customed clothes and resistance can become a habit rather than

a strategic choice. Shirlow and Murtagh (2004, p. 68), writing about Northern Ireland, for example, describe a voluntary and community sector shaped by 'victimhood'.

But it is also possible to get stuck on the inside. Barnes, in her research with mental health service users (1999, pp. 85–6), argues that community involvement in partnership can dissipate energies and encourage a reactive rather than active stance. Dependence on government funding, which often accompanies partnership, she goes on to argue, can also inhibit campaigning activities and promote self-censorship. A respondent in my own recent research commented that it was easy to get comfortable on the inside and to 'lose that cutting edge which may have been the creative force in the first instance'. The balancing act between collusion and influence is a difficult one. In the same study, one respondent confessed:

> We get privileged information, so we moderate our relationships with [key players] because we don't want to jeopardise getting hold of privileged information in the future. And so we collude. And this is how we get controlled ... it takes up all the agenda time ... we get utterly distracted from what we want to do ... and we never get our business done. (Author's unpublished research)

While community players should not be criticised for taking a pragmatic approach, therefore, Barnes, Newman and Sullivan warn (2007, p. 195) that it is easy to become removed from the day-to-day experience of the public they claim to speak for, as I have argued earlier in this volume.

The best strategy might therefore be a combination of 'insider' and 'outsider' tactics. Mitchell Dean – a seminal Foucault scholar – argues that 'one can simultaneously work together and be restive'. Alinksy too (1971, p. xix) argues the need to work inside the system, although he is talking more generally about the need for reform before revolution – changing public opinion is, he argues the precursor to more dramatic change:

> As an organiser, I start from where the world is ... not as I would like it to be. That we accept the world does not in any sense weaken our desire to change it into what we believe it should be – it is necessary to begin where the world is if we

are going to change it to what we think it should be. That means working in the system.

'Outsiders' force issues on to public agendas. They keep the power holders at the table and extend the boundaries of what is allowed on to that table. 'Insiders' make use of this opportunity to achieve concrete gains. Chapter 3, for example, described how the critique provided in the UK by the 1970s Community Development Projects was an important counterpoint to more consensual forms of community practice at the time and it is an analysis that still has resonance for many today.

Several times in this volume, I have argued that 'popular spaces', where people can find their independent voice and where they will be held accountable, are essential if they are to maintain a critical perspective when they do enter 'invited spaces'. Sometimes organisations can operate in both, but this can be a difficult balancing act, as many who try to combine service delivery with campaigning have found. Alliances can provide alternative, popular spaces, allowing organisations to move from inside to outside, or to work alongside others who use different tactics. Conversely, insiders can act as a resource for outsiders. In the research on this issue cited earlier (Craig, Taylor and Parkes 2004), one particularly important finding was the extent to which established 'insider' organisations provided training and development resources for community groups that wanted to maintain their autonomy and remain 'outside' the system in their own 'popular spaces'. Insiders also used their privileged access to policy networks to provide 'docking points' which allowed these autonomous groups to engage in the policy process at strategic times without losing their independence or power to disagree.

Summary

In their study of community leadership in neighbourhood renewal in the UK, Purdue *et al.* (2000, p. 3) comment that 'Much of the leadership behaviour we have observed has in practice been grappling with the complexity, diversity and conflict embedded in the concept of "community"'. The same applies to the other tensions addressed here. While it would be good to be able to wave a wand and spirit them away, they are inherent in the nature of community and its relationship with the state. As such, naming them helps – simplistic and idealistic notions of community do not prepare communities or their partners for the complexities of practice. And while there are many useful handbooks and guidelines that can help community members and workers to address the challenges they pose, there are no absolute answers, only balancing acts. Earlier in the book, I introduced the concept of 'community' as a 'variable' or 'aspiration' (Hunter 1974; Warburton 2009). Communities are dynamic entities, constantly reconstructing themselves in image and identity. Achieving a balance between cohesion and diversity, leadership and participation, between focusing inwards and scaling up to act in the wider environment, between forcing change from the outside and negotiating it from within: these will all likewise be moving targets.

Chapter 13

The Institutional Challenge

In the course of this book I have drawn on a number of meta-
phors: power circuits, trees, journeys. For this chapter, I want
to introduce one more: the metaphor of jazz, which I have borrowed from Wynton Marsalis, the jazz musician, via a pamphlet
produced by the US-based Pew Foundation. In an interview for
The American Heritage magazine, he described jazz as a social
invention (Marsalis 1996). He saw in it both musical and non-
musical elements. The first of the non-musical elements is the
desire to think about an issue in a new light, to play with an
idea. Second, he refers to the need to 'make room': jazz, he argues, is about participation, dialogue and reaction. His third
non-musical element is respect for individuality: 'Playing jazz
means learning how to reconcile differences, even when they're
opposites'. He calls it 'dialogue with integrity'.

Turning to the non-musical elements, jazz, says Marsalis,
must have 'blues': an optimism that is not naive, a willingness
to work through pain and move forward. Jazz, after all, is a
music born of oppression. Second, in those time-honoured words,
it 'don't mean a thing if it ain't got that swing', which means
'constant co-ordination, but in an environment that's difficult
enough to challenge your equilibrium'. This is about adapting
to something that is always shifting and changing. Third, jazz is
collective improvisation: 'people getting together and making up
music as a group', a risky business. Finally, there is syncopation:
'you're always prepared to do the unexpected'.

Communities have been invited into governance arrangements
because of the knowledge and legitimacy they bring to problems
that public-sector partners have found difficult to resolve – 'wicked
issues' that have complex roots and need to draw on a range
of energies and ideas if they are to be successfully addressed.
But working in partnership across different cultures is itself
a tricky business. So how can the elements above – dialogue,
respect for difference and a willingness to take risks together – be

266

institutionalised into partnership working, creating new norms, new rules of the game that address the problems highlighted in Chapter 9? In this section I address three aspects of change: changing people, changing cultures and changing structures.

Changing people

Reform often starts with structures. But, as a respondent in research I carried out on neighbourhood renewal argued, while 'People can overcome structures; structures cannot overcome people' (Taylor 2000b, p. 41). Evaluating the US Empowerment Zones, Marilyn Gittell (2001, p. 92) agreed: 'Reforms that devolve power to state and local governments without changing the participants', she wrote, 'fail to produce more responsive policies or contribute to the revitalisation of the democratic process'. The drive for change from international institutions and national governments has been important in opening doors that, as I argued in Chapter 11, will be difficult to close again. But research across the globe shows that, whatever reforms are thrown at them, public servants are good at 'doing what they've always done in a different wrapping' (Taylor 2000b).

Understanding barriers

To achieve change, therefore, we first need to understand what prevents it. Two major sources of resistance stand out from the literature. The first is the many conflicting demands that cut across the commitment to participation and engagement; the second is the threat that community participation is seen to represent to traditional power structures and ways of doing things.

Firstly, public servants are governed by conflicting demands that vie for attention and are often in tension. The rhetoric of partnership, engagement and decentralisation is one set of demands, but it sits uneasily with other drivers of public-sector performance: the language of the market, performance and risk control, and – particularly as I write – the need to make efficiency savings. The enormous growth in central monitoring, audit and risk management that I have described in earlier chapters leaves little room for the manoeuvre needed if power is to be shared. Nor does it encourage the flexibility and innovation that change requires. At the same time, despite the rhetoric about collaboration and joint working, rewards, career structures and sanctions are embedded in departmental and professional structures. They rarely reward joint working across public agencies, let alone joint working with communities. The resistance of middle managers, while it may not be condoned, is at least understandable when their day-to-day working lives are already 'governed by performance targets, output measures, league tables, service standards and tight budget constraints' (Taylor 2000b, p. 8). The targets that have to be met and cuts that have to be accommodated easily trump the messiness and complexity of partnership working.

Meanwhile, the advance of the market into the public sphere brings with it an emphasis on competition and the commodification of services, which conflicts with the collaboration and holistic approaches that partnership is meant to bring to bear. Box 13.1 illustrates the extent to which market principles can cut across the values of collaboration and empowerment discussed

---

BOX 13.1   The hegemony of competition

In an article for *Voluntas*, a university lecturer describes a group exercise in a third-sector studies programme she ran. In one of her sessions, students from both the public and the third sector were asked to role play a commissioning process. They were divided into four groups, three of which were asked to take the role of tendering consortia, the fourth the role of the commissioners themselves. These were students who had already expressed concerns about the impact of the 'the contract culture': the tendency for commissioning to favour larger organisations over those that are closer to the community; the short timescales; the preference for performance management over creativity and flexibility. And yet the tendering consortium with the most in-depth knowledge of the service required and a real commitment to collaboration still lost out to the one that ticked the managerial boxes and spoke the market language. The smallest consortium found itself completely ignored in the competitive and time-pressured environment that the exercise was able to replicate.

Source: Milbourne and Murray 2010.

in this chapter, securing 'willing compliance' even amongst those who are well aware of the problems it causes (see Chapter 7). The rules governing competition and procurement practice also discourage the sharing of information and knowledge, whether between commissioner and tenderer or between those competing in the same field, who will want to keep privileged information to themselves.

Furthermore, with increasing pressure on public expenditure, public services and public servants have found themselves consistently undermined and treated as second-rate, especially in the most disadvantaged neighbourhoods (see Chapter 6). To officials and politicians already under siege, community and service-user engagement can easily be seen by local state actors as a form of discipline introduced by central government to limit their powers and legitimacy (Lowndes and Sullivan 2004, p. 55). In these circumstances, it is perhaps not surprising if public servants hang on to the vestiges of power that remain. Many elected politicians are also unclear about how the new drive for engagement relates to the formal representative system and what their roles in new hybrid partnership bodies will be (Taylor and Seymour 2000; Howard and Taylor 2009). Who ultimately represents the community?

For officials, community engagement may seem to require 're-laxing and deviating from strategies and approaches that have served them well in the past' (Rich, Giles and Stern 2007, p. 138). But 'doing that we have always done' will not create change. And even if the will to engage exists, public-sector partners – politicians, policymakers, professionals and officials – often lack the basic skills they need to work effectively with communities. So what will encourage them to try a different approach? Is it a matter of sanctions and incentives – finding the right carrots and sticks? Of evidence? Of toolkits and examples of best practice? Or of capacity building within the public sector itself?

Incentives

If participation as to be taken seriously it may need to be subjected to the same rigorous audit as that required to account for public money (Burns and Taylor 2000). This has not been the case in the past. Goetz and Gaventa (2001, p. 50) remark, for example, that the rhetoric about participation in the US Empowerment Zones did not translate into performance management: 'the benchmarks of success on which program managers were required to report to Washington failed to include a single indicator of success in fostering participation'. Since then, in the UK, attempts have been made to build indicators on community participation and third-sector development into local government performance regimes, along with 'beacon' schemes, which reward authorities that they see as performing strongly. There is some evidence that this is having an impact (IVAR and UWE 2010). But such schemes have to override the 'tick-box' mentality that has beleaguered much participation practice. Audit cultures generate their own culture of deception and counter deception (Amman 1995), which means they risk catching the sprats while the bigger fish go free.

Evidence and 'best practice'

Rather than rely solely on carrots and sticks therefore, it is necessary to persuade public decision makers and practitioners of the 'business case' for community engagement. Evidence-based practice is a very strong discourse in current policy and in different parts of the globe much effort is going into the development of effective evaluation tools, using a wide range of approaches: from traditional positivist approaches, thorough design experiments (Stoker and John 2009), to more participatory approaches developing measures with communities themselves. This is important work. But it can still only take us so far. Community approaches are concerned with 'intermediate outcomes of connectedness, trust and other features of social life that can be difficult to measure as well as social outcomes that are often difficult to change significantly' (Briggs 2007, pp. 38–9), especially in the short term. Furthermore, 'complex processes of chain and effect make the tracking of these efforts, not to mention the task of attributing their effects, difficult indeed'. There is growing evidence to suggest that community participation is cost-effective (SQW 2005; Burton *et al.* 2005; Pratchett *et al.* 2009) and that 'the high costs of community involvement are negligible when set against the gains of better decision making and improved outcomes' (Gilchrist 2009, p. 31). But there is much more to be done to produce a robust evidence base that is also valid for those most closely involved.

Another form of evidence that can support change comes from examples of what has worked elsewhere. This is made easier nowadays by the Internet, which, as Chapter 10 suggested, can be a significant channel for communicating such examples across localities, agencies, partnerships and, indeed, countries. This sharing has provided inspiration and innovative ideas across the globe. It has undoubtedly raised the bar in terms of policy. But there is a limit to how far what is often called 'best practice' can simply be downloaded from the web and replicated in different settings. Context matters. Writing about democratic innovations in Brazil, for example, Cornwall, Romano and Shankland (2008, p. 50) warn that: 'These institutions cannot be exported wholesale to countries that lack the preconditions – either in terms of radical democratic actors within the state, or mobilised social movements outside the state – to make them viable'. Chapter 10 described how the wholesale application of participatory appraisal techniques had attracted criticism from those who saw them being applied indiscriminately, divorced from the values of their originators and failing to engage with power and politics (Cooke and Kothari 2001). While there are plenty of more positive examples of their application (Hickey and Mohan 2004), it is important to remember that applying 'best practice' is not simply a technical exercise. Ideally, participants from the different sectors need opportunities to discuss together – if possible along with facilitators with first-hand experience – how ideas and practices from elsewhere can best be used in a particular situation and by different stakeholders.

Toolkits

A similar argument applies to toolkits. Recent years have seen an explosion of toolkits and handbooks to aid effective practice. They can play a valuable role in alerting their users to the steps that need to be taken and the dangers that need to be avoided in engaging effectively with communities (or conversely with official partners). Like best practice examples, however, they are likely to be most effective when accompanied by hands-on support, which can help communities reflect on their relevance and adapt them to the context in which they are to be used. And they can be a distraction. In recent years there has been a tendency to commission more and more toolkits in relation to participation and partnership practice – many of which tend to say much the same thing under different NGO, government department or consultancy brands – to the extent that, as a colleague of mine put it, we are 'drowning in a sea of toolkits'. Perhaps less attention needs to be paid to the production of ever more toolkits and reviews of best practice, and more to both evaluating their usefulness and also providing the support that both authorities and communities need to apply them effectively.

Capacity

Capacity building is a popular term in the community policy field these days. But it is usually applied to communities, rarely to public servants themselves. And yet it is important, as Gaventa has said, to 'work on both sides of the equation'. It is amazing how little thought has gone into evaluating and accrediting the skills that make partnerships work. Effective partnership working requires investment in skills that have not always been valued in public service in the past: mediation, brokerage, conflict resolution, networking, negotiation, listening and sharing. Public servants will also need to be given support to work in new ways, not just thrown in at the deep end. If working across boundaries is the future, as some claim, it will need to be rewarded in career terms and at a professional level, with performance targets and output measures for professionals that are as robust as those which govern their service delivery and budget management tasks. And capacity building does not stop with front-line staff or even managers; it needs to reach the auditors, accountants and contract managers whose behind the scenes decisions ultimately affect the work that is done at the front line. It also needs to reach the politicians, many of whom have proved resistant to this kind of capacity building in the past (IVAR and UWE 2010).

Capacity building needs to be understood as more than the transfer of skills and competencies. Robert Chambers (1997, p. 189) emphasises the importance also of learning and judgement. Capacity building is about knowledge, confidence, aptitude and understanding. This is built through action, reflection, dialogue and joint learning – the kind of communicative action that Habermas sought to promote. In an arena where many of the answers are still not known, it is important to maximise opportunities for people – on both sides of the equation – to reflect on their learning together, to spread rather than to protect knowledge, and to challenge the cultural assumptions that lie

> **BOX 13.2 Crossing the boundaries**
>
> In the UK an unprecedented two-year consultation over the National Strategy for Neighbourhood Renewal brought senior civil servants into direct contact with community professionals and activists through 18 joint 'policy action teams', field visits and workshops. The implementation of the strategy was then assisted by the secondment of staff from community organisations and with other relevant experience into key government departments and government regional offices, and through the formation of a Community Forum to advise on the implementation of the programme.

behind the status quo (see Box 13.2). Joint training and learning opportunities, which bring together community, private and public sector players, will be particularly important, as will initiatives such as secondments, shadowing, 'twinning' and 'mentoring' across the sectoral divide. Capacity building for professionals also needs to value community knowledge and use community trainers, who can reflect the realities of life in the communities they serve rather than assumptions based on professional lifestyles and aspirations.

All the mechanisms discussed in this section have a role to play in changing the way people operate and rechanneling circuits of power. But Perri 6 and his colleagues (1999) argue that ultimately what they call the 'weak tools' of persuasion, learning, training and dialogue – the kinds of approach Chambers promotes above – are likely to be the most effective. While the 'strong tools' associated with the new public management – regulation, inspection and sanctions are useful for 'short sprints', they argue that the weaker tools are the 'long-distance runners', necessary to bring the doubters on board and bed down new ways of working that can last long after the initial fanfare has died down.

Changing cultures

Changing people is necessary, therefore, but it is still not sufficient. Experience from across the world suggests that there are champions within the public sector who have made great strides in sharing power with communities (CDRC and Logolink 2008). But champions and leaders are not enough. It is no good if champions of change are lone rangers within their organisations and the sheriff and the troops are going on 'as before'. And champions eventually move on. Change cannot rely on individuals therefore; it needs to be cultural, institutionalised change, which goes beyond the 'walk-on-water school principal or human services manager' (Briggs 2007, p. 38). It will also involve more than a few training programmes, fine words from the top or a few dedicated posts. I argued in Chapter 9 that the failure of partnership working to engage adequately with communities is not necessarily a conscious process but ingrained in everyday assumptions about the way things work. Culture change therefore needs to encompass the rules, norms and values that determine how public agencies are run and the hidden, taken-for-granted workings of power. Discussion so far in this volume suggests three in particular that affect the capacity of public bodies to engage with communities: the 'silo'-driven nature of public bureaucracies; a preoccupation with public accountability that drives out risk and change; and the consensus culture that accompanies much partnership working.

The silo mentality

Diana Leat (1999) has argued that: 'the waste of information and knowledge in public sector organisations would be a public scandal if it were money'. Whether it comes packaged in a training course, toolkits or best practice case studies, new knowledge needs to be embedded and spread if it is to be sustainable. So change will depend on new ways of generating and communicating information that can free up the knowledge that is silted up in separate agencies and break down the cultures of secrecy that are endemic within government. This departmentalism has proved resistant to attempts to modernise government in different parts of the world. UK experience also suggests that, even if local administrations are committed to 'joined-up working', they frequently run up against the silo mentality that continues to plague central government.

Risk

Several times in this book, I have highlighted the dominance of new managerialist cultures, whose emphasis on targets and outputs is in danger of excluding communities, destroying trust and social capital, stifling innovation and taking the politics out of policy. I have also emphasised that this is in no way intended to dispute the importance of accounting for public money. The mishandling of public funds not only causes major scandals, but denies desperate communities the funds that they need. But, as whole new professions and career structures develop around the monitoring and auditing requirements of government and other funders, it is important also to hold the auditors and account-ants themselves to account and balance their demands with those of others.

Burton *et al.* (2006, p. 302) remind us that community inter-ventions, by their nature are 'complicated, complex and unpre-dictable'. They involve many different partners, they operate in a constantly changing environment and they are tackling complex issues. Conventional performance management approaches based on linear models of change fail to capture this. Liz Richardson (2008, p. 54), for example tells the story of a failed attempt to speed up a community-based initiative to meet the external targets set by a contract. She comments that groups do many amazing things but not necessarily to the level of contract delivery.

I argued in Chapter 9 that communities need to be given a say both in what counts and how it is counted. Communities are well placed to develop their own targets and jointly owned performance measures are more likely to carry weight than outputs defined by administrators and funders, let alone by a distant consultant working for a central government department. Communities are also well placed – and highly motivated – to monitor outcomes, if they believe in them. But, as Goetz and Gaventa (2001, p. 25) have argued: 'Citizen auditing strikes right at the heart of practices which preserve the powers and privileges of bureaucrats and politicians'. It is likely to be strenuously resisted.

Nonetheless, developing community-based criteria for success can be a powerful tool for developing common agendas between partners and for understanding the assumptions and constraints that different partners bring to the table. For community partici-pants it can also turn the weary task of filling in other people's forms into a jointly owned enterprise and learning experience, so long as monitoring is a learning process and not a punish-ment for 'failure'.

Similar arguments apply to the level of risk that can be accepted in any community initiative. I argued in Chapter 9 that upwards accountability always takes precedence over downwards accountability. Monitoring requirements are driven by the need to avoid risk. But if communities are to be at the centre of change, they need to have a say in the risks that they are prepared to take and how the balance is struck between risk and security (Taylor, Langan and Hoggett 1995).

Beyond consensus

Conflict, for Bent Flyvbjerg (1998), is the sign of a strong democratic society. Earlier chapters have described how disempowering a consensus culture can be to communities and, conversely, how some of the most effective partnerships are honed through the successful negotiation of conflict. Acknowledging and working with creative tension can be one of the major achievements of partnership, and participation – if it is effective – will require differences to be expressed and frustrations to be aired. Conflict, creatively handled, can bring about a richer, more equal and more dynamic dialogue.

There are many examples from modern history – from the anti-slavery campaign onwards – of the role of struggle in achieving progress. Citing a range of literature, Flyvbjerg (1998, p. 206) claims that 'The very constitution of the public sphere' derives 'not solely from rational discourse and consensus, but "from a field of conflict, contested meanings and exclusion"'. He goes on to argue that 'resistance and struggle, rather than consensus are the most solid basis for the practice of freedom' and that 'social conflicts produce themselves the valuable ties that hold modern democratic societies together and provide them with the strength and cohesion they need' (Flyvbjerg 1998, pp. 203, 209).

Organisational development experts argue that conflict is an inevitable and important stage of group development. The sequence of *forming, storming, norming* and *performing* is one that is frequently used in their field and illustrates how groups often go through a period of dissent before agreements can be forged. In one renewal initiative I have referred to in this volume (Taylor and Parkes 2001), a respondent described how there 'was blood on the carpet' in the early days, with conflicts within communities and agencies as well as between the two. But, with time, she reported, people learnt to work together, despite their differences: 'We have gone through a Greek tragedy. Because we do have very, very different and very vocal opinions. I wouldn't say that all passion is now spent, but we can now all get on and we do achieve'.

When badly handled, conflicts can be extremely destructive, cementing divisions between and within communities as well as between partners. If partnerships are to generate creativity out of the tensions within them, they will need the institutional capacity to handle difference and diversity, along with the skills discussed earlier: mediation, negotiation and conflict resolution. But these skills are still all too rare in most partnerships and even more rarely rewarded.

Gilchrist (2009, p. 90) highlights the important mediating role that can be played by community workers, who are often located at the margins of organisations and have a special concern with boundaries and barriers. Indeed, as boundaries become more porous, there are an increasing number of people working across boundaries who can help to bridge the gaps in understanding between the very different cultures of communities and public authorities. In many countries people now move across the divide from community action to positions within the state and vice versa. My own recent research provides several examples: people from the community sector who become advisors to government ministers (see Box 13.2); local authority officers who service community partnerships and see their primary accountability as being to the community rather than the authority; a councillor who also ran an ethnic minority advocacy organisation; the leader of a third-sector intermediary body who used to work for the local authority (Howard and Taylor 2010). Councillors and officers from BME communities can also break down barriers between power holders and these communities, as long as they maintain their roots there. While some of those who cross these boundaries melt seamlessly into their new environment, scarcely noticing how their values and culture have changed, others are able to become change agents, spanning boundaries, highlighting cultural barriers and challenging traditional ways of operating that continue to exclude communities. These boundary spanners can be critical to the new ways of working that are needed in contemporary governance.

Changing structures

Partnerships that are created at community level often adopt traditional decision-making methods (see Box 7.1) and communities adjust their expectations accordingly. Monitoring requirements and performance measures imposed from outside reinforce these 'isomorphic' tendencies, as do drives to establish 'best practice', if narrowly defined and interpreted. However, Rich, Giles and Stern remind us (2007, p. 138) that bureaucracies, as well as some of the other barriers that communities come up against in their attempts to engage, are responses to 'real organisational needs for structuring authority and maintaining accountability'. While structural innovation is needed, there is no need to throw out the baby with the bathwater.

There are some simple ways in which the imbalances of power that are engrained in existing structures can be reduced. A good beginning is to make power visible and bring to the surface the practices that privilege the views of particular constituencies. For example, in one English case, after countless meetings had been bogged down in procedural matters, a Process Group was set up which brought process issues out into the open and involved both communities and partners in resolving them in a setting outside the formal decision-making meetings. Such issues might include: how meetings are run, who chairs, how bids for funding are appraised and funding dispersed, how needs and priorities are defined, how conflicts of interest are handled, how agendas are defined and structured, and so on (Taylor and Parkes 2001).

The question of chairing is particularly interesting. The people who take the chairing role in partnerships are often appointed or elected there because of their status rather than any skills in group dynamics. An alternative, which leaves the high-status chair to be the external face of the partnership but ensures that the process of the group is run effectively, is to bring in an independent professional facilitator to manage the process of the group.

Clarity of purpose follows on from this. Perri 6 and his colleagues (1999) argue that partnerships are a scarce resource that needs to be used efficiently. The promotion of partnership and participation initiatives runs the risk of becoming the victim of its own success, in that it has placed enormous strain on the community infrastructure and also on public agencies themselves. It is important, therefore, to be clear what partnerships are trying to do and what different assumptions are being brought to the table, a recommendation that has been made in virtually every study ever made of partnerships but which is still woefully lacking in practice. Then it is easier to judge whether partnerships are the most appropriate way of tackling the issue at hand and what kind of partnership will be useful.

Clarity is needed first about the nature of the enterprise and why people are working together. Pratt, Gordon and Plamping (1999) distinguish between four types of inter-agency working, based on whether goals are shared or individual, and whether they are known and predictable or open-ended. The four types are competition, co-ordination, collaboration and co-evolution (see Figure 13.1).

In later developments of this model they used the metaphor of a single mountain to describe competition, of a jigsaw to describe co-ordination, of game theory – where the different parties calculate when their individual interest is best served by joint working – to describe collaboration, and a mountain range (with all its ups and downs) for co-evolution. The best strategies for known and predictable goals are likely to be co-operation and co-ordination, where partners maintain their boundaries and separate identities. Where goals are difficult to predict, however, Pratt, Gordon and Plamping argue that partners need co-evolutionary approaches, which bind partners together more closely and shares risk among them. Otherwise there is a danger that partners will opt in and out.

Clarity is also needed about the functions that partnerships are carrying out and where responsibility lies for each of these functions, of which the most obvious are: strategy, commissioning, delivery, facilitation and monitoring. Different accountabilities,

FIGURE 13.1 *Partnership behaviour*

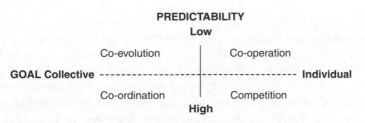

PREDICTABILITY
Low

Co-evolution		Co-operation
GOAL Collective -------------------	------------------	**Individual**
Co-ordination		Competition

High

Source: Pratt *et al.* (1999, p. 100).

relationships and skills may be needed for these different functions. In designing an appropriate model it will therefore be necessary to consider whether they can be integrated within one body or whether they may be best performed by different bodies. Putting too many functions into one body can make it unwieldy and create role confusion and conflicts of interest.

Chapter 12 discussed the value of 'nested' structures within communities, which can address conflicts of interest, involve more people and address tensions between scaling up and the need to stay close to the community. The same applies to cross-sector partnerships. Uphoff, Esman and Krishna (1998, pp. 66, 67) conclude from their studies in the South that:

> The most effective programs have had systems of 'nested' organisations that start from a base-level group or association ... Small organisations by themselves may be beautiful, but their impact will be limited if they are not joined in some larger enterprise. Any programme that aims to produce widespread benefits must address the question of how to organise a hierarchical structure that is animated from below rather than above.

Nested structures can also allow a partnership to access different kinds of money and maximise its income through covenanting and cross subsidy.

Complex structures can, however, be administratively costly and difficult to hold together. They can also be inflexible. Wilcox and Mackie (2000) argue that in some places where partnerships have been introduced, the complexity of working arrangements and community involvement makes it almost impossible to produce results. In any case, effective working arrangements need to be given time to develop. Communities that engage in partnerships will need time to get their heads round the implications of different institutional arrangements; official partners meanwhile need time to open up to new ways of organising decision making. Institutional frameworks will therefore need to be designed to adapt and evolve as the capacity of local residents and professionals develops, based on a view of where everyone wants to be in the long run and the steps that are needed to get there. The leader of the organisation described in Box 11.1 – one of the most successful community development trusts in the

UK – argued: 'It is a process rather than an administrative structure which is required: something more messy, a continuous process of relationships constantly being renegotiated, where risk and failure are accepted as inevitable, and where success is rewarded, especially when it arises from the addressing of social needs' (Tuckett 1999).

There are many who argue for a more informal approach to partnership design, based on networks. Haynes (1999) draws on chaos and complexity theory to argue that, by allowing for elements of instability, organisations can generate a new form of order. This requires a rich pattern of connections within and across organisations and subsystems and the mix of formality and informality that Chapter 12 began to discuss. Gilchrist (2000, p. 269) expands on this, suggesting that systems with low levels of connectivity and high homogeneity become stagnant because they are unable to adapt. Instead, she argues for systems that create: opportunities for interaction, mutual learning and the development of relationships based on trust as well as respect [leading to] the development of 'flexible, self-reliant networks which contain a "sufficient diversity" of skills, knowledge, interests and resources for the formation of any number of potential groups and initiatives'. On the ground this means creating space for discussion around the edges of meetings, where people can check out informally where they stand. 'Conversations held at intersections and exits, where people have easy routes and excuses to depart', she argues (2009, p. 110), 'can often be the most interesting, probably because people can take risks with what they reveal'. It is also easier to build trust in these informal settings and to develop the linking social capital in which effective democratic practice can be developed (see Box 13.3).

The notion of footloose connections, which are light on resources, light on their feet, highly adaptable and can create change at the intersections of the system, is an attractive one. Its advocates would see such connections as having the potential to tackle many of the tensions we have been discussing. But all these approaches raise questions about the sustainability and institutionalisation of change. Can bursts of power from the edges and intersections of the system be transformed into sustainable change rather than being colonised and absorbed back into existing systems, or will they spin out of the loop altogether? The arguments for informality are persuasive, but, as I have argued in earlier chapters, informal structures can still be dominated by powerful partners, with informality rendering their power less visible and accountable. They can exclude those who do not know the ropes and the ways in. They can be vulnerable to take-over if membership is too open, or to being used as the forum for perpetual conflict between different community or political factions. There is potential for considerable role confusion and conflict of interest as the different 'hats' that people are wearing become mixed up. They are formidably difficult to hold to account and depend on the integrity of key players. Can a new institutional settlement hold the virtues of both informality and formality without succumbing to their inherent weaknesses?

Lowndes and Skelcher (1998) suggest that partnerships move through life cycles, adopting different forms at different stages: looser

---

Box 13.3   Formality and informality in a partnership setting

A partnership I was involved in as a community representative in Central London had a difficult start. Meetings went on until all hours, many of us were unfamiliar with the procedures that others took for granted and very little seemed to happen as a result. This changed radically after about 18 months. To me, it seemed that four things were critical in making this change. The first was the development of a plan with clear targets, which allowed us to monitor progress from meeting to meeting. The second was that the Leader of the Council and the Mayor (who happened to be our local councillors) separately called meetings of all the Committee Chairs and Heads of Departments in the local authority and told them they had to take the partnership seriously. The third was that a member of staff was appointed to service the partnership, acting as a repository of information and a progress chaser. But the fourth was unplanned. It was simply that, as meetings got a bit shorter, we all repaired to the local pub afterwards. Things we felt we could not say in the meeting were checked out in this more informal setting. We got to know some of the key players and they got to know us. We found out who our allies were. And we all began to understand each other better and work collaboratively.

and more like networks at the beginning and end, more formal in the planning and delivery stages. As well as building in change over time, however, it is essential that community policies pay as much attention to developing informal networks and links across the sectors in parallel to the more formal structures, because it is in these settings that stereotypes are broken down and people learn that they can work together. It is likely, therefore, that the institutional forms of the future will need articulated and interlocking systems, which combine the best of formality and informality. This requires a 'whole systems' approach which seeks to understand policy and its implementation 'in terms of the interaction between each part of the system and its environment' (Stewart 2002, p. 158).

What does this mean in practice? First, that such processes require connections between communities and their partners to flow through many passages rather than through bottlenecks. This has the potential to build both 'bridging' and 'linking' 'social capital' (see Figure 11.1).

Second, that such an approach requires new kinds of mediators and brokers whose role would be to work horizontally rather than vertically (Wilkinson and Applebee 1999) – including the 'boundary spanners' who featured earlier in this chapter – in order to:

- Stimulate the exchange of knowledge across boundaries
- Make connections between potential allies across boundaries
- Build on assets, rather than focusing on needs
- Encourage joint learning.

Third, that this approach would need to be dynamic, to 'search for negotiated, collaboratively arrived at rules and practices', rather than relying on 'formal legal and procedural rules embedded in established organisations' (Healey *et al.* 2002, p. 213). Healey and her colleagues acknowledge, however, that this has to be a form of freedom within boundaries: 'The formal boundaries can never be ignored. They structure the invention of new practices, while the struggles to escape their parameters generate mobilisation campaigns to change the law'.

Fourth and finally, that this approach requires time. In earlier work, Lucy Gaster and I wrote of the learning curve involved in partnership working (Gaster and Taylor, 1993) (see Figure 13.2). There is a tipping point along this learning curve, which

FIGURE 13.2   *The learning curve in partnership*

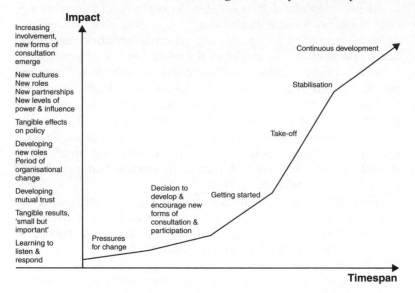

Source: Gaster and Taylor (1993, p. 17).

we called 'take-off', after which progress begins to accelerate and tangible outputs begin to be achieved. Much of my own work has suggested that this usually takes two years, before which there is relatively little to be seen (although policy makers have learnt to build in 'quick wins' nowadays), but after which the endeavour begins to bear fruit (see also Gilchrist 2009, p. 124).

Bringing the state back in?

The role of the state

If the mix of formality and informality advanced in the previous section is to work, it is likely to need an honest broker to 'hold' the tensions and provide a framework within which the system can operate. In principle, this is the role a democratic government is supposed to play and the language of enabling and govern-ance that has come to the fore in the twenty-first century em-phasises this role. It also has a critical role to play in balancing out inequalities and supporting the inclusion of marginalised people (Cornwall and Coelho 2004, p. 18). Thus Keane (1988b, p. 15) defines the state as a device for: 'containing inevitable conflicts between particular interests within well-defined legal limits, and preventing civil society from falling victim to new forms of inequality and tyranny'. The state also serves as a focus. Sidney Tarrow (1994), in his work on social movements, underlines the importance of the state as a fulcrum for groups to position themselves in society, to compare their situations to others and, where necessary, to advance their claims against those others. It provides a target for mobilisation; it can also provide cognitive frameworks within which groups can find allies and position themselves in relation to more favoured constituencies.

States may serve as a positive or negative focus. But they often fail to act as the kind of honest brokers outlined above. Whaites (2000, p. 131) voices the ambivalence of many in both North and South when he writes: 'I am caught in the paradox of seeing the state as part saviour, a vehicle for social change and equality, and part villain, an intrusive monolith with a propensity to lose sight of the common good in pursuit of its own bureaucratic agenda'. Can we trust the state to play this role?

The overall weakening of the state in the context of neo-liberal policies affects its ability to do so. Michael Storper (1998, p. 245) argues that 'progressive community activists have become unwitting allies of the withdrawal of the state from public policy'. He cites the US Empowerment Zone programme, which

> is all dressed up in the ideology of 'bottom-up' community-led development; but its structure is fundamentally defined by the withdrawal of the Federal government from an active, universalising role in urban matters and the whole program does little to restore the Reagan-era cutbacks of two-thirds of the federal funding for urban policy.

This is an argument that remains highly relevant today and Storper's call for a relegitimation of the state is one that is echoed by many writers across the globe. Some share his view that only the state has the capacity to address social exclusion. Geddes (1998, p. 92), for example, in his study of partnerships in Europe, argues that 'the involvement of the public sector is almost universal in partnerships' and that this is essential since 'the problems of unemployment, poverty and social exclusion still remain primarily the responsibility of public authorities'. Indeed, over the months in which I have been revising this book, financial recession and the global economic crisis have, momentarily at least, reminded us of role of the state in balancing the excesses of capitalism.

Development scholars – especially those who have observed the consequences of weak states in the South – are among those who argue that an effective government structure is just as essential to empowerment as a strong civil society. Thus, despite their disillusionment with the state as it is, the Commonwealth Foundation study of civil society (1999) reports that poor people would like to see strong government, insofar as it can provide services, facilitate their involvement and promote equal rights and justice. Similarly, Dey and Westendorff (1996, p. 1), referring to research for the UN Research Institute for Social Development (UNRISD) and the UN Volunteers (UNV), report that: 'One of the findings to emerge most forcefully from the UNV–UNRISD project was that community responses to urban social problems could achieve much greater impact if they occurred in a context of genuine support from a stronger, more open local government'.

The UK experience over the 1970s and 1980s illustrates this further. While, in the 1970s, much community action saw local government and public services as the enemy, in the 1980s communities were fighting alongside local government to defend public services against the depredations of the Thatcher government. This did not represent any change of heart. The opposition came from people's belief that public services were not delivering; the support from the belief that only the state could deliver the rights, services and redistribution that excluded communities need. Indeed, from the US, Fairbanks (2007, pp. 103–4) summarises a range of research to show how decentralisation of the responsibility of welfare to non-profit organisations, along with an increasing reliance on philanthropy and volunteering, has had highly regressive effects. Fundamentally the need for the state derives from the insufficiency of other actors.

We need in this discussion to differentiate between the nation state and the local state. Decentralisation is a strong part of the community discourse. But, while there are many who announce the hollowing out of the nation state in the context of globalisation, the fact remains that its ability to tackle the structural causes of exclusion remains far stronger than that of isolated communities. De Filippis and Saegert argue that devolution has limited the potential for federal spending when economic downturns create increased social demand. The 'pitiful response to Hurricane Katrina', they suggest, is 'related to devolution of responsibilities to local levels without adequate provision of resources or coordination of levels of government' as well as 'the decreased efficacy of federal agencies in performing core missions' (2007, p. 331). Amazingly in this richest of countries, they report that foreign governments stepped in, both in New Orleans and elsewhere. I write from the UK, a very centralised country, where central government has nonetheless recognised the need – in principle at least – to allow more decisions to be taken at local level. But the role of the central state in funding community initiatives over the past decade or so has been critical in both driving change and ensuring that community engagement does not become a postcode lottery. Getting the balance right between driving change from the centre and devolving decisions to the local level has proved tricky. For example, some years ago the New Labour government introduced a programme of funding to support community representation in local strategic partnerships. But before the programme had run its course, the decision was taken that the funding should be devolved to local level, with the result that much of this newly developing democratic infrastructure disappeared (CLG 2005; Urban Forum 2008). A frustrated national commentator remarked:

> The government is nationally elected but is giving up all the levers to implement its policies. We are not just electing bureaucrats. There needs to be a debate about the practical implications of a devolution agenda, a new agreement between central and local government.

Getting the balance right

We do not really have the structures that can make partnership work, that can satisfy the needs of public accountability and yet be flexible enough to take risks and represent the diversity in communities. In these circumstances, the frequent juxtaposition between 'top-down' and 'bottom-up' is not helpful. Gaventa argues that real change comes from working at the interstices between bottom-up (popular) and top-down (invited) spaces (see p. 230, this volume). 'Navigating the intersections of relationships', he argues (2004, p. 38), may 'in turn create new boundaries of possibility for action and engagement'. We need to generate a new middle ground: a new public space where the tensions I have discussed can be addressed. But what sort of spaces are these?

In their analysis of citizenship and social movements, Leach and Scoones (2007, p. 15, 18) argue that, 'in a world increasingly influenced by the dispersing and fragmented effects of globalisation, there is a need to go beyond state-centred or even pluralist accounts of citizenship'. Citing Ellison (1997) they go on to argue that 'the multiplication of identities, affiliations and forms of solidarity' in contemporary society will require 'the dissolving of more conventional boundaries between the public and private, the political and the social', with a more 'practised social engagement through social solidarities'. Mike Saward, too, argues that in a post-statist context that has no single centre of authority, it is necessary to think in new ways, with mechanisms across boundaries that are changeable, temporary and sporadic (2005).

How far do new governance spaces fit this bill – or at least provide a springboard on which to build? Healey *et al.* (2002, p. 213) accuse the bodies that are being set up in the move to governance as being 'chronically deficient in formal procedures for legitimacy and accountability'. In the UK, many partnerships are constituting themselves as companies limited by guarantee with charitable status (not-for-profit companies), which begs all sorts of questions about precisely what kind of animal they are. The fact that many of them were set up by government and have substantial government representation could create a dangerous path out of political accountability for governments themselves.

Nor do these spaces address the relationship between representative and participatory forms of government – as I argued earlier, elected representatives in these spaces are often highly uncertain about their status and liabilities (Howard and Taylor 2010). However we may judge the performance of elected politicians and the formal democratic system over the years, the new institutions of governance do not yet provide a robust alternative and are vulnerable to capture. Some see deliberation as enabling more subtle feedback to politicians and public institutions, but Melucci argues that the multiplicity of spaces in which people and interests can be represented only serves to increase the tension between the structures of representation and the interests of those represented (Barnes *et al.* 2007, pp. 49, 186).

The relationship between the elected representative and participatory forms of democracy merits more attention than I have been able to give it in these pages. I have written briefly in Chapter 9 about the wounded 'lions' and their resistance to change and later about the uncertainty that surrounds their role. But over the years I have come across local councillors who have been real champions of their communities, working tirelessly alongside residents, identifying resources, championing their communities in places the communities themselves could not reach and establishing their own legitimacy by working closely with local people so that they knew the communities they represented inside out. In the UK, the increasing centralisation of political parties and their falling membership, along with the crisis of representation – with elected local councillors increasingly atypical of the population at large – put considerable pressure on this relationship and recent government initiatives have done little to address this. This relationship is likely to become an increasingly vexed issue over the coming years.

Saward (2005, p. 181) argues that representation is a blunt medium for the expression of the diverse preferences in society: 'Traditional geographical constituencies do not have characteristics, faultlines and policy preferences that can be simply ... read-off by would-be elected representatives.' Instead, he advocates new forms of stakeholder governance and calls attention to the role of representation in constituting identities and issues within consultative, participative, or implementation processes. He makes a case for new, more flexible types of representative claim, which can give prominence to marginalised interests, emergent interests and what he calls 'intense interests'. While this encourages us towards new, more fluid ways of grappling with this difficult concept, however, it is not clear how his ideas would translate into practice on the ground.

Discussion

Community policies have a habit of appearing in short bursts of enthusiasm and commitment followed by years in the doldrums.

This chapter has discussed the need to develop a stronger institutional and cultural underpinning that can sustain community engagement in the mainstream of governance processes. In doing so, it has urged the need for more flexible and co-evolutionary processes that can encompass complexity, risk and diversity, echoing the jazz metaphor with which the chapter started. This will require imagination and innovation in institutional design as well as new ways of approaching the thorny question of democratic accountability. While moving from government to governance is a phrase that trips lightly off the tongue, it represents a considerable challenge.

This chapter has also underlined the role of a democratic state in the negotiation of competing interests and in providing an accountable framework for governance. However, governments in many countries and in many localities have a lot of work to do to convince their citizens that they can be trusted with these roles. If the state is to be relegitimated as Storper suggested, this will require informed communities to hold it to account and inform its actions. Howell and Pearce argue that, rather than stressing the separation between state and civil society, we should be defining them in a symbiotic relationship (see also Chapter 5). Using Nancy Fraser's concept of strong publics (1994), they argue that: 'from strong publics could come new thinking about the state and its role in development and about ways of ensuring that a developmental state is also a democratic state, a debate that needs to be re-opened, after being buried in our view, by the emphasis on civil society' (Howell and Pearce 2002, p. 7). The task for effective community policies is to create the environment within which those strong publics can emerge and be fully engaged in that debate from the basis of experience on the ground.

Chapter 14

Community Empowerment: Myth or Reality?

A global world

This book began with the many challenges that commentators across the globe have identified for the twenty-first century. The giant among these has been 'globalisation'. It is a phenomenon that brings many new opportunities, but the ideological dominance of market capitalism, with the convergence of global markets, has costs too. It has seen a widening chasm between the winners and the losers. The middle classes may have expanded, giving more of us access to the fruits of economic growth, but the gap between the rich and the poor has grown inexorably and social mobility is in decline (Judt 2010). The excessive earnings of the wealthy pull the threshold of inclusion up to ever higher levels. And while, at the one end of the scale we have global citizens, whose influence extends across continents; at the other, growing numbers of people are dispossessed by war, environmental catastrophe, and political and economic oppression.

Globalisation, say its critics, has taken power away from the nation state and fragmented communities. It has led to the abandonment of the public sphere, the erosion of public responsibility, the loss of public space and the eclipse of the public realm. Instead, we have the shopping mall – under the constant gaze of CCTV – in a consumer society that is seen by its critics as both impoverishing culture and prejudicing the future sustainability of the planet (Friedmann 1998). This consumer culture has also impoverished political life, as we have moved from the politics of class to the consumerist politics of identity, reflected in a preoccupation with style and 'message' rather than substance. In a shop-around society, those who can are increasingly choosing 'off the shelf' identities, politics and moralities, while those who cannot risk being seduced into exclusive sectarian, racist and fundamentalist politics, which render the dispossessed vulnerable as both followers and targets.

In the conclusion to my first edition, I discussed a spate of campaigns against paedophiles on public housing estates in England at the time and the way that they threw into relief the paradoxes in the community agenda. There were stories of innocent people, who happened to have the wrong names, being hounded from their homes. Social commentators were horrified. But there is no doubt that these communities had really got their act together: their campaigns caught the headlines in a way that most community activists can only dream of. A sense of empowerment – of finally taking the initiative – was obvious from many of the media interviews, and local authorities were moving mountains to meet the community leaders. In a similar way waves of racial unrest over the decades – and the recent rise of the far right – have focused political minds and brought investment into divided communities.

Writing about similar demonstrations in the 1990s, one journalist looked beyond the headlines. 'What we haven't asked', she said, 'is whether these protests have anything to do with paedophiles' (Decca Aikenhead, *The Guardian* 1998). Or are they more to do with the insecurity that is inherent in contemporary society and the need for someone to blame as an outlet for long-accumulated anxiety (Bauman 1999)? The more privileged in society lobby more subtly and more successfully to ensure that the most vulnerable, or threatening, people do not end up in their backyard; or they simply buy their way out of that kind of risk. They/we make sure, too, that incinerators, waste dumps and other unwanted or potentially unsafe items are sited far away. However, this means that risk is displaced onto those least able to bear it, with communities that are already stressed expected to take on extra pressure, without the resources to do so. Seen in this light, communities that have dumped on them everything and everyone that the rest of society does not want in its backyard do have a case.

The rise of the far right in recent years is an issue that is exercising politicians' minds across Europe. Perhaps it has something to do with the fact that, in disadvantaged neighbourhoods, far-right groups may now be the only people organising at a local level – going from door to door to ask what people's concerns are, just like community workers used to do. Mainstream political parties no longer have much of a local presence in the UK. And who else, at a time when professionals complain of having to spend more and more time meeting targets and filling in forms, finds the time to listen? It is instructive to read, in a recent survey of community workers in the UK, that one-third of respondents said they spent less than a quarter of their time in direct contact with communities (Glen *et al.* 2003).

Can community deliver?

This paints a rather gloomy picture. But it is against this background that concern in governments and global institutions about the persistence and possible effects of poverty and exclusion has led to a resurgence of interest in 'community'. Associated with community are ideas of empowerment, participation and partnership, with communities expected to take their place in radically new forms of service delivery and governance. This set of ideas (social capital and civil society prominent among them) form part of the armoury that, it is hoped, will redress the imbalances of the global economy – or perhaps ameliorate its worst effects. Community is seen to offer the prospect of reinstating social and moral cohesion, mediating between global forces and what Richard Sennett has called 'the tyranny of intimacy' that has resulted from the demise of the public sphere (Sennett cited in Misztal 2003).

While this renewed interest in community and the stable of ideas associated with it is welcome, however, it is necessary to exercise some caution before hailing it as a potential answer to the world's woes. Pitting the David of community against the Goliath of international capital requires a huge leap of imagination or at least a healthy dose of realism, especially when the Davids in question are the very people whom international capitalism has rejected. On the other hand, David did prevail. I could fill this page with many positive stories of campaigns won, people's lives transformed and links formed between people across the world. But if policy is to build social capital and draw on the strengths of community, mutuality and civil society to tackle social exclusion, it needs a tough, rigorous and realistic understanding of how these concepts operate in the real world as well as the conditions that allow them to flourish.

It is instructive in this respect to go back to the last time that community and empowerment enjoyed a resurgence in the North. Several times in this book I have referred to Marris and Rein's seminal analysis of the US War on Poverty in 1967 – a government programme that combined resources, community development and research to tackle the persistence of poverty in an affluent society. Much of their analysis – which highlighted the 'dilemmas of social reform' – remains true in the twenty-first century. I want to focus on three of those dilemmas, which have also been central to the discussion in this book. The first is the 'intransigent autonomy of public and private agencies, at any level of government'; the second is the contradiction within the idea of community itself; the third is how to build an informed and evidence-based approach to change.

Firstly, many writers over the years and across the globe have commented on the resistance of many public authorities to the sharing of power with communities. This appears to be the case even when parts of the public sector are fighting for their lives and communities are potential allies, as anxious to support the continued role of the state in welfare as the authorities themselves. Sometimes this intransigence is overt: Marris and Rein report that city mayors were particularly resistant in the US to a federally imposed programme. But it is often more subtle than this. Marris and Rein (1967, p. 218) identify two fundamental contradictions in the administration of the War on Poverty. The first was that, while it was supposed to be run *by* poor communities, its implementation depended on the powers and resources of government. The second was that this programme to tackle social exclusion had to be paid for and mandated by the 'included'. This gives those within the system who do not want to change ample opportunity for resistance. It is worth quoting Marris and Rein (1967, p. 218) at length here, since so much of what they say mirrors the dilemmas discussed in Chapter 9 of this book:

> Community action has still to be contained within bureaucracies which answer to the community at large. ... Unless the representatives of the poor are satisfied with gradual change ... their demands seem likely to be more than social agencies can assimilate, without antagonising those who pay for most of their functions. Unable to serve two masters with incompatible

claims upon them, bureaucracies will surely seek to evade unwelcome commitments. By delay and obstruction, by the authority of their professional knowledge, by reinterpreting intentions, they will out-manoeuvre the radicalism of the poor. ... And in this they will probably meet, as a democratic administration must, the wishes of the majority.

Encouraging poor communities to organise, they argued, was seen to be 'unsettling politics' and the outcome was that many cities received considerable funding without involving poor people in policymaking at all (p. 219). Diversity in funding addressed some of these problems by allowing piecemeal reform, but meant abandoning the dream of a coherent strategic programme . There was no critical mass; reform was incremental.

The settlement between central and local government, and independent institutions –whether business or the third sector – will of course be different from country to country. But Marris and Rein's analysis resonates with experience in other Northern countries, while analysis from the South identifies similar issues, depending on the strength or weakness of government (Edwards and Hulme 1995c).

The second dilemma surrounds the nature of 'community' itself and its struggle to reconcile contending ideals. Marris and Rein (1967, pp. 185–6) underline the particular difficulties of organising a coherent constituency around poverty: to be poor, they argue, is not a status that defines a common political interest. In these circumstances, 'the pressure for reform becomes fragmented, unsure of itself, and easily patronised'. Other writers highlight the inherent parochialism of many communities – rich and poor – and the constant challenge that is posed by the need to find ways of reconciling diversity and mediating potential conflict.

The third dilemma that Marris and Rein identify pits the requirements of a sound evidence base against the high-pressure demands of politics. Is it possible, they ask, to develop a rational process of reform which is informed, evidence-based and carefully planned while accommodating the twists and turns of the real world and meeting the needs of politicians and residents for quick returns? This is a dilemma that has moved to centre stage since Marris and Rein carried out their analysis. A recurring theme in this volume has been the advance of the technical over the political, a measurement and audit culture that threatens not only to exclude those that community programmes are meant to help but also to swamp genuine attempts to learn and develop. Again Marris and Rein (p. 207) make an important contribution to the debate. Describing the original intention as 'a blue-print of planned intervention, articulate theory, rigorous method and objective measurement', they found that:

> The final outcome cannot simply be related to the initial aim and method. The whole process – the false starts, frustrations, adaptations, the successive recasting of intentions, the detours and conflicts – needs to be comprehended. Only then can we understand what has been achieved and learn from the experience.

Careful and informed planning is important, as is the search for evidence to back up the claims made for community policy and practice. But this search has to acknowledge the near impossibility of producing the clear-cut evidence that politicians require and the limitations of too simplistic an approach. The focus today on 'evidence based' and 'best' practice makes assumptions about the transferability of practice and how people learn, which the above critique does not support. It also raises questions about who is defining 'best practice'. Edwards and Hulme cite Carroll's argument (1992, p. 164) that long-term institutional support requires a 'continual dialogue about objectives and strategies, rather than simply a specification of outputs and targets' and, I might add, the hasty retrospective evaluations by consultants that often characterise local interventions. This is the difference that Habermas draws between instrumental rationality and communicative action (see Chapter 8). It also reminds us that policymaking is a political process and cannot be reduced to management and accounting procedures. Benjamin Barber (1992, p. 52) argues that the rational scientific approach 'voids politics of its essential meaning altogether'. Solving the 'wicked issues' of policy is a process that needs to draw on the dialogue between different forms of knowledge that can inform, complement and challenge each other.

These dilemmas, identified by Marris and Rein over 40 years ago, reflect the particular make-up of US society: a mixture of tolerance and competition which tends, they argue, to end in a frustrating stalemate for those who wish to introduce strategic reform: 'the hundred flowers bloom, but they do not make a garden' (Marris and Rein 1967, p. 237). But they are not pessimists. They credit the War on Poverty with the birth of what they call the social reformer: the professional expert who, at best, acts as a broker between government and people. They also argue (p. 223) that, despite the programme's disintegration, it left behind a permanent achievement:

In those five years, community action developed a range of skills, concepts, organisations, models of action, which equipped the search with much more sophisticated means. And by this, it ... stimulated a realignment of resources and ideas which powerfully influenced the variety of initiatives that now competed for priority in the exploration of reform.

Pessimist, optimist or pragmatist?

In the opening chapter of this book, I set out the possible views of pessimists, optimists and pragmatists in response to the contemporary interest in 'community'. How are these different perspectives affected by the theory and practice discussed in this volume?

The pessimistic scenario

The 'pessimists' might argue that nothing has changed in the past five decades. They would point to the successive fashions in community policies in the intervening years: the regular re-emergence of policies that blame the poor and the belief that social inclusion is ultimately all about getting people into jobs (important though this is as part of a wider strategy). They would cite the facility with which successive bureaucracies adapt to whatever new regimes can throw at them; the continuing and widening polarisation between rich and poor; the failure to learn from the past; and the tendency to reinvent the wheel.

A pessimistic analysis would see power as a zero-sum game. It would argue that the state will always work to shore up capitalism and the power of the global economy. Habermas (Ambrose 2000) has argued that many of the programmes that are presented by governments to tackle endemic structural inequalities are presented in one of two ways. The first is to present them as something confined to marginal groups; the second as problems that can be solved by better management. This form of presentation is required so that the legitimacy of the system is not endangered. In this analysis, the call for community is a way of reducing costs, a primary strategy for managing economic decline, for anticipating and controlling potential social unrest and for getting 'the poor' to manage their own exclusion. Communities, the pessimists might argue, are being set up to fail. Involvement in participation, community management and other initiatives diverts the attention of communities away from the issues that contribute to their exclusion and focuses attention away from the inexorable march of global power. They might also draw attention to the way in which acceptance into governance spaces has been accompanied by increasing intolerance of those who choose to stay outside the system and engage in traditional forms of dissent.

O'Connor (2007, p. 10) describes how, 'having encouraged the trends that impoverish communities in the first place, the federal government steps in with modest and inadequate interventions to deal with the consequences ... and then wonders why community development so often "fails"'. The use of 'community' and associated terms in current policy is reminiscent of Wolfgang Seibel's theory of 'mellow weakness' (1989). Seibel developed this theory in relation to the non-profit or voluntary sector, arguing that the state displaces on to this sector the responsibilities that it cannot fulfil. In doing so, it deflects responsibility away from itself. Certainly, there are many who see the current interest in 'community' as what members of the governmentality school, in their rather formidable terminology, call 'responsibilisation', making communities responsible for the gaps that the withdrawal of the state leaves behind.

Pessimists might also argue that society is never going to allocate the resources needed to address poverty seriously: in a democratic society, those who have benefited from progress will not allow it. Tax breaks will always be preferred by the electorate over welfare reforms and, with the marketisation of welfare, the support of the middle classes for public provision – always essential if the state is to invest in welfare – will melt away, leaving poorly resourced, residual provision for those who cannot afford to buy their way out. In this argument, the logic of capitalism will always be to create 'marginal people' (Harman 1993). The forces of the global economy will exclude faster than any policy can include. Even in the wake of the recent crisis of global capitalism, many commentators feel that nothing has been learnt and politicians are too weak – or too embedded in the system – to rein in its excesses.

Pessimists might also stress the limitations of community action as a driver for change. They would argue that neighbourhood action tends to be parochial, and not concerned with what goes on at city and wider regional levels. They would bear witness to the increasing fragmentation that characterises society today and expose the conflicts and struggles within communities. They would add that community empowerment, in any case, only extends to the few – an unrepresentative minority who can be as oppressive as the market or the state or who become irrelevant, as they are seduced into the system and away from their constituencies. They might agree with Edwards (2004, p. 79) that the reality of dialogic politics is still likely to be 'one of entrenched inequality in voice and access'. They might also argue that creating change within a fluid and complex system requires considerable sophistication and that traditional forms of opposition are stuck in a game that is far removed from – and largely irrelevant to – the realities of today's society.

A further set of arguments would despair of the current hegemony of technocratic cultures – and the way in which the new managerialism and the audit culture have taken politics out of the public sphere and policymaking. Participation and partnership initiatives, the pessimist would add, are creating an industry that largely benefits the professionals and the consultants who have flooded into the field, with communities as unpaid accessories that need to have their 'capacity built' to fit in. Following Michel Foucault, they would see the growth of toolkits, guidelines and consultancy as an industry that is reinventing central, top-down control in more subtle forms, specialising in 'off-the shelf' technical fixes. Participation in this view is a veneer, a game, even a 'tyranny', rather than a genuine attempt to give a voice to the disenfranchised.

Finally, critics would probably take the arguments for 'inclusionary argumentation' (Healey 1997), for communicative action (Habermas 1984), for dialogue and whole-system approaches, for 'practised social engagement through social solidarities' (Ellison 1997) and for 'networking to the edge of chaos' (Gilchrist 2000), and demand to know what these actually mean in practice. They would have little time for 'process', arguing with Green (1998, p. 72), that: 'A productless process is a very Western, upper middle class intellectual and psychological amenity good'.

These are powerful arguments and need always to be the counterfactual against which practice and policy is tested. But pessimism is fatalist, allows little room for change and few guidelines for effective practice at community level. Cynicism is a luxury, which abandons those who are excluded to their fate. There has to be a place for optimism or at least for a pragmatic reworking of the lessons of the past.

An optimistic scenario

Optimists would argue that there has been a seismic shift in discourse and practice that will leave the landscape permanently altered, even if there are occasional reversals. They would marvel at the conversion of such powerful institutions as the World Bank and the International Monetary Fund to the cause of participation and the leverage that this has provided for change in the most intransigent governments.

At ground level, they would call attention to the thousands of people who, through engaging with various forms of community activity and action, have enriched the quality of their lives and those around them. They would point to allies in the state – and perhaps also the private sector – and those whose thinking and practice has changed. They would cite the gains that have been made through community-based action, the expertise that communities have acquired in navigating the tensions of engagement, and the instances where communities have broken free of the empowerment industry and taken control themselves. They would also stress the importance of small incremental changes to those who have benefitted. Optimists would also see the growing dialogue between North and South as a positive sign, with the recognition in the North of what it can learn from the inventiveness that has characterised grass-roots developments in the South. They would see the spread of practices such as participatory budgeting from South to North as evidence of the potential for changing the balance between state and citizen when the state is genuinely committed to empowerment.

Another school of optimists would point to the increasing prevalence of 'globalisation from below', the growing evidence that people are no longer accepting the inevitability of the economic growth argument, the costs that are associated with it or explanations that blame individuals for not being able to keep up. The wave of protests that have begun at least to sting the Leviathan of international capital and the ease with which their image is carried around the world by new technology gives new cause for hope. Indeed, Marris' argument in the 1990s – that the scope for influence at international level is potentially greater than at national level – still carries conviction:

> At both the Cairo conference on population and development in 1994 and the fourth world conference on women in Beijing in 1996, nongovernmental organisations largely defined the issues and drafted the resolutions, and by their parallel participation in these events acted as an informal Parliament, representing the women of the world more immediately than did the delegates of their governments. (Marris 1998, p. 12)

Optimists would also celebrate the potential of the communications revolution and the power of the Internet. The protests described above are only the most visible aspects of a network of linkages between local action in all parts of the globe that is allowing communities to learn and draw strength from each other. They would also celebrate the success of Barack Obama's campaign for the US presidency as an example of what community organising can achieve when married with new technologies – perhaps even as the harbinger of a new form of politics.

A pragmatic scenario

Pragmatists – and I count myself as one – would probably echo Gramsci's call to combine 'pessimism of the intellect' with 'optimism of the will'. They would acknowledge the advances claimed by the optimists, but they would inject these claims with a healthy dose of realism. They would remind us of the force with which the state has come down on anti-globalisation protests and the leeway that the events of 11 September 2001 have given for governments to increase the repression of dissent. With Saul Alinsky (1971, p. 12), they might argue that 'the basic requirement for the understanding of the politics of change is to recognise the world as it is'. On the other hand, they would still, on balance, see power as a positive-sum game and one where dominant ideas about the way the world works can be refashioned personally or through collective endeavour, as Chapter 7 suggested. With Popple and Shaw (1997, p. 194), they would acknowledge that community development has often been used to maintain the status quo, but argue that the 'the spaces created by community development have also been used to foster and sustain resistance'.

The task for the pragmatists is not to promote a blueprint or 'grand narrative' for change. It is to open up and exploit the gaps and tensions in a fluid and complex system. Pragmatists would emphasise the importance of using the new political opportunities that have developed to create new political spaces, at the interstices between 'invited' and popular' spaces. They would work with those who are politically, socially and economically excluded to develop the 'strong publics' (Fraser 1994) with which we ended Chapter 12, ensuring that there are a variety of ways into engagement. The role for those who want to support change at community level, in this analysis, is to make power visible, identify the opportunities for change and to ensure that communities are ready and have the skills to exploit them.

This means working with communities over the long term, linking people up, creating the spaces and energies for co-operative enquiry and exploration, sharing and understanding experience. It means spreading involvement, and keeping things going through the thin times, so that the organisational intelligence, the 'abeyance structures' and networks are there when they are needed. It means acting as a 'social relay' to link up the people across different systems who can mobilise to exploit opportunities for change. It means finding the allies whose external resources provide communities with resources they cannot command on their own (Tarrow 1994, p. 185) and pushing at the edges of what is possible, as Kuti (1999) suggested was the case in Central and Eastern Europe. It also means linking local communities together at local, regional and national level, and encouraging dialogue between communities of place and communities of identity.

The very complexity of the policy world today works against rigidity and total control. Some of the theories now being applied to policymaking and implementation betray this very well: complexity theory, chaos theory and even 'garbage can' theory (see Chapter 8). Neither policymaking nor even power is as neatly sewn up as some of the pessimists suggest. There are windows of opportunity and cracks in the system; there are allies in the most uncompromising institutions. There are also significant opportunities to link up communities across localities, regions and countries, and combat the isolation that makes communities invisible. There is enormous potential in such alliances for learning, for the development of new community-based narratives and for the development of new networks of power which can be deployed at all levels. The communications revolution, in particular, opens up significant new opportunities but, if these are to be realised they must be shared much more effectively than they have been to date.

Making pragmatism work

Pragmatism is not a soft option. To make all this possible requires a sophisticated understanding both of the nature of community and of the way power and policy works in today's society, so that communities can assess the strategies available to them in different political circumstances and widen the cracks that do appear. It means finding answers to the difficult institutional and community dilemmas that I outlined in Chapters 12 and 13. It requires a rediscovery of the public sphere and relegitimation of the role of the state. It also requires the skill and creativity to work on the inside and the outside of the system.

Power

Central to effective community engagement is a sophisticated understanding of power. Cairncross, Clapham and Goodlad (1994) build on Stewart Clegg's analysis, which I discussed in Chapter 7, to construct tenant participation as a series of relational games. Power can become fixed through 'obligatory passage points' or 'the rules of the game', but people can gain power by playing the game effectively or by resisting or even redefining the rules of the game presented to them. To do this effectively, communities need to understand how power is constituting and reconstituting itself, and to be able to identify the windows of opportunity for engagement and resistance.

Understanding power means not only understanding how power elites hang on to their own power: it also means that communities need to recognise and realise the potential power that they have. Across the world, an increasing number of communities are being courted by official agencies anxious to fill in the 'community involvement line' in bids for funding or for debt relief. This is powerful leverage. But communities still have difficulty making that leverage count. Too often, 'community involvement' is just treated by partners as a box to tick. Community players may need to make hard choices and say 'No' more often if they are to gain entry to the decision-making circuit. Indeed, demands from the World Bank and other major institutions for evidence of participation will only be effective if communities are prepared to blow the whistle when that evidence is not there. On the other hand, communities can only make their voices count if institutions are prepared to listen to that whistle and to be realistic in their expectations of representation and legitimacy.

In an increasingly fragmented policy environment, power is more difficult to locate and address than it was when, for example, the formal institutions of government at national and local level were the only players. But this fragmentation also creates potential, as cracks open up within the system to be exploited. The new political opportunities have empowered allies within the system as well as communities on the outside. These allies may be looking to community groups to create the pressures for the changes they themselves want to see. Communities need to develop a practice that can work with these allies across the institutional map to find the possibilities for change in an increasingly turbulent environment. New alliances can also be developed as different players begin to work together and come to understand each other. Change agents need to resist partnership bottlenecks and recognise that this may mean putting as much work into the *informal* networks and links across the sectors as the formal ones.

Clegg (1989, p. 221) argues that isolation and division increases the chances that communities will be 'outflanked' by those who are in control of the game. Sharing experience and creating alliances across communities themselves is therefore needed to build both consciousness and confidence, and also to redefine the way in which the game is played. Divisions deliver power into the hands of opponents. Alliances and networks across communities and across countries deliver power into the hands of communities. In the same way that individuals gain strength from sharing their knowledge and experience with each other, so alliances create a space where communities can recognise that the problems they are encountering are shared and pool experience as to how they can be tackled.

Another advantage that alliances and networks give to local communities is the ability to refer to good practice in other settings. The concern in governments and international bodies with national and international 'best practice' gives considerable leverage to those communities that can point to innovation and effective power-sharing initiatives elsewhere. Communities also have an unprecedented opportunity to build up their own definitions of good practice if they are prepared (and can find the resources) to link up with their counterparts across the globe.

A post-modern analysis would argue that the future lies with those who are adept at working across conventional boundaries. Certainly, increasing fragmentation, complexity and fluidity is likely to create more of these precious creatures. It will also, as I have suggested in earlier chapters, place a premium on new skills: of networking, mediation, negotiation, facilitation and conflict resolution. Boundary spanners can command respect across conventional boundaries; but they will need considerable resilience – the boundary spanner will often be perceived as 'not one of us' by both 'sides', despite his or her best efforts (Howard and Taylor 2010).

However, what my own and other research has underlined in recent years is that 'invited spaces', while welcome are not enough. For, if 'invited spaces become the only legitimate channel for citizens to press their demands on the state', there will be costs not only to the quality of democratic citizenship but for those who never find their way in (Cornwall, Romano and Shankland 2008, p. 53). Communities need their own independent 'popular' spaces, where they can find their voice and their feet. They can then enter invited spaces from this springboard if they feel it is appropriate. But ultimately, it is from the spaces that citizens define for themselves and from the solidarity developed there that change comes:

> History suggests that the impetus for radically progressive change must come from civil society. ... Political and business elites have little incentive to initiate the reallocation of power, resources and privilege. (Lawrence 2007, p. 292)

A recent Commission on the Future of Civil Society in the UK and Ireland (Carnegie UK 2010) develops this point in relation to the media. It highlights the increasing concentration of media power across the globe, the lack of transparency in news production and the threat to public-service broadcasting values, only partly balanced, it argues, by the use of the web. It sees a crucial role for civil society in regrowing local and community news media but also in holding the bigger players accountable and scrutinising the quality and authenticity of information they produce.

Community

If we need a more sophisticated idea of power, we certainly need a more sophisticated understanding of 'community' and the concepts associated with it, as well as a stronger empirical base to inform debate. In my previous edition, I argued that the community studies tradition of the 1960s needed to be renewed and extended in order to create a more robust analysis of what value 'community' and its related concepts do or do not add in a multi-ethnic and multi-faith society. In the UK, the term super-diverse is becoming increasingly common as a way of describing multi-ethnic, multicultural communities. What will this mean for notions of community? De Filippis and Saegert (2007b), for example, claim that immigration is transforming the meanings of both community and development, with diaspora communities relating as strongly to their place of origin as to their place of residence. Will the notion of community become detached from place? The growth of social networking raises a similar question, as people increasingly forge their identities and develop significant relationships online.

We also need to know more about what it is that makes some communities work effectively together and others not. We still know too little – beyond 'best practice examples' – about the networks and capacities within communities and how these affect what works and what does not. Policy needs to be based in a much deeper understanding of how people in communities actually engage with each other and with the outside world in different political and economic circumstances.

Work on collective efficacy in relation to crime (Sampson, Raudenbusch and Earls 1997) and community resilience in relation to emergencies and disasters has addressed this issue by seeking to define the characteristics of communities that can pull together in the face of hazards or threats to their well-being. We might need to be wary of introducing yet more terms into the community lexicon – especially if by focusing on what communities can do, they absolve the wider society of its responsibilities. But insofar as these new terms provoke interest, promote debate and stimulate new thinking, they have a role to play. The empirical search to identify the characteristics that make a difference between those communities that can rise to the challenges they face and those that are destroyed by them, certainly has the potential to take thinking forward.

Gilchrist (2010) argues that community resilience as a concept is capable of bringing together different aspects of the community portfolio – capacities, capabilities, context and connectivity – into an interdependent and integrated whole. She sees it as a combination of psychological mindsets, connectivity and practical capability 'enabling communities to innovate, adapt and reorganise in order to survive', in much the same way as, in engineering, the term refers to the way in which materials or a system can adapt to distortion or damage. It cannot, she argues, be taught or delivered by experts – she cites the 'second tsunami' in Sri Lanka of 'well-meant and generously given help which nonetheless swamped the efforts of the indigenous voluntary and community groups' and 'undermined local initiative'. What it does emphasise is the need to find the most appropriate way of supporting communities in developing their own resilience rather than abandoning them to their fates.

An encouraging development in our understanding of community practice over recent years has been the increased exchange of learning between North and South – between social policy traditions in the North and development studies in the South. An understanding of the importance of political and historical context, both between and within world regions, has the potential to bring a new critical edge to policy in any individual country, as well as to challenge assumptions and introduce new ideas. Research can also be enriched by a participatory approach, which is open to different forms of knowledge and insight. Both will be essential if informed policy interest in community is to be sustained.

Institutional dilemmas

The new political opportunities that exist in the twenty-first century have swept away some of the persistent problems of the past; while progress is still fragile, recent initiatives in the UK, for example, have allowed more time and resources for communities to engage effectively. By clearing away a lot of the undergrowth that suffocated previous initiatives, these opportunities have exposed some of the more persistent tensions of partnership. If they are serious about sharing more power with communities, public agencies need to look seriously at the way they operate and the cultures that they take for granted and how they might break down the barriers that have prevented change. Communities themselves and those who are committed to supporting them have difficult decisions to make about how they work with external actors, how they address difference and diversity, how to engage people at different levels and how to take their concerns into wider arenas.

Perhaps the key challenge for community policy is to accommodate – and indeed celebrate – diversity and yet forge the common bonds that we need to survive. Community and civil society are the places where we want to have it both ways. We want social cohesion and a sense of belonging, but also the freedom to be individuals. This is not just a problem for excluded communities – it is a reflection of the wider dilemma within society as a whole, as John Gray (1996, p. 23) has argued:

> After all necessary constitutional reforms, the real task is the political one of searching for the elusive thread of common life through the labyrinth of intractably conflicting interests and ideals.

Understanding of both the 'public' and the 'public sphere' needs to be reconstructed in ways that can encompass diversity but are not swamped by it. At an institutional level, this requires new forms of governance that can mediate conflict and diversity effectively without succumbing to a bland consensus or denying the emotions and passions that motivate many citizens to take action at local level (Gaventa 2006). The participatory world, as Jenny Pearce reminds us, will never be a pristine universe of easy consensus building. Indeed, Powell (2009, p. 52) compares the bucolic Tocquevillian vision of Americans associating in a Utopian world, which has generated much contemporary thinking about community and social capital, with the more robust European notion of a democracy based on conflict. But resolution is still needed. Key to this, several scholars have argued, is the notion of civility, which, Edwards argues (2004), is absolutely not about avoiding debate and political controversy, but about respect for strangers and resolving disagreements peacefully. Effective community policy needs institutions and institutional players who can achieve the difficult task of reconciling these different ideas.

A second challenge at both community and institutional level is between leadership and representation on the one hand and participation on the other. Partnerships need to find ways of engaging people that can reach well beyond the most articulate and committee-literate. They need to draw on the energies and ideas of people whom earlier programmes have not begun to reach: those who are excluded within 'community'. At the same time, complex and large-scale programmes will also require effective organisation and informed leadership: people who can 'hit the ground running'. Balancing participation with effective representation and entrepreneurial leadership will require dynamic, responsive and accountable community structures, which have the confidence of all parts of the community and can also deliver. There is still a lot to learn about how such structures can be built.

A third challenge is that between accountability for public money and the flexibility and risks that are essential if new solutions to the problems of exclusion are to be found. I have in this book been highly critical of the obsession with monitoring and measurement that accompanies every attempt at participation, and also of the tendency for risk to be pushed down to those who are least equipped to handle it. In this I am certainly not alone. Public accountability is not simply an unnecessary

barrier put up by bureaucratic government officials: it is important. Nonetheless, there are very real tensions between accountability for public money and the need to be flexible, to think and
act in new ways, and to take risks. I have argued in these pages
that the balance is going too far in the direction of accountability, to the extent that it is difficult to know what happens
to all the information that is produced. More attention needs
to be given to the claims of downwards (opposed to upwards)
and strategic (as opposed to procedural) accountability, both
of which are equally important but sadly neglected – perhaps
because they are more difficult to achieve. Otherwise, power will
remain 'top-down', but in a more insidious and less transparent
way than in the days of more overt state control.

Finding the middle ground

Another theme of these pages has been the need to get beyond the
common distinction that is made between 'top-down' and 'bottom-up' (Wilkinson and Applebee 1999; Putnam 2000, p. 413).
We need instead to populate the middle ground. There is a tendency in too much of the rhetoric about community and civil
society to see the forces of community, social capital and civil
society as an alternative to, or even substitute for, the state, especially in the US. The task of tackling social exclusion is one
that needs all the resources that society can muster; and it has
become clear through the social capital literature that the state
has an important role both in creating the conditions in which
social capital, and indeed civil society, can thrive and in recognising and avoiding policies that destroy them. However, years
of criticism and financial cuts have demoralised public servants,
especially at local level, and potentially deprived the local state
of the energy and people with new ideas that it needs if it is to
address past failures and move forward into new ways of working. Public authorities need to change radically if they are to
take on the new roles expected of them, including orchestrating
and enabling policy development, implementation and review,
engaging citizens and balancing different interests to ensure
social justice.

A major gap in the debates about participation and governance is the failure to address the relationship between representative and participatory democracy. At the international level

this is understandable, but at the local level it creates all sorts of tensions between potential partners and raises huge questions in relation to legitimacy and accountability. The legitimacy of traditional forms of representative democracy has been much criticised, especially given falling voting figures. But more thought needs to be given to the ways in which the two forms of democracy can work effectively together. And, if more participatory forms of democracy are not to evolve into the survival of the fittest, much more attention needs to be given to the ways in which they are legitimated, how diverse views are balanced, and how change is institutionalised.

Zygmunt Bauman argues that, rather than being seen as an antithesis to the state, civil society – if it is to make safe the individual freedom that the liberal society demands – needs to be seen as 'a code-name for the "great compromise" between state and society which is the hub of the liberal/democratic project and practice' (Bauman 1999, p. 155). Bauman's compromise, which would have to be a dynamic one, could reconstruct the public, opening up again the public space whose loss so many writers have lamented, and supplying the public presence, which can, at least in a democratic setting, reduce uncertainty and fear. It could generate the strong publics that Nancy Fraser and others are looking for.

The experience that has been described in this book, however, suggests that managing this great compromise is not a simple task; we have had too many grand narratives of how the perfect society will be achieved (Deakin 2001). The reality is likely is likely to be a great deal messier. Bob Jessop, in his discussions of governance, argues that 'failure is the most likely outcome of all attempts to govern'. He suggests that there are three prerequisites therefore in pursuing these attempts. The first is intellectual: thinking critically about the intentions and outcomes of policy and acting on lessons learnt, which he describes as 'requisite reflexivity'. The second is practical: a flexible repertoire, which he describes as 'requisite variety'. The third is philosophical: 'requisite irony', in which participants recognise the likelihood of failure but always proceed as if success were possible, seeking creative solutions, while always acknowledging and engaging with the limits of any such solution (2003, pp. 7, 9).

In a similar vein, I have referred to Diane Warburton's (1998) definition of community as an aspiration. Seeing community in this way implies three things: that there is something to work towards, that the process of working towards it is ongoing and that there is no finishing point. The search for Bauman's compromise is therefore likely to be a dynamic process, one that is far from straightforward, and one that has neither a map nor a finishing point. What is important is that it is a shared journey and particularly one in which the people who continue to be excluded from economic, social and political life can take a full part.

References

Abah, O.S. (2007) 'Vignettes of communities in action: an exploration of participatory methodologies in promoting community development in Nigeria', *Community Development Journal*, 42.4, 435–48.

Abbott, J. (1996) *Sharing the City: Community Participation in Urban Management* (London: Earthscan).

Abers, R. (1998) 'Learning democratic practice: distributing government resources through popular participation in Porto Alegre, Brazil', in Douglass and Friedmann (1998).

Acheson, N. and Milofsky, C. (2010) 'Derry exceptionalism and an organic model of sustained dialog', in R. Lohmann and J. Van Til (eds), *Sustained Dialogue* (New York: Columbia University Press).

Addy, T. and Scott, D. (1988) *Fatal Impacts? The MSC and Voluntary Action* (Manchester: William Temple Foundation).

Allen, C., Camina, M., Casey, R., Coward, S. and Wood, M. (2005) *Mixed Tenure Twenty Years on: Nothing Out of the Ordinary* (Coventry: Chartered Institute of Housing/JRF).

Alcock, P., Craig, G., Dalgleish, K. and Pearson, S. (1995) *Combating Local Poverty* (London: Local Governance Innovation and Development).

Alexander, J. (1998) *Real Civil Societies: Dilemmas of Institutionalisation* (London: Sage).

Allan, G. (1983) 'Informal networks of care: issues raised by Barclay', *British Journal of Social Work*, 13, 417–33.

Alinsky, S. (1971) *Rules for Radicals* (New York: Random House).

Ambrose, P. (2000) *A Drop in the Ocean* (Brighton: Health and Social Policy Research Centre).

Amman, R. (1995) 'Research in universities', *The Times Higher Educational Supplement*. 1 September, p. 11.

Anastacio, J., Gidley, B., Hart, L., Keith, M., Mayo, M. and Kowarzik, U. (2000) *Reflecting Realities: Participants' Perspectives on Integrated Communities and Sustainable Development* (Bristol: The Policy Press).

Anheier, H. and Kendall, J. (2002) 'Interpersonal trust and voluntary associations: examining three approaches', *British Journal of Sociology*, 53.3, 343–62.

Arendt, H. (1958) *The Human Condition* (Chicago, IL: University of Chicago Press).

Arnstein, S. (1969) 'A ladder of participation in the USA', *Journal of the American Institute of Planners*, 35, July.

Ascoli, U. and Ranci, C. (eds) (2002) *Dilemmas of the Welfare Mix: The New Structure of Social Care Policies in an Era of Privatization* (New York: Plenum Press).

Atkinson, R. (1999) 'Discourses of partnership and empowerment in contemporary British urban regeneration', *Urban Studies*, 36.1, 59–72.

Atkinson, R. (2000a) 'Combating social exclusion in Europe: the new urban policy challenge', *Urban Studies*, 37: 5/6, 1037–55.

Atkinson, R. (2000b) 'Narratives of policy: the construction of urban problems and urban policy in the official discourse of British government 1968–98', *Critical Social Policy*, 20.2, 211–32.

Atkinson, R. (2001) 'The emerging "urban agenda" and the European spatial development perspective: toward and EU urban policy?' *European Planning Studies*, 9.3, 385–40.

Atkinson, R. (2003) 'Addressing urban social exclusion through community involvement in urban regeneration', in R. Imrie and M. Raco (eds), *Urban Renaissance? New Labour, Community and Urban Policy* (Bristol: The Policy Press), pp. 109–19.

Atkinson, R. and Carmichael, L. (2007) 'Neighbourhood as a new focus for action in the urban policies of West European states', in I. Smith, E. Lepine and M. Taylor (eds), *Disadvantaged by Where You Live?* (Bristol: The Policy Press).

Atkinson, R. and Eckardt, F. (2004) 'Urban policies in Europe: the development of a new conventional wisdom', in F. Eckhardt and P. Kreisl (eds), *City Images and Urban Regeneration* (Frankfurt: Peter Lang).

Audit Commission (1999) *Listen Up! Effective Community Participation* (London: Audit Commission).

Bachrach, P. and Baratz, M.S. (1962) 'Two faces of power', *American Political Science Review*, 56, 947–52.

Baker, W. (1992) 'The network organization in theory and practice', in Nohria and Eccles (1992).

Bandura, A. (1994) 'Self-efficacy', in V.S. Ramachudaram (ed.), *Encyclopedia of Human Behaviour*, vol. 4 (New York: Academic Press).

Bang, H. (2005) 'Among everyday makers and expert citizens', in J. Newman (ed.), *Remaking Governance: Peoples, Politics and the Public Sphere* (Bristol: The Policy Press).

Banks, S. (2007a) 'Working in and with community groups and organizations: processes and practices', in Butcher *et al.* (2007).

Banks, S. (2007b) 'Becoming critical: developing the community practitioner', in Butcher *et al.* (2007).

Barber, B. (1992) *Strong Democracy: Participatory Politics for a New Age* (Berkeley: University of California Press).

Bardach, E. (1989) 'Social regulation as a generic policy instrument', in L.M. Salamon (ed.), *Beyond Privatization: The Tools of Government Action* (Washington, DC: Urban Institute Press).

Barnes, M. (1999) 'Users as citizens: collective action and the local governance of welfare', *Social Policy and Administration*, 33.1, 73–90.

Barnes, M., Newman, J. and Sullivan, H. (2007) *Power, Participation and Political Renewal: Case Studies in Public Participation* (Bristol: The Policy Press).

Bauman, Z. (1999) *In Search of Politics* (Cambridge: Polity).

Bauman, Z. (2001) *Community: Seeking Safety in an Insecure World* (Cambridge: Polity).

Bellah, R., Madsen, R., Sullivan, W., Swidler, A. and Tipton, S. (1985) *Habits of the Heart: Individualism and Commitment in American Life* (New York: Harper and Row).

Ben Ner, A. and van Hoomissen, J. (1993) 'Non-profit organizations in the mixed economy: a demand and supply analysis', in A. Ben Ner and B. Gui (eds), *The Non-Profit Sector in the Mixed Economy* (Michigan: University of Michigan Press).

Benington, J. and Geddes, M. (2001) 'Social exclusion, partnership and local governance – new problems, new policy discourses in the European Union', in M. Geddes and J. Benington (eds), *Local Partnerships and Social Exclusion in the European Union*, (London: Routledge).

Bewley, C. and Glendinning, C. (1994) *Involving Disabled People in Community Care Planning*, (York: Joseph Rowntree Foundation).

Bhalla, A. and Lapeyre, F. (1997) 'Social exclusion: towards an analytical and operational framework', *Development and Change*, 28, 413–33.

Birkholzer, K. (1998) 'A philosophical rational for the promotion of local economic initiatives', in Twelvetrees (1998a).

Black, A. (1984) *Guilds and Civil Society in European Political Thought from the Twelfth Century to the Present* (London: Methuen).

Blackburn, J. and Holland, J. (eds) (1998b) *Who Changes? Institutionalising Participation in Development* (London: Intermediate Technology Publications).

Bocock, B.J. (1986) *Hegemony* (London: Tavistock).

Bourdieu, P. (1986) 'The forms of capital', in J.G. Richardson (ed.), *Handbook of Theory and Research for the Sociology of Education* (New York: Greenwood Press).

Bourdieu, P. (1990) *In Other Words: Essays towards a Reflexive Sociology* (Stanford, CA: Stanford University Press).

Branagan, M. (2007) 'The last laugh: humour in community activism', *Community Development Journal*, 42.4, 470–81.

Brennan, G. (1997) 'Selection and the currency of reward', in R. Goodin (ed.), *The Theory of Institutional Design* (Cambridge: Cambridge University Press).

Briggs, X. (2007) 'Community building: new (and old) lessons about the politics of problem-solving in America's cities', in De Filippis and Saegert (eds) (2007).

Broady, M. (1956) 'The organisation of Coronation street parties', *Sociological Review*, 4, 223–42.

Brower, S. (1996) *Good Neighbourhoods* (Westport, CT and London: Praeger).

Brundtland Commission (1987) *Our Common Future* (Oxford: Oxford University Press).

Buchanan, James M., and Tullock, G. (1962) *The Calculus of Consent: Logical Foundations of Constitutional Democracy* (Ann Arbor: University of Michigan Press).

Bulmer, M. (1988) *Neighbours: The Work of Philip Abrams* (Cambridge: Cambridge University Press).

Bunyan, P. (2010) 'Broad-based organising in the UK: reasserting the centrality of political activity in community development', *Community Development Journal*, 45.1, 111–27.

Burns, D. and Taylor, M. (1998) *Mutual Aid and Self-Help: Coping Strategies for Excluded Communities* (Bristol: The Policy Press).

Burns, D. and Taylor, M. (2000) *Auditing Community Participation: An Assessment Handbook* (Bristol: The Policy Press).

Burns, D., Hambleton, R. and Hoggett, P. (1994) *The Politics of Decentralisation: Revitalising Local Democracy* (London: Palgrave Macmillan).

Burns, D., Forrest, R., Flint, J. and Kearns, A. (2001) *Empowering Communities: The Impact of Registered Social Landlords on Social Capital*, Research report 94 (Edinburgh: Scottish Homes).

Burton, P., Goodlad, R., Croft, J., Abbott, J., Hastings, A., MacDonald, G. and Slater, T. (2005) 'What works in community involvement in area-based initiatives? A systematic review of the literature', Home Office Online Report 53/04.

Burt, R. (1992) *Structural Holes: The Social Structure of Competition* (Cambridge, MA: Harvard University Press).

Butcher, H. (1993) 'Introduction: some examples and definitions', in H. Butcher *et al.* (1993), pp. 3–21.

Butcher, H. (2007a) 'Power and empowerment: the foundations of critical community practice', in H. Butcher *et al.* (2007).

Butcher, H. (2007b) 'Towards a model of critical community practice', in H. Butcher *et al.* (2007).

Butcher, H. and Mullard, M. (1993) 'Community policy, citizenship and democracy', in H. Butcher *et al.* (1993).

Butcher, H. and Robertson, J. (2007) 'Critical community practice: organisational leadership and management', in Butcher *et al.* (2007).

Butcher, H., Glen, A., Henderson, P. and Smith, J. (eds) (1993) *Community and Public Policy* (London: Pluto Press).

Butcher, H., Banks, S., Henderson, P. with Robertson, J. (2007) *Critical Community Practice* (Bristol: The Policy Press).

Cabinet Office (2010) www.cabinetoffice.gov.uk/media/407789/building-big-society.pdf, accessed 16 September 2010.

Cairncross, L., Clapham, D. and Goodlad, R. (1994) 'Tenant participation and tenant power in British council housing', *Public Administration*, 72.2, 177–200.

Campbell, A., Hughes, J., Hewstone, M. and Cairns, E. (2010) 'Social capital as a mechanism for building a sustainable society in Northern Ireland', *Community Development Journal*, 45.1, 22–38.

Caniglia, B. and Carmin, J. (2005) 'Scholarship on social movement organizations: classic views and emerging trends', *Mobilization*, 10.2, 201–12.

Capital Action (2001) *Placemaking* (Brighton: East Brighton New Deal for Communities).

Carley, M. (2001) 'Top-down and bottom-up: the challenge of cities in the new century', in Carley, Jenkins and Smith (2001).

Carley, M. and Bautista, J. (2001) 'Urban management and community development in Metro Manila', in Carley, Jenkins and Smith (2001).

Carley, M., Jenkins, P. and Smith, H. (eds) (2001) *Urban Development and Civil Society: The Role of Communities in Sustainable Cities* (London: Earthscan).

Carley, M. and Smith, H. (2001) 'Civil society and new social movements', in Carley, Jenkins and Smith (2001).

Carmel, E. and Harlock, J. (2008) 'Instituting the "third sector" as a governable terrain: partnership, procurement and performance in the UK', *Policy and Politics*, 36.2, 155–71.

Carpenter, M. (2009) 'The capabilities approach and critical social policy: lessons from the majority world?' *Critical Social Policy*, 29.3, 351–73.

Carroll, T. (1992) *Intermediary NGOs: The Supporting Link in Grassroots Development* (West Hartford, CT: Kumarian Press).

Cars, G., Healey, P., Madanipour, A. and de Magalhaes, C. (eds) (2002) *Urban Governance, Institutional Capacity and Social Milieux* (Aldershot: Ashgate).

Castells, M. (1996) *The Rise of the Network Society* (Oxford: Basil Blackwell).

Castells, M. (1998) *The Information Age: Economy, Society and Culture*, 3 vols (Oxford: Basil Blackwell).

Cattell, V. (2001) 'Poor people, poor places, and poor health: the mediating role of social networks and social capital', *Social Science & Medicine*, 52.10, 1501–16.

Cernea, M. (1994) 'The sociologist approach to sustainable development', in I. Serageldin (ed.), *Making Development Sustainable: From Concepts to Action* (Washington, DC: The World Bank).

Chambers, R. (1997) *Whose Reality Counts? Putting the Last First* (London: Intermediate Technology Productions).

Chanan, G. (1992) *Out of the Shadows: Local Community Action in the European Community* (Dublin: European Foundation for the Improvement of Living and Working Conditions).

Chandler, D. (2001) 'Active citizens and the therapeutic state: the role of democratic participation in political reform', *Policy and Politics*, 29.1, 4–14.

Chari-Wagh, A. (2009) 'Raising citizenship rights for women through microcredit programmes: an analysis of MASUM, Maharashtra, India', *Community Development Journal*, 44.3, 403–14.

Chatterton, P. and Bradley, D. (2000) 'Bringing Britain together? The limitations of area-based regeneration policies in addressing regeneration', *Local Economy*, 15.2, 98–111.

CDRC (Citizenship Development Research Centre) and Logolink (2008) *Champions of Participation: Engaging Citizens in Local Governance* (Brighton: Institute for Development Studies).

Clark, D. and Southern, R. (2006) 'Comparing institutional designs for neighbourhood renewal: Neighbourhood management in Britain and the Regies de Quartier in France', *Policy and Politics*, 34, 173–91.

Clarke, G. (1995) *A Missed Opportunity: An Initial Assessment of the 1995 Single Regeneration Budget Approvals and their Impact on Voluntary and Community Organisations* (London: National Council for Voluntary Organisations).

Cleaver, F. (2004) 'The social embeddedness of agency and decision-making', in Hickey and Mohan (2004).

Clegg, S. (1989) *Frameworks of Power* (London: Sage).

Clegg, S. (1990) *Modern Organisations: Organisational Studies in the Post-Modern World* (London: Sage).

CLG (2005) *Making Connections: An Evaluation of the Community Participation Programmes* (London: Communities and Local Government).

CLG (2010) *2008–9 Citizenship Survey: Volunteering and Charitable Giving Topic Report* (London: Communities and Local Government).

Coaffee, J. and Healey, P. (2003) '"My voice: my place": tracking transformations in urban governance', 40.10, 1979–99.

Cockburn, C. (1991) *In the Way of Women: Men's Resistance to Sex Equality in Organisations* (London: Palgrave Macmillan).

Cohen, J. and Fung, A. (2004) 'Radical democracy', *Swiss Political Science Review*, 10.4, 23–34.

Cohen, J. and Rogers, J. (1992) 'Secondary associations and democratic governance', *Politics and Society*, 20.4, 393–472.

Coin Street Community Builders (2010) www.coinstreet.org, accessed 28 September 2010.

Cole, I. and Smith, Y. (1993) *Bell Farm in the Midst of Change* (Sheffield: Centre for Regional, Economic and Social Research, Sheffield Hallam University).

Coleman, J. (1990) *Foundations of Social Theory* (Cambridge, MA: Harvard University Press).

Carnegie UK (2010) *Making Good Society: Report of the Commission of Inquiry into the Future of Civil Society in the UK and Ireland* (Dunfermline: Carnegie UK Trust).

Commonwealth Foundation (1999) *Citizens and Governance: Civil Society in the New Millennium* (London: The Commonwealth Foundation).

Community Development Project (1977) *Gilding the Ghetto: The State and the Poverty Experiments* (London: Community Development Project).

Connell, J., Kubisch, A., Schorr, L. and Weiss, C. (1995) *New Approaches to Evaluating Community Initiatives: Concepts, Methods and Contexts* (Washington, DC: The Aspen Institute).

Cooke, B. and Kothari, U. (2001) *Participation: The New Tyranny?* (London: Zed Books).

Cornwall, A. (2004a) 'New democratic spaces? The politics and dynamics of institutionalised participation', *IDS Bulletin*, 35.2, 1–10.

Cornwall, A. (2004b) 'Spaces for transformation? Reflections on issues of power and difference in participation in development', in Hickey and Mohan (2004).

Cornwall, A. (2008a) 'Unpacking "participation": models, meanings and practices', *Community Development Journal*, 43.3, 269–83.

Cornwall, A. (2008b) *Democratising Engagement: What the UK can Learn from International Experience* (London: Demos).

Cornwall, A. and Coelho, V. (2004) *Spaces for Change? The Politic of Citizen Participation in New Democratic Arenas* (London and New York: Zed Books).

Cornwall, A., Romano, J. and Shankland, A. (2008) *Brazilian Experiences of Participation and Citizenship: A Critical Look* (Brighton: Institute of Development Studies).

Craig, G. (1989) 'Community work and the state', *Community Development Journal*, 24.1, 3–18.

Craig, G. and Mayo, M. (eds) (1995) *Community Empowerment: A Reader in Participation in Development* (London: Zed Press).

Craig, G., Mayo, M. and Taylor, M. (1990) 'Empowerment: a continuing role for community development', *Community Development Journal*, 25.4, 286–90.

Craig, G., Mayo, M. and Taylor, M. (2000) 'Globalisation from below: implications for the *Community Development Journal*', *Community Development Journal*, 35.4, 323–55.

Craig, G., Taylor, M., and Parkes, T. (2004) 'Protest or partnership? The voluntary and community sectors in the policy process', *Social Policy and Administration*, 38.3, 221–39.

Craig, G., Taylor, M., Bloor K. and Wilkinson. M., with Syed, A. and Monro, S. (2002) *Contract or Trust: The Role of Compacts in Local Governance* (Bristol: The Policy Press).

Crossley, N. (2003) 'From reproduction to transformation: social movement fields and the radical habitus', *Theory, Culture and Society*, 20.6, 43–68.

Dahrendorf, R. (1995) 'Can we combine economic opportunity with civil society and political liberty?' *The Responsive Community*, 5.3.

Dale, A. and Newman, L. (2010) 'Social capital: a necessary and sufficient condition for sustainable community development?' *Community Development Journal*, 45.1, 5–21.

Dalrymple, J. and Burke, B. (1995) *Anti-Oppressive Practice, Social Care and the Law* (Buckingham: Open University Press).

Dalton, R. and Wattenberg, M. (2000) *Parties Without Partisans* (Oxford: Oxford University Press).

Daly, M. (2003) 'Governance and social policy', *Journal of Social Policy*, 32.1, 113–28.

Dasgupta, P. and Serageldin, I. (eds) (1999) *Social Capital: A Multi-Faceted Perspective* (Washington, DC: World Bank).

Deakin, N. (2001) *In Search of Civil Society* (London: Palgrave Macmillan).

Dean, J. and Hastings, A. (2000) *Challenging Images: Housing Estates, Stigma and Regeneration* (Bristol: The Policy Press).

De Filippis, J. (2007) 'Community control and development: the long view', in De Filippis and Saegert (2007).

De Filippis, J. and Saegert, S. (2007) 'Communities develop: the question is how?' in De Filippis and Saegert (2007).

De Filippis, J. and Saegert, S. (2007) *The Community Development Reader* (New York: Routledge).

De Filippis, J. and Saegert, S. (2007) 'Conclusion' in De Filippis and Saegert (2007).

De Filippis, J., Fisher, R. and Shragge, E. (2009) 'What's left in the community? Oppositional politics in contemporary practice', *Community Development Journal*, 44.1, 38–52.

Dekker, P. (2009) 'Civicness: from civil society to civic services?' *Voluntas*, 20.3, 220–38.

Della Porta, D., Andretta, M., Mosca, L. and Reiter, H. (2006) *Globalization from Below: Transnational Activists and Protest Networks* (Minneapolis, MN: University of Minnesota Press).

Dey, K. and Westendorff, D. (1996) *Their Choice or Yours: Global Forces or Local Voices* (Geneva: United Nations Research Institute for Social Development).

De Zeeuw, C. (2010) 'The rationales of resident participation in the Netherlands: a case study of The Hague', unpublished PhD thesis, University of the West of England.

Dhesi, A.S. (2000) 'Social capital and community development', *Community Development Journal*, 35.3, 199–213.

Diamond, J. (2001) 'Managing change or coping with conflict? Mapping the experience of a local regeneration project', *Local Economy*, 16.4, 272–85.

Diani, M. (1997) 'Social movements and social capital: a network perspective on movement outcomes', *Mobilization*, 2, 129–48.

DiMaggio, P. and Powell, W.W. (1983) 'The iron cage revisited: institutional isomorphism and collective rationality in organizational fields', *American Sociological Review*, 48, 459–62.

Disraeli, B. (1925) *Sybil* (Oxford: Oxford University Press).

Dore, R. (1983) 'Goodwill and the spirit of market capitalism', *British Journal of Sociology*, 34.4, 459–82.

Dorling, D., Rigby, J., Wheeler, B., Ballas, D., Thomas, B., Fahmy, E., Gordon, D. and Lupton, R. (2007) *Poverty and Wealth across Britain 1968–2005* (Bristol: The Policy Press).

Douglass, M. and Friedmann, J. (eds) (1998) *Cities for Citizens* (Chichester: John Wiley).

Dreyfus, H. and Rabinow, P. (1982) *Michel Foucault: Beyond Structuralism and Hermeneutics* (Brighton: Harvester).

Driver, S. and Martell, L. (1997) 'New Labour's communitarianisms', *Critical Social Policy*, 17.3, 27–46.

Dryzek, J. (1990) *Discursive Democracy: Politics, Policy and Political Science* (Cambridge: Cambridge University Press).

Duncombe, S. (2007) '(From) cultural resistance to community development', *Community Development Journal*, 42.4, 490–500.

Durose, C., Greasley, S. and Richardson, L. (2009) *Changing Local Governance, Changing Citizens* (Bristol: the Policy Press).

Edwards, J. and Batley, R. (1978) *The Politics of Positive Discrimination* (London: Tavistock).

Edwards, M. (2004) *Civil Society* (Cambridge: Polity).

Edwards, M. and Hulme, D. (1995a) 'Beyond the magic bullet: lessons and conclusions', in Edwards and Hulme (1995c).

Edwards, M. and Hulme, D. (1995b) 'NGO performance and accountability: introduction and overview', in Edwards and Hulme (1995c).

Edwards, M. and Hulme, D. (eds) (1995c) *Non-Governmental Organisations – Performance and Accountability: Beyond the Magic Bullet* (London: Earthscan).

Ellison, N. (1997) 'Towards a new social politics: citizenship and reflexivity in late modernity', *Sociology*, 31.4, 697–717.

Equalities Review (2007) '*Fairness and freedom: the final report of the Equalities Review*' (London: The Equalities Review), http://archive.cabinetoffice.gov.uk/equalitiesreview/publications.html.

Esman, M. and Uphoff, N. (1984) *Local Organisations: Intermediaries in Rural Development* (Ithaca, NY: Cornell University Press).

Etzioni, A. (1998) *The Essential Communitarian Reader* (Lanham, MD: Rowman & Littlefield).

Evers, A. (2003) 'Social capital and civic commitment: on Putnam's way of understanding', *Social Policy and Society*, 2.1, 13–21.

Evers, A. and Laville, J-L. (2004) 'Introduction', in A. Evers and J-L. Laville (eds), *The Third Sector in Europe* (Cheltenham: Edward Elgar).

Fainstein, S. and Hirst, C. (1995) 'Urban social movements', in Judge, Stoker and Wolman (1995).

Fairbanks, R. (2007) 'The political-economic gradient and the organization of urban space', in R. Cnaan and C. Milofsky (eds), *Handbook of Community Movements and Local Organizations* (New York: Springer).

Fischer, C. (1982) *To Dwell Among Friends: Personal Networks in Town and City* (Chicago, IL: University of Chicago Press).

Fischer, F. (1990) *Technocracy and the Politics of Expertise* (London: Sage).

Flyvbjerg, B. (1998) 'Empowering civil society', in Douglass and Friedmann (1998).

Foley, M. and Edwards, R. (1996) 'The paradox of civil society', *Journal of Democracy*, 7.3, 38–52.

Foley, M. and Edwards, R. (1999) 'Is it time to disinvest in social capital?' *Journal of Public Policy*, 19.2, 141–72.

Forrest, R. and Kearns, A. (1999) *Joined-Up Places? Social Cohesion and Neighbourhood Regeneration* (York: Joseph Rowntree Foundation).

Foster, J. (1995) 'Informal control and community crime prevention', *British Journal of Criminology*, 35.4, 563–83.

Foucault, M. (1980) *Power/Knowledge* C. Gordon (ed.). (Brighton: Harvester Press).

Foucault, M. (1984) 'Polemics, politics and problematisations: an interview with Michel Foucault', in P. Rabinow (ed.), *The Foucault Reader* (London: Penguin).

Foucault, M. (1991) 'Governmentality', in G. Burchell, C. Gordon and P. Miller (eds), *The Foucault Effect: Studies in Governmentality* (London: Harvester Wheatsheaf).

Foweraker, J. and Landman, T. (1997) *Citizenship Rights and Social Movements: A Comparative and Statistical Analysis* (Oxford: Oxford University Press).

Fowler, A. (2000) 'Beyond partnership: getting real about NGO relationships in the aid system', *IDS Bulletin*, 31.3, 1–11.

Fraser, J., Lepowsky, J., Kirk, E. and Williams, J. (2007) 'The construction of the local and the limits of contemporary community building in the United States', in De Filippis and Saegert (2007).

Fraser, N. (1992) 'Rethinking the public sphere: a contribution to the critique of actually existing democracy', in C. Calhoun (ed.), *Habermas and the Public Sphere* (Cambridge, MA: MIT).

Frazer, E. (2000) 'Communitarianism', in G. Browning, A. Hacli and F. Webster (eds), *Understanding Contemporary Society: Theories of the Present* (London: Sage).

Freeman, J. (1973) *The Tyranny of Structurelessness* (New York, NY: Falling Wall Press).

Freire, P. (1972) *Pedagogy of the Oppressed* (Harmondsworth: Penguin).

Friedmann, J. (1998) 'The new political economy of planning: the rise of civil society', in Douglass and Friedmann (1998).

Fukuyama, F. (1989) 'The end of history', *The National Interest*, 19, 3–18.

Fukuyama, F. (1995) *Trust* (Harmondsworth: Penguin).

Gaster, L. and Taylor, M. (1993) *Learning from Citizens and Consumers* (London: The Local Government Management Board).

Gaventa, J. (1980) *Power and Powerlessness: Quiescence and Rebellion in an Appalachian Valley* (Urbana: University of Illinois Press).

Gaventa, J. (1998) 'Poverty, participation and social exclusion in North and South', *IDS Bulletin*, 29.1, 50–7.

Gaventa, J. (1999) 'Crossing the great divide: building links and learning between NGOs and community based organisations in North and South', in D. Lewis (ed.), *International Perspectives on Voluntary Action: Reshaping the Third Sector* (London: Earthscan).

Gaventa, J. (2004a) 'Towards participatory governance: assessing the transformative possibilities', in Hickey and Mohan (2004).

Gaventa, J. (2004b) 'Strengthening participatory approaches to local governance: learning the lessons from abroad', *National Civic Review*, 93.4, 16–27.

Gaventa, J. (2006) 'Triumph, deficit or contestation? Deepening the "deepening democracy" debate', IDS Working paper in conjunction with Logolink and the Citizenship DRC, Institute for Development Studies, University of Sussex.

Geddes, M. (1998) *Local Partnership: A Successful Strategy for Social Cohesion* (Dublin: European Foundation for the Improvement of Living and Working Conditions).

Giddens, A. (1990) *Consequences of Modernity* (Cambridge: Polity Press).

Giddens, A. (2000a) *Runaway World* (London: Profile Books).

Gilchrist, A. (1995) *Community Development and Networking* (London: Community Development Foundation).

Gilchrist, A. (2000) 'The well-connected community: networking to the edge of chaos', *Community Development Journal*, 35.3, 264–75.

Gilchrist, A. (2009) *The Well-Connected Community: A Networking Approach to Community Development* (Bristol: The Policy Press).

Gilchrist, A. (2010) 'Community resilience: a shared capacity for resistance and recovery', *New Start*, February.

Gilchrist, A. and Taylor, M. (1997) 'Community networking: developing strength through diversity', in Hoggett (1997b).

Gilchrist, A. and Taylor, M. (2011) *A Short Guide to Community Development* (Bristol: The Policy Press).

Gittell, M. (2001) *Empowerment Zones: An Opportunity Missed: A Six-City Comparative Study* (New York: The Howard Samuels State Management and Policy Centre, The Graduate School and the University Centre of the City University of New York).

Glen, A. (1993) 'Methods and themes in community practice', in Butcher *et al.* (1993).

Glennerster, H., Lipton, R., Noden, P. and Power, A. (1999) *Poverty, Social Exclusion and Neighbourhood: Studying the Area Basis of Social Exclusion*. CASE Paper 22 (London: Centre for the Analysis of Social Exclusion, London School of Economics).

Goetschius, G.W. (1969) *Working with Community Groups: Using Community Development as a Method of Social Work* (London: Routledge).

Goetz, A.M. and Gaventa, J. (2001) *From Consultation to Influence: Bringing Citizen Voice and Client Focus into Service Delivery*, Working Paper 138 (Brighton: Institute of Development Studies).

Gosden, P. (1973) *Voluntary Associations in Nineteenth Century Britain* (London: Batsford).

Gouldner, A. (1960) 'The norm of reciprocity: a preliminary statement', *American Journal of Sociology*, 25.2, 161–78.

Granovetter, M. (1973) 'The strength of weak ties', *American Journal of Sociology*, 78.6, 1360–80.

Granovetter, M. (1985) 'Economic action and social structure: a theory of embeddedness', *American Journal of Sociology*, 91.3, 481–510.

Gray, J. (1996) *After Social Democracy: Politics, Capital and the Common Life* (London: DEMOS).

Green, R.H. (1998) 'Problematics and pointers about participatory research and gender', in Guijt and Shah (1998a).

Grimshaw, L., and Lever, J. (2009) 'Citizens' participation in policy making', www.cinefogo.org.

Gruba, J. and Trickett, E. (1987) 'Can we empower others? The paradox of empowerment in the governing of an alternative public school', *American Journal of Community Psychology*, 15.3, 353–71.

Guijt, I. and Shah, M.K. (eds) (1998a) *The Myth of Community: Gender Issues in Participatory Development* (London: ITDG Publishing).

Guijt, I. and Shah, M.K. (1998b) 'Waking up to power, conflict and process', in Guijt and Shah (1998a).

Gyford, J. (1976) *Local Politics in Britain* (London: Croom Helm).

Habermas, J. (1984) *The Theory of Communicative Action* (Boston, MA: Beacon Press).

Hall, P.A. (1997) 'Social capital: a fragile asset', *DEMOS Collection*, 12, 35–7.

Hall, S. (2000) 'The way forward for regeneration? Lessons from the Single Regeneration Budget Challenge Fund', *Local Government Studies*, 26.1, 1–14.

Halpern, D. (2005) *Social Capital* (Cambridge: Polity).

Hambleton, R., Savitch, H. and Stewart, M. (2002) *Globalism and Democracy* (London: Palgrave Macmillan).

Hampden-Turner, C. (1996) in The *Independent*, 5 February, cited by Penny Mitchell in 'News and Views', *Public and Social Policy*, 1.1, 1–10.

Harman, W.W. (1993) 'Rethinking the central institutions of modern society: science and business', *Futures*, December, 1063–70.

Harris, V., Howard, J., Lever, J., Mateeva, A., Miller, C., Petrov, R., Rahbari, M., Serra, L. and Taylor, M. (2008) *Understanding Partnership Working: A Pack for Participants* (Bristol: University of the West of England).

Hastings, A., McArthur, A. and McGregor, A. (1996) *Less than Equal: Community Organisations and Estate Regeneration Partnerships* (Bristol: The Policy Press).

Hausner, V. and associates (1991) *Small Area-Based Urban Initiatives: A Review of Recent Experience, Vol. 1: Main Report* (London: V. Hausner and Associates).

Haynes, P. (1999) *Complex Policy Planning: The Government's Strategic Management of the Social Care Market* (Aldershot: Ashgate).

Healey, P. (2006) *Collaborative Planning: Shaping Places in Fragmented Societies* (London: Palgrave Macmillan).

Healey, P., Cars, A., Madanipour, A. and de Magalhaes, C. (2002a) 'Transforming governance, institutionalist analysis and institutional capacity', in Cars *et al.* (2002).

Healey, P., Cars, G., Madanipour, A. and de Magalhaes, C. (2002b) 'Urban governance capacity in complex societies: challenges of institutional adaptation', in Cars *et al.* (2002).

Held, D. (1996) *Models of Democracy* (Cambridge: Polity Press).

Henderson, P. and Salmon, H. (1998) *Signposts to Local Democracy: Local Governance, Communitarianism and Community Development* (London: Community Development Foundation and Warwick: The Local Government Centre).

Hickey, S. and Mohan, G. (eds) (2004) *Participation: From Tyranny to Transformation* (London: Zed Books).

Hickey, S. and Mohan, G. (2004) 'Towards participation as transformation: critical themes and challenges', in Hickey and Mohan (2004).

Hill, M. (1997) *The Policy Process in the Modern State,* Third edition (New York: Prentice Hall/Harvester Wheatsheaf).

Hillery, G. (1955) 'Definitions of Community: areas of agreement', *Rural Sociology,* 20.

Hillier, J. (1997) 'Going round the back? Complex networks and informal associational action in local planning processes', paper for *Planning Theory Track.* ACSP, Fort Lauderdale, Florida.

Hirschman, A.O. (1970) *Exit, Voice and Loyalty* (Cambridge, MA: Harvard University Press).

Hirschman, A.O. (1994) 'Social conflicts as pillars of democratic market society', *Political Theory,* 22.2, 203–18.

Hirst, P. (1994) *Associative Democracy: New Forms of Economic and Social Governance* (London: Polity Press).

Hoch, C. and Hemmens, G. (1987) 'Linking formal and informal help: conflict along the continuum of care', *Social Service Review,* September. 432–46.

Hoggett, P. (1997a) 'Contested communities', in Hoggett (1997b).

Hoggett, P. (ed.) (1997b) *Contested Communities: Experience, Struggles and Policies* (Bristol: The Policy Press).

Home Office (2003) *2003 Home Office Citizenship Survey: People, families and communities,* Home Office Research Study 289 (London: The Home Office).

Horton, M. and Freire, P. (1990) *We Make the Road by Walking: Conversations on Education and Social Change* (Philadelphia: Temple University Press).

Howard, J. and Taylor, M. (2010) 'Hybridity in partnerships: Managing tensions and opportunities', in D. Billis (ed.) *The Erosion of the Third Sector? Hybrid Organisations in a New Welfare Landscape* (London: Palgrave Macmillan).

Howard, J., Grimshaw, L., Lipson, B., Taylor, M. and Wilson, M. (2009) *Alternative Approaches to Capacity Building – Emerging Practices Abroad* (Birmingham: Capacitybuilders).

Howell, J. and Pearce, J. (2002) *Civil Society and Development: A Critical Exploration* (Boulder, CO: Lynne Rienner).

Hulme, D. and Edwards, M. (1997) 'NGOs, states and donors: an overview', in Hulme and Edwards (eds) *NGOs, States and Donors: Too Close for Comfort* (London: Macmillan).

Hunter, A. (1974) *Symbolic Communities: The Persistence and Change of Chicago's Local Communities* (Chicago University Press).

Hunter, A. (2007) 'Contemporary conceptions of community', in Cnaan, R. and Milofsky, C. (eds) *Handbook of Community Movements and Local Organizations* (New York: Springer).

Hutton, W. (2002) *The World We're In* (London: Little, Brown).

Hyatt, S. (1994) 'Tenants' choice or Hobson's choice? Housing the poor in the enterprise culture', paper presented at the European

Association of Social Anthropologists Conference, Oslo, Norway, 25 June.

Ingamells, A. (2007) 'Community development and community renewal: tracing the workings of power', *Community Development Journal*, 42.2, 237–50.

Innes, J., Gruber, J., Thompson, R. and Newman, M. (1994) *Planning through Consensus Building: A New Review of the Comprehensive Planning Ideal* (Berkeley: University of California).

IVAR (Institute for Voluntary Action Research) and UWE (University of the West of England) (2010) *Evaluation of the National Empowerment Partnership: an interim report in year three – September 2010* (London: Community Development Foundation).

Jackson, K. (1995) 'Popular education and the state: a new look at the community debate', in M. Mayo and J. Thompson (eds), *Adult Education, Critical Intelligence and Social Change* (Leicester: National Institute of Continuing Education).

Jackson, L.S. (2001) 'Contemporary public involvement: toward a strategic approach', *Local Environment*, 6.2, 135–47.

Jacob, M. (2002) 'An Exploration of the Routes to Empowerment for Older Women', PhD Thesis, University of Brighton.

Jenkins, P. (2001) 'Relationships between the state and civil society and their importance for sustainable development', in Carley, Jenkins and Smith (2001).

Jessop, Bob (2003) 'Governance and metagovernance: on reflexivity, requisite variety, and requisite irony', in Bang, H. (ed.) *Governance, as Social and Political Communication* (Manchester: Manchester University Press).

John, P. (2009) 'Citizen governance: where it came from, where it's going', in Durose, Greasley and Richardson (2009).

Jones, E. and Gaventa, J. (2002) *Concepts of Citizenship: A Review* (Brighton: Institute of Development Studies).

Jones, P. (2003) 'Urban regeneration's poisoned chalice: is there an impasse in (community) participation-based policy?' *Urban Studies*, 40.3, 581–601.

Judge, D., Stoker, G. and Wolman, H. (eds) (1995) *Theories of Urban Politics* (London: Sage).

Judt, T. (2010) *Ill Fares the Land* (London: Allen Lane).

Jupp, B. (1999) *Living Together: Community Life on Mixed Tenure Estates* (London: DEMOS).

Kale, P., Singh, H. and Perlmutter, H. (2000) 'Learning and protection of proprietary assets in strategic alliances: building relational capital', *Strategic Management Journal*, 21, 217–37.

Kane, D., Clark, J., Lesniewski, S., Wilton, J., Pratten, B. and Wilding, K. (2009) *The UK Civil Society Almanac 2009* (London: NCVO).

Keane, J. (1988a) *Democracy and Civil Society* (London: Verso).

Keane, J. (1988b) 'Introduction', in Keane (1998a).

Kendall, J. and 6, P. (1994) 'Government and the voluntary sector in the United Kingdom', in S. Saxon-Harrold and J. Kendall (eds), *Researching the Voluntary Sector*. Vol. 2 (Tonbridge: Charities Aid Foundation).

Kingdon, J. (1984) *Agendas, Alternatives and Public Policies* (Boston, MA: Little, Brown).

Kinloch, V. (2007) 'Youth representations of community, art and struggle in Harlem', *New Directions for Adult and Continuing Education* (Wiley Online Publishing), pp. 37–49.

Klein, N. (2000) *No Logo* (London: Flamingo).

Klijn, E and Koppenjan, J. (2000) 'Politicians and interactive decision making: institutional spoilsports or playmakers', *Public Administration*, 78.2, 365–87.

Kretzmann, J. and McKnight, J. (1993) *Building Communities from the Inside Out: A Path Toward Finding and Mobilising a Community's Assets* (Evanston, IL: Center for Urban Affairs and Policy Research, Northwestern University).

Kubisch, A., Auspos, P., Brown, P., Chaskin, R., Fulbright-Anderson, K. and Hamilton, R. (2007) 'Strengthening the connections between communities and external resources', in De Filippis and Saegert (2007).

Kumar, S. (1997) *Accountability Relationships between Voluntary Sector 'Providers', Local Government 'Purchasers' and Service Users in the Contracting State* (York: York Publishing Services).

Kuti, E. (1999) 'Different Eastern European Countries at Different Crossroads', *Voluntas*, 10–11, 51–60.

Laguerre, M. (1994) *The Informal City* (Basingstoke: Palgrave Macmillan).

Larner, W. and Butler, M. (2005) 'Governmentalities of local partnerships: the rise of a "partnering" state', *Studies in Political Economy*, 85–108.

Lawrence, K. (2007) 'Expanding comprehensiveness: structural racism and community building in the United States', in De Filippis and Saegert, (2007).

Leach, M., and Scoones, I. (2007) *Mobilising Citizens: Social Movements and the Politics of Knowledge* (Brighton: Institute of Development Studies).

Leadbeater, C. (1999) *Living on Thin Air* (London: Viking).

Leadbeater, C. and Christie, I. (1999) *To Our Mutual Advantage* (London: DEMOS).

Leat, D. (1999) 'Holistic Budgets', unpublished.

Levitas, R. (1998) *The Inclusive Society? Social Exclusion and New Labour* (London: Macmillan).

Ledwith, M. (2005) *Community Development: A Critical Approach* (Bristol: The Policy Press).

Lipsky, M. (1979) *Street Level Bureaucracy* (New York: Russell Sage Foundation).

Lloyd, L. and Gilchrist, A. (1994) 'Community caremongering: principles and practices', *Care in Place*, 1.2, 133–44.

Lo, J. and Halseth, G. (2009) 'The practice of principles: an examination of CED groups in Vancouver, BC', *Community Development Journal*, 44, 80–110.

London Citizens (2010) http:// www.londoncitizens.org.uk. Accessed 11 March 2010.

Loney, M. (1983) *Community Against Government* (London: Heinemann).

Lowery, D., de Hoog, R. and Lyons, W.E. (1992) 'Citizenship in the empowered locality', *Urban Affairs Quarterly*, 28.1, 69–103.

Lowndes, V. (2000) 'Women and social capital: a comment on Hall's "Social Capital in Britain"', *British Journal of Political Science*, 30, 533–40.

Lowndes, V. (1995) 'Citizenship and Urban Polities', in Judge, Stoker and Wolman (1995).

Lowndes, V. and Skelcher, C. (1998) 'The dynamics of multi-organizational partnerships: an analysis of changing modes of governance', *Public Administration*, 76, 313–33.

Lowndes, V. and Sullivan, H. (2004) 'Like a horse and carriage or a fish on a bicycle: how well do local partnerships and public participation go together? *Local Government Studies*, 30.1, 51–73.

Lowndes, V. and Wilson, D. (2001) 'Social capital and local governance: exploring the institutional design variable', *Political Studies*, 49, 629–47.

Lukes, S. (2005) *Power: A Radical View*, Second edition. (London: Palgrave Macmillan).

Lupton, C., Peckham, S. and Taylor, P. (1998) *Managing Public Involvement in Healthcare Purchasing* (Buckingham: Open University Press).

Lyons, M. (2001) *Third Sector: The Contribution of Nonprofit and Cooperative Enterprises in Australia* (Crows Nest, NSW: Allen & Unwin).

MacFarlane, R. (1997) *Unshackling the Poor: A Complementary Approach to Local Economic Development* (York: Joseph Rowntree Foundation).

Maginn, P. (2002) 'Community power in a cosmopolitan city: an ethnographic study of urban regeneration in three ethnically diverse localities in London', PhD thesis (London: South Bank University).

Maloney, W., Jordan, G. and McLaughlin, A. (1994) 'Interest groups and public policy: the insider/outsider model revisited', *Journal of Public Policy*, 14, 17–38.

Maloney, W., Smith, G. and Stoker, G. (2000) 'Social capital and urban governance: adding a more contextualised "top-down perspective"', *Political Studies*, 48, 823–41.

March, J. and Olsen, J. (eds) (1976) *Ambiguity and Choice in Organizations* (Oslo: Universitetesforlaget).

Marris, P. (1982) *Community Planning and Conceptions of Change* (London: Routledge & Kegan Paul).

Marris, P. (1996) *The Politics of Uncertainty* (London: Routledge).

Marris, P. (1998) 'Planning and civil society in the twenty-first century', in Douglass and Friedmann (1998).

Marris, P. and Rein, M. (1967) *Dilemmas of Social Reform* (New York: Atherton Press).

Marsalis, W. (1996) 'The Music of Democracy', cited in S. Morse *Building Collaborative Communities* (Charlottesville, PA: Pew Partnership for Civic Change).

Marsh, A. and Mullins, D. (1998) 'The social exclusion perspective and housing studies: origins, application and limitations', *Housing Studies*, 6, 749–59.

Marsh, D. and Rhodes, R. (1992) *Policy Networks in British Government* (Oxford: Oxford University Press).

Marshall, T.H. (1950) *Citizenship and Social Class* (Cambridge: Cambridge University Press).

Martin, G. and Watkinson, J. (2003) *Rebalancing Communities: Introducing Mixed Incomes into Existing Rented Housing Estates* (York: Joseph Rowntree Foundation).

Maslow, A.H. (1943) 'A theory of human motivation', *Psychological Review*, 50.4, 370–96.

Matarasso, F. (2007) 'Common ground: cultural action as a route to community development', *Community Development Journal*, 42.4, 449–58.

Mathers, J., Parry, J. and Jones, S. (2008) 'Exploring resident (non) participation in the UK New Deal for Communities Regeneration Programme, *Urban Studies,* 45.3, 591–606.

Mayo, M. (1975) 'Community development as a radical alternative', in R. Bailey and M. Brake (eds.) *Radical Social Work* (London: Edward Arnold).

Mayo, M. (1997) 'Partnerships for regeneration and community development: some opportunities, challenges and constraints', *Critical Social Policy*, 17.3, 3–26.

Mayo, M. and Annette, J. (2010) *Taking Part: Active Learning for Active Citizenship and Beyond* (Leicester: National Institute for Adult and Continuing Education).

Mayo, M. and Taylor, M. (2001) 'Partnerships and power in community regeneration', in S. Balloch and M. Taylor (eds), *Partnership Working: Policy and Practice* (Bristol: The Policy Press).

McCulloch, A. (2000) 'Evaluations of a community regeneration project: case studies of Cruddas Park Development Trust, Newcastle-pon-Tyne', *Journal of Social Policy*, 29.3, 397–420.

McLaughlin, K., Osborne, S. and Ferlie, E. (2002) (eds) *New Public Management: Current Trends and Future Prospects* (London: Routledge).

Mead, L. (1985) *Beyond Entitlement* (New York: Basic Books).

Meekosha, H. (1993) 'The Bodies Politic – equality, difference and community practice', in Butcher *et al.* (1993).

Melucci, A. (1988) 'Social movements and the democratisation of everyday life', in J. Keane (ed.), *Civil Society and the State* (London: Verso).

Michels, R. (1915; reprinted 1962) *Political Parties* (New York: Free Press).

Milbourne, L. and Murray, U. (2010) 'Negotiating interactions in state-voluntary sector relationships: competitive and collaborative agency in an experiential workshop', *Voluntas*, 2011, 22.1, 70–92.

Miller, C. and Bryant, R. (1990) 'Community work in the UK: reflections on the 80s', *Community Development Journal*, 25.4, 316–25.

Milofsky, C. (1987) 'Neighbourhood-based organisations: a market analogy', in W.W. Powell (ed.), *The Nonprofit Sector: A Research Handbook* (New Haven, CT: Yale University Press).

Milofsky, C. (2008) *Smallville: Institutionalizing Community in Twenty-First-Century America* (Medford, MA: Tufts University Press).

Milofsky, C. and Hunter, A. (1994) 'Where non-profits come from: a theory of organisational emergence', paper presented to the Association for Research on Nonprofit Organisations and Voluntary Action, San Francisco, October.

Mingione, E. (1997) 'Enterprise and exclusion', *DEMOS Collection*, 12, 10–12.

Misztal, B. (2000) *Informality: Social Theory and Contemporary Practice* (London: Routledge).

Misztal, B. (2005) 'The new importance of the relationship between formality and informality', *Feminist Theory*, 6.2, 173–94.

Monbiot, G. (1994) *No Man's Land: An Investigative Journey in Kenya and Tanzania* (London: Palgrave Macmillan).

Morison, J. (2000) 'The government-voluntary sector compacts: governance, governmentality and civil society', *Journal of Law and Society*, 27.1, 98–132.

Morison, J. (2003) 'Modernising government and the e-government revolution: technologies of government and technologies of democracy', in P. Leyland and N. Bamforth (eds), *Public Law in a Multi-Layered Constitution* (Oxford: Hart Publishing).

Morrissey, J. (2000) 'Indicators of citizen participation: lessons from learning teams in rural EZ/EC communities', *Community Development Journal*, 35.1, 59–74.

Morrow, V. (1999) 'Conceptualising social capital in relation to the well-being of children and young people: a critical review', *The Sociological Review*, 47.4, 744–65.

Mosca, G. (1939) *The Ruling Class* (New York: McGraw-Hill).

Mouffe, C. (1992) *Dimensions of Radical Democracy: Pluralism, Citizenship, Democracy* (London: Verso).

Mowbray, M. (2000) 'Commentary on *Community Development Journal* Special Issue "Community Development in Canada"', *Community Development Journal*, 35.3, 306–9.

Moynihan, D. (1969) *Maximum Feasible Misunderstanding: Community Action in the War on Poverty* (New York: Free Press).

Mulgan, G. (1991) 'Citizens and Responsibilities', in G. Andrews (ed.), *Citizenship* (London: Lawrence & Wishart).

Murphy, P. and Cunningham, J. (2003). *Organizing for Community Controlled Development: Renewing Civil Society* (Thousand Oaks: Sage).

Murray, C. (1990) *The Emerging British Underclass*, Choice in Welfare Series no. 2 (London: IEA Health and Welfare Unit).

Naidu, R. (2008). 'Deepening local democracy and governance – an experiential perspective', *The Governance Link*, Issue 4, Action Aid.

New Economics Foundation (2010) *Ten Big Questions about the Big Society* (London: New Economics Foundation).

Narayan, D., Chambers, R., Shah, M. and Petesch, P. (2000) *Voices of the Poor: Crying Out for Change* (Washington, DC: World Bank).

Navarria, G. 'Transparency, accountability and representativeness in the age of blogging: the complex case of beppogrillo.it', paper presented to 'The normative implications of new forms of participation for democratic policy processes, CINEFOGO conference, Grythyttan, Sweden, 8–10 May.

Newman, J. (2001) *Modernising Governance: New Labour, Policy and Society* (Bristol: The Policy Press).

Newman, J. (ed.) (2005) *Remaking Governance: Peoples, Politics and the Public Sphere* (Bristol: The Policy Press).

Nisbet, R. (1953) *The Quest for Community* (Oxford: Oxford University Press).

Nisbet, R. (1960) 'Moral Values and Community', *International Review of Community Development*, 5.

Nohria, N. and Eccles, R. (eds) (1992) *Networks and Organizations: Structure, Form and Action* (Boston, MA: Harvard University Business Press).

O'Brien, D., Wilkes, J., de Haan, A. and Maxwell, S. (1997) *Poverty and Exclusion in North and South*, IDS Working Paper, 55 (Brighton: Institute of Development Studies).

O'Connor, A. (2007) 'Swimming against the tide: a brief history of federal policy to poorer communities', in De Filippis and Saegert (2007).

O'Donnell, D. and McCusker, P. (2007) 'Enhancing political knowledge in the public sphere through eParticipation: where is the value?' paper presented to 'Citizen Participation in Policy Making, CINEFOGO conference, Bristol, February 2007.

O'Donovan, O. (2000) 'Re-theorising the interactive state: reflection on a popular participatory initiative in Ireland', *Community Development Journal*, 35.3, 224–32.

O'Neill, M. (1992) 'Community participation in Quebec', *International Journal of Health Services*, 22.2, 287–301.

Offe, C. and Heinze, R. (1992) *Beyond Employment* (Cambridge: Polity Press).

Ohlemacher, T. (1992) 'Social relays: micro-mobilisation via the meso-level', Discussion Paper FS III 92–104 (Berlin: Wissenschaftzentrum).

Ohmer, M. and Beck, E. (2006) 'Citizen participation in neighbourhood organisations in poor communities and its relationship to neighbourhood and organizational collective efficacy', *Journal of Sociology and Social Welfare*, 23.1, 179–202.

ONS (Office of National Statistics) (2003) www.statistics.gov.uk/CCI/nuggetasp?ID=314, accessed 16 September 2010.

Onyx, J. and Dovey, K. (1999) 'Celebration in the time of cholera: praxis in the community sector in the era of corporate capitalism', *Community Development Journal*, 34.3, 179–90.

Open Democracy (2010) http://www.opendemocracy.net/ourkingdom/guy-aitchison/what-can-london-citizens-teach-left, accessed 11 March 2010.

Osborne, D. and Gaebler, T. (1992) *Reinventing Government: How the Entrepreneurial Spirit is Transforming the Public Sector* (Reading, MA: Addison-Wesley).

Ouchi, W.G. (1980) 'Markets, bureaucracies and clans', *Administrative Science Quarterly*, 25.1, 129–41.

Page, D. (2000) *Communities in the Balance: The Reality of Social Exclusion on Housing Estates* (York: York Publishing Services).

Pahl, R. (1970) *Patterns of Urban Life* (London: Longman).

Parliament of the Commonwealth of Australia (1995) *Discussion Paper on a System of National Citizenship Indicators* (Canberra: Senate Legal and Constitutional References Committee).

Parsons, W. (1995) *Public Policy* (Cheltenham: Edward Elgar).

Pateman, C. (1988) 'The fraternal social contract', in J. Keane (ed.), *Civil Society and the State: New European Perspectives* (London: Verso).

Pearce, J. (2000) *Development, NGOs and Civil Society* (Oxford: Oxfam GB).

Pearce, J., Howard, J. and Bronstein, A. (2010) 'Editorial: Learning from Latin America, *Community Development Journal*, 45.4, 265–75.

Peillon, M. (1998) 'Bourdieu's field and the sociology of welfare', *Journal of Social Policy*, 27.2, 213–29.

Perkin, H. (1989) *The Rise of Professional Society* (London: Routledge).

Peters, B. and Pierre, J. (2001) 'Developments in intergovernmental relations: towards multi-level governance', *Policy and Politics*, 29.2, 131–5.

Pitcoff, W. (1997) 'Comprehensive community initiatives: Redefining community development', retrieved 4 October 2005 from: http://www. nhi. org/online/issues/96/ccis. html.

Piven, F.F. and Cloward, R. (1977) *Poor People's Movements: Why They Succeed, How They Fail* (New York: Pantheon Books).

Plant, R. (1974) *Community and Ideology: An Essay in Applied Social Philosophy* (London: Routledge & Kegan Paul).

Plant, R. (1990) 'Citizenship and rights', in R. Plant and N. Berry, *Citizenship and Rights in Thatcher's Britain* (London: IEA Health and Welfare Unit).

Popple, K. (1995) *Analysing Community Work: Its Theory and Practice* (Buckingham: Open University Press).

Popple, K. and Shaw, M. (1997) 'Social movements: reasserting community', in *Community Development Journal*, 32.3, 191–8.

Portes, A. (1995) 'Economic sociology and the sociology of immigration: a conceptual overview', in A. Portes (ed.), *The Economic Sociology of Immigration* (New York: Russell Sage Foundation).

Portes, A. and Landolt, P. (1996) 'The downside of social capital'. *The American Prospect*, 26, 18–21.

Powell, F. (2009) 'Civil society, social policy and participatory democracy: Past, present and future', *Social Policy and Society*, 8.1, 49–58.

Powell, F. and Geoghegan, M. (2004) *The Politics of Community Development* (Dublin: A&A Farmer).

Powell, W.W. (1990) 'Neither market nor hierarchy: network forms of organization', *Research in Organizational Behaviour*, 12, 295–336.

Power, A. and Tunstall, R. (1995) *Swimming Against the Tide* (York: Joseph Rowntree Foundation).

Power, M. (1994) *The Audit Explosion* (London: DEMOS).

Power, M. (1997) *The Audit Society* (Oxford: Oxford University Press), reprinted 1999.

Pratchett, L., Durose, C., Lowndes, V., Stoker, G and Wales, C. (2009) *Empowering Communities to Influence Local Decision Making: A Systematic Review of the Evidence* (London: Communities and Local Government).

Pratt, J., Gordon, P. and Plamping, D. (1999) *Working Whole Systems* (London: King's Fund).

Prime, D., Zimmeck, M. and Zurawan, A. (2002) *Active Communities: Initial Findings from the 2001 Home Office Citizenship Survey* (London: Home Office).

Purdue, D., Razzaque, K., Hambleton, R., Stewart, M. with Huxham, C. and Vangen, S. (2000) *Community Leadership in Area Regeneration* (Bristol: The Policy Press).

Putnam, R. (1993) *Making Democracy Work* (Princeton, NJ: Princeton University Press).

Putnam. R. (2000) *Bowling Alone: The Collapse and Revival of American Community* (New York: Simon and Schuster).

Rappaport, J. (1998) 'The art of social change: community narratives as resources for individual and collective identity', in X.B. Arriaga and S. Oskamp (eds), *Addressing Community Problems: Psychological Research and Interventions* (London: Sage).

Reid, B. and Iqbal, B. (1996) 'Redefining housing practice: inter-organisational relationships and local housing networks', in P. Malpass (ed.), *The New Governance of Housing* (Harlow: Longman).

Revill, G. (1993) 'Reading Roshill', in M. Keith and S. Pile (eds), *Place and the Politics of Identity* (London: Routledge).

Rhodes, R. (1988) *Beyond Westminster and Whitehall: The Subcentral Governments of Britain* (London: Unwin Hyman).

Rhodes, R. (1997) *Understanding Governance* (Buckingham: Open University Press).

Rich, M., Giles, M. and Stern, E. (2007) 'Collaborating to reduce poverty: views from city halls and community based organizations', in DeFilippis and Saegert (2007).

Richardson, L. (2008) *DIY Community Action: Neighbourhood Problems and Community Self-Help* (Bristol: The Policy Press).

Robertson, J. (1998) *Transforming Economic Life: A Millennial Challenge* (Schumacher Briefings, Dartington: Green Books).

Room, G. (1995) 'Poverty in Europe: competing paradigms of analysis', *Policy and Politics*, 23.2, 103–13.

Rorty, R. (1998) *Achieving a Country: Leftist thought in Twentieth Century America*, Harvard University Press.

Rose, N. (1999) *Powers of Freedom: Reframing Political Thought* (Cambridge: Cambridge University Press).

Rose, S. (1998) *From Brains to Consciousness* (London: Allen Lane).

Rosenvallon, P. (1995) 'The decline of social visibility', in J. Keane (ed.), *Civil Society and the State* (London: Verso).

Rothman, J. (2000) 'Collaborative self-help community development: when is the strategy warranted?' *Journal of Community Practice*, 7.2, 89–105.

Rothman, J. and Tropman, J. (1993) 'Models of community organizations and macro practice perspectives: their mixing and phasing', in F. Cox, J. Erlich, J. Rothman and J. Tropman (eds), *Strategies of Community Organisation*, 4th edn (first published 1987) (Itasca, IL: F.E. Peacock).

Rupp, L. and Taylor, V. (1987) *Survival in the Doldrums: The American Women's Rights Movement, 1945 to the 1960s* (Oxford: Oxford University Press).

Sabatier, P. (1988) 'An advocacy coalition framework of policy change and the role of policy-oriented learning therein', *Policy Sciences*, 21, 129–68.

Saez, E. (2009) 'Striking it richer: the evolution of top incomes in the United States', Institute for Research on Labor and Employment, Working Paper Series (Berkeley: Institute of Industrial Relations, University of California).

Salamon, L. (1995) *Partners in Public Service: Government–Nonprofit Relations in the Modern Welfare State* (Baltimore: The Johns Hopkins University Press).

Sampson, R. (2004) 'Neighbourhood and community: collective efficacy and community safety', *New Economy*, 11, 106–13.

Sampson, R. (2007) 'What community supplies', in DeFilippis and Saegert (2007).

Sampson, R. J., Raudenbush, S. and Earls, F. (1997) 'Neighborhoods and violent crime: a multilevel study of collective efficacy', *Science* 277, 918–24.

Saunders, H. (1999). *A Public Peace Process: Sustained Dialogue to Transform Racial and Ethnic Conflicts* (New York: Palgrave Macmillan).

Saward, M. (2005) 'Governance and the transformation of political representation', in J. Newman (2005).

Schattschneider, E. (1960) *The Semi-Sovereign People* (New York: Holt, Rinehart & Winston).

Schmitter, P. (1974) 'Still the century of corporatism?' *The Review of Politics*, 36.1, 85–131.

Schofield, B. (2002) 'Partners in power: governing the self-sustaining community', *Sociology*, 36, 663–83.

Seibel, W. (1989) 'The function of mellow weakness: non-profit organisations as non-problem solvers in Germany', in E. James (ed.), *The Nonprofit Sector in International Perspective* (Oxford: Oxford University Press).

Seligman, A. (1992) *The Idea of Civil Society* (New York: Free Press).

Seligman, M. (1975) *Helplessness* (San Francisco, CA: W.H. Freeman).

Sen, A (1999) *Development as Freedom* (Oxford: Oxford University Press).

Sen, A. (2000) 'Freedom's market', The *Observer*, 25 June, 29.

Sending, O. and Neumann, I. (2006) 'Governance to governmentality: analyzing NGOs, states and power', *International Studies Quarterly*, 50.3, 651–72.

Senge, P. (1990) *The Fifth Discipline* (New York: Doubleday).

Servian, R. (1996) *Theorising Empowerment: Individual Power and Community Care* (Bristol: The Policy Press).

Shaw, M. and Martin, I. (2000) 'Community work, citizenship and democracy: re-making the connections', *Community Development Journal*, 35.4, 401–13.

Shepherd, A. (1998) 'Participatory environmental management: contradiction of process, project and bureaucracy in the Himalayan foothills', in Blackburn and Holland (1998b).

Shils, E. (1997) *The Virtue of Civility* (Indianapolis: Liberty Fund).

Shirlow, P. and Murtagh, B. (2004) 'Capacity-building, representation and intracommunity conflict', Urban *Studies*, 41.1, 51–70.

Shore, C. and Wright, S. (1997a) *Anthropology of Policy: Critical Perspectives on Governance and Power* (London: Routledge).

Shore, C. and Wright, S. (1997b) 'Policy: a new field of anthropology', in Shore and Wright (1997a).

6, P. (1997a) *Escaping Poverty: From Safety Nets to Networks of Opportunity* (London: DEMOS).

6, P. (1997b) 'Social exclusion: time to be optimistic', *DEMOS Collection*, 12, 3–9.

6, P., Leat, D., Seltzer, K. and Stoker, G. (1999) *Governing in the Round: Strategies for Holistic Government* (London: DEMOS).

Skelcher, C., McCabe, A., Lowndes, V. and Nanton, P. (1996) *Community Networks in Urban Regeneration: 'It all depends who you know!'* (Bristol: The Policy Press).

Skidmore, P., Bound, K. and Lownsbrough, H. (2006) 'Do policies to promote community participation in governance build social capital?' (York: Joseph Rowntree Foundation).

Skocpol, T. (1996) 'Unravelling from above', *The American Prospect*, 25, 20–5.

Smith, A., Schlozman, K., Verba, S. and Brady, H. (2009) *The Internet and Civic Engagement* (Washington DC: Pew Foundation), accessed on http:// www.pweinternet.org/Reports/2009/15-The-Internet-and-Civic-Engagement.aspx.

Smith, M.J. (1993) *Pressure, Power and Policy* (Brighton: Harvester Wheatsheaf).

Smock, K. (2003) *Democracy in Action: Community Organizing and Urban Change* (New York: Columbia University Press).

Social Exclusion Unit (1998) *Bringing Britain Together: A National Strategy for Neighbourhood Renewal* (London: The Stationery Office).

Social Exclusion Unit (2000) A *National Strategy for Neighbourhood Renewal: A Consultation Document* (London: The Stationery Office).

Social Exclusion Unit (2001) *A New Commitment to Neighbourhood Regeneration: The Action Plan* (London: The Stationery Office).

Somerville, P. (2005) 'Community governance and democracy', *Policy and Politics*, 33.1, 117–44.

SQW (2005) *Improving Delivery of Mainstream Services in Deprived Areas: The Role of Community Involvement* (London: Communities and Local Government).

Stewart, M. (1999) *Local Action to Combat Exclusion* (London: Department of the Environment, Transport and the Regions).

Stewart, M. (2002) 'Compliance and collaboration in local government', in Cars *et al.* (2002).

Stewart, M. and Taylor, M. (1995) *Empowerment and Estate Regeneration: A Critical Review* (Bristol: The Policy Press).

Stoecker, R. (2007) 'The CDC model of urban development: a critique and an alternative', in De Filippis and Saegert (2007).

Stoker, G. (1995) 'Regime theory', in Judge, Stoker and Wolman (1995).

Stoker, G. (1998) 'Governance as theory: 5 propositions', *International Social Science Journal*, 155, 17–28.

Stoker, G. and John, P. (2009) 'Design experiments: Engaging policy makers in the search for evidence about what works', *Political Studies* 57, 2, 337–73.

Stone, C. (1989) *Regime Politics: Governing Atlanta 1946–1988* (Lawrence, KS: University Press of Kansas).

Stone, D. (1989) 'Causal stories and the fixation of policy agendas', *Political Science Quarterly*, 104.4, 281–300.

Storper, M. (1998) 'Civil society: three ways into a problem', in Douglass and Friedmann (1998).

Suttles, G. (1972) *The Social Construction of Community* (Chicago, IL: University of Chicago Press).

Swyngedouw, E. (2005) 'Governance innovation and the citizen: the Janus-face of governance-beyond-the-state', *Urban Studies*, 42, 11, 1991–2006.

Tajfel, H. (1981) *Human Groups and Social Categories: Studies in Social Psychology* (Cambridge: Cambridge University Press).

Tam, H. (1998) *Communitarianism* (London: Palgrave Macmillan).

Tarrow, S. (1994) *Power in Movement: Social Movements, Collective Action and Politics* (Cambridge: Cambridge University Press).

Tarrow, S. (1996) 'Making social science work across time and space: a critical reflection on Robert Putnam's *Making Democracy Work*', *American Political Science Review*, 90.2, 389–97.

Tarrow, S. (1998) *Power in Movement: Social Movements and Contentious Politics*, 2nd edn (Cambridge: Cambridge University Press).

Tawney, R. (1926) 'Adult Education and the History of the Nation', paper read at the Fifth Annual Conference of the British Institute for Adult Education.

Taylor, M. (1995a) 'Community work and the state: the changing context of UK practice', in Craig and Mayo (1995).

Taylor, M. (1995b) *Unleashing the Potential: Bringing Residents to the Centre of Estate Regeneration* (York: Joseph Rowntree Foundation).

Taylor, M. (1998) 'Combating the social exclusion of housing estates', *Housing Studies*, 13.6, 819–32.

Taylor, M. (2000a) 'Communities in the lead: power, organisational capacity and social capital', *Urban Studies*, 37.5/6, 1019–35.

Taylor, M. (2000b) *Top Down Meets Bottom Up: Neighbourhood Management* (York: Joseph Rowntree Foundation).

Taylor, M. (2001) 'Partnership: insiders and outsiders', in M. Harris and C. Rochester (eds), *Voluntary Organisations and Social Policy in Britain: Perspectives on Change and Choice* (London: Palgrave Macmillan).

Taylor, M. (2006) 'The nature of community organizing: social capital and community leadership', in R. Cnaan and C. Milofsky (eds), *The Handbook of Community Movements and Local Organizations* (New York: Springer).

Taylor, M. (2007a) 'Community participation in the real world: opportunities and pitfalls in new governance spaces', *Urban Studies*, 44. 2.

Taylor, M. (2007b) *Neighbourhood Management and Social Capital*, Neighbourhood Management Pathfinder Programme National Evaluation: Theme Report I (London: SQW).

Taylor, M. and Hoggett, P. (1994) 'Trusting in networks? The third sector and welfare changes', in P. 6 and I. Vidal (eds), *Delivering Welfare* (Barcelona: Centre d'Iniciatives de l'Economia Social).

Taylor, M. and Parkes, T. (2001) *Brighton Urban: Draft Report on Phase III of the Evaluation* (Brighton: Health and Social Policy Research Centre).

Taylor, M. and Seymour, L. (2000) *Brighton Urban: Draft Report on Phase II of the Evaluation* (Brighton: Health and Social Policy Research Centre).

Taylor, M. and Warburton, D. (2003) 'Legitimacy and the role of UK third sector organizations in the policy process', *Voluntas*, 14.3, 321–39.

Taylor, M., Barr, A. and West, A. (2000) *Signposts to Community Development* (London: Community Development Foundation).

Taylor, M., Craig, G. and Wilkinson, M. (2002) 'Co-option or empowerment: the changing relationship between the state and the voluntary and community sectors', *Local Governance*, 28.1, 1–11.

Taylor, M., Harris, V., Howard, J., Lever, J., Mateeva, A., Miller, C., Petrov, R., Serra, L. (2009) *Dilemmas of Engagement: The Experience of Non-Governmental Actors in New Governance Spaces*, Non-Governmental Public Action Programme (NGPA), Research Paper 31 (London: London School of Economics).

Taylor, M., Howard, J. and Lever, J. (2010) 'Citizen participation and civic activism in comparative perspective', *Journal of Civil Society*, 6.2, pp. 145–64.

Taylor, M., Kestenbaum, A. and Symons, B. (1976) *Principles and Practice of Community Work in a British Town* (London: Community Development Foundation).

Taylor, M., Langan, J. and Hoggett, P. (1995) *Encouraging Diversity: Voluntary and Private Organisations in Community Care* (Aldershot: Arena).

Taylor, M., Wilson, M., Purdue, D. and Wilde, P. (2007) *Changing Neighbourhoods: Lessons from the JRF Neighbourhoods Programme* (Bristol: Policy Press).

Taylor, P. and Lupton, C. (1995) *Consumer Involvement in Health Care Commissioning*, Report no. 30 (Portsmouth: Social Services Research and Information Unit, University of Portsmouth).

Taylor, V. (1995) 'Social reconstruction and community development in the transition to democracy in South Africa', in Craig and Mayo (1995).

Tester, K. (1992) *Civil Society* (London: Routledge).

Thake, S. (1995) *Staying the course: The Role and Structures of Community Regeneration Organisations* (York: York Publishing Services).

Thane, P. (1982) *The Foundations of the Welfare State* (Harlow: Longman).

Thekaekara, S. (2000) 'Does Matson matter? Assessing the impact of a UK neighbourhood project', *Development in Practice*, 10.3/4, 556–72.

Thomas, D. (1983) *The Making of Community Work* (London: Allen & Unwin).

Thompson, E.P. (1963) *The Making of the English Working Class* (London: Victor Gollancz).

Thompson, G., Frances, J., Levacic, R. and Mitchell, J. (1991) *Markets, Hierarchies and Networks: The Co-Ordination of Social Life* (London: Sage).

Tilly, C. (1999) *Durable Inequality* (Berkeley: University of California Press).

Tönnies, F. (1955) *Community and Association* (London: Routledge & Kegan Paul).

Tuckett, I. (1988) 'Coin Street – there is another way', *Community Development Journal*, 23.4, 249–57.

Tuckett, I. (1999) 'Some issues for government and development trusts', in *Development Trusts Association, Making Regeneration Stick: Symposium Report* (London: Development Trusts Association).

Tungaranza, F. (1993) 'Social networks and social care in transition', *Social Policy and Administration*, 27.2, 141–50.

Twelvetrees, A. (ed.) (1998a) *Community Economic Development: Rhetoric or Reality* (London: Community Development Foundation).

Twelvetrees, A. (1998b) 'Preface', in Twelvetrees (1998a).

Twelvetrees, A. (1998c) 'Towards comprehensive community economic development', in Twelvetrees (1998a).

Twelvetrees, A. (1998d) 'The growth of CED in the UK', in Twelvetrees (1998a).

UK Coalition Against Poverty (1998) *Eradicate Poverty!! A Resource Pack for Community Organisations* (London: UK Coalition Against Poverty).

UNDP (1993) *Human Development Report* (Oxford: Oxford University Press).

Unger, R. (1987) *False Necessity* (Cambridge: Cambridge University Press).

Uphoff, N. (1995) 'Why NGOs are not a third sector: a sectoral analysis with some thoughts on accountability, sustainability and evaluation', in Edwards and Hulme (1995c).

Uphoff, N., Esman, M. and Krishna, A. (1998) *Learning from Instructive Experiences in Rural Development* (West Hartford, CT: Kumarian Press).

Urban Forum (2008) *Urban Forum CEN Research 2008* (London: Urban Forum).

Vinson, T., Baldry, E. and Hargreaves, J. (1996) 'Neighbourhoods, networks and child abuse', *British Journal of Social Work*, 26, 523–43.

Wacquant, L. (1993) 'Urban outcasts: stigma and division in the black American ghetto and the French urban periphery', *International Journal of Urban and Regional Research*, 17.3, 365–83.

Waddington, M. and Mohan, G. (2004) 'Failing forward: going beyond PRA and imposed forms of participation', in Hickey and Mohan (2004).

Waddington, P. (1979) 'Looking ahead: community work in to the 1980s', *Community Development Journal*, 14.3, 224–34.

Walker, M. (1995) 'Community spirit', *The Guardian*, 13 March.

Walzer, M. (1992) 'The civil society argument', in Mouffe (1992).

Warah, R. (1997) 'The partnership principle', *Habitat Debate*, 3.1, 1–5 (United Nations Centre for Human Settlements).

Warburton, D. (2009) 'A passionate dialogue: community and sustainable development', in D. Warburton (ed.), *Community and Sustainable Development: Participation in the Future*, Second edition (London: Earthscan).

Warren, C. (1996) 'Family support and the journey to empowerment', in C. Carman and C. Warren (eds), *Social Action with Children and Families* (London: Routledge).

Watson, D. (1994) *Putting Back the Pride: A Case Study of a Power-Sharing Approach to Tenant Participation* (Liverpool: Association of Community Technical Aid Centres).

Wellman, B. (1979) 'The community question: the intimate networks of East Yorkers', *American Journal of Sociology*, 84.5, 1201–31.

Whaites, A. (2000) 'Let's get civil society straight: NGOs, the state and political theory', in Pearce (2000).

White, S. (1996) 'Depoliticising development: the uses and abuses of participation', *Development in Practice*, 6.1, 6–15.

Wilcox, D. and Mackie, D. (2000) 'Making the internet work for partnerships', *Town and Country Planning*, 69.5, 161–3.

Wilkinson, D. and Applebee, E. (1999) *Implementing Holistic Government: Joined up Action on the Ground* (Bristol: The Policy Press).

Wilkinson, R. (1997) *Unhealthy Societies: The Afflictions of Inequality* (London: Routledge).

Wilkinson, R. and Picket, K. (2009) *The Spirit Level* (London: Allen Lane).

Williams, C. and Windebank, J. (2000) 'Helping each other out? Community exchange in deprived neighbourhoods', *Community Development Journal*, 35.2, 146–56.

Williams, C. and Windebank, J. (2001) 'Beyond social inclusion through employment: harnessing mutual aid as a complementary social inclusion policy', *Policy and Politics*, 29.1, 15–27.

Williams, F. (1993) 'Women and community', in J. Bornat (ed.), *Community Care: A Reader* (London: Palgrave Macmillan).

Willmott, P. (1986) *Social Networks, Informal Care and Public Policy* (London: Policy Studies Institute).

Wilson, J. (1995) *Two Worlds: Self-help Groups and Professionals* (Birmingham: British Association of Social Workers).

Wilson, W.J. (1996) *When Work Disappears* (New York: Knopf).

Wistow, G., Knapp, M., Hardy, B. and Allen, C. (1992) 'From providing to enabling: local authorities and the mixed economy of social care', *Public Administration*, 70, 24–45.

Wolfe, A. (1992) 'Democracy versus sociology: boundaries and their sociological consequences', in M. Lamont and M. Fournier (eds), *Cultivating Differences: Symbolic Boundaries and the Making of Inequality* (Chicago, IL: University of Chicago Press).

Woliver, L. (1996) 'Mobilising and sustaining grass-roots dissent', *Journal of Social Issues*, 52.1, 139–52.

Woolcock, M. (1998) 'Social capital and economic development', *Theory and Society*, 27.2, 151–207.

Woolcock, M. (2001) 'The place of social capital in understanding social and economic outcomes', *Canadian Journal of Policy Research*, 65–82.

World Bank (2010a) http://go.worldbank.org/3RB76M9CU0, accessed 9 April 2010.

World Bank (2010b) http://go.worldbank.org/COQTRW4QFO, accessed 16 September 2010.

World Bank (2010c) http://siteresources.worldbank.org/INTEMPOW-ERMENT/Resources/14657_Partic-Budg-Brazil-web.pdf, accessed 9 April 2010.

Yeo, S. (2001) 'Co-operative and mutual enterprises in Britain: a usable past for a modern future', unpublished, but available at s.yeo@pop3.poptel.org.uk and summarised in S. Yeo (2001) 'Making membership meaningful: the case of older co-operative and mutual enterprises (CMEs) in Britain', in N. Deakin (ed.), *Membership and Mutuality*, Report no. 3 (London: Centre for Civil Society).

Young, I.M. (2007) 'Five faces of oppression', in De Filippis and Saegert (2007).

Young, J. (1971) *The Drugtakers: The Social Meaning of Drug Use* (London: McGibbon & Kee).

Zdenek, R.O (1998) 'An overview of CDCs in the US', in Twelvetrees (1998a).

Zucker, L. (1986) 'Production of trust: Institutional sources of economic structure 1920–1940', in S. Bacharach (ed.) *Research in Organizational Behavior* (Greenwich, CA: JAI Press).

Author Index

Subject Index